The Network Society

JAN VAN DIJK

The Network Society

3rd Edition

SAGE Publications Ltd
1 Oliver's Yard
55 City Road
London EC1Y 1SP

SAGE Publications Inc.
2455 Teller Road
Thousand Oaks, California 91320

SAGE Publications India Pvt Ltd
B 1/I 1 Mohan Cooperative Industrial Area
Mathura Road
New Delhi 110 044

SAGE Publications Asia-Pacific Pte Ltd
3 Church Street
#10-04 Samsung Hub
Singapore 049483

Library of Congress Control Number: 2012935784

British Library Cataloguing in Publication data

A catalogue record for this book is available from the British Library

ISBN 978-1-4462-4895-9
ISBN 978-1-4462-4896-6 (pbk)

Typeset by C&M Digitals (P) Ltd, India, Chennai
Printed by MPG Books Group, Bodmin, Cornwall
Printed on paper from sustainable resources

CONTENTS

Contents

ABOUT THE AUTHOR

Jan A.G.M. van Dijk is an internationally recognized communication scientist and sociologist in the field of new media studies. He is full professor of the University of Twente, the Netherlands on the teaching chair *Sociology of the Information Society*. He is Chair of the *Department of Media, Communication and Organization* and of the *Center for eGovernment Studies*.

Van Dijk is the author of a series of books about the social aspects of the new media. Four Dutch editions of this book, and three English have appeared since 1991. He is the author of *Digital Democracy: Issues of Theory and Practice* (2000) co-edited with K. Hacker, *Information and Communication Technology in Organizations* (2005) co-authored by H. Bouwman, B. van den Hooff and L. van de Wijngaert and *The Deepening Divide, Inequality in the Information Society* (2005). All these books are SAGE publications. Forthcoming is the book *Digital Skills, The Key to the Information Society*, co-authored by A. van Deursen.

The author earned his PhD in the Social Sciences at the University of Nijmegen (1984) and worked for the University of Utrecht from 1980 through 2000.

Van Dijk is an advisor of the European Commission and a number of Dutch ministries, administrative government organizations and municipalities.

His personal website called *Welcome to the Network Society* contains more author information and backgrounds to this book: http://www.utwente.nl/gw/vandijk/

 **INTRODUCTION**

About this chapter

- This chapter presents basic concepts for the book and for the location of the new digital media in social and communication science.

- It starts with a description of the daily life of people in contemporary developed societies which have become completely dependent on networks as some kind of lifeline.

- Most people think that our life and our mediated world change faster and deeper than ever before. Here it is claimed that the first communications revolution of about a century ago was just as sweeping as the current second communications revolution – the digital. But what constitutes a communications revolution?

- What are the characteristics of the new media that make us call them new? Why do we call them interactive media, multimedia or digital media?

- What are the uses of the new media as compared to the old media? To answer this question in this chapter the concept of communication capacities will be developed.

- What kind of book is this? What is its approach and what are the background theories used by the author?

A NEW INFRASTRUCTURE FOR SOCIETY

The age of networks

A new lifeline is being added to all the ones we already had. Today, we no longer only depend on roads, electricity cables, water pipes, gas lines, sewers, post-boxes, telephone wires and cable television to conduct our daily lives and manage our households. We now also need networks of electronic communication. Young people in rich countries can no longer imagine a world without mobile telephony, the Internet and Facebook or any of the other social networking sites. Missing them for only a day would cause serious withdrawal symptoms. This dependence does not only apply for individuals. It also goes for organizations and society at large. This observation is the start of this book. How can this dependence have grown so fast? After all, it has only been in the last two decades that the main networks of the Internet and mobile telephony have been used by the majority of people in the developed world.

Contemporary literature abounds with expressions such as 'we live in a connected world', 'a connected age', a 'human web' and a 'web society'. At first sight this dependence seems rather peculiar because simultaneously there is much talk about individualization, social fragmentation, freedom and independence. But on second thought, this coincidence is not that strange because both tendencies might be two sides of the same coin – at least, that is what is argued in this book: 'The world may never have been freer, but it has also never been so interdependent and interconnected' (Mulgan, 1997: 1).

At the individual level the use of networks has come to dominate our lives. Counting the time spent on broadcast networks, telephony and the Internet we can add between five and seven hours of leisure time a day on average in a developed society. Not to mention the hours spent at work or at school. Observing social networking by individuals, we could add several hours spent in all kinds of social networking sites (SNS), chat-boxes, email conversations, texting, instant messaging and blogging. So, individualization and smaller households packed with technology to make us more independent from others, have not made us less social human beings.

Almost every organization in the developed world has become completely dependent on networks of telephony and computers. When they break down, the organization simply stops working. 'The network is down' is an expression needing no further explanation.

At the level of society and on a global scale we can see that media networks, social networks and economic networks reach into the farthest corners and edges of the world. Our world has become truly globally connected. With the swift spread of satellite TV, mobile telephony and the Internet, developing countries such as China and India are rapidly transforming from pre-industrial societies into mass industrial societies and partly even post-industrial network societies. Online communication networks have become so vital for the management of all other infrastructures of society that in future wars it would be far more effective to switch them off than to bombard other material infrastructures.

With little exaggeration, we may call the 21st century the age of networks. Networks are becoming the nervous system of our society, and we can expect this infrastructure to have more influence on our entire social and personal lives than did the construction of roads for the transportation of goods and people in the past. The design of such basic infrastructures is crucial for the opportunities and risks to follow. In the early 20th century we did not foresee what the consequences would be of our choice of predominantly small-scale private transportation instead of large-scale public transport. But now we are only too well aware of the consequences. Traffic congestion, environmental degradation and global warming are all too evident. The potential consequences of choosing a certain kind of communication infrastructure and embedding this infrastructure in our social and personal lives may be less visible, but it will be just as severe.

Continuing this line of argument, at stake here is not only the ecology of nature – that is, transportation of information and communication will partly replace transportation of goods and people – but also 'social ecology'. When the new media arrived in the 1980s, some people were concerned about the 'pollution' of our social environment by the new media penetrating our private lives. According to them, the new media were reducing, diminishing and even destroying the quality of face-to-face communications and were making human relationships more formal (Kubicek, 1988). They would result in privacy reduction and total control from above. In the 1990s these *dystopian* views were replaced by *utopian* views of the new media substantially improving the quality of life and of communication. A 'new economy' and a new era of prosperity, freedom and online democracy was looming ahead.

In the first Dutch edition of this book (van Dijk, 1991), I championed a wide public debate about such presumed outcomes of the new media. This call was partly heeded. Especially between 1994 and 1998, a huge boost was given to the discussion of the opportunities of the Internet and the perspective of the so-called electronic highway, a term introduced in the United States in 1993 as 'information superhighway'. The discussion in those years was largely theoretical and philosophical. Utopian and dystopian views were listed and opposed in an abstract and rather speculative manner.

In the first decade of the 21st century we have been able to develop a more balanced or *syntopian* view (Katz and Rice, 2002) of new media development after more than 25 years of experience. This time we are able to draw conclusions based on facts and empirical investigations. This is the main objective of this book.

Values at stake

This book demonstrates how the most fundamental values of our society are at issue when it comes to the development of new information and communication technologies, in which networks are already setting the tone.

Social equality is at stake, since certain categories of people participate more than others in the information society. Some profit from its advantages, while others are deprived. Technology allows for a better distribution of knowledge. Its complexity and costs, however, may serve to intensify existing social inequalities, or even create large groups of 'misfits' – people who do not fit in with the information society.

The fact that the new media enable well-informed citizens, employees and consumers to have more direct communication with, and participation in, institutions of decision-making should, in principle, strengthen *democracy*. On the other hand, because the technology is susceptible to control from above, democracy could be threatened. Some would argue that *freedom* – for example, the freedom of choice for consumers – will increase because of the interactivity offered by this technology. Others paint a more pessimistic picture, predicting that freedom will be endangered by a decrease in privacy for the individual as a registered citizen, a 'transparent' employee and a consumer screened for every personal characteristic, and by the growing opportunities for central control.

For certain groups of people (disabled, sick and elderly people) as well as for society as a whole, *safety* can be improved by all kinds of registration and alarm systems. At the same time, safety seems to decrease because we have become dependent on yet another type of technology, and a very vulnerable technology at that.

The *quantity and quality of social relationships* might improve if communication technology enables us to easily get in touch with almost everybody, even over long distances. On the other hand, our social relationships might decrease because particular people may withdraw into computer and telephone communication and only interact in safe, self-chosen social environments. For example, Sherry Turkle (2011) has observed that many American teenagers no longer call each other, not only because this is more expensive, but also because this is a personal confrontation. Instead, they prefer texting which allows greater control. In this way new media communication may become a complete substitute for face-to-face communication, causing the quality of communication to diminish in certain respects.

The *richness of the human mind* may increase owing to the diversity of impressions we gather through these new media. On the other hand, it may also be reduced because these impressions are offered out of context in schematic, (pre-)programmed and fragmented frames. And because it is available in huge amounts, information can never be fully processed by the recipient.

A SECOND COMMUNICATIONS REVOLUTION
What is a communications revolution?

Most descriptions of media history suggest an evolutionary development of a large number of new media in succession. In reality, media development in the last two centuries has been more like two concentrations of innovations, of which the first can be placed roughly in the last decades of the 19th century and the early decades of the 20th century, and the second is to be observed in the last decade(s) of the 20th century and the first decades of the 21st century. James Beniger was the first to describe and analyse the first concentration and its background in his book *The Control Revolution* (1986); Frederick Williams first identified the second concentration in his book *The Communications Revolution* (1982). I dare to speak of the *first and second communications revolutions of the modern age*. 'Revolution' is a big word, all too readily referred to in the history of industry and technology, whether it is appropriate or not. Every so-called revolution in fact took decades to complete. The major technological developments are seldom revolutionary; the technological process is usually much more evolutionary. Innovations are preceded by a long process of preparation. It would be misleading to suggest that new technologies arise suddenly. Rather they are a combination of techniques developed earlier. It would be wise to ask ourselves what exactly is new about the new media and why the term 'revolution' can be used here. If there was merely a considerable quantitative acceleration of the arrival of innovations in the two concentrations mentioned before, I would not dare to mention the word 'revolution'. *Structural changes* or *qualitative technical improvements* in mediated communications must take place in order for something to be called a revolution in communications.

A structural communications revolution

In the history of the media, several communications revolutions have taken place. These can be divided into structural and technical communications revolutions. In *structural* revolutions, fundamental changes take place in the coordinates of space and time. Media can be a form of communication fixed in space (in one place) or they may allow communications between different places. Furthermore, they can fix the moment of communication to a certain time or enable us to bridge time.

The switch from communication fixed in space and time to communication bridging space and time marks the two first communications revolutions in the (pre-)history of man: sending smoke, drum and fire signals over long distances, and sending messengers in order to bridge places. Time was transcended by making illustrations on pottery and inside caves – signs that passed to future generations.

The next and presumably most important structural communications revolution was the development of writing, which enabled humans to overcome both space and time. The most recent communications revolution – the subject of this book – is primarily a structural revolution. It signals an end to the distinction between media that are fixed in space and time and media that bridge these dimensions. The new media, after all, can be used for both purposes. Even though the purpose of bridging time and space is predominant, the new media can also be used in offline environments, for example, in consulting an electronic book or a DVD. The new media are a combination of online and offline media, such as the Internet, personal computers, tablets, smart-phones and e-readers. They are a combination of transmission links and artificial memories (filled with text, data, images and/or sounds) that can also be installed in separate devices.

Therefore, the new media require a step outside the scheme of revolutions bridging space and time that have described media history until now (see Figure 1.1). The combination of online and offline applications of the new media, used both in traditional social environments fixed to a particular time and space and in online media environments bridging these dimensions, produces the structurally new characteristics of these media. This book will demonstrate that this combination helps to realize perhaps the most promising social perspective of the new media, which is not a replacement of local face-to-face communication by online mediated communication but a potentially fruitful interplay between them.

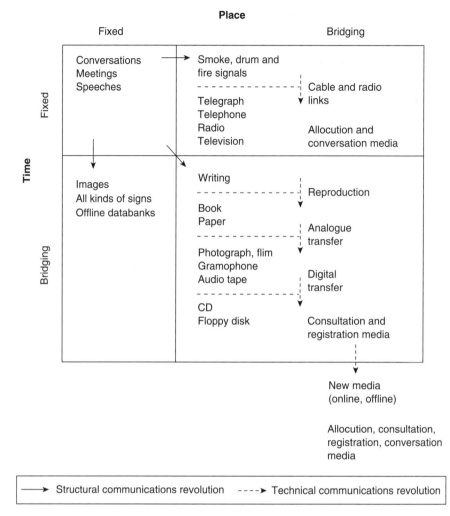

FIGURE 1.1 Communications revolutions in media history

A technical communications revolution

In a technical communications revolution, a fundamental change takes place in the structure of connections, artificial memories and/or the reproduction of their contents. The development of the printing press was a revolution in the reproduction of writing. In the second half of the 19th century, a second revolution took place. It was mainly a technical revolution, based on the invention and construction of long-distance connections by cable and air, the introduction of new analogue artificial memories (photograph, film, gramophone record and audio recording tape), and new techniques for reproduction (the rotary press in particular). Qualitatively new was the development of media for a direct transfer of sound/speech, text/data and images by separate channels and over long distances. The *invention* of the telegraph and telephone date from a long time before the turn of the 19th to the 20th century, and radio and television started from the years immediately after. Their *innovation*, which means a first introduction in usable form, took place between 1890 and 1925. *Large-scale introduction* needed another 50 years. The most recent technical communications revolution is characterized by the introduction of digital artificial memories, and digital transmission and reproduction. The term 'digital revolution' is appropriate in this context.

Developments in the current communications revolution follow the same pattern. The inventions took place during the past 50 years. In the first decades after the Second World War, large mainframe computers, serving as number-crunching machines or database processors, and satellite telecommunications were fabricated. Then, from the 1960s onwards, smaller and yet more powerful computers were introduced that served as general symbolic machines. They dealt with the interactive manipulation of information and with communication. Increasingly, they were connected in networks.

In the meantime we have passed the phase of innovations through the introduction of several generations of personal computers, computer networks, terminal equipment, programs and services. Currently, their large-scale introduction in workplaces, schools, households and public places is happening all over the world. This process will probably continue until about 2040.

Now we are able to answer the key question: how has quality improved in the current structural and technical communications revolution? It is not because the crucial coordinates of space and time seem to be reduced to insignificant proportions, or because it is possible to communicate with everyone all over the world within seconds if you have access to the means to do so. In other words, it is not the fact that 'the world is turning into a village', to use a popular phrase. This would simply mean an evolutionary development along the axes of space and time, which had already taken place with the communications revolution of the 19th century. It would 'merely' be an acceleration of this evolution. No, the essence of the current revolution can be summarized in the structural terms of *integration* and *interactivity* and in the technical terms of *digital code* and *hypertext* as the defining characteristics of the new media.

CHARACTERISTICS OF THE NEW MEDIA

In this section I characterize the new media in three ways. First, I supply a definition of the new media as a combination of the four characteristics just mentioned; then I discuss the typical patterns of information and communication to be observed in their application; and finally, I describe their strong and weak usage qualities, called communication capacities.

Integration or convergence

The most important *structural* new media characteristic is the integration of telecommunications, data communications and mass communications in a single medium. It is the process of *convergence*. For this reason, new media are often called multimedia. Integration can take place at one or more of the following levels:

1   infrastructure – for example, combining the different transmission links and equipment for telephone and computer (data) communications;

2 transportation – for example, Internet telephony and web TV riding on cable and satellite television;

3 management – for example, a cable company that exploits telephone lines and a telephone company that exploits cable television while both offer Internet connections;

4 services – for example, the combination of contacting services and marketing in social networking sites;

5 types of data – putting together sounds, data, text and images.

This integration has led to a gradual merging of telecommunications, data communications and mass communications; the separate meaning of these terms is already disappearing. We will use terms such as 'multimedia', 'broadband', 'the Internet' or 'the network'. We believe that these terms will also eventually replace the term 'new media'.

The integration process is enabled by two revolutionary techniques:

1 full digitalization of all media (the general use of digital code);

2 broadband transmission through all connections by cable and by air.

While the first technique enables a complete integration of telecommunications and data communications, the second is more relevant for the integration of mass communications in the process of convergence. The concept of integration is summarized in Box 1.1.

BOX 1.1
Levels of integration

1 *Infrastructure*: combining different types of connections.
2 *Transportation*: connections carrying different types of media.
3 *Management*: companies managing different kinds of media.
4 *Services*: media offering a combination of information, communication, transaction and entertainment services.
5 *Types of data*: multimedia containing sound, text, images and data.

Interactivity

The second structural new media characteristic of the current communications revolution is the rise of interactive media. In a very general definition, interactivity is a sequence of action and reaction. It is remarkable how poorly this crucial concept is (further) defined and made operational for research in media and communication studies. Jensen (1999) has produced an exhaustive account of the laborious search by social and communication scientists for a suitable definition. Jensen himself wishes to reserve the concept of interactivity for mediated communication. Van Dijk and de Vos (2001) offer an operational definition that is supposed to be valid for face-to-face communication as well. These authors define interactivity at four accumulative levels, acknowledging, like many other authors, that this concept is a multidimensional construct. The levels of interactivity are supposed to be appropriate to define how interactive a particular digital medium is.

The most elementary level of interactivity is the possibility of establishing two-sided or multilateral communication. This is the *space* dimension. All digital media offer this possibility to a certain extent. However, most often, the downloaded link or the supply side of websites, interactive television, and computer programs is much wider than the uplink or the retrieval made by their users.

The second level of interactivity is the degree of synchronicity. This is the *time* dimension. It is well known that an uninterrupted sequence of action and reaction usually improves the quality of interaction. However, some interactive media, such as electronic mail (email), are used for their lack of synchronicity. Producing and receiving messages can be done at self-chosen times and places, and one is allowed to think longer about a reply. Yet this goes at the expense of immediate reactions and of the ability to send all kinds of verbal and non-verbal signs simultaneously.

When multilateral and synchronous communication are available, a higher level of control by the interacting parties is possible. So, the third level of interactivity is the extent of control exercised by the interacting parties. This *behavioural* dimension is defined as the ability of the sender and the receiver to switch roles at any moment. Furthermore, it is about the control over the events in the process of interaction. Interactivity in terms of control is the most important dimension in all interactivity definitions of media and communication studies (see Jensen, 1999). It means attention to the division of power in the interface of media and humans or between humans in both mediated and face-to-face communication. At this level, interactivity means, among other things, that the user is able to intervene into the program or representation itself and to make a difference. What the user does has to create a substantial change at the other side – it has to make a difference. As digital media are more interactive than traditional media, potentially they enable a shift in the balance of power to the user.

The fourth and highest level of interactivity is acting and reacting with an understanding of meanings and contexts by all interactors involved. This *mental* dimension is a necessary condition for full interactivity, for example, in physical conversation and computer-mediated communication. Currently, this level of interactivity is reserved for mediated and face-to-face interaction between human beings and animals with a consciousness, except by those who have much confidence in interactions directed by artificial intelligence. The concept of interactivity is summarized in Box 1.2.

BOX 1.2
Levels of interactivity

1 *Place*: multilateral exchange.
2 *Time*: synchronicity and equally long turns.
3 *Action*: equal control in action and reaction.
4 *Mental*: mutual understanding.

Digital code and hypertext

Digital code is a technical media characteristic only defining the form of new media operations. However, it has great substantial consequences for communication. Digital code means that in using computer technology, every item of information and communication can be transformed and transmitted in the form of bytes (strings of 1s and 0s, with every single 1 or 0 being a bit). This artificial code replaces the natural codes of the analogue creation and the transmission of items of information and communication (e.g. by beams of light we can see and vibrations of sound we can hear).

The first substantial effect of the transformation of all media contents in the same digital code is the uniformity and standardization of these contents. Form and substance cannot be separated as easily as many people think they can. Digital code is not a neutral form (see Chapter 8). It starts with initially cutting into pieces a number of undivided analogue items of information and communication (signs) and then recombining them in the digitized forms of images, sounds, texts, and numerical data. These forms are produced using not only the same basic code but also the same languages, such as HTML (hypertext markup language), a graphic code for pages of the World Wide Web (www). The resulting forms are known for their great similarities in menu and navigation structures when they are programmed in computer software. Another effect of using uniform digital code is the increase in the quantity of items of information and communication. This code makes their production, recording and distribution much easier. Supported by the exponentially rising storage capacity of computers and their disks, unlimited amounts of items are produced.

A final and perhaps most important effect of using digital code is the break-up of the traditional linear order of large units of information and communication, such as texts, images, sounds, and audiovisual programs, in such a way that they can be transformed into hyperlinks of items liable to be perceived and processed in the order that the reader, viewer, or listener wants. This transformation from linear to hypertext media would have been impossible without digital code. However, it is fully justified to call the hypertext form a second technical characteristic defining the new media. The social and cultural consequences of the 'hypertext revolution' in media production and use will be big. They will be fully described in this book, primarily in Chapters 8 and 9. The concepts of digital code and hypertext are summarized in Box 1.3.

BOX 1.3

Digital code and hypertext

1 *Digital code*: uniform code of bits and bytes for all types of data in digital media.
2 *Hypertext*: uniform code for linking different chunks of all types of data in digital media.

Finally, we can say that the new media be defined by all four characteristics simultaneously: they are media at the turn of the 20th and 21st centuries which are both integrated and interactive and use digital code and hypertext as technical means. It follows that their most common alternative names are multimedia, interactive media and digital media. By using this definition it is easy to identify media as old or new. For example, traditional television is integrated as it contains images, sound and text, but it is not interactive or based on digital code. The plain old telephone was interactive, but not integrated as it only transmitted speech and sounds and it did not work with digital code. In contrast, the new medium of interactive television adds interactivity and digital code. Additionally, the new generations of mobile or fixed telephony are fully digitalized and integrated as they add text, pictures or video and they are connected to the Internet.

Information traffic patterns

As stated, the first level of interactivity is two-sided or multilateral communication. Bordewijk and Van Kaam (1982) had this concept in mind when they designed their typology of the four *information traffic patterns* of allocution, consultation, registration and conversation. They have proved very useful in social and communication science, as will be shown in this book. They illuminate the structures of communication and the aspects of power these structures contain. Finally, they show that the new media evolve from the pattern of allocution, characterizing the old media, to the patterns of consultation, registration and conversation. In this way they become more interactive and more integrated as they converge into fully integrated networks.

In the 20th century, the pattern of *allocution* has gained most importance in communication media. Radio, television and other mediated performances have come to the fore in this century of scale extension and massification. They perform important coordinating functions in society, because they are based on a pattern of allocution: *the simultaneous distribution of information to an audience of local units by a centre that serves as the source and decision agency in respect of its subject matter, time and speed* (Figure 1.2a). The new media do not enhance this pattern, though sometimes new allocution media are introduced such as weblogs and Twitter. The only exceptions are where 'old' broadcasting media offer more opportunities of choice for viewers and listeners, such as by means of pay-per-view and video on demand with feedback channels at freely chosen times. Here, within the limits and menus offered, the local unit is able to co-decide about the information to be received: the subject, the time the information is consumed, and the agenda of future broadcasting. Further, reactions to current programmes and answers to questions posed in the mass media become possible. However, these innovations do more to damage the pattern of allocution than to enhance it. Therefore this pattern transforms into the next one in the new media environment.

The pattern of *consultation* certainly is enhanced by the new media. Consultation is *the selection of information by (primarily) local units, which decide upon the subject matter, time and speed, at a centre which remains its source* (Figure 1.2b). Old consultative media are books, newspapers, magazines, audio and video. Examples of new consultative media are CDs or DVDs with information sources such as encyclopaedias, electronic program guides in digital and interactive television and, of course, numerous online information sites. Because they add new routes and a seemingly endless number of sources, these media are to be viewed as a basic improvement to the pattern of consultation. Often they are online connections enabling more consultation at the centre than the old media. For example, the gigantic, ever-expanding Wikipedia offers many more search terms and pages than classical encyclopaedias.

The opportunities for *registration* also grow in the new media. Registration is the *collection of information by a centre that determines the subject matter, time and speed of informa-tion sent by a number of local units, who are the sources of the information and who sometimes take the initiative for this collection themselves (to realize a transaction or reservation)* (Figure 1.2c). In old media and data collection instruments, often the centre not only decides but also takes the initiative and requests the transfer of information. Examples of these media and instruments are enquiries, elections, examinations, archives and visual observation by cameras. To a large extent, these activities were already performed by the old media. The new media offer more opportunities for registration as they are built on computers. The initiative often comes from the centre that offers a web questionnaire or asks for votes and opinions in an online referendum. The new media, however, offer even more chances of registration by the centre at the initia-tive of the local units, for example, in electronic reservations, online shopping and Internet banking. A more serious problem arises when the reverse is the case – when the registration initiative is taken by the centre, without the agreement of the local units. This might be the case with privacy intruding tracking technologies, electronic surveillance from a distance and all other kinds of observations of personal data without the individual concerned knowing or wanting it.

The most fundamental change takes place in the pattern of *conversation*. Conversation is *an exchange of information by two or more local units, addressing a shared medium instead of a centre, and determining the subject matter, time and speed of information and communication themselves* (Figure 1.2d). In the new media, the existing channels for conversation are not only enlarged, but they can also contain more kinds of data. The old media (telegraph and telephone) only offered room for speech and a limited amount of data. Local computer networks and data communication over

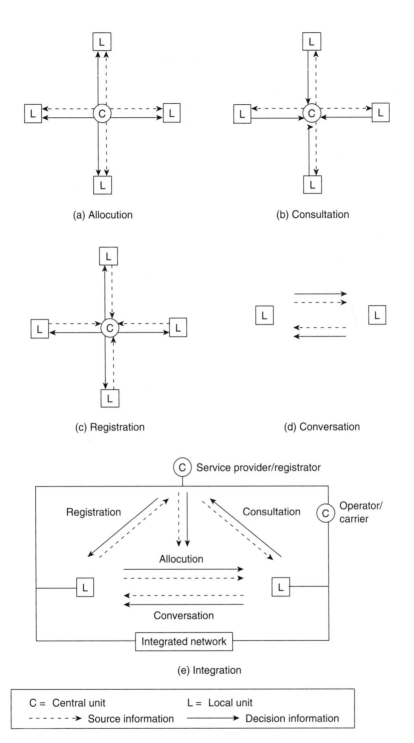

FIGURE 1.2 The integration of information traffic patterns in networks

telephone lines caused an explosive growth in the capabilities for transporting data and text. The new media added a substantial new quality: the possibility to *combine* speech, data and text *in one message*. Then pictures could be added, and since a number of decades we can even add moving images to these messages. This qualitative enlargement of the range of options for conversation is enabled by broadband facilities.

The birth of integrated networks for telephony, broadcasting and Internet implies a combination of allocution, consultation, registration and conversation in a single medium (Figure 1.2e). This would make such a medium important enough in social communications to enable us to speak of a communications revolution, the results of which will be the central theme of this book.

The evolution of the four information traffic patterns involves a clear shift of patterns towards local units. The new media cause a shift from allocution towards consultation, registration and conversation. The initiative and selection by local units, and the interactivity between these local units and the centre, and between these local units themselves, have increased the opportunities in communications. They will cause a revolution in mediated communications, and perhaps even in all communications in our society. *For the first time in history, the new media will enable us to make a deliberate choice between mediated and face-to-face communication in a large number of social activities.* The implications of this choice will form a prime focus of this book.

COMMUNICATION CAPACITIES OF THE NEW MEDIA
Approaches to mediated communication

In the last 25 years, a lot of research has been carried out on the opportunities and limitations of mediated communication as compared with face-to-face communication. In social-psychological experiments among small groups using different media, the modes of communication and the accomplishment of tasks have been investigated systematically. Two approaches are prevalent. The first takes the *objective* characteristics of media and channels as a point of departure. The second emphasizes the *(inter)subjective* characteristics of the use of them, mainly as a reaction to the first approach. In this book, an *integrated* (objective and subjective) approach is taken to develop the concept of communication capacities. This concept is developed to answer the question of what can be done with the new media. What are the special characteristics of new media compared with the old media? The general properties of integration and interactivity have been described in the previous section. Nine so-called communication capacities of the new media will now be introduced, but first the origin of the concept of communications capacities must be briefly explained.

The oldest social-psychological approach in this area mainly stresses the limitations of all media and channels as compared with face-to-face communication.

It emphasizes that all media take away or filter cues as compared to face-to-face communication. Short et al. (1976) introduced the influential concept of *social presence*. This refers to the sociability, warmth, personal information and sensitivity of face-to-face communication that media are only able to transmit in a limited way. By means of these characteristics, presumed to be objective, all media and face-to-face communications produce a different experience of presence among communication partners. For example, the video-phone offers more social presence than the audio-phone.

An almost identical approach is the one that refers to the so-called *reduced social context cues* of the media of telecommunications and network computing (Kiesler and Sproull, 1992; Kiesler et al., 1984; Sproull and Kiesler, 1986, 1991). According to the psychologists concerned, media more or less lack the space for crucial non-verbal and contextual signs. In the somewhat further elaborated concept of *information or media richness,* Daft and Lengel (1984) have distinguished the following four objective characteristics of media: feedback capacity (immediate, fast, slow); channel used (audio, visual); nature of the source (personal, impersonal); and language richness (spoken, written and/or body language).

In the second half of the 1980s this kind of classical social-psychological research was increasingly criticized. A large number of phenomena could not be explained using its objective approach. It appeared that media which are lacking in social presence and information richness, e.g. email and SMS-messaging, are frequently used for social-emotional and even erotic communications. The same phenomenon arose with phone sex and phone helplines. After a period of habituation, the quantity of informal and intimate communications in computer networks increases (Rice and Love, 1987; Walther, 1992). Eventually there arises a (sub)culture of electronic communication with new norms, language and behaviour.

In reaction to the social-psychological approaches just described, largely confining social reality to communication that is interpersonal and tied to place, a more social-cultural or sociological approach emphasizing (inter)subjective social construction processes has appeared. Fulk et al. (1987) were the first to develop a *social information processing model.* They wanted to know how the media are really used in daily practice and how humans shape them (inter)subjectively in their social information processing. This is supposed to be conditioned by the opinions about and attitudes towards media of people themselves and of others in their immediate social environment, most often colleagues at work, in the early phase of computer-mediated communications (CMC). See Fulk and Steinfield (1990) for a summary of this view.

Walther (1992; 1996) has presented a comparable approach. In his *relational perspective,* the media are used differently in relation to particular functions (tasks, goals) and contexts. According to the results of his experiments, after some time the quality of CMC approaches that of face-to-face communications. This conclusion is diametrically opposed to the claims of the social presence and reduced social context cues approaches.

The experiments of Spears and Lea (1992) support Walther's conclusion. According to their *social identity theory*, the reason for the approximate equivalence of mediated and face-to-face communication is that people take their whole social, cultural, personal and groups identity with them as baggage into computer network communications. The smallest cue is then sufficient to compensate for the limitations of the medium, using the mental construction and imaginative power derived from this identity.

I have proposed an integrated approach, one that is both objective and (inter) subjective (van Dijk, 1993b). According to this view, it remains important to start the analysis with the structural, more or less objective properties of the media, old and new. Their (inter)subjective interpretation and their use in practice differ too much to allow any kind of generalization. Besides, the suggestion that media have no objective characteristics is incorrect. One event in an American computer discussion of women about intimate female affairs should be convincing enough: When it transpired, after some time, that a male psychiatrist using the pseudonym 'Julie' had been taking part, the women were extremely shocked and insulted (see Stone, 1991: 82ff). In most other media this event just could not have happened.

So, media do have particular potentialities and limitations that cannot be removed (inter)subjectively. In this book they are called communication capacities – a concept which carries the connotation of both defining (objective) and enabling (subjective) features. Using the following nine communication capacities, we are able to compare old and new media in a systematic way: speed, reach, storage capacity, accuracy, selectivity, interactivity, stimuli richness, complexity and privacy protection. A short introduction to these capacities follows. Old and new media are compared in Table 1.1 in terms of these capacities.

TABLE 1.1 Communication capacities of old and new media

| Communication capacity | Old Media | | | | New Media | |
	Face-to-face	Print	Broadcasting	Telephone	Internet	Multimedia (offline)
Speed	Low	Low/ medium	High	High	High	High
Reach (geographical)	Low	Medium	High	High	High	Low
Reach (social)	Low	Medium	Variable	Variable	Variable	Low
Storage capacity	Low	Medium	Medium	Variable	High	Medium
Accuracy	Low	High	Low/medium	Variable	High	High
Selectivity	Low	Low	Low	High	High	High
Interactivity	High	Low	Low	Medium	Medium	Medium
Stimuli richness	High	Low	Medium	Variable	Medium	Medium
Complexity	High	High	Medium	Medium	Medium	Medium
Privacy protection	High	Medium	Medium/High	Low	Low	High

The *speed* of bridging large distances in communication is one of the strongest capacities of the new media. In this respect they are similar to the telephone and broadcasting. Using the Internet and email, one is able to send a message to the other side of the world within one minute. Face-to-face communication and print media are only able to connect quickly to proximate others.

The potential *geographical and social reach* of the new media is very large. The whole world might be connected to them and with them in the future. Geographic reach indicates the number or places you can reach with the medium, and social reach the number of people. Currently, almost every place in the world is connected to the Internet. However, the social reach of the Internet is variable – it ranges from less than 5 per cent home access in some developing countries, to more than 90 per cent in some developed countries. Social telephone reach also remains very unequally divided in the world, though currently developing countries are catching up fast via the diffusion of mobile telephony.

Another strong quality of the new media is their huge *storage potential*. This potential is low in face-to-face communication, which depends on inadequate human memory. It was also low in telephony before the invention of answering devices. Presently, it is variable as we have both very simple mobile phones, and smart phones that are actually computers. In digital media one can store much more than in printed media and analogue broadcast media.

The *accuracy* or exactness of the information transmitted is an important advantage of the new media as compared with the traditional telephone and face-to-face communication. Signals in the latter media are often ambiguous. Historically, accuracy has also been an advantage of print media. The new media add the exactness of data or numbers and the informativeness of images. Both the storage capacity and the accuracy of the new media enable governments, politicians and managers to control the rising complexity of society and organizations. Without ICT, many processes would become out of control and bogged down in paperwork and bureaucracy (see Chapters 4 and 5).

The *selectivity* of messages and addresses is another strong capacity of the new media, contrasting with face-to-face communication of groups and other collectives, in which it is rather low. Here individuals have to make appointments and separate themselves from each other. Much of the communication using print media is not addressed, except for personal letters of course. The same goes for broadcasting. The telephone was the first fully selective medium used to address people. The new media advance this capacity by enabling us to systematically select (parts of) groups using email lists and the like. In this way, one can address very specific target groups. This is a capacity that is already used frequently in the corporate world (telemarketing) and Internet politics.

One refers to the new media as interactive, but actually their *interactivity* does not reach the high level that can be attained in face-to-face communication. The new media's general characteristic of interactivity described earlier has to be specified in terms of the concrete levels and types of interactive capacities to be observed in old and new media. Some new media do not offer anything more than two-way traffic and a central store-and-forward agency serving as some kind of answering device or voicemail. Clearly this goes for email. In other new media such as the interactive press and broadcasting, or digital information services, the user has very little control over content. Though ever more room is made for user-generated content, most users do not take this opportunity. The majority does not (inter)act much; instead it chooses from menus, consumes and reacts. Moreover, fully fledged new media conversation that is equal to face-to-face communication is still lacking. One is not able to exchange all the signals (often) desired. Even video conferences, which partly enable the participants to see each other, have their limitations. So-called kinaesthesis (the sense of movement) is largely absent and the sense of distance between conference people is still present.

In terms of *stimuli richness,* no other medium is able to beat face-to-face communication. The reason is clear: all current new media are sensory poor in natural human perception. This is especially so for computer networks transmitting only lines of text and data. Multimedia offer a greater richness of stimuli, often even an overload, in all kinds of combinations: images, sounds, data and text. However, the combination of these stimuli is not natural but artificial. Some stimuli can be strengthened while others recede, but there is still a clear lack of the movement and body language provided by someone who is close. So the most advanced kind of teleshopping will remain different from going to shop in town for a day.

As a consequence of the last two capacities described, the *complexity* that one is able to achieve collectively by using them is not high. Research indicates that one is able to make contacts, ask questions, exchange information and make appointments very well using computer networks, but it appears to be difficult to negotiate, decide, explain difficult issues and really get to know someone (see Rice, 1998).

The biggest minus of the present design of the new media is the low capacity for *privacy protection* that they offer. Face-to-face communication can be secluded to a large degree. Current broadcasting and the press can be received anonymously. This does not apply for the new interactive broadcasting and electronic press media. In fact, all usage, and often the personal characteristics of users, are registered in the new media. This is certainly the case for computer networks. For stand-alone computers and multimedia it is less so, because they are under the control of the user, but these media have internal memories which can be accessed.

THE NATURE AND DESIGN OF THIS BOOK
An interdisciplinary outline of social aspects

This book contains an outline of a large number of social aspects of the new media compiled in a particular framework. For the original first Dutch edition of this book, written at the end of the 1980s, an inventory was made of all social aspects that appeared to be relevant at that time. With every new edition, the inventory was extended and reduced. At the time of writing (2011) it is scarcely possible anymore to be complete. The new media have merged so much in society that they touch about every aspect of it. So, this book is no encyclopaedia of new media social aspects. It is very comprehensive, but it does not discuss all the literature. It has been updated, but the overview simply cannot be complete. A library full of books and articles on the topic of this book has been published in the past two decades.

What I do attempt is to be extremely interdisciplinary in the treatment of social aspects. This is for fundamental reasons. I will explain that in the network society the so-called micro, meso and macro levels are closely connected and that many dividing lines between the fields of disciplines simply dissolve. To get a grip on the causes and consequences of the introduction and use of the new media in contemporary society one simply has to be interdisciplinary. Of course, this will provoke the comment of specialists in technology, economy, political science, law, culture and psychology that the treatment is not complete. I am prepared to take this risk for the benefit of reaching a better understanding of the whole picture.

Theoretical Framework

The outline is made against the background of a theoretical framework that has been made more explicit in this edition as compared to previous ones. This framework has found sources of inspiration in four theories of social and communication science.

The first source of *inspiration* is network theory. This has been known for decades now in social and communication science, but in the last fifteen years it has made considerable progress. Social scientists have reached for the help of natural scientists and mathematicians in discovering the 'laws' or regularities of networks. In the following chapter I will also present a number of 'laws' of the Web that will return in about every chapter. The latest versions of network theory have made it possible to extend the framework linking the social aspects and to improve the coherence of the book. Here I defend a moderate network approach in social science. It is moderate because I not only focus on relations, but also on the characteristics of the units that are related in networks (people, groups, organizations and societies).

The second source is *(adaptive) structuration theory*. The axiom of this theory is that social structures and communicative action are mutually changing each other (structures are adapted continually). My general view of technology is that it is both defining and enabling, and that technologies and human beings are mutually shaping. These assumptions define another part of the nature of this book. Again and again both the opportunities and risks, optimistic and pessimistic views or utopian and dystopian perspectives of the new media for man, society and organization, are portrayed. The assumptions also explain why this book not only contains observation and analysis, but also policy perspectives based upon a number of explicit social values.

The third insight comes from so-called *medium theory* (inspired by Innis, Ong and Meyrowitz). This theory says that media and technologies in history are not only enabling but also defining. They have a number of objective characteristics that must have a particular influence on users in their social environments. The communication capacities elaborated above provide an example. The core argument is that media and technologies themselves are social environments. This clearly goes for media networks. The clearest case in this book is the Internet, which has become a society by itself. The fact that social and media networks are becoming a single reality is one of the main statements in this book.

The final source of inspiration is contemporary *modernization theory* (note that this is not the one followed in the 1950s and 1960s hailing the superiority of western civilization). Current modernization theory observes the conflict of western and other cultures in the world (see, for example, Barber, 1996 and Castells, 1997, 1998). In this book, modernization theory appears in basic statements about networks linking global and local social relations and processes of scale extension and reduction in society.

Chapter division

The book contains three parts. In the first part, comprising Chapters 1 to 3, basic terms and statements are explained. Chapter 1 contains the basic terms. Chapter 2 provides the most important part of the theoretical framework: network theory and an explanation of the network society concept. Chapter 3 describes the technological infrastructure of the network society. I have tried to do this in a manner that should be understandable for a non-technical reader.

The heart of the book is the exposition of the social aspects of the new media in several spheres and levels of society: the economy, politics, the law, the social infrastructure of society, culture and individuals (psychology). In this third English edition, I have added chapter contents and conclusions to the chapters and provided them with explanation and listing boxes. I hope this will improve the coherence and didactic quality of the book.

Every book I have published in this field contains policy perspectives at the end. I am not satisfied with only providing scientific analysis to my readers. I do not want them to feel helpless after they have grasped the overwhelming impact of the new media on their society. The opportunities of the new media for society can be taken and the risks can be reduced.

- Communication networks have become a lifeline for people in modern society. Increasingly, they are merging with social networks in the offline world, in this way creating a network society.

- The rise of the new media constitutes a second communications revolution. The influence on society and daily life of the first revolution, which brought the mass media about a century ago, was just as sweeping as the impact of this second revolution. New media technology is revolutionary. However, their impact on society rather is evolutionary, reinforcing existing trends in society.

- The new media can be defined by four characteristics, two structural and two technical: they are media at the turn of the 20th and 21st centuries which are both *integrated* (multimedia) and *interactive*, and use *digital code* and *hypertext* as technical means.

- In the new media, the information traffic patterns of allocution, consultation, registration and conversation come together, making them very powerful in information retrieval, processing and exchange.

- The new media are also characterized by a number of communication capacities that are both enabling and defining their use. Strong capacities are speed, geographical reach, storage capacity, accuracy and selectivity. Weak capacities are (full) interactivity, (natural) stimuli richness, complexity of tasks to be achieved with them and privacy protection.

- This is an interdisciplinary book that explains what is going on in the new media in many domains and with several theories: network theory, structuration theory, medium theory and modernization theory.

2 NETWORKS: THE NERVOUS SYSTEM OF SOCIETY

About this chapter

- How can the network society be defined? What is the difference between this concept and the concepts of the information society and the mass society? Why do we need these concepts anyway? Are traditional classifications such as capitalist society, (post)modern society or (un)sustainable society no longer adequate?

- It is told that social networks are as old as mankind. A short history of networks in past human societies as compared to their role in contemporary society is presented.

- How can the exceptional rise of networks in contemporary society be explained? Evolution theory, systems theory and adaptive structuration theory will come forward as explanations.

- Networks currently appear at every level (individual, organizational and societal). A multilevel theory of the network society will explain why this happens and why these levels are more and more linked.

- How can the network society and the mass society be compared?

- According to network theory, networks operate according to particular scientific laws. Social science is able to apply some of these laws in seven so-called 'laws of the Web'. Formulating these 'laws' is one of the most important objectives of this book – they will return as explanations for things happening on the Internet in almost every chapter.

WHAT IS A NETWORK SOCIETY?

Definitions of the information society, network society and mass society

Several concepts are available to indicate the type of society that evolves under the influence of information and communication technology. The most popular concept is the 'information society', which is used in this book in combination with the concept 'network society' to typify contemporary developed and modern societies marked by a high level of information exchange and use of information and communication technologies (ICTs). In the concept of an information society, the changing *substance* of activities and processes in these societies is emphasized. In the concept of a network society, attention shifts to the changing organizational *forms* and (infra)structures of these societies.

I start with my own complete definitions of these types of society and continue with a number of qualifications of these definitions and their relationships with other classifications such as capitalist society and (post)modern society. My definition of the information society is listed in Box 2.1.

It is the intensity of information processing in all these spheres that allows us to describe it as a new type of society. The common denominator of the changes produced by the increasing information intensity of all activities is the semi-autonomous character of information processing. Most activities in contemporary society are dedicated to *means*, in this case means of processing and producing information. These activities tend to keep a distance from their ultimate aims and to gather their own momentum and reason to exist. Manuel Castells (1996) even claims that information has become an independent source of productivity and power.

BOX 2.1
Definition of the information society

A modern type of society in which the information intensity of all activities has become so high that this creates:

- an organization of society based on science, rationality and reflexivity;
- an economy with all values and sectors, even the agrarian and industrial sectors, increasingly characterized by information production;
- a labour market with a majority of functions largely or completely based on tasks of information processing requiring knowledge and higher education (hence, the alternative term *knowledge society*);
- a culture dominated by media and information products with their signs, symbols and meanings.

While the information society points to the content, the network society concept emphasizes the form and organization of modern society. An infrastructure of social and media networks takes care of this. The definition is given in Box 2.2.

> **BOX 2.2**
> ## Definition of the network society
>
> A modern type of society with an infrastructure of social and media networks that characterizes its mode of organization at every level: individual, group/ organizational and societal. Increasingly, these networks link every unit or part of this society (individuals, group and organizations). In western societies, the individual linked by networks is becoming the basic unit of the network society. In eastern societies, this might still be the group (family, community, work team) linked by networks.

This book compares the network society with the so-called mass society preceding it. The definition of this type of society is given in Box 2.3.

> **BOX 2.3**
> ## Definition of the mass society
>
> A modern type of society with an infrastructure of *groups, organizations* and *communities* (called 'masses'), that shape its prime mode of organization at every level (individual, group/organizational and societal). The basic units of this society are all kinds of relatively large collectivities (masses) organizing individuals.

Other classifications

Later in this chapter, in the section 'From Mass Society to Network Society', and in the remaining chapters of this book, I will elaborate the network and mass society concepts. Here I want to draw attention to a number of qualifications of the information and network society concepts. With good reasons, both concepts are contested. Webster (2001) concludes that all definitions of the information society refer to more *quantity* of information, information products, information occupations, communication means and so on, but are unable to identify the *qualitatively* new (system) character of this type of society. Manuel Castells (1996) also rejects the concept of information society as all societies in the past have been based on information. Instead, he proposes the concept of 'informational society': 'a specific form of social organization in which information generation, processing and transmission become the fundamental sources of productivity and power' (Castells, 1996: 21).

In the next section we see that all human societies since the invention of speech have been partly organized in networks. The idea of the network society as something particularly new has been called a fashionable and shallow concept with no theoretical basis. The fact that I try to improve the status does not deny that currently this statement still applies.

These qualifications suggest that other classifications of contemporary society remain valid anyway. All of them are abstractions. Concrete human societies are always combinations of abstract relationships on several fields grasped with similar abstract concepts. From an economic point of view, almost every contemporary society is capitalist. One type is called developed, the other developing. In political terms, a society is more or less democratic. Government might be called 'statist' as in the few remaining communist countries; a 'developmental state' such as in most East Asian countries; a welfare state such as in most European countries; and a (neo) liberal state serving a market economy such as the United States. From a social and cultural perspective, present-day societies may be called modern, post-modern and late-modern (whichever term one prefers), or traditional. In ecological terms, contemporary societies may be more or less sustainable.

In this book the general classifications of information and network society will be related to these other classifications. For example, in Chapter 4 we will see that a network economy changes capitalism, in Chapter 5 it will be argued that a network state and digital democracy are able to alter government, and in Chapters 7 and 8 that networks such as the Internet transform social living and culture in (post)modern society. In some parts of the book it will be questioned whether ICT favours or harms a sustainable society.

A final qualification to add is that the information and network society concepts indicate long-term evolutionary processes of human society. They are not concrete societal forms with precise historical beginnings and ends. To clarify this one might say that the information society did not start in 1751 with the appearance of the first part of the *Encyclopédie* of Diderot and d'Alembert and the network society did not appear with the installation of the first telegraph line by Samuel Morse in 1844. Both are much older (McNeill and McNeill, 2003; Gleick, 2011). In the 19th century, after the industrial revolution, modernizing western societies gradually became information societies (Beniger, 1986). In the 20th century, their social structure, modes of organization and communication infrastructure together typifying a mass society progressively changed into a network society (Castells, 1996; Mulgan, 1991; van Dijk, 1991, 1993a). So, contemporary societies are in the process of becoming information and network societies. Developed, high-tech societies have gone further down this road than developing societies that predominantly still are in the stage of being mass societies. However, the history of human networking is much older than the last two centuries.

A SHORT HISTORY OF THE HUMAN WEB
Five successive worldwide webs

Social networks are as old as humanity. Human individuals have always communicated more with some people than with others since the time they lived in small bands and tribes. The bands and tribes of ancient human history consisted of a few dozen (bands) to hundreds (tribes) of people. This number was big enough for people to maintain very intensive relations with some members (direct family and kin) and less intensive relations with other members of the band or tribe. The obvious biological necessity was a scale of coupling and mating that prevented inbreeding.

According to the historians J.R. and W. McNeill (2003), the human web dates back at least to the development of human speech. 'Our distant ancestors created social solidarity within small bands by talking together, and exchanging information and goods. Furthermore, bands interacted and communicated with one another, if only sporadically' (2003: 4). Their 'bird's eye view of world history' as a series of expanding and thickening webs, published in their brilliant book *The Human Web* (2003), is this section's guide.

The McNeills portray world history as a succession of five worldwide webs. The extension of these webs was not only driven by biological necessity, but also by the need and desire to make new discoveries and material conquests to improve the conditions of life. In these webs, not only speech and information in general were exchanged, but also goods, technologies, ideas, crops, weeds, animals and diseases.

In the *first worldwide web*, human kind spread around the world in hunting and gathering tribes. The exchange of ideas and cultural expressions (song and dance), technologies (bows and arrows, the control of fire) and genes (exogamous marriages between members of different bands and tribes) swept across Africa, Asia, and Europe and into the Americas and Oceania. This first human web remained very loose until the invention of agriculture about 12,000 years ago. Settling enabled humans to sustain more continuous interactions among a larger number of people at a local level.

About 6000 years ago, the local webs of settlements grew into *metropolitan* or *city webs*. They served as storehouses of information, goods and infections. In this way, the first civilizations of Mesopotamia, Egypt, the Indus, the Yellow River (China), Mexico and the Andes were created. These civilizations first established connections among thousands and then among millions of people. This was the first time in history that those connected actually remained strangers for each other: 'For the first time, key relationships and important everyday transactions routinely transcended the primary communities within which human beings had previously lived' (McNeill and McNeill, 2003: 41). These civilizations were connected by transport caravans of pack animals and vehicles across land and by ships along sea coasts and rivers.

The third human web was the *Old World Web* that grew out of the contact between and partial fusion of civilizations in Eurasia and North Africa around 2000 years ago. It caused the rise of large bureaucratic empires in India, China, the Mediterranean (Greece and Rome), Mexico and the Andes. Transport and communication improved considerably with the invention and spread of hub and spoke wheels, better roads, ships with higher capacity and alphabetic writing. The first tensions in the worldwide web appeared as epidemics spread, religions clashed and different civilizations and their rural hinterlands not only borrowed ideas, habits and customs from each other, but also rejected them, defending their own.

From about 1450 onwards, oceanic navigation brought the Eurasian and American civilizations into contact with each other to produce a truly worldwide *cosmopolitan web*. It was a violent clash of European civilizations overruling the native American ones. The result was an exchange of everything these civilizations had to offer, including lethal diseases. Between 1450 and 1800, more and more people moved to cities and became enrolled in larger and larger social networks. The result was that information circulated faster and more cheaply than ever before. However, the majority of people in 1800 still lived on the land as farmers: 'they knew little about the world beyond their own experience, because they could not read and they only occasionally met strangers' (McNeill and McNeill, 2003: 212).

The fifth type of human web changed this last point: the *global web* that covers the last 160 years. This period is characterized by urbanization and population growth. The human web was not so much widening anymore, but thickening. The volume and velocity of communication increased markedly. The number and use of new means of transport and communication exploded with trains, automobiles and aeroplanes, together with telegraphs, telephones, radios, televisions and, finally, computers and networks.

In this book, the first period of this era of the global web is characterized as the mass society marked by mass communication networks. In the second period, the network society evolves. With the thickening of the global human web, it has turned inwards into society. It is no longer only quantitatively extending across the globe and becoming more voluminous, but it is also qualitatively changing the infrastructure and working of current societies. This comes to rest upon social and media networks of all kinds and at all levels of society.

Conclusions from network history

Before I explain the role of networks and the characteristics of the network society in detail, I want to focus on the four important conclusions the McNeills have drawn from the history of the human web (McNeill and McNeill, 2003: 5–8). The first conclusion is that all webs have combined cooperation and competition. Communication sustains cooperation among people. Within a cooperative framework, specialization and division of labour are able to make a society richer and more powerful. They also make it more stratified and unequal. This inequality within society, together with the inequalities between societies, has always produced competition. Rivals share information too. It urges them to respond, for instance by cooperation with others.

The second conclusion is that the general direction of history has been toward greater social cooperation – both voluntary and compelled – driven by the realities of social competition. Groups and societies who cooperated most improved their competitive position and chances of survival. It gave them economic advantage (by the specialization of labour and exchange), military advantage (quantity and quality of warriors and the organization of armies) and epidemiological advantage (building immunities against diseases by close contact).

A third deduction from history is that, over time, the scale of human webs has tended to grow. So too has their influence on history. The current global web is truly worldwide. Practically no human society exists in isolation any more. The volume, velocity and importance of messages exchanged have become so large that their impact on contemporary society is incomparable to the effect of communication systems in ancient societies. This impact is a major reason for the emphasis of the network society concept in this book.

Finally, it has to be concluded that the power of human communication, both in its cooperative and competitive forms, has also affected the earth to an ever larger degree. Increasingly, economic and population growth, urbanization and technology have produced an ecological impact. 'We would not be 6 billion strong without the myriad of interconnections, the flows and exchanges of food, energy, technology, money that comprise the modern worldwide web' (McNeill and McNeill, 2003: 7).

NETWORKS AT ALL LEVELS
Networks of nature and society

What actually is a network? This question comes to mind after this broad description of networks in human history. After all, the concept appears in both natural and social sciences. Unfortunately, the following definition and account has to be rather abstract, but a precise definition and elaboration of the network concept here will enable better future understanding. A network can be defined as *a collection of links between elements of a unit*. The elements are called nodes. Units are often called systems. The smallest number of elements is three and the smallest number of links is two. A single link of two elements is called a relation(ship). Networks are a mode of organization of complex systems in nature and society.

In simple systems of nature and society, a static and hierarchical organization characterizes the relation of elements. For example, the relation between the elements or parts of atoms, molecules and chemical substances is fixed and has a particular order. Change means a transition to another (kind of) unit. When matter gets more complicated, especially when it becomes life, the elements have to be organized in more complicated ways. Life organizes these ways while it exchanges energy with the environment and adapts to this environment for survival. Networks are relatively complicated ways of organizing matter and living systems. They produce order out of chaos, linking elements in a particular way. Chaotic situations always appear as soon as the elements of matter and living systems become less fixed.

Emphasizing the organization and the relation of elements entails less attention to the elements and units themselves. The characteristics of units and elements, among them human individuals, and the way they are made up, are not the focus of attention. Instead every network approach in the natural and social sciences stresses the relations of elements. It is opposed to atomistic views of reality and methodological individualism in research (measuring social reality by adding individual attributes).

So, networks occur both in complicated matter and in living systems at all levels (see Table 2.1). Buchanan (2002) mentions a couple of examples of physical networks. The first one is an ecosystem of earth surfaces, flora and fauna and the second one a river network organizing its downward water flow in branches adapting to the ground and all kinds of obstacles. Examples become more numerous in living systems. All organisms with many cells organize these cells in networks. When they become larger they create special (network) systems such as a nervous system and a blood stream. As a matter of fact, cells themselves contain networks. The most important one is the DNA string of genes (molecules). Nowadays it is common scientific understanding that the complexity of life is not determined by the number of genes but by their relationships.

The largest nervous system of organisms on earth is to be found in the human brain. An increasing number of neurobiologists and psychologists agree that the human mind works with neuronal networks that are organized on a higher level using mental 'maps' in particular regions of the brain. The connection between these maps (themselves being neuronal networks) also reveals a network form. Gerald Edelman, one of the best known of these neurobiologists, argues that even human consciousness emerges from such connections of mental maps (Edelman and Tononi, 2000).

Human beings have created social networks at least since the invention of speech, as was explained in the previous section. In these networks, the elements are social agents (individuals, groups, organizations and even societies at large) and the links are created by communicative (inter)actions. Below I argue that social networks figure at all levels and subsystems of society. In the course of history, humans have also created a number of technical networks. Examples are roads, canals, all kinds of distribution networks and the telecommunication and computer networks that are an important subject matter in this book. When the latter networks are filled

TABLE 2.1   Types of network

Physical networks	Natural systems of higher complexity: ecosystems, river networks
Organic networks	Organisms: nervous system, blood circulation, strings of DNA in cells
Neuronal networks	Mental systems: neuronal connections, mental maps
Social networks	Social systems with concrete ties in abstract relationships
Technical networks	Technical systems: roads, distribution networks, telecommunication and computer networks, etc.
Media networks	Media systems connecting senders and receivers and filled with symbols and information

with symbols and information to connect human senders and receivers, they become media networks.

This book is about the relationship between social, technical and media networks – together they shape the infrastructure of the network society. Even organic and neuronal networks receive some attention, for instance in Chapter 9, which discusses the psychology of new media use. However, the primary focus of attention is social networks supported by media networks.

Networks at all social levels

Social networks supported by media networks are available at all levels and sub-systems of society. Four levels can be distinguished. They are portrayed in Figure 2.1, which shows the first picture of the abstract concept of the network society in this book.

The first and most basic level is the level of *individual relations*, not that of the individual because units and elements are not the prime focus of attention in a network perspective (Brass, 1995; Wellman and Berkowitz, 1988). This level corresponds to the common-sense meaning of (social) networking: individuals creating ties to

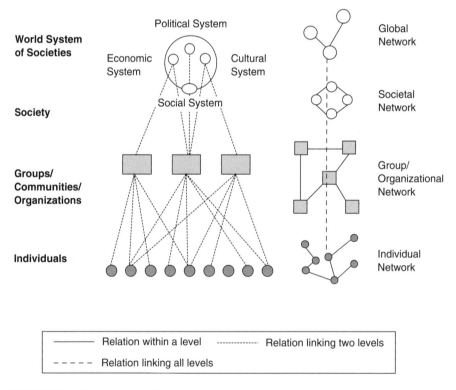

FIGURE 2.1 Four social units and levels linked by networks

family members, friends, acquaintances, neighbours, colleagues, fellow sportsmen, and so on. Currently, this level is supported and intensified by the rise of the media networks of the Internet (email) and mobile or fixed telephony.

The second level is that of *group and organizational relations*. Individuals create all kinds of groupings or collective agencies, some of them temporary and loose (such as project teams and mailing lists) and others permanent and fixed (institutions and corporations). All contemporary groupings are supported by telecommunications and computer networks. They tend to loosen fixed group and organizational structures because they enable virtual organizing at every scale. Internally, many organizations have become network organizations of largely independent teams and projects. Externally, they assemble to form network organizations cooperating in the execution of a particular task. They may even become virtual organizations that are more or less independent from spatial, temporal and physical conditions as these conditions are substituted by networks of information and communication technology.

The third is the level of *societal relations*. Individuals, groups and organizations shape a society that is built on, and linked by, social and media networks. This goes for all subsystems of society. One increasingly uses the phrase 'network(ed) economy', which is sometimes called a 'new economy'. In politics, some people talk about a 'network state'. Internally, this state links the bodies and institutions of the government and the public administration at every level. Externally, it maintains strong relationships with organizations of citizens and with semi-autonomous or privatized public institutions (Castells, 1997; Fountain, 2001; Goldsmith and Eggers, 2004; Guéhenno, 1993; van Dijk, 2000a). In the cultural sphere, the Internet has created a vast hyperlink structure of sources and artefacts of human activity (de Kerckhove, 1998). Finally, the societal infrastructure of interpersonal and group relationships has been intensified by the ever-stronger links between social networks and telecommunication networks using email and mobile or fixed telephony (Katz and Rice, 2002; Wellman, 2001; Wellman and Haythornthwaite, 2002).

The final level is the level of *global relations* in the world system of societies and international organizations (Slaughter, 2004; Urry, 2003). We have entered the era of the global web as it was explained in the previous section. This is created by expanding international relations and a scale extension of organization. Both are strongly supported by international broadcasting, telecommunications and computer networking.

A multilevel theory of networks

It is vital for the understanding of the network society to analyse it in terms of levels of networking. In their helpful overview of contemporary *Theories of Communication Networks* (2003), Monge and Contractor have made a strong argument for multilevel theories of networks. The word theory is used in the plural as they also defend a combination of theories to explain phenomena at the different levels distinguished.

An important part of their argument is that the levels are linked themselves. They build their own theory relating statements at the level of the individual, the dyad, tryad, group, organization and at the interorganizational level.

Previously, I also advocated a multilevel theory of the network society (van Dijk, 2001). This advocacy did not only lean on the historical rise of media networks that are used at every level, but also on basic views on the composition and (infra) structure of society. Such a basic view is developed in Kontopoulos' methodological and conceptual book *The Logics of Social Structure* (1993). According to him, the world must be analysed as a level structure: 'Levels are not juxtaposed layers; every level is rooted to lower levels, down to the chemical and physical ones. Therefore, same-level or intra-level analysis must be supplemented and enriched by cross-level or inter-level analysis' (1993: 63). At every level, particular properties emerge that only apply to that level (the individual, group, organization, society, world system). Examples of such properties are the personality of an individual, the measure of formality of a group, the extent of centralization of an organization and the phase of development of a society.

In this book about the network society, such a basic view is needed to explain the character of networks as a particular mode of social organization. Kontopoulos makes a distinction between hierarchical and heterarchical modes of organization of the world. Networks clearly belong to the last mode. In a hierarchical mode, the lower levels are fully included in the higher levels. The units at these levels are simply aggregated to form units at a higher level. Individuals add to groups and organizations and both add to society. A second property of the hierarchical mode is that the lower levels are superseded by the higher ones. This might mean that the higher level controls the lower one. This is the common meaning of the term hierarchy.

In a heterarchical mode of organization, the lower levels are only partially included in the higher levels. The units concerned contain relations and structures that overlap with those at higher levels. Networks belong to these relations and structures. They cut right through all levels, and they connect these levels (see Figure 2.1 again). Networks realize complex interactions within and between levels. In this way, they increase the flexibility of organization.

In terms of determination, the heterarchical mode means that neither the higher nor the lower levels are in control. Instead, a very complicated picture appears of determination from below, determination from above and determination at the semi-autonomous level in focus itself (Kontopoulos, 1993: 55).

Examples of this cutting through all levels of networks are individuals who pass the borders of the units they belong to (families, groups, departments, organizations) to establish links with other individuals in groups, organizations and societies they do not belong to, in this way creating their own structures. The same goes for organizations passing the borders of their societies or nation states.

The use of telecommunication and computer networks strongly supports these practices. They also link the types and levels of interpersonal, organizational and mass communication. For the first time in history we have a medium, called the Internet, directly linking them simultaneously. Telephones, letters, documents, computer files and meetings served interpersonal and organizational communication, and mass communication was realized by broadcasting and the press. However, with the Internet, this traditional split has dissolved, as it is used for communication at all levels.

So, networks organize relations within and between levels or units of social reality. As has been argued before, every network approach stresses the importance of the relations as compared to the units that are linked. The traditional network approach defends this position in a radical way. It gives priority to forms instead of substances. The social network analysis following this approach emphasizes the morphology of ties and nodes to such an extent that it downplays the attributes of the social units and what happens inside or between them, that is, the communicative action of people who are using and creating rules, resources and meanings. In this book, I reject this formalistic and superficial approach. Instead, I defend a moderate notion of a network approach. This means that, first, not only relations are stressed, but also the characteristics of the units they link. The most interesting things occur when relations and the characteristics of units come into conflict. This happens, for example, when the new digital communication networks, with relations transcending space and time in the global 24-hour economy, collide with the limitations of the biological human organism (unit), with its daily rhythms and routines or needs for rest that cannot fulfil the 24/7-expectations of the technology and economy concerned.

A second qualification of the radical network approach is that, in this book, networks are not supposed to be the basic units of contemporary society as they are in the view of Manuel Castells (1996, 2000, 2001). Instead, these basic units are held to be individuals, households, groups and organizations *increasingly linked by social and media networks*. In modern western societies, the individual is becoming the most important basic unit of society. In others, this frequently is the family, kinship group or local community. The combination of social and media networks produced by both organizational and technological innovation forms the all-embracing network structure of modern societies. This combination justifies the use of the strong metaphor of networks shaping the nervous system of advanced high-tech societies.

CAUSES OF THE RISE OF NETWORKS
Historical and social causes

What are the causes of the rise of networks in contemporary societies? It is relatively easy to describe a number of historical and social reasons. It is far more difficult to uncover the basic social infrastructures and modes of organization of societies explaining the rise of network structures. Let us start with the historical and social reasons. The McNeills would explain the current rise of information and communication networks as the last stage of the evolution of the global web. This web is no longer primarily widening, but it is thickening. Ever more persons, animals, plants, diseases, goods, services, pieces of information, messages, new ideas and innovations are exchanged globally and at ever faster rates.

Social explanations will emphasize the social need and appropriateness of the creation and use of networks at all levels. At the *individual* level we are witnessing the rise of networking as an explicit and increasingly systematic method of making contacts and improving social relations. Below, the concept of network individualization is used to describe this phenomenon. The use of networking is an evident social need in an individualizing society. Networks can be seen as the social counterparts of individualization. At the level of *organizations*, corporations and institutions are no longer working alone. They have become a part of a comprehensive division of labour. Increasingly, this division is organized in networks of cooperating organizations. Moreover, organizations have to open themselves more and more to their environment to survive in competition (business) and societal demand (government and non-profit organizations). Traditional internal structures of organizations are crumbling and external structures of communication are added to them. Acquiring new combinations of internal and external communication, they are better equipped to adapt to a swiftly changing environment.

Networks also cause a comprehensive restructuring of *society at large*. They are breaking old modes of organization as they help organizations in their search for new scale levels, new markets and new ways to govern and control. Networks link the processes of scale extension and scale reduction occurring simultaneously in modern society. At the one side they support globalization and socialization, and at the other side localization and individualization. In this way, they have accelerated modernization (Barber, 1996; Castells, 1996; van Dijk, 1993a).

All of these historical and social explanations are valid, but they fail to answer the question of why networks are built to satisfy these social needs. What is the presumed superior organizational quality of networks and networking? To answer these questions we have to dig deeper and consult network theory, a theory that has made considerable progress in the last fifteen years. Unfortunately, this means that the exposition has to become fairly abstract again.

Systems causes: Adaptation, evolution and managing complexity

Networks are structures and they organize systems. Network theory is usually some kind of structural theory and systems theory. The most general one is systems theory. In terms of this theory a network can be defined as *a relatively open system linking at least three relatively closed systems*. The relatively closed system is the unit. As we have seen, we need at least three of them to create a network. These units can be conceived as relatively closed systems because they contain elements that primarily act among themselves to reproduce the unit in a (pre)determined way. As soon as these closed units are forced, for one reason or another, to interact with their environment and to link themselves to other units in a network, they create an open system. In an open system, complete determination is lost and replaced by chance and random events. That allows change and new opportunities. This process of opening up closed systems is the secret of networks or networking as an organization principle.

This propensity of change is explained differently by two versions of systems theory that have inspired network theory. The first version has a biological inspiration and the second a physicist and mathematical inspiration. According to the biological inspiration, systems are conceived as organisms that have to adapt to a physical environment to survive (among others, Maturana and Varela, 1980, 1984; Prigogine and Stengers, 1984). This is the propensity of change here. In this reading, networks can be seen as adaptive systems. Our brain is a complex adaptive system and the same goes for our bodies. Increasingly, our organizations and societies are also complex adaptive systems. All of them are relatively closed. However, they have to adapt to an ever more complex environment. Here they get the assistance of networks as relatively open systems. According to Axelrod and Cohen (1999), adaptation occurs in three successive processes, which they derive from evolution (systems) theory: variation, interaction and selection. However, I think the right order in this theory is interaction, variation, selection and retention and I will treat them in this order.

First there is *interaction*. Networks support interactions within and between system units. For example, inside organizations they help to break through the divisions of departments to enable the communication of more members than before in shifting teams and projects. This offers them opportunities for changing and (self-)steering the organization. Between organizations, networks, particularly telecommunication and computer networks, are reducing the limits of time and place that were formerly keeping their members' communicative (inter)actions apart.

Increasing or intensifying interaction leads to more *variation*. First of all, there is variation of scope as the reach of information retrieval and communication is enlarged by new network connections. Everyone engaged in networking will recognize this idea: one has to break out of one's own small circle of people to obtain experiences and contacts outside, even when they are very superficial. Granovetter (1973) called this idea the strength of weak ties. Accepting the value of weak ties, one should not deny the importance of strong ties. Variation also reaches into depth. Our own familiar environment offers opportunities of interaction and information by means of intensive ties and high-quality communication. It is the combination of variation in scope and in depth that makes networks strong as relatively open systems emerging from relatively closed systems, but always remaining linked to them. A person engaged in networking is not a roaming nomad, but someone who keeps a home base.

The final process is *selection*. Here the goal of networking is reached: choosing the most successful actions and actors. This serves the adaptation and survival of the particular system concerned: *retention*. For example, an unemployed individual gets a job, a company finds the best chain of suppliers and customers and a society adopts a particular policy, organization and provision to uphold itself in the process of globalization.

The second version of systems theory reveals a mathematical and physicist inspiration. Here systems are conceived as units, both in nature and in society, containing elements that can be connected in ordered (clustered) and disordered (random) ways. Here the propensity to change is the tendency of nature to produce order out of chaos. For ages now, networks have been studied as mathematical objects called graphs. Graphs depict the potential links between a collection of elements in a particular unit. A social-scientific application is the discovery by the psychologist Stanley Milgram (1967) that on average every inhabitant (element) of a given unit, in this case the United States, is linked by six intermediary persons, in the so-called *six degrees of separation,* to every other inhabitant. This peculiar fact can only be explained by the other fact that groups of people are closely linked and organized in clusters. These clusters are often linked by so-called weak ties, a phenomenon described by the sociologist Granovetter (see above). In the tradition of Milgram and Granovetter, a number of mathematicians and physicists have made their way to social science to produce important discoveries in network theory that will be represented in the sections and chapters that follow (Barabási, 2002; Barabási & Albert, 1999; Buchanan, 2002; Watts, 2003; Watts and Strogatz, 1998).

This version of network and systems theory tries to explain how randomly distributed elements of a unit or system link to each other in clusters and these clusters in a single whole (a particular order). In this way, a complex system is created, in this case a complex society that is highly adaptable to environmental change. The question remains how order appears in a system without a pre-existing centre but with a number of interacting equals. The answer is connectivity: at a critical point, a phase

FIGURE 2.2   Picture of a network connecting small worlds (clusters)

transition in the system, 'all parts of the system act *as if* they can communicate with each other, despite their interactions being purely local' (Watts, 2003: 63). This critical point appears as a sufficient number of (random) long-distance links connects a large number of local individual units ordered in all kinds of clusters (groups, communities, organizations). In this way a so-called *small world* is created within a large-scale or global environment. These small worlds have internal links and reveal order because two elements that are connected to a common third element are more likely to establish a link to each other than two elements picked at random. You will more easily become acquainted with a friend of a friend than with a stranger. Figure 2.2 portrays a network connecting a number of small worlds (clusters with strong ties) with long-distance (weak) ties.

Social and media networks in contemporary society increasingly create small worlds and clusters in such a way that any pair of individuals or organizations can be connected via a short chain of intermediaries. This leads to statements, almost platitudes in the mean time, that we live in a connected world and that society is ever more connected. In short, that it is becoming a network society.

THE SEVEN 'LAWS' OF THE WEB

To understand what networks really are and how they 'behave', we have to realize that they have particular structural properties. These can be summarized in a number of 'laws' of the Web (an expression first made by Huberman, 2001). They are not some kind of natural laws. They are defining and enabling conditions that exert pressure on human behaviour in networks, but that can also be changed, as usually happens to structures according to structuration theory. Understanding these 'laws' helps to explain things we can observe on the Web and it assists in finding mechanisms to intervene in the network structures concerned. Seven laws summarize a large part of the general theoretical argument in the following chapters of this book.

BOX 2.4
The law of network articulation

In the network society, the social *relations* are gaining influence as compared to the social *units* they are linking.

The first and most important law is the law of network articulation. In the network society, relations are getting more important in comparison to the units or nodes they are linking. Relations float to the surface in every subsystem of society. They are realized by a combination of social and media networks. Their effect substantially changes the economy, politics, government, culture and daily life.

In Chapter 4, we will see that a network economy is created. In Chapter 5, it will be observed that institutional politics and public administrations transfer power to other units, directly getting into touch with each other via networks: transnational corporations, international bodies, non-governmental organizations (NGOs), local corporations, individual citizens and their social and political organizations. In this way, the national state may be bypassed as the traditional centre of politics. Reacting to this shift of power, the state itself transforms into a 'network state' linking increasingly independent and privatized government agencies. In Chapter 6, we will find out that our current law system based on the notion of independent actors, acts and property items is undermined by networks. In Chapter 7, it will be established that we increasingly select and compose our own social relationships as a matter of network individualization. These relationships are less and less imposed by the social environment. Finally, in Chapter 8, we will observe the rise of a digital culture of hyper-linked creations that will completely transform our current culture of separate creations and media practices. The enormous variety of reactions to the articulation of networks in all fields of society – that we will come across in the following chapters – testifies to the fact that the laws of the Web have no deterministic effects.

BOX 2.5
The law of network externality

Networks have effects on things/ people external to the network. The more people participate in a network, the more others are likely to join. There is a pressure to connect.

The second law is the law of network externality. Networks have effects, called 'network effects' on people and things around them. The more people participate in the network the bigger the effects are. As a network grows it exerts pressure on people to join. This pressure is stepped up at two tipping points. The first occurs when a critical mass of users is reached. When about 20 to 25 per cent of a population is connected, it makes ever more sense for others to join. This happens most of all in communication networks such as email and social networking sites (SNS). After some time, when about two-thirds is connected, a second tipping point arrives. Saturation sets in and connection rates slow down. Yet, from this point onwards, people are more or less forced to participate on the risk of social exclusion. In developed countries, both tipping points have already occurred for email. For SNS the second is fast approaching in the year 2011. This second law partly explains the extraordinarily fast growth of the Web.

Networks also exert influence on things, not only computers, telephones and TV-sets but all kinds of objects as they become increasingly linked by tags with embedded chips. There is a pressure to connect all of them to speed-up and control production and distribution processes. As networks are systems, their connections have to follow common standards. A network with standards which are accepted by many people has power (Grewal, 2008). This is the power to decide who is able to connect to the network and use it for communication with others. Generally, people prefer a general standard because in that case they can reach many others in the same system. In this way, critical mass can be reached. This is one of the reasons for the steady popularity of Microsoft's operating systems and other software. Next to TCP/IP operating systems such as Windows, Mac OS and Linux, browsers such as Internet Explorer, Mozzilla Firefox and Google Chrome, mark-up languages such as HTML and search engines such as Google, Bing and Yahoo are important software standards.

BOX 2.6
The law of network extension

When networks such as the Web grow, they tend to become too big. Network units lose oversight and do not reach each other anymore. To solve this problem, *intermediaries*, such as search engines, portals and social networking sites are necessary.

The third law of the Web reveals the internal dimension of network growth. The law of network extension holds that networks quickly become too big to directly link every unit or node to every other. When this happens, they form internal structures of clusters of units that can reach each other more easily – see Figure 2.2 for an image. They also create bridges between clusters and central meeting places: these are intermediaries. They characterize the Web as it grows. While in the early days of the Internet many people thought that intermediaries were no longer required, as people would serve themselves and link to each other, the contemporary Internet is dominated by all kinds of intermediaries, from search engines, portals, price comparison sites and market places (such as eBay) to SNS and dating services.

BOX 2.7
The law of small worlds

In large-scale networks, most units are not neighbours, but still can reach almost every other unit in a few steps (six degrees of separation) creating a *small world*. Explanation: units are grouped in clusters with *strong ties*, and they reach people in other clusters by long-distance and often *weak ties*.

Taking these steps, the influence of people by contagion reaches three degrees.

In large-scale networks such as the Web, most units are not neighbours. Nevertheless, they still can reach almost every other connected unit in a few steps, in this way creating a *small world*. This has been demonstrated by among others Stanley Milgram (1967) with his famous observation of the *six degrees of separation*. This means that, on average, every world inhabitant is connected to every other in only six steps when all available social networks of these inhabitants are used. The secret that explains this phenomenon is that actors are grouped in clusters with *strong ties*, and that they reach people far away in another cluster by long-distance ties, often *weak ties*. See pages 2–15 and Figure 2.2. Examples of clusters with strong ties are extended families, neighbourhoods, groups of colleagues and school classes.

When not only social networks are used, but also new media networks, the number of six steps could be reduced to five or even four as has been demonstrated in research using email, web-page links, SNS and Twitter messages for a test (Albert et al., 1999; Cheng, 2010; Watts, 2003).

An important question is how far actions and communication carry on this average of six degrees of separation. According to Christakis and Fowler (2009) the answer is three. According to the *three degrees of influence* rule, they show that the phenomenon of contagion on average reaches three steps further than the source and then gradually dissipates. Think about friends of friends. This goes for attitudes, feelings and behaviour and for a very broad range of phenomena such as political views, obesity, emotions or non-verbal behaviour – laughing, coughing and dancing are contagious – and even happiness.

The law of small worlds explains why our world is ever more connected and interactive using the Web and other communication networks.

BOX 2.8
The law of the limits to attention

As everybody in a network is able, in principle, to connect and communicate to everyone else in the network, there is a limit to attention because the time to read, listen or view for receivers runs out. The more people write/produce content on the Web, the smaller on average their audiences become.

Many people think that everything is available on the Internet as the number of senders and receivers is endless. They suppose that there is an audience for every new voice. However, this is a basic mistake. People forget that sending may be boundless, but attention is limited. It is easy to speak on the Internet, but difficult to be heard (Hindman, 2008). Let us suppose that every new Internet user has the same period of time to read and to write online. In that case, the new Internet user would on average find only an audience of one. Fortunately, most Internet users take more time to read, listen and view than to write and to produce. Moreover, it takes more time to produce than to consume messages on the Internet. So, fortunately, the audience for a new voice is larger than one. However, it still is limited. The more people generate content on the Internet, the smaller their audiences become. Most weblogs are read by very few people; the majority of Twitter messages are never read; and most personal web-pages have a very small audience.

The limitation of Web audiences is strongly reinforced by 'Googlearchy', the rule of the most heavily linked (Hindman, 2008). Google and other search engines rank the most popular websites at the top of their results page. In this way they become even more popular (this is an instance of the power law discussed below). Because of the law of network extension we simply have to use search engines and other intermediaries.

So, in theory, the Web may offer equal chances to numerous senders, but in practice audiences are unequally divided. Hindman (2008) has even shown that media concentration on the Internet is bigger than in the traditional mass media (see Chapter 8). The largest part of the Internet audience goes to a few big players such as Google, MSN, Yahoo, Facebook and MySpace. At the other end of the scale, another large part goes to the numerous senders with very small audiences. This is the so-called 'long tail' (Anderson, 2006). But the middle is missing: surprisingly few middle-sized media in terms of audience can be observed on the Internet (Hindman, 2008: 82–102).

BOX 2.9
The power law in networks

In large, scale-free networks those units already having many links acquire even more, while most units keep only a few links. The mechanisms are a continuous growth of links, preferential attachment and contagion.

This distribution of a small number of units or nodes with many links, a large number of units or nodes with a few links and the missing middle is explained by the so-called power law. This is a statistical regularity for large-scale, so-called scale-free networks – scale-free means that there is no assumption on the number of nodes and links in the network. Nor is it assumed that every node is linked to every other or that the distribution is normal. The Internet, for example, does not have a fixed number of nodes, every user is not linked to everybody else and the distribution is not normal (this would mean a fat middle: a Bell curve). Instead, there is a power law distribution. This is marked by many nodes with a few links and a few nodes with a very large number of links: 'They have the power'. In more common-sense language it is called 'the rich are getting richer and the poor are getting poorer effect' on the

Internet. Yes, the poor are also getting poorer, mostly not in absolute but in relative measures. The law of the limits to attention is responsible. Those with few links have increasing problems finding an audience.

There are three mechanisms explaining the appearance of this regularity. First, there should be a large and growing number of units and links that forces people to choose according to the law of network extension. Second, the new units decide to choose links to other units in the network following preferential attachment. In social networks this means that people tend to flock round the 'most popular guy'. In media networks such as the Web, the most conspicuous example is that search engine users tend to go to the first hits on the list. In this way the most popular links become even more popular. This also goes for Facebook and Twitter. Those that already have most friends and followers regularly assemble most new connections. The third mechanism is contagion. Observing and simulating the behaviour of others stimulates people to follow each other and flock to the most popular.

The power law helps to explain inequality in networks. In this book it will be shown that networks tend to increase inequality, despite the fact that they are also able to spread knowledge, information, contacts and other valuable things.

BOX 2.10
The law of trend amplification

Networks are relational structures that tend to amplify existing social and structural trends. When technologies such as ICT networks and computers are used, they serve as reinforcing tools.

The last 'law' of the Web returns in about every chapter of this book. It is the main contribution of this book to the known laws of the Web in network theory. A basic statement of this book is that networks such as the Internet tend to reinforce existing structures of society instead of overthrowing them. The effects of the Internet and the new media on society are evolutionary rather than revolutionary. The technology of networks might be revolutionary, but its social effects on society are not (van Dijk, 2010a). A very popular view is that things have never changed so fast and as deeply as they have in contemporary society, by the current communications revolution among others. However, already at the start of the following chapter we will see that changes in the former communications revolution of modern history, about a century ago, were perhaps even more pervasive for society and everyday life in those days than they are today. Remember that a communications revolution is not equal to a societal revolution! This also goes for the network society that gradually evolved from the mass society and did not, for example, put an end to capitalism.

In this book many examples will be given to show that the Internet and the new media reinforce existing social trends – they are trend amplifiers. The background reason is that networks are relational structures that emphasize and reinforce existing relations between people embedded in social structures. The relation between units is reinforced in particular when people use the new media as tools. For example, social inequality in most developed and developing societies was already increasing when a type of information inequality arrived that is marked by unequal digital skills (see Chapter 7). It happens to be that the higher educated, who usually have the best digital skills, increase their advantage on the lower educated with less.

FROM MASS SOCIETY TO NETWORK SOCIETY
A systematic comparison

Finally, we are ready to understand the main characteristics of the network society as compared to that of the mass society. This comparison is made in Table 2.2. It will serve as a summary of the argument in this section and an introduction to the following chapters where the network society is described in detail.

The mass society was defined earlier in this chapter as a social formation with an infrastructure of groups, organizations and communities ('masses') that shapes its prime mode of organization at all levels. The main components of this formation are all kinds of relatively large collectivities. Historically, the mass society characterizes the first phase of the era of the global web as it is called by the McNeills (2003). This society evolved during the industrial revolution when large concentrations of people came

TABLE 2.2 A typology of the mass society and the network society

Characteristics	Mass Society	Network Society
Main components	Collectivities (Groups, Organizations, Communities)	Individuals (linked by networks)
Nature of components	Homogeneous	Heterogeneous
Scale	Extended	Extended and Reduced
Scope	Local	'Glocal' (global and local)
Connectivity and Connectedness	High within components	High between components
Density	High	Lower
Centralization	High (few centres)	Lower (polycentric)
Inclusiveness	High	Lower
Type of community	Physical and unitary	Virtual and diverse
Type of organization	Bureaucracy	Infocracy
	Vertically integrated	Horizontally differentiated
Type of household	Large with extended family	Small with diversity of family relations
Main type of communication	Face-to-face	Increasingly mediated
Kind of media	Broadcast mass media	Narrowcast interactive media
Number of media	Low	High

together in industrial towns and trading centres. Typical of these concentrations was that the traditional communities already existing in neighbourhoods and villages were largely maintained when they were combined on a larger scale in cities and nations.

The basic components of mass society are large households and extended families in the rather tight communities of a village or a city neighbourhood. In large companies, other mass associations appear, such as closely cooperating shifts and departments. The basic components or units of the mass society are homogeneous. This does not mean that internal conflict or opposition is absent, but that all units concerned largely reveal the same characteristics and social structures. For example, the large households consist of standard nuclear families with a mother, father and many children. Local communities also are relatively homogeneous or unitary and they are marked by physical proximity.

The mass society is marked by scale extension. Corporations, governments and other organizations grow larger and larger and they become bureaucracies. They spread across nations and the world at large to create a global web of 19th-century empires and multinationals. However, the scope of the mass society remains local: the organization of its basic components is tied to particular places and communication is still overwhelmingly local. The mass society is an assembly and connection of relatively homogeneous separate localplaces. These basic components or units of the mass society are marked by the physical co-presence of their members. This means

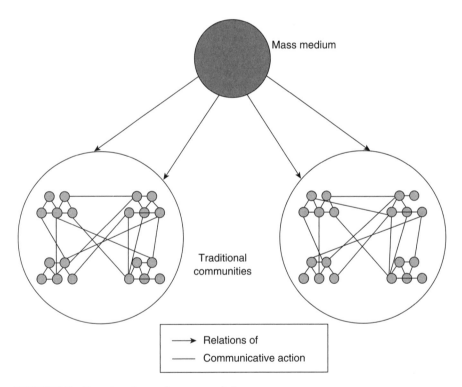

FIGURE 2.3 The structure of mass society

high connectivity inside and relatively low connectivity outside. The mass society is very much clustered with strong ties of high density (in local communities and extended family structures) and it contains relatively few weak ties connecting these clusters at long distances in diffuse network structures.

The internal relations in the units of the mass society are centralized. Bureaucratic and vertically integrated modes of organization prevail. There are relatively few very influential centres: the national, regional and local state, the army, a number of large corporations, churches or other cultural institutions and a limited number of mass media. The complement of centralization is that the inclusiveness of relations is high as well. The number of connected members is high and few of them are isolated or excluded. The mass society is marked more by solidarity than the network society.

In the mass society, every unit (community, household) has access to only one or perhaps a few of each type of mass media, such as one local newspaper, followed by one national newspaper and one or a few radio and television channels. So, the number of media is relatively low as compared to the current standards in network societies. Essentially, they are all broadcast media. However, generally speaking, face-to-face communication is much more important than mediated communication in the mass society.

In Figure 2.3 an attempt is made to depict the social and communicative structure of the mass society.

In the course of the 20th century, the structures of the mass society were gradually replaced by the structures of the network society. This happened first of all in developed or modern societies. The reasons for this replacement will be discussed in the following chapters, as they derive from problems of organization and communication in the economic, political and cultural systems and the general social infrastructure of these societies. The characteristics of the network society are described below in order to compare them with the mass society.

Characteristics of the network society

As has been argued above, in the contemporary process of individualization, the basic unit of the network society has become the individual who is linked by networks. Traditional local collectivities such as communities, extended families and large bureaucracies are fragmenting. This is caused by simultaneous scale extension (nationalization and internationalization) and scale reduction (smaller living and working environments). Other kinds of communities arise, consisting of people who on the one hand continue to live and work in their own families, neighbourhoods and organizations, but on the other hand frequently move around in large-scale social networks that are much more diffuse than the traditional ones. Daily living and working environments are getting smaller and more heterogeneous, while the range of the division of labour, interpersonal communications and mass media extends. So, the scale of the network society is both extended and reduced as compared to the mass society. The scope of the network society also is both global and local, sometimes indicated as 'glocal'. The organization of its components (individuals, groups, organizations) is no longer tied to particular times and places. Aided by information and communication technology, these coordinates of existence can be transcended to create virtual times and places and to simultaneously act, perceive and think in global and local terms.

The social units of the network society are fragmented and dispersed. This means that the density of contacts and ties *within* these units is relatively low as compared to traditional families, neighbourhoods, communities and organizations in the mass society. Instead, the elements of these units, the individuals, select their own contacts and ties *beyond* these units. Using all kinds of telecommunication they develop an extremely high level of connectivity between themselves as individuals and accordingly between the units of the network society of which they are a part.

Networks are relatively flat and horizontal, so-called heterarchical social structures. However, this does not mean that they do not have centres. Think about the spider in the web. Networks usually do not have a single centre – they are polycentric, as some nodes are (much) more important than others. For this reason, the network society is less centralized in the sense of having single centres in the economy, politics, government, culture and community life. They are replaced by a multitude of centres cooperating and competing with each other.

The network society is less inclusive than the mass society. You may be a member of some part of the mass society by birth or ascription. In the individualized network society you have to fight for a particular place. You have to show your value for every network, otherwise you will be isolated within it, or even excluded from it. In the network society, you have to stand firm as an individual. You are not that easily taken along in solidarity by proximate people.

In the network society, face-to-face communication remains the most important kind of communication in many ways. However, gradually it is also partly replaced and supplemented by mediated communication. A multitude of interpersonal and mass communication media are used for this purpose. Broadcast mass media reaching everyone are accompanied by, and partly replaced by, narrowcast interactive media reaching selected audiences. They lead to all kinds of new communication forms and groupings between interpersonal and mass communications, such as chat and instant messaging groups, virtual teams at work and virtual communities of interest. Virtual communities add to the thinned out physical communities of the network society with their small and diversely composed households. Figure 2.4 represents the complicated social and communicative structure of the network society.

The advent of another structure of a society implies that the relations between its parts are changing. In the network society, both abstract relations and concrete ties between individuals, groups and organizations are transformed. Often these changes run against popular views about social and media networks. For instance, one popular view is that networks are not a hierarchic but are a 'flat' mode of organization. Most often, horizontal and flexible networks are opposed to vertical and ponderous columns of organizations. Some people even suggest that networks are democratic by nature. Or they suppose that they are more transparent than the institutions they partly replace. Another popular view is that networks are open and accessible to all, contrary to fixed and closed organizations with their memberships. A less positive popular connotation is that networks are breaking the social cohesion of modern societies. They cut right through existing institutions and everyone appears to communicate alongside each other in their own subcultural network. A final popular view is that computer networks are no longer tied to place, time and physical conditions and that they are offering us more freedom in this way. In this book, it is argued that all these popular views are one-sided, to say the least. Networks are not necessarily more 'flat', democratic, open, free, accessible, physically unconditional or less socially coherent than other modes of organization and communication.

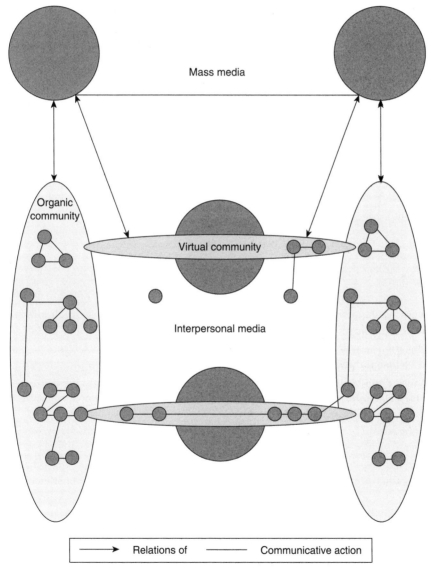

FIGURE 2.4 The structure of network society

CONCLUSIONS

- The network society should be defined as a modern type of society with an infrastructure of social and media networks that characterizes its *mode of organization* at every level: individual, group/organizational and societal. This can be compared to an information society that is marked by a particular *substance*: a high information intensity of all activities in society. It can also be contrasted with the mass society: a previous type of modern society with an infrastructure of groups, organizations and communities (called 'masses').

- Social networks are as old as human kind. First trade networks were added and subsequently transportation and production networks. In the course of the 20th century, information and communication became so important that it has now become possible to speak of a network society.

- Currently, networks serve at every level of society and they connect these levels. The Internet, for example, simultaneously serves individuals, organizations, communities and societies. We have never had such a medium in history before.

- The growing importance of networks can be explained by historical and social causes and by systems causes. Historically, it can be shown that individuals, organizations and societies needed them to realize their social, cultural and economic objectives. Systems theory adds deeper causes defining networks as relatively open systems linking closed systems of individuals and organizations. In the biological inspiration of evolution theory, networks are seen as structures that help social units to better adapt to their environment. In a mathematical and physicist inspiration, networks are a way to create order out of chaos. They consist of long-distance links connecting a large number of local individual units ordered in all kinds of clusters (groups, communities, organizations). In this way, a 'small world' is created with a decreasing number of degrees of separation and a growing number of degrees of influence via higher connectivity.

- Following these deeper causes, network theory has formulated seven 'laws' of the Web. These laws are no natural necessities as they are continually changed by human beings. Nevertheless, they exert pressures that are able to explain many trends of the network society in the following chapters.

- With the distinctions and theories formulated in the first part of this chapter a systematic and recognizable comparison can be made between the network and mass society.

3 TECHNOLOGY

About this chapter

- What are the technical characteristics of the computer, the Internet and other digital media that people who do not have a technical background should know in order to understand the social aspects of their use and the effects discussed in the remainder of this book? The first characteristics are a number of technical foundations for the network society such as micro-electronics, digitalization, the store and forward principle, the layered organization of networks and new connections.

- On top of these foundations a number of important current trends are described: the convergence of all information and communication networks (telephony, broadcasting and the Internet); the miniaturization of digital media devices; the embedding and the merging of these media into everyday-life; the turn to mobile, wireless and broadband connections; and finally the rise of cloud computing.

TECHNICAL FOUNDATIONS OF THE NETWORK SOCIETY

Micro-electronics

The technical foundations of the network society and the second communications revolution were prepared in five revolutionary developments all happening in the last part of the 20th century. The first, and most important, development was a series of successive revolutions in micro-electronics. It led to five generations of computers in the last 25–30 years of the 20th century. This series was characterized mainly by a miniaturization of parts. The most important breakthrough was the invention of the integrated semiconductor, a chip consisting of hundreds of thousands of connections on a plate with a surface of just a few square millimetres.

The capacity of chips increased exponentially; it doubled on average every 18 months. Chips enabled a complete computerization of telephone networks, from the central exchange to local switches and terminal equipment. At the same time, they caused a drastic decentralization of computer processing, turning data communication into an important phenomenon. Eventually, chips and processors were also used in audiovisual equipment for transmission and reception on a large scale. Thus, the foundation was laid for a uniform micro-electronic technology for telecommunications, data communications and mass communications. It is the basis for the improvement of the communication capacities of speed, storage capacity, accuracy, stimuli richness and complexity of operations in the new media, as discussed in Chapter 1.

Digitalization

The second foundation is inextricably linked to the first. Micro-electronics uses a uniform language for all signals exchanged in its components. This uniformity is the language of digital signals. Digitalization is the binding structure for all new media networks in tele-, data and mass communications. Telecommunications and mass communications have always used natural analogue signals for sound and images. Before transmission, these signals are converted into electrical signals. At the receiving end, they are converted back to analogue signals. Although analogue signals are realistic, they are also open to flaws and misinterpretations. As a result, switching is relatively slow and transmission causes some interference.

Digitalization means that all signals are chopped into little pieces, called bits, consisting of nothing but ones and zeros. With the aid of micro-electronics, these bits can be transported and connected fast and without interference. The best result is achieved when the entire link, from transmitter to receiver, consists of digital signals. Data are easily processed, texts are prepared for word processing and sounds and images achieve higher quality. Yet this technical superiority is not the primary cause of the swift digitalization of all mediated communications. It is rather the need to assimilate the explosive growth of the entirely digitized data communications into the completely converging infrastructure. With digitalization, data communication and computer technology become the dominant factors in all communication infrastructures.

Digitalization supports the communication capacities of accuracy, selectivity and stimuli richness of the new media. Its uniform language makes content more accurate: fewer faults and replication of mistakes and more opportunities for exact processing and calculation. It facilitates the selection of sources, contents and destinations as they are all framed and assembled in the same language. Finally, all data types (sound, text, numerical data and video) can be added in the same multimedia source to increase the stimuli richness of the new media.

Store and forward principle

The next technical foundation of the network society is the store and forward principle that is realized in digital micro-electronic equipment. This means the use of electronic memories and storage in databases of all types. Traditionally, the content of telephone calls could not be stored. Telephone operators in central exchanges simply switched the lines by hand. It was only much later that calls could be stored on the tapes of answering devices. Broadcast messages were only stored on tape; they were not accessible for both senders and receivers simultaneously. The storage of digitalized contents in electronic memories and databases, accessible by software programs, is a strong stimulus for all interactive media. They can be filled by producers and users and forwarded to all those connected to the medium. The insertion of the store and forward principle enriches telecommunications with a large number of new facilities and is the basis for all email use, all retrieval of web-pages on the Internet, all use of computer software and all interactions with audiovisual multimedia programs. In short, it is the basis of all interfaces with online and offline new media.

The store and forward principle sustains the communication capacities of accuracy, selectivity and interactivity. Databases and electronic memories enable these capacities of control. However, they also are a potential threat to privacy protection, as every single action is registered and stored.

Layered organization

The fourth technical foundation of the network society is the layered organization of the technology of computers and computer networks. This characteristic is often unnoticed, but in this book it will become evident that it is extremely important for making choices and for information and communication freedom in the network society. The layered organization of computers is the distinction between hardware, software and applications. This distinction turns computers into multifunctional machines. Software is divided into operating systems, browsers and specific programs.

Computer networks also reveal a layered organization. The least number of layers is three: the layer of network infrastructure, the layer of transport and operations and the layer of application services. According to the standard open systems interconnection (OSI) model, in computer networks these three layers are in fact divided into seven. By means of this standard, the rules for seven layers of a network are defined. They are extremely important for an understanding of what happens in the media sector, both technically and in the perspective of business and power, as we will see later on in this book. See Table 3.1.

The two bottom layers consist of infrastructure specifications for networks and their equipment. The *physical layer* specifies the rules for the hardware of network computer centres, cables or transmission lines by air, terminal equipment and connectors such as Bluetooth and USB. The *data link layer* on top of this bottom layer defines the physical addressing required for all network components. Here switching techniques are standardized such as circuit-switching for telephony and packet-switching for the Internet.

Four layers on top of the infrastructure layers define the software required to operate networks. Software code is standardized for the following functions.

TABLE 3.1 Seven technical O.S.I. network layers enabling network use

Nature	Network Layer	Function
Content	Application	Enables the use of the content of applications (telephone conversation, Internet exchange, broadcasting, etc.) determining the identity and availability of communication partners and synchronizing communication.
Software code	Presentation	Formats and encrypts data of applications using a different data language in order to be readable across networks.
	Session	Controls sessions ('dialogues') between different computers or hosts.
	Transport	Reliable transmission of data between end-users. Control of data streams. E.g. TCP (Transmission Control Protocol).
	Network	Path determination and addressing of data (packages) between different networks. E.g. Internet Protocol (IP4, IP6, IPsec).
Infrastructure	Data link	Physical addressing between multiple devices and a transmission medium.
	Physical	Electrical and physical specifications for devices and for the connection between devices and transmission media.

The *network layer* organizes the path of messages, which includes packages of data between network nodes and the addressing system. For example, the Internet uses the Internet Protocol, currently available in a number of versions (IP4, IP6 and IPsec). By means of this protocol, packages of Internet traffic can be delivered in the fastest, most indiscriminate ('net-neutral': see below) or secure way. Right on top of this layer the *transport layer* organizes and controls the transmission of messages of data between nodes or end-users. One of the protocols defined here is the TCP (Transmission Control Protocol) that rules the Internet. One has to emphasize that the contemporary Internet in fact *is* the combination of the protocols of IP and TCP. Without them this network would not have the decentralized character it currently has. Peer-to-peer networking, anonymous communication, social media and many other applications of the Internet would not be possible. Any change in these protocols might substantially change the nature of the Internet. See the last section of this chapter.

Two software code layers on top of the former arrange the communication between network components such as computers and telephones that do not have the same software specifications or that use different data languages: the *session layer* and the *presentation layer*. They act as translators.

The top network layer is the *application layer* which enables the content of network applications and the synchronization of network communication. It sets rules for the technical determination of the availability and identity of users, among others by address names such as HTTP. Finally, it has to be emphasized *that this layer does not contain the software of applications themselves.* This comes on top of all seven layers that have to work together to realize all network operations.

The layered organization of computers and their networks supports the capacities of selectivity and interactivity as choices can be made at every level. It offers the opportunity to both centralize and decentralize information and communication flows in networks. It offers the best opportunities for the management of computers and their networks. In Chapters 5 and 6 we will see that the division of labour in the operations of network layers also provides better opportunities for privacy protection.

New connections

The fifth technical foundation is improvements in the connections by cable and by air. They do not only concern the transmission capacity of the wires and beams used, but also the capacity of senders and reception equipment and all switchers and routers used in passing. In networks, the progress in micro-electronics and digitalization cannot engender real changes until the connections are able to transport large amounts of digital signals. The transmission capacity of wires has considerably increased in the last century. The copper wires of telephony were accompanied by coaxial cables,(twisted into a bundle) and used for cable TV. For computer networks they were progressively replaced by *fibre-optic or plastic wires.* These are extremely thin wires made out of glass or new plastics, transporting light signals instead of electric signals. The capacity of fibre-optic wires increases up to four or five times the capacity of a six-wire-coaxial cable and many times the capacity of an ordinary copper wire. In the meantime, the capacity of connections by air has been improved by the use of higher frequencies. From the low frequencies used for radio and the medium frequencies used for television, the evolution was to high frequencies used for satellite broadcasting at a long distance and laser or infrared technology reaching short distances in broadband and wireless computer communications.

However, the capacity of transmitters, receivers and switchers is far more important. Gradually they have become computerized technology with ever stronger micro-electronic capacities. The embedded software is capable of compressing signals to such an extent that even the capacity of copper wires can be extended considerably. Another major improvement is the progress made in the optical transmission of satellites and antennas used for broadcasting, telephony and broadband computer traffic. In the future, all connections may consist of optical computers, fibre-optic wires or high-frequency transmission by air and satellites, all transporting signals of light (at the speed of light).

Obviously, better connections by cable and air improve the new media's communication capacities for speed and geographical reach. In the course of the 20th century, an increasing variety of connections by cable and by air were interconnected to create a global system of telecommunications, computer networks and broadcasting.

The last technical foundation to be discussed is the convergence of the technologies of telecommunication, data communication and mass communication to create one single digital communications infrastructure. This process rests upon all five foundations discussed above. It is so important that it deserves a special section presented below. Convergence has a major influence on the infrastructure of the network society. For the first time in history we will have a single communications infrastructure that links all activities in society. Online and offline communications will be linked in all kinds of ways. We will have the choice of conducting more and more activities either online or offline, or both: work, education, information retrieval, conversation, decision-making, cultural expression, entertainment and more. The convergence of communications is producing the tangible nervous system for society that was discussed in Chapter 2. It is time to explain how it has evolved.

CURRENT TECHNICAL TRENDS

Convergence

The epochal trend of convergence is the most important trend in the evolution of the new media in the last 30 to 40 years. It stands for the gradual integration of three types of communication: tele-, data- and mass communication, symbolized by the telephone, the computer, and radio or television respectively.

The process has started with the digitization of telecommunication. This type of communication exchanges sound (speech) and text over relatively long distances using central exchanges and terminal equipment (telephone devices). The main communication pattern is conversation (see Chapter 1). Digitization of telecommunication stands for a link with data communication that can be defined as the exchange by computer equipment of data and text in the form of the computer language of bits and bytes. Here the main communication patterns are registration and consultation. The first parts of telecommunication to be digitized were the central telephone exchanges that in fact became large computer centres. The transmission switches in local telephone houses were the ones to follow. Finally, transmission lines were digitized together with telephone equipment. An early digital telephone transmission service in the 1980s and 1990s was ISDN to be followed by DSL.

An important boost to the digitization of telecommunication came from the arrival of manageable mobile telephony using digital technologies since the 1980s. The first generation of digital mobile telephony was GSM, the second was GPRS. In the first decade of the 21st century the third generation, called 3G, was introduced to be followed by UMTS or 4G. The last two generations do not only offer increasing capacity but also applications coming from all three types of communication.

The first application emerging from the convergence of tele- and data communication was the fax, actually a successor of the age-old telex for offices. Other applications symbolizing this convergence were email and instant messaging realized by computer networks (notably the Internet) as these applications are digital and textual

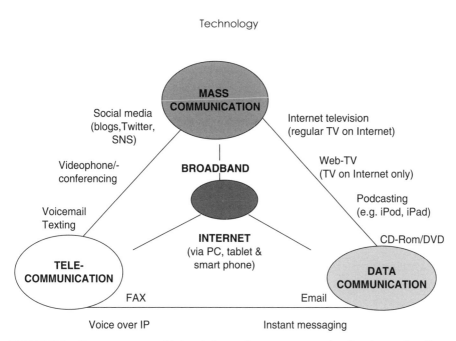

FIGURE 3.1 Convergence of tele, data and mass communication in applications

alternatives for telephone messages of speech and texting. As soon as telephone lines and Internet connections were integrated in DSL or cable connections, the last application symbolizing this convergence came forward: Voice over IP, which means telephony via the Internet. The convergence of tele- and data communication is portrayed in Figure 3.1.

The convergence of tele- and mass communication is technically realized by the digitization of telephone networks and their increasing bandwidth. This enabled the exchange of images and video in telecommunication – in this way partly becoming mass communication. The latter can be defined as a communication type *that distributes sound, text, images and video among a relatively large audience*. The main communication pattern is allocution. The first applications added to digitizing telecommunication were texting (SMS) and voicemail replacing the answering machine. Texting can also be used to distribute messages to a large number of telephone subscribers. A second series of applications was adding images (MMS) and video calls to be followed by video-conferencing. MMS and video-conferencing can reach larger audiences than a pair of individuals. The final series of applications between telecommunication and mass communication is social media. They are used for telecommunication-like interpersonal communication (Social Networking Sites) or for mass communication on the Internet (weblogs and Twitter). See the left-hand side of Figure 3.1.

Finally, the convergence of data communication and mass communication has evolved with the introduction of the multimedia PC and broadband computer networks. First, stand alone multimedia players and carriers such as CD-Rom and DVD arrived containing, among others, videos, movies and games. Shortly afterwards, the capacity of Internet connections was enlarged to offer broadcasting (regular TV on the Internet and Web-TV) and online newspapers and magazines with pictures and videos. Recently, newspapers, magazines, music, videos and other mass media sources have been podcasted to all kinds of devices connected to the Internet. See the right-hand side of Figure 3.1.

The convergence between tele-, data and mass communication seems to end in a single final destination: a broadband or high-speed Internet. However, it is a big mistake to think that the Internet will swallow all traditional media. Currently, we still have telephone networks for plain old speech and text conversation and we have cable and satellite networks for broadcasting, both of which we will continue to have for a long time. The printing press will not disappear either. Convergence will go on in the combination of ever-widening high-speed networks and a multitude of terminal devices with multimedia capacities (from multimedia PCs to tablets and smart phones). The Internet will primarily become a public switching facility linking all kinds of networks and media, as will be explained in the last section of this chapter.

Miniaturization

A second most important current trend, undoubtedly, is the further miniaturization of information and communication technology. In 1965, Gordon Moore published a general conclusion that has become known as *Moore's Law*: every 18 months the memory and processing capacity of chips doubles. This 'law' still holds and will continue to work in the near future. Eventually, we will reach the limits of electrical currents that can run on the smallest amount of physical material used for chips, but then the optical computer might appear, working with small beams of light instead of electricity. A further prospect is the integration of *nanotechnology* – the science of building devices at the molecular and atomic level. This would lead to the smallest chips, computers and communication devices you can imagine, built-in almost everywhere, from objects to human bodies and brains. Perhaps the chips will even be linked to human cells. In this way, ICT will be integrated with the other two great technologies of the first part of the 21st century: biotechnology and nanotechnology.

In terms of networking, miniaturization means that the potential elements or units to be linked are getting smaller. This goes for both social and media networks. In this book, it is argued that computer and telephone networks support the process of network individualization, which means social scale reduction. When the new media are miniaturized they will become available and portable everywhere. Social and media networks will be fully integrated together producing a network society, the basic theme of this book.

Embedded technology

Miniaturization enables so-called embedded technology. Currently, chips are not only a part of computers and electronic communication devices, but also of an increasing number of other devices and physical objects, from watches to cars, houses and clothing. A popular example is the refrigerator that sends signals to the supermarket that the milk is almost finished, prompting a new delivery. The built-in chips can be processors, but they can also act as small transmitters of signals to other devices. The result is called *ubiquitous computing*. In the future, both people and their physical objects will use information processing and transmitting technologies almost everywhere. A general term for this is 'information appliances'. According to Donald Norman (1999), information appliances should serve as invisible computers.

Embedded technology means an enormous extension of the scale of networking. Henceforth, not only are people connected, but also objects, which are able to exchange signals without human intervention. When human intervention occurs, we also have a connection between people and objects. In this way we create an all-embracing network infrastructure.

Mobile and wireless technology

A fourth trend is the transition from ICT, which is tied to fixed devices or places and uses wires for transmission, to a technology that is used when we are mobile and which uses atmospheric beams for transmission. In mass communication, there has been a return to atmospheric (satellite) networks after the dominance of cable in many developed societies. In telecommunications, fixed telephony is partly replaced by cellular telephony; in developing countries, large-scale telephone distribution even starts in wireless formats. Finally, data communication is increasingly exchanging computer cables for wireless connections, first in local house or office environments and subsequently in mobile and wide area spaces.

The capacity of wireless communication is still limited as compared to high-speed cable connections. A second limitation is the scarcity of frequencies in the air and a third is the problem of keeping the increasing number of atmospheric connections apart. So, the combination that is most likely to appear is a connection of long-distance cable with access points for wireless communication in a growing number of local places.

The significance of the rise of mobile and wireless communication in terms of networking is the considerable extension and expansion of it. First there is the expansion of geographical reach. Rural areas in developed countries and all territories of developing countries acquire relatively easy and cheap access to telephony, satellite broadcasting and the Internet. Second is the extension of use from homes and workplaces to uses in transport and in leisure time. In all these environments, the room to move and to use the technology is no longer limited by wires and fixed access points. This significantly increases the scale and scope of networking. Mobile and wireless technology will spread the network society to the most remote places and the deepest pores of the world.

Broadband technology

Another trend that widens the technical foundation of a fully developed network society is the advance of broadband connections. The multimedia PC power and applications provided in the 1990s were gradually extended in broadband connections by cable and by air in the years that followed. George Guilder even maintains in his so-called *Guilder's Law* that bandwidth grows at least three times faster than computer power. This means that if computer power doubles every 18 months, communications power doubles every six months.

Whether this is true or not, broadband has an enormous influence on the daily use of computers and their networks. New usage patterns have appeared and a new lifestyle has developed after the year 2000 according to surveys of the Pew Internet and American Life Project (Horrigan and Rainie, 2002) and the UCLA *Internet Report* (UCLA, 2003). Gradually the use of computers and the Internet has become embedded in everyday life. With the 'always on' feature of broadband, people do not have to worry about the cost of connection time any more. The result is that the connection is used for the smallest occasions to inform and to communicate. A 'broadband elite' has appeared that uses this connection for at least ten different applications a day (Horrigan and Rainie, 2002). Not only the elite, but also average users are increasingly online all of the day. Moreover, they use ever more network applications substituting offline activities. So, broadband will also extend the scale and scope of networking in society.

Cloud computing

A fifth trend partly runs opposite to the former four that all have a decentralizing effect on computer and Internet use. Cloud computing centralizes computer processing in 'clouds' of central servers containing most software used and all data stored. Companies such as Microsoft, Google, Yahoo, Amazon and Salesforce offer this service on demand. The desktop computer disappears or is stripped from office programs and computing power, only keeping a display and perhaps a minimal web browser and operating system. The main advantage of cloud computing is much more efficient use of processing power because independently working computers use only a tiny part of their capacity. A second advantage might be energy saving, though this depends on the usage conditions and has yet to be proven. Other advantages are that data can be safely and professionally stored and that updates and software patches can be added without bothering end-users.

Of course, the big disadvantage is that companies and individual users partly lose control of their own data. Computer development from the 1980s onwards started with independent PCs, which later on connected to Local Area Networks and to the Internet. This has stimulated autonomous work and innovation by end-users themselves (Zittrain, 2008). However, in the last 15 years, software providers have already partly taken control of the user's computer at a distance by all kinds of security software and continuous updating. Local IT operators started to manage all computers in company networks. Additionally, companies such as Google offer to store and process email and cooperative work. Cloud computing only extends this trend.

Critics in companies and governments fear the loss of independent IT policy, control and innovation capacity to private software businesses, though this largely depends on the centres where the data are stored. These centres can be private and internal or public and external. Critics on behalf of individual users fear both privacy and security loss. This is because all personal data can be monitored by private companies that work under different international privacy jurisdictions. They also run more risks from professional hackers than individual users as there is more to steal. Finally, clouds drift away: cloud companies can go bankrupt. In any case, cloud computing is an extremely important trend for the Internet that will decide its future as a free medium. Much attention will be paid to this trend in the remainder of this book.

CONCLUSIONS

- The network society has a number of technical foundations that should be known to understand what effects media networks might have on society. The enormous capacity of micro-electronics to store and process data and information supports both the information and network society. The digitalization of media leads to the convergence of all media. Without the store and forward principle no mediated information and communication would be possible. The layered organization of networks is crucial to understand, for example, what constitutes the Internet (the TCP-IP protocol on the transport and network layers actually is the Internet) and what happens in the new media business sector (Chapter 4).

- Additionally, we have observed a number of important technological trends that set the parameters for an *ever more pervasive* network society: the convergence of all information and communication networks (telephony, broadcasting and the Internet); the miniaturization of digital media devices and the embedding of these media in everyday-life; the turn to ubiquitous and always-on mobile, wireless and broadband connections; and finally the rise of cloud computing where all of our networked life can be stored.

4 ECONOMY

About this chapter

- This chapter starts with the historical background of the present communications revolution (the 'digital revolution') as compared to the former, about a century ago, that brought mass communication.

- The network economy is called a 'flow economy' as all parts of the economy, production, distribution and consumption are linked by networks inside and between companies creating a superior form of logistics and adaptation to market circumstances.

- The rise of Enterprise 2.0 as a Web 2.0 perspective for organizations (factories, service providers and offices) has introduced new ways of working based on flexible working conditions and knowledge networks.

- There has been an evolution of a new mode of organization between the traditional modes of hierarchy or bureaucracy and the market – it is known as the network mode of organization.

- The characteristics of a network and information economy, which are partly new to the capitalist economy without creating a crisis-free 'new economy'. On the contrary, ICTs are accessories to the recent economic and credit crisis.

- This chapter provides a systematic analysis of the producers of public networks (telephony, broadcasting and the Internet) at every level: from producers of infrastructure and network operators or carriers to service providers of content.

- We will study the big players on the Internet (Microsoft, Apple, Google and Facebook) that are engaged in heavy platform competition trying to control the Internet.

- Why are some new media successful while others fail? We analyse the position of the consumers of networks, primarily individual and household consumers, to try to answer this question.

CAUSES OF THE CURRENT COMMUNICATIONS REVOLUTION

General background

The acceleration, in some cases even the explosion, in demand for communication media over the past three or four decades cannot be explained simply by looking at *general* tendencies in society, economy and culture or at the availability of new technologies (van Dijk, 1993b). Saunders and Warford (1983) and Metcalfe (1986) were among the first to identify the following factors governing the increasing need for information and communication media in developed economies:

1 scale extension in production processes;

2 an increase in the division of labour and the complexity of organizations;

3 a rise in standards of living;

4 information production gaining its own dynamics.

This list is not entirely correct (in this book, scale reduction is stressed in addition to scale extension) and it is not complete either, because it is mainly based on economic aspects. For example, it omits the social-cultural aspects of individualization and the reduction of household size, which have a direct influence on the need for communication media. However, the most important objections to an explanation using these factors are the lack of historical specification – even from an economic point of view – and the assumption of linear evolution. Contrary to this, I will describe a combination of several background factors that produce their effects with varying speed and strength in the long, medium and short term. The American scientist James Beniger initiated such a description in a detailed, historic-economic analysis of technological developments in the United States in the 19th and early 20th centuries (*The Control Revolution*, 1986). And since I want to apply his argument to the current state of affairs, it is important to briefly repeat his account.

The first communications revolution

Beniger demonstrates that, during the period just mentioned, a veritable information and communications revolution took place. He considers it to have been a reaction to the faltering industrial revolution owing to its poor infrastructure. Many points of friction arose halfway through the 19th century. Together they produced a *control crisis*. This term describes a period in which the organizational and communication means of control lagged behind the size, speed and complexity of physical production, energy extraction and transportation. Beniger describes the control crisis in the industrial revolution as follows: 'Suddenly – owing to the harnessing of steam power – goods could be moved at the full speed of industrial production, night and day and under virtually any conditions, not only from town to town but across entire continents and around the world' (1986: 12). The crisis was visible in numerous frictions: problems of coordination in factories, in mass transportation (trains colliding, mistakes made in freight transfers, missing vehicles, divergent time-tables) and in the distribution and sale of bulk goods in department stores. In the second half of the 19th century, the crisis was solved by a *control revolution* marked by three series of innovations summarized in Box 4.1.

BOX 4.1
Innovations of the first communications revolution

1 *Bureaucratic organization*: the rise of bureaucratic functions, sharp task divisions and hierarchies, rationalization by formal procedures, preparations (for example, paper forms) and time synchronization.
2 A new *infrastructure* of transportation and communication (paved roads, trains, telegraph, telephone and so on) to handle the explosive growth in mass transportation of goods and people.
3 *Mass communication and mass research* (national press, film, radio, advertising, market research, opinion polls) as ways to reach and map an elusive new mass of consumers.

Beniger describes the rapid development, within a lifetime, of a whole series of new communication means still controlling everyday life. He lists: photography and telegraphy (1830–40), the rotary press (1840–50), the typewriter (1860–70), the transatlantic cable (1866), the telephone (1876), film (1894), wireless telegraphy (1895), magnetic tape recording (1899), radio (1906) and, somewhat later, television (1923). Beniger considers them to be the means of a (very broadly defined) control revolution. Considering the list supplied, we prefer to speak of the *first communications revolution* of the modern age, for the innovations of the control revolution are much more than simply new means or media: they also contain basic techniques of organization and programming.

All the means mentioned were invented, developed and introduced on a small scale in the period indicated. In the decades between 1920 and 1970, they were diffused on a large scale as the main technologies of an economic age characterized by mass production and mass consumption.

A similar, but shorter, period of invention, development and innovation, with the computer as its central medium, resulted from the Second World War and the race in arms and in space that followed. Now, with a staggering speed of development, computers are already in their fifth generation since 1950. With their miniaturization and chip technology, the third and fourth generations (from 1965 onwards) were the most important. They paved the way for large-scale digitalization and integration of communication media.

The second communications revolution

According to Beniger, the computer has replaced bureaucracy as the most important instrument of control since the Second World War. He considers the introduction of the computer, the revolution in micro-electronics and the information society in general to be only a new – albeit much faster – phase in the control revolution of modern times (1986: 427). To us this is an under-estimation of the meaning of current innovations. However, it is productive to apply Beniger's analysis to the present situation, defending the thesis that we are now going through a *second* control crisis which is partly being solved using the media of a *second communications revolution*. We can see that the three series of innovations, which Beniger considers to be the solution to the control revolution, have run their course. They have even become impediments to present development. This applies to certain bureaucratic modes of organization, to the congesting and polluting system of the transportation of goods and people, to the fragmented types of mass communication and to the growing problems for mass research and marketing in an individualizing and differentiating society. New media networks can be important *means* to solve these problems: They are able to support the flexibility, efficiency and productivity of organizations; to improve all kinds of logistic processes; to replace transportation of goods and people by transportation of information; and to reach effectively a segmented public of communicating consumers.

The question arises as to whether this technology is just as much a reaction to the frictions and congestions in processes of production, distribution and consumption as 19th-century technology was to the control revolution of those days.

BOX 4.2
Innovations of the second communications revolution

1 *Flexible network organization*: flexible modes of production and distribution (a just in time or flow economy); network forms of organization rise in between markets and hierarchies; infocracy replaces bureaucracy.
2 A new *infrastructure of transport and communication*: computer networks partly replace road transport; logistic improvement; more communication channels with better communication capacities.
3 *Segmented and personalized communication*: one-to-one and customer relationship marketing; interactive narrowcasting instead of broadcasting; multiplication of media forms.

A FLOW ECONOMY

A network structure between corporations

In the United States, the turning point in the scale extension of production processes had already been reached before the Second World War (Jerome, 1934). Up to that time, production had been concentrated in ever larger units. Since the Second World War companies have slowly started decreasing in size, not only in the United States, but also in other western countries. This should not overshadow a second process that has been going on simultaneously: the centralization of capital and strategic control over production processes (Castells, 1996; Harrison, 1994). These trends appear in the growth of international corporations and conglomerates of financial capital, and in the tendencies towards business monopolization or oligopolization, which are dealt with in this chapter. A present-day example of the convergence of both trends is the concentration of media in the hands of tycoons such as Murdoch, Berlusconi, Malone and Bertelsmann. These people have no wish to merge the media they appropriate: on the contrary, more often they are diversifying them in order to gain a larger share of a growth market.

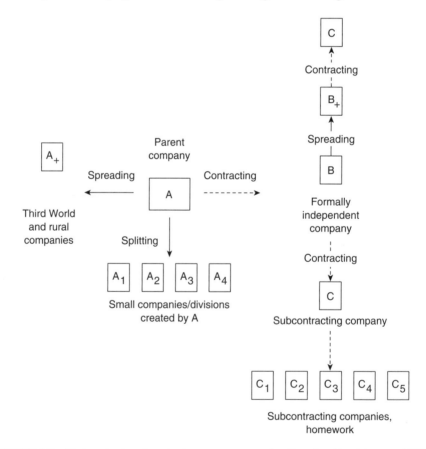

FIGURE 4.1 Network structure between companies (inspired by Murray, 1983)

If the all-embracing parent company of the past is taken as a starting point, the decentralization of production can be portrayed as in Figure 4.1. The first phase of this process was the spread of western transnational corporations over the rest of the world. Subsequently, a division in depth took place in the western countries themselves: a split in formally independent and regional departments first and in subcontracting business activities afterwards.

Over the past 25 years, decentralization of executive power has also taken place inside western governments and public administrations, by means of a regional spread of activities, privatization and subcontracting. In contrast to this, the commercial service sector has always been marked by small-scale organizations. In recent times, the emphasis has shifted to scale extension. For example, cleaning agencies, IT companies and other service organizations are getting bigger. However, activities are still performed locally.

Behind these trends of predominant decentralization are specific *economic* motives that become more urgent in times of economic recession: rationalization and redistribution of added value towards the place(s) where all the money is concentrated (see below). A more general reason is the necessity to *control* the extending scale and organization of large corporations. This is also related to increasing *geographical restraints*. Formerly, centralization of production led to high costs of establishment, traffic congestion and other problems with regard to transportation.

Decentralized economic organization was a reaction to all these organizational and financial problems. However, the result was a huge increase in the need for communications, and thus capacity problems in existing infrastructures (Palvia et al., 1992). The lack of capacity and flexibility in public networks has been the most important reason for large companies to construct their own (inter)national networks and to install advanced private branch exchanges, for which they have been willing to make large investments. This comes as no surprise if one realizes how many *strategic opportunities of choice* are created by this technology. Companies are able to choose the best place for all their specific activities of production, distribution, information, management, support and maintenance. So, production can take place in regions/countries with the best trained and most reliable personnel available. Subsequently, assembly is located in low-wage countries or near markets; distribution is based on the best infrastructure; and information is concentrated in centres of high technology. The preferred place for management, which requires high-quality internal communication and support services, is a metropolitan area close to financial centres. Thus, a spread of activities can be combined with extreme centralization and specialization (Castells, 1989, 1994, 1996; Harrison, 1994; Nicol, 1985). The spatial proximity of business activities seems to have lost its importance. A geography of places is replaced by a geography of flows (Castells, 1989, 1996; Martin, 1978). The conclusion is obvious: this corporate network structure, representing both scale extension and scale reduction, can exist only with the help of advanced communication networks.

A network structure within companies

The conclusion reached in the previous paragraph is underlined by trends *within* separate corporate departments, that is, production processes. Within companies, a network structure of functions, tasks and activities also arises (Dutton et al. 2005). This is a fundamental transformation described variously as a movement 'from just-in-case to just-in-time production' (Sayer, 1986), 'from mass production to flexible specialization' (Piore and Sabel, 1984) and 'from Fordism to post-Fordism' (Aglietta, 1979). The first part of these distinctions refers to the modern industrial production process based on Taylorism and the system of assembly lines (Fordism) that was predominant in industrialized countries until recently. Here, the goal was to achieve the highest production at the greatest speed. Machines had to work for as long as possible on a single (part of a) mass product. A high level of specialization between and within divisions was prevalent. Assembly lines and other systems of transportation took care of transit. Parts, components and personnel had to be kept in store ('just-in-case') to keep production going during breakdowns. However, this system, so devoted to the speed of continuous mass production, in fact suffered delays in almost every link (De Sitter, 1994). The linear structure had too many phases and links working at different speeds. So, numerous logistical problems were created. The structure was vulnerable to the smallest malfunction. An extensive hierarchical line structure was needed to coordinate all the processes and divisions. The more complicated the end product, the longer and more complicated the route between all the divisions. The results were long and delivery times unreliable. Only two decades ago a (part of a) product was processed only 5 per cent of the time it spent in the factory; 30 per cent of production costs were used for storage, coordination and transportation inside the factory (Balance and Sinclair, 1983: 148). To summarize: this type of production process was characterized by optimizing *partial aspects*, to allow separate machines and workers to work faster. The advancing complexity of products and differentiation of demand slowed this process and reduced the growth of productivity in the 1960s. However, it took the economic crisis of the 1970s and the model of the Japanese economic system to make manufacturers face the facts.

The alternative, developed in large Japanese assembly companies, optimized the production process *as a whole*. The process was not split into stations, tasks and activities, but in parallel streams in which entire products and components, all similar to each other, were produced. Of course, the phases in these streams were divided into segments too, but these segments were homogeneous and they were supported by production groups working relatively independently. These production groups were multifunctional; they constantly improved their work and were charged with quality control of their own products. Hence the name 'quality circles'. The number of segments was limited and they could be coordinated by a small staff 'recruited' from the quality circles themselves. In order to make this system succeed, the work done in the segments had to fit closely ('just-in-time'). Waiting periods were unacceptable. Information always had to be where it was needed. Therefore, direct communication

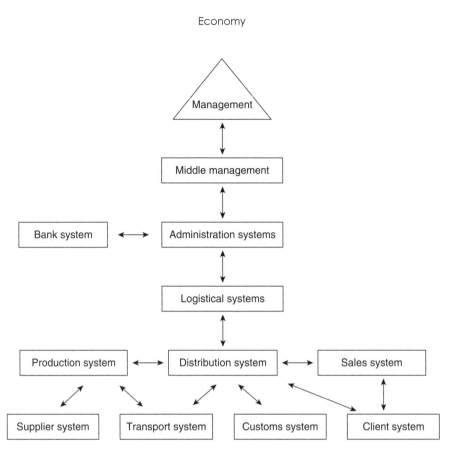

FIGURE 4.2 Network structure inside companies

between production groups was vital. However, soon production processes became so complicated, and distances increased so much, that media networks became indispensable for the integration of all types of communication required. They were needed to integrate computer-aided design and computer-aided manufacturing in a single cybernetic system: computer-integrated manufacturing. In turn, this system had to be connected to distribution and supply systems, office systems, personnel information systems and management information systems (see Figure 4.2).

Over the past 30 years, this method of flexible specialization mediated by information and communication networks has spread across the world and become the dominant mode of production. The next step was a transition to the world of distribution, circulation and consumption. The first thing required was a transformation of office work and the processing of information and knowledge.

Streamlined offices

Even though it is hard to measure and compare differences in productivity in factories and offices, it is well known that, during the 20th century, productivity in factories increased far more than productivity in offices (for data see Gershuny and Miles, 1983). The difference was experienced as a growing economic problem: whereas the costs per single product gradually decreased, the share of administration and management in the total costs kept increasing both in absolute and in relative figures. The reasons are obvious: office work is, and always has been, highly informal, unstructured and little mechanized or automated. But this has rapidly changed in the last 20 to 25 years. Traditional office work has been automated, in fits and starts, and with many organizational problems. The Italian computer manufacturer Carlo de Benedetti expressed a clear view of this process: 'Essentially, information technology is a technology of control and coordination of workers – in particular white-collar workers – not yet reached by Taylorism' (cited in Rada, 1980: 106). Soon it became evident that a more Tayloristic, or even a factory-like, organization could be created for office work when an office is viewed as a *system of information processing* passing through stages of generating, producing, collecting, processing, multiplying, distributing, storing, retrieving and interpreting data (see Hawryskiewicz, 1996).

Such a concept of office work is necessary in order to first structure and then formalize and standardize this particular type of work. This will enable automation as soon as the necessary techniques are available. High-grade technology for offices is still a fairly new phenomenon. Take, for example, the copier: this was introduced only 40 years ago. Clearly, several separate phases of the above-mentioned process have been automated through ICT in the past 20 to 25 years. But in the average office, this has not yet produced an increase in productivity that can be measured. The changes seem to have been too basic and introduced too swiftly for personnel and organization to respond to them adequately. Much more information is processed and many more communication channels and sources are used, but it is questionable whether the quality of office products has increased and real savings in terms of resources have been made. Anyway, the 'paperless office' will continue to be a utopia for some time.

The really fundamental changes will be brought about by network technology. One should not expect major changes in the productivity, efficiency and structure of office work until either integrated office systems are introduced or all existing equipment and software are connected in networks. The first step in this process will be to connect activities such as word processing and graphical design to databases and documentary systems or electronic supply management. The next step is very aptly called *workflow automation*. The entire administrative procedure of an office is divided into separate tasks to be performed successively by the departments/workers in the network. A list of tasks for the day is displayed in a window on the monitor. All tasks performed are marked and passed on to the next station in the network. The process of office streamlining will not be completed until it is extended to the office environment of suppliers and customers by means of integrated tele- and data communication networks. The network will be the assembly line of the office, an assembly line not stopping at the door, but continuing outside to be connected to other lines. Therefore, the effects of networks in offices will be even greater than the effects that assembly lines had in factories.

Of course this does not mean that networks will lead to the same standardization and division of tasks that occurred in factories. It will still be possible to work in teams and on all-round sets of activities. Special programs have been developed for *groupware* or *computer-supported cooperative work* emphasizing cooperation (see Greiff, 1988; Hawryskiewicz, 1996). Furthermore, activities such as generating, producing, collecting and, above all, interpreting office information are difficult to formalize. Therefore, the network as the assembly line of the office can have different consequences for various groups of office employees: those who keep managing and communicating informally and those whose tasks are formalized in a factory-like way.

ENTERPRISE 2.0

Knowledge networks and knowledge management

Gradually, flows of information and communication have become more important to the modern economy than flows of physical products. Initially, they only accompanied the flows of physical products in transport and assisted in their coordination, but later they became increasingly independent. All developed countries now have a so-called service and knowledge economy. In this economy, information exchange and communication are predominant economic activities. Detailed and timely information has to be available for all operations at every level of economic activity. Increasingly, electronic networks are used to accomplish this. A particular kind of network specializes in the creation, distribution and exchange of a certain type of information: knowledge networks. They are ICT networks designed for the creation, accumulation, distribution, exchange and use of knowledge.

Knowledge networks actually consist of people who use both social and media networks to create, exchange and apply all kinds of knowledge. Knowledge that can be exchanged easily is so-called migratory knowledge, to be distinguished from embedded knowledge (Badaracco, 1991). Migratory knowledge is the explicit and codified knowledge contained in books, reports, designs, programs, databases and other files. ICT has made the creation, exchange and use of this type of knowledge in digital and accessible formats much easier.

It is a lot more difficult to use knowledge networks for embedded knowledge, also called tacit knowledge. This is the accumulated know-how, unique individual skill, craftsmanship and group expertise that rests with people, in this case with employees. This type of knowledge is becoming not less but more important in the complex flow economy based on cooperation. Here, knowledge creation is less and less an individual affair, rather it is increasingly a social affair of communities of practice and learning (Brown and Duguid, 2000). Moreover, knowledge production is not a static thing, but a process (Hakken, 2003). Finally, knowledge exchange is mostly informal, not using official channels but informal social networking (Davenport and Prusak, 1997, Wenneker, 2009).

Social, changeable and informally embedded or tacit knowledge has to be extracted with special effort. This is attempted by knowledge management in organizations. It uses ICT and ICT networks, in particular computer-supported collaborative work (CSCW) and online learning communities, to create expert systems and knowledge databases extracting and making explicit all the professional knowledge of available employees. This requires the cooperation of these employees – they have to be motivated to pass their main asset as individual professional workers (their explicit knowledge and implicit skill and expertise) to the collectivity of the organization. For this purpose, all kinds of material and immaterial rewards are appearing, from bonuses and career advancement to status increase and corporate identity or job satisfaction (Thomas, 1996). However, a fundamental problem is that the flow economy of flexible jobs and subcontracting reduces attachment to the organization and the motivation to pass on one's personal expertise (Nonaka and Takeuchi, 1995).

The arrival of social media in organizations

After the arrival of Web 2.0, knowledge management in organizations has reached increasing support by social media use. This has been labelled as Enterprise 2.0 (McAfee, 2009). This concept means that Web 2.0 technologies and social media are used to support business processes by all kinds of exchange between employees and managers or between businesses and customers. As will be explained in Chapter 7, knowledge networks are one type of social media. The perspective of Enterprise 2.0 enables so-called 'new ways of working' in organizations with the goals listed in Box 4.3.

BOX 4.3
Goals of the 'new ways of working' in organizations

- Innovation (creation of new designs and products)
- Collaboration (of colleagues across departments or with partners and customers)
- Knowledge-sharing (exchanging *existing*, ideas, experience, contacts)
- Collective intelligence (creating *new* ideas in discussion)
- Search and discovery (seeking and finding information of other parts of one's own organization)

These goals can be achieved by the following social media applications. Because *profiles* are the pivotal part of social networking sites (SNS), they can be used to search and find the right persons or experts and the best teams for particular tasks both inside and outside the organization. LinkedIn is one of the most popular applications here. Knowledge networks under the social media names of *corporate wikis* and *community platforms* enable collaboration, knowledge sharing and collective intelligence to create new ideas (Dutton, 2008, Dutton, W.H. and Eynon, R., 2009). Finally, *corporate blogs* are used more and more, both for internal and external corporate communication and to show the innovativeness of an organization.

The perspective of Enterprise 2.0 is often linked to the broader perspective of more flexible ways of working in organizations. In that case it means working on flexible places and times, instead of a fixed desk or office floor and nine-to-five schedules. Increasingly, small and wireless equipment serves a highly mobile and autonomously performed type of work. In this meaning the concept of Enterprise 2.0 comes close to the so-called *virtual organization*. A virtual organization is an association of people linked by ICTs. In this way it can function without constraints of time, place and physical conditions. To paraphrase the words of a popular AT&T commercial in the 1990s: it is an organization that works anytime, anywhere and anyhow.

The perspective of Enterprise 2.0, based on Web 2.0 technologies and flexible, virtual types of organization, offers the following opportunities:

- compensation for a division of labour that has gone too far in organizations steered by hierarchies instead of network management;

- faster and better adaptation of organizations to the environment;

- attraction of young professionals that have grown up with the Internet and mobile or social media.

However, the perspective also contains a number of risks:

- a clash with existing organizational divisions and hierarchies;

- a perspective which requires a lot of time and effort to be realized;

- a departure from particular idealistic assumptions such as the preparedness of people to give away their own main assets and the things they know in sharing knowledge – employees with traditional attitudes are less likely to do this;

- a dependence on the flexibility of persons while many people, not only seniors, prefer their own personal space, relatively fixed working hours and certainty;

- a probability of early splits of knowledge organizations: why not start your own Enterprise 2.0 with colleagues you like most?

MARKETS, HIERARCHIES AND NETWORKS
Networks between markets and hierarchies

In the flow economy described above, ICT networks are used as *channels* to exchange goods and services. In this section, the question to be answered is whether they also

TABLE 4.1 Forms of economic organization (adapted from Powell (1990))

Characteristics	Forms		
	Markets	Networks	Hierarchies
Organizational basis	Contracts, property rights	Complementary strengths	Employment relationship
Relation of actors	Independent	Interdependent	Dependent
Goals of organization	Profits	Reciprocal gains	Careers
Means of organization	Prices	Relationships	Routines
Mode of organization	Competition	Competition and cooperation	Cooperation
Control	Horizontal	Horizontal and vertical	Vertical
Coordination	Horizontal	Horizontal and vertical	Vertical
Conflict resolution	Dealing, going to court	Trust, reputation	Administrative fiat, supervision
Flexibility	High	Medium	Low

help to create a new *form of economic organization*. The next section will discuss whether they create an altogether new economy, as was claimed in the 1990s.

In 1990, Walter Powell published a well-known article called *Neither Market Nor Hierarchy: Network Forms of Organization*. In this article, he compared three typical forms of contemporary economic organization: markets, hierarchies and networks. This comparison will serve as a source of inspiration for this section. It will be claimed that networks are a form of economic organization that is not new, as networks of production, trade, circulation and distribution have evolved in human history over thousands of years (McNeill and McNeill, 2003), but that they are now coming to the fore as a form of organization and technology that takes its place between the forms that have dominated the economy since the industrial revolution: markets and hierarchies. I want to locate this form *between* markets and hierarchies, even though it is distinctively different (Powell, 1990: 299). These three forms are ideal types. Real economies are combinations of these three forms. In my view, they also characterize whole economies from the organizational point of view. A communist or so-called command economy is dominated by hierarchies, and a free-market economy by markets. In the so-called 'mixed economy', networks achieve special importance. However, these simplifications require several qualifications.

I have adapted Powell's typology and made it more general and appropriate to the argument in this chapter. The result is summarized in Table 4.1.

Organizational characteristics

The organizational basis of markets is a free exchange of values between independent actors. This exchange can only survive under a law that gives the actors property rights and binds them to the agreements made in contracts of buying and selling. In a hierarchy, actors are no longer independent. They are employed and become part of a relationship between employers and employed. They are dependent on each other. In networks, actors make agreements and more or less freely engage in associations. They cooperate on the basis of complementary strengths and they become *inter*dependent.

After the industrial revolution, independent producers (farmers, craftsmen) and traders were increasingly subsumed under a wage condition in the ever larger hierarchies of corporations and government agencies. In communist societies, this was/is even the rule for everybody. The rise of networks as an economic form entails that more and more actors become semi-independent as they both have an employment relationship and their own business. Clear examples are freelance workers, semi-autonomous professionals and subcontracting firms.

The primary goal of the market form of economic organization is to make profits. This is realized by particular means of production, distribution, circulation and trade that are ruled by prices. Hierarchies are forms of organization that have departed from this goal in the general social division of labour in order to manage necessary tasks and conditions separately. Their familiar names are management and government. Here, the actual goals of the actors engaged shift to their own personal advancement in the organization, that is to say their careers. Their actions are not ruled by prices, but by organizational routines. The rise of networks fulfils the growing organizational need to achieve common goals in a division of labour that has gone very far. However, this is not realized by the invisible hand of the market and its prices, nor by the visible hand of management and its routines, but by reciprocal gains to be achieved in conscious agreements of interdependent actors and their relationships. This is considered to be an ideal compromise between freedom and control in an increasingly complex environment.

The history of the human web has always been a combination of cooperation and competition (see Chapter 2). Contemporary networks of organization and communication in the economy bring this combination to perfection. The modern capitalist economy is a mixture of strategic alliances, federations, oligopolies and even monopolies on the one side and heavy competition on the other. The free market of independent producers and traders manufacturing and exchanging a single product all by themselves has ceased to exist, if it has ever existed. Production and trade have become parts of an extensive value chain that requires a sharp division of labour and a smooth cooperation of all those concerned. Competition only exists in sections of this value chain, most often sections close to consumers. Auctions, stock markets and all kinds of retail markets are still highly competitive. However, the large chains of production and distribution are ruled by strategic alliances and divisions of labour based on cooperation in relations of contracting and subcontracting. The previous section explained that networks between and inside corporations have contributed to this trend. In the sections below, we see that the modern capitalist economy, among others, the media sector itself, remains highly organized and regulated, despite all calls for liberalization and deregulation to bring more competition; except that this organization increasingly adopts a network form.

Control and coordination characteristics

All forms of economic organization reveal a particular type of control and coordination. Control is the management of economic processes by decisions to allocate resources. It requires power, authority and accountability. Coordination is the division and synchronization of tasks. It involves the operation, communication and consent of those engaged. A common theme in the literature on new organizational forms is that a reduction in vertical *control* mechanisms is linked to an increase in horizontal *coordination* mechanisms (Fulk and DeSanctis, 1999: 18). This link is attributed to networks as they are considered to be 'flat' horizontal structures. However, I think this is partly a mistake. All organizational forms require both control and coordination. There is no shift from control to coordination, only the types of control and coordination are changing.

In markets, control is achieved by contracts, and coordination is realized by prices. Both are horizontal as, in principle, all actors are equal. However, they do involve so-called transaction costs. Historically, the hierarchy of corporations and government departments has traded transaction costs between actors on the market for coordination costs within these organizations (Watts, 2003: 263). 'The visible hand of management supplants the invisible hand of the market in coordinating supply and demand' (Powell, 1990: 303).

In hierarchies, management attempts control by command, authority and supervision. This often means centralization of decision-making. Coordination is achieved by formalization, standardization and specialization of tasks in a sharp division of labour. The resources of the organization and the skills and time of employees are allocated according to fixed schemes. This combination of vertical control and coordination is called bureaucracy.

The network form of organization is a smart combination of both horizontal and vertical control and coordination. It is no surprise that in the previous section, a combination of decentralization of production and centralization of capital and control was established. In a labour survey of more than 500 managers from firms of all sizes located throughout the world, Lynda Applegate (1999) observed that ICTs permit simultaneous centralization and decentralization. Hierarchical reporting and authority structures between top-management and employees were maintained, but middle-management layers were removed. The span of control of top-management increased. All kinds of incentives and boundary systems (limits of action) for employees remained. At the same time, organizations became more flexible, adaptive and locally responsive because the employees and the remaining line managers were provided with powerful information systems. These systems enabled them to coordinate and control operations locally themselves, albeit within clearly defined limits. Additionally, the 'adoption of a more information-intensive approach to control resulted in a shift in emphasis from standardization and supervision to learning' (Applegate, 1999: 43).

Information and communication networks enable new types of combined vertical and horizontal control in organizations. Human supervision is replaced by the technical control of information systems. Infocracy takes the place of bureaucracy (see Chapter 5 for an explanation of the concept of infocracy). Coordination is achieved by communication and knowledge networks. They have both horizontal and vertical characteristics. Horizontal are all kinds of cross-functional and virtual teams within and across organizational units, computer-supported collaborative work (CSCW) and so-called concurrent engineering (working in parallel instead of linearly). Vertical characteristics are identity and performance controls, personnel registration systems and password-protected databases.

Forms of economic organization should not be viewed in a narrow economic sense: they have a number of social, ethical and juridical ramifications. For instance, conflict resolution happens in different ways. When normal procedures for dealing in markets do not work anymore, because the parties engaged do not agree, they can only go to court or to another mediation agency. In hierarchies, conflicts are solved by administrative fiat, which means a higher level supervising a lower one. In networks, the parties engaged have to solve their own problems. Cooperation emerges out of mutual interests and is guided by common standards. These standards are built during a long process of generating reputations and mutual trust. With these means, the actors in networks try to prevent conflicts and solve problems more quickly than in markets and hierarchies. Trust and reputation are vital in networks.

The last characteristic of the three forms of economic organization is flexibility. The gradual replacement of markets by hierarchies in the economic development of the last two centuries has produced a bureaucratic organization with low flexibility. This increasingly became a problem when the environments of corporations changed ever faster and when demand and supply revealed sharp fluctuations. A new control crisis appeared (see above). Compared to hierarchies, networks are much more flexible because they combine centralization and decentralization, as we have seen several times now. Markets are the most flexible form of organization, as they quickly react to changing prices. However, the simple price mechanism is no longer sufficient to rule the extremely complex contemporary economy. Other mechanisms of adaptation have been added to run a kind of mixed economy on a capitalist basis. Networks are a form of organization that serves this interest. In fact, a particular combination of markets, hierarchies and networks rules all contemporary economies. In some economies, markets are prevalent, in others hierarchies. In network societies, networks come forward as increasingly important forms of economic organization.

Networks added to the mixed economy

In the course of the 20th century three main economic systems have evolved: market economies, state-planned economies and mixed economies. The mixed economy is supposed to be a market economy with much regulation and state intervention. Evidently, this is a mixture of the market and the hierarchy as forms of organization. Some observers see networks as some kind of mixture of hierarchies and markets too (see Borgatti and Foster, 2003). Others see them as a unique and independent organizational form added to hierarchies and markets (Powell, 1990 and to a lesser extent Thompson, 2003). I agree with the latter observers. The consequence for the macro economy of the 21th century is that networks as an organizational form for the economy at large have to be added to the mixed economy of a market economy and state intervention. This form has come forward in the flow economy previously discussed. Superior logistics and adaptive capacity to the environment are the main contributions to the mixed economy. Other characteristics are the co-creation of producers and consumers and a number of new features of the network economy to be discussed below. As compared to state regulation the network economy has more horizontal ways of control and coordination and as compared to the market economy it follows more social interests (cooperation and exchange) and less individual interests. Finally, networks entail enduring interaction, while markets focus on one-time transactions.

Concrete network configurations

The abstract ideal-type analysis of the network form of organization in this section is substantiated in a large number of very different concrete network configurations. Some concrete networks are very informal and open, while others are formal and closed. Though public opinion is familiar with the first type (informal and open), the second type (formal and closed) occurs just as frequently. The concrete configurations of networks mainly differ according to their emphasis on horizontal or vertical control and coordination. They can be put on a scale between two poles. See Box 4.4.

BOX 4.4
Network configurations, formal and closed versus informal and open

FORMAL AND CLOSED
Vertical control/coordination

- TERRORIST/CRIMINAL NETWORKS
- INTRACOMPANY AND INTRAGOVERNMENTAL NETWORKS
- SHARED SERVICES CENTRES (more than one organization)
- INTERGOVERNMENTAL ORGANIZATIONS
- MULTI-STAKEHOLDER NETWORKS (public and private)
- RESEARCH AND KNOWLEDGE NETWORKS
- ISSUE NETWORKS/MOVEMENTS
- PEER-TO-PEER NETWORKS

INFORMAL AND OPEN
Horizontal control/coordination

On the top pole networks are real alternatives for institutional organizations; on the pole below they are more like loose associations. The first type of configurations is relatively formal – it has to keep to particular organizational rules – and it is closed because not everyone can become a part of it. It is also less transparent because operations are only visible to the management of the network. This still largely uses vertical ways to control and coordinate the network from above.

Examples of the most extreme configuration are criminal and terrorist networks. Al Qaida is considered to be a terrorist network. It has all the characteristics of a network (see Table 4.1) but it is secret and closed. Members have to strictly follow the rules that are made and supervised by the leadership that is even called number one, two, etc. of Al Qaida. This aspect of centralization is compensated by an organization in decentralized cells. The extinction of a cell only means that somewhere else another one is created in the same (network) structure. Networks within companies and governments (see the section 'A flow economy' and Chapter 5 for governments) also follow the rules of their company and government. Though they are relatively autonomous being network organizations, they work within the strategy and division of labour of the institution at large. Shared services centers are most often IT organizations or financial and personnel organizations that serve different organizations needing the same kind of operations. It goes without saying that they also work within the limits of their principles.

In the middle of the scale of configurations one finds networks that combine formal and informal, closed and open ways of working. Intergovernmental organizations (in global or United Nations structures) have to represent their nation states, but they have some room for manoeuvre. They largely work in the public sphere when they are not engaged in closed negotiations. This also goes for multi-stakeholder networks in the public and private sphere (so-called public-private partnerships). They are organizations offering the same kind of products and services in a particular domain. Or they are networks of producers and consumers together trying to improve a certain product or service. Multi-stakeholder networks are both engaged in competition and cooperation.

At the other pole we have the networks that are best-known to Internet users. The most formal here are knowledge and research networks. They follow particular rules of operation and they have no unlimited access. Think about Wikipedia. Some of them are relatively closed because they are very specialist or are engaged with license and patent issues. More open and informal are issue networks that have to mobilize as many people as possible. They do not have many formal rules and act horizontally being, for example, activist networks. Finally, we have the most open and informal networks currently available: peer-to-peer networks. They are open and transparent. 'Members' can come and go when they want as their only job is to exchange sources between everyone engaged.

CHARACTERISTICS OF A NETWORK ECONOMY

A new economy?

Does this combination of organizational forms lead to an altogether new economy? Are the flow economy and the mixed economy including the network form of organization also shaping a 'new economy'? This expression became quite popular in a short period of time in the year 1999. Under the label 'a new economy', both strong and weak claims were made. A strong claim was the statement that this economy causes a permanent rise of labour productivity and economic growth without recessions or high unemployment and high inflation. The assumption was that this economy would push aside the 'old economy' in a short period of time (Kelly, 1998). A weak claim was that the 'new economy' temporarily increases economic growth and that it launches a wave of innovations that first make the processes in our economy faster and more efficient (a 'flow economy') and afterwards, perhaps, cause a breakthrough of new products. According to this claim, the economy keeps working according to the old rules of capitalism. This means periods of downturns in economic growth, rising unemployment, recessions and inflation. Those who defend this weak claim prefer not to use the term 'new economy', instead using terms such as 'information economy' and 'network economy' (Shapiro and Varian, 1999).

Ten years after it had been created, the strong claim was completely refuted by economic development. The biggest economic and financial crisis turned up in the world since the 1930s. In this section it will be claimed that ICTs did not ease this crisis. On the contrary, they partly caused and reinforced it. However, first it will be argued that there is some justification for the weak claim as information and networks bring real changes to the economy.

Characteristics of the information and network economy

In the first place, the products of the information economy are characterized by *high development costs* and *low (re)production costs*. The major part of labour is spent in the development and design of products such as software and information files. Creating many digital copies of them takes only a small effort. This is the opposite of goods in the material economy that can be designed, developed and produced much faster, but require additional labour, capital, raw material and transport when (re)production is increased. This characteristic causes a further shift towards an information services economy, already appearing in the 'old economy'. It also explains how a software company such as Microsoft is able to make continual high profits after it has once developed Windows.

A second attribute of the information economy is that information is an *experience good*. One first has to taste or know something of this good to ensure that it has sufficient worth to purchase it, in this case that it offers useful information. The only alternative is to trust in advance that the supplier is a provider of useful information. This is the main reason why so many services are given away free on the Internet and the reason why building a reputation for providing quality has become a prerequisite for any information business.

Third, *information is a special good or product* because the producer is able to sell and transfer the good to a purchaser without losing it himself. Information is shared by producer and consumers. In a digital shape, it is easy to copy nowadays. This explains the current problem of safeguarding intellectual property rights in a digital environment and the frenetic efforts of the owners to maintain these rights (see Chapter 6).

The fourth and fifth characteristics belong to a network economy. They are a consequence of the most important attribute of networks: being a system of elements with links and some coherence. Networks create information *systems*, combining devices (nodes and terminals), connections and information flows inside. This attribute first of all leads to *high switching costs* in cases where users want to change systems as products. Switching from Microsoft to Apple means a replacement of all programs, files and operating skills. This attribute explains all the fighting *over standards* and the continuous threat of *monopolization* in the sector of ICT. Standards are necessary in networks according to the law of network externality (see Chapter 2); moreover, they are very useful for most users. This is the main reason why, perhaps unwillingly, the Microsoft standards are so popular among users.

The fifth and last characteristic is the existence of *network effects*, which also belong to the law of network externality. A network becomes both less expensive and more effective when more units or people are connected. The more people have access to the Internet and email, the more valuable these media become for those connected. At a particular time a new medium reaches the stage of so-called *critical mass*; from that moment onwards the medium seems to diffuse as a matter of course until all potential users are connected. This characteristic explains why telephone, cable and Internet companies long to have the highest potential number of subscribers or clients and to get them as quickly as possible. It is a prime reason for the frequent fusions and take-overs in the new media sector.

In fact, these five characteristics are not new (Shapiro and Varian, 1999). The 'old economy' also makes information products (e.g. broadcasting and the press), experience goods (if only a piece of cake could be tasted before purchasing) and network systems (railways, telephony). However, the characteristics do become increasingly important in the information and network economy.

Two new characteristics of the network economy

Only two characteristics of the network economy can really be called new. The first one is the so-called *reversal of the value chain*. This is a process running from production via distribution and marketing to consumption. In the network economy, the traditional preponderance of supply shifts to demand and the value chain is reversed (Rayport and Sviokla, 1999). Increasingly, consumers give the first signals and producers deliver on demand. It also becomes easier for consumers to make large-scale price comparisons with the aid of software on the Internet. Moreover, they are able to organize electronically as groups of purchasers to push down prices and to command conditions, for example, by means of rating and filtering systems (see Chapter 6). Finally, consumers contribute to the production and distribution in the fast growing practices of co-creation. The service economy has transformed into a self-service economy where consumers themselves partly realize the service by filling in web forms, making selections in menus and adding own knowledge and information (such as reviews and ratings) on a massive scale. On the other hand, producers also get the opportunity to organize and to collectively buy parts of their products online. Besides, they are able to reach much more understanding of their own opportunities to sell and the patterns of spending among individual consumers.

A fundamental consequence of the reversal might be that stocks can get smaller and that the periodic crises of over-production in capitalism will be mitigated. Opposed to this, we more often observe the destabilizing effects of increasingly fast and massive buying and selling in electronic markets. Clearly, the rapid exchanges enabled by electronic networks are partly responsible for the continuous yo-yo movements on the stock markets. They boost financial speculation and proliferate crises and upturns. See Watts (2003: 195–219) for the social and psychological backgrounds of sudden shifts on markets using networks as channels.

A second fundamental change is a continuing *division and dematerialization of the value chain* (Rayport and Sviokla, 1999). Increasingly, all available information about the production, distribution and consumption process is detached from the process itself, both with material and immaterial products. This information is processed electronically and sold separately. In this way, the information-based organization of the different parts of the value chain can be split in many parts, detached from the process of material production and handled purely electronically by different companies. This is the core of e-commerce. For example, the Internet shop Amazon.com is able to uncouple the most profitable part of, among others, the book industry – marketing and selling – from the largely material process of producing, printing and distributing books and other goods. Amazon.com itself only possesses an electronic catalogue, a database of customers and suppliers, and distribution houses with small stocks of popular books. It mainly uses the stocks of other companies.

In an increasing number of value chains of the network economy, the organization and the information of the production process can be detached. In this way, the most profitable parts are creamed off. However, the material process and the production or distribution companies do not disappear at all. As many traders in e-commerce have learned the hard way, they are extremely dependent on the fast and reliable supply of their products to keep their customers satisfied and to guarantee their success. An important consequence of this division and dematerialization is the partial disappearance of traditional distributive trade to be replaced by all kinds of information brokers. The result is an increasing shift in the economy from material to informational goods. One of the problems with this shift is the difficulty of private appropriation of information, as we will see in Chapter 6. This explains the intensifying struggle for copyright, standards, codes and regulations (see the next section).

These two characteristics of the network economy might have a large impact on the capitalist economy of the future. However, they will certainly not cause the end of crises, recessions, inflation, unemployment and exploitation. The flow economy, with the growing support of ICT, has led to all kinds of *process innovation* enabling the economy to recover from the crises of the 1970s and 1980s and to remove a long list of bottlenecks in production, distribution and consumption (see, among others, van

Tulder and Junne, 1988). In the 1980s, direct cutbacks in production costs had the highest priority; in the 1990s, the emphasis shifted towards improvements in the efficiency and effectiveness of production and a better strategic control of production.

However, these two innovations have a counterpart. The uncoupling of 'virtual' from 'real' economic processes also creates excessive complexity and instability in the system, despite the stabilisation brought by the mitigation of over-production. Complexity is increased because the real value of financial products is very difficult to detect in the current far-reaching dematerialization of the value chain. The network society in general and the financial markets in particular have become very unstable because all social and economic processes are accelerated in electronic networks. Behind this acceleration, two 'laws' of the Web are working: the power law and the law of trend amplification (see Chapter 2). On account of these 'laws', rumours, hypes and contagions are spreading much faster than before.

Networks and the credit crisis

A good example of more instability in the economic system and the role of ICT as a trend amplifier is the credit crisis of 2007–09. ICT certainly was not innocent to this crisis. However, it was not the deeper cause of it that lies in the nature of contemporary advanced capitalism with its extended financial sphere. In at least three basic ways, networks of ICT have amplified the credit crisis:

1 Networks of ICT reinforce the volatility and speed of change in the economy. ICT enables yo-yo-movements on the stock market and a crowd behaviour of ever faster selling and buying on this market aided by computer programs. This complicates government and regulatory reaction in case of problems. Fortunately, government reaction was faster than ever before in the crisis of 2007–9. However, as a result, governments that saved the banks and lost billions of tax revenues in the slump of economic growth ran into debt crises. In this way, they came under the pressure of volatile financial markets working with the same technologies.

2 As has been argued before, ICT reinforces the virtuality and immateriality of economic processes. Without ICTs, no financial derivatives (the packing, selling and securitization of loans, the introduction of credit default swaps, etc.) would have been possible to the extent they were used before (and after) the crisis.

3 ICT delivers the software for all financial trade and product innovations, including automatic selling and buying.

Long waves of the economy

Possibly, ICT has assisted in the gradual recovery of the world economy after the previous crisis of the 1970s and 1980s by means of a better organization of the production process. This conjecture would match very well with the *theory of long waves of economic development* particularly known through the work of the Russian economist Kondratieff (1929) and extended by very different economists, from the Marxist

Mandel (1980) to mainstream economists such as Forrester (1976) and van Duijn (1979). According to this theory, the economy not only reveals short trade cycles between five and seven years long, but also long waves of about 50 years with an upturn and a downturn phase that are mainly launched by the arrival of new technologies. In the last two centuries, we have witnessed four waves dominated by:

1   the steam engine (roughly 1800–50);

2   electricity and the media of the first communication revolution (1850–1900);

3   oil, steel, chemicals and the combustion engine (1900–50); and finally

4   electronically-controlled machines followed by the transistor and the computer (1950–2000).

All these technologies had a great and lasting impact on production, transport and communications. However, not until decades after their first application did they appear to have a clear influence on economic growth and labour productivity. Apparently, technology has to be incorporated and domesticated in organizations and households before it has a greater impact. The same seems to be happening at this very moment, with the introduction of ICT. The computer has existed for a long time, but only after its miniaturization, exponential capacity growth and connection in networks is it entering organizations and households on a massive scale. Here, the computer is helping them to remove bottlenecks and to develop all kinds of new products and applications.

The last long wave in the world economy started after the Second World War with an upturn that lasted until the early 1970s, when it changed into a downturn. In the middle of the 1990s, a new upturn appeared. Perhaps this has launched a new long wave that is stimulated by ICT in general and network technology in particular and, to a lesser degree (yet), by biotechnology and nanotechnology. In the upturn phase of a long wave, periods of boom are long and on average they reach high growth figures, while recessions are relatively mild and short. The credit crisis of 2007–09 might be a partial exception as it was relatively short, but certainly not mild, at least not for the western countries. The credit crisis and the ensuing debt crisis of governments might be a disturbance of the current long way upward for western countries while eastern countries keep growing fast. Clearly, the balance of economic growth is shifting to the East that reaps the benefits of global economic recovery, while the West enters a stage of stagnation. However, the growing financial instabilities of capitalism are bound to aggravate any future long wave downturn.

Every upturn is characterized by numerous innovations, as has been emphasized by Schumpeter (1942), another advocate of long waves in the economy. According to him, the history of capitalism is a long succession of destruction and innovation. In the innovative upturn, young, creative entrepreneurs start a series of daring innovations that will be partly adopted by the whole economy later on. It is not difficult to recognize this process in the advent of Internet companies and the Internet hype around the turn of the century. The same can be argued for a second rise of the market value of Internet companies that currently happens for a number of typical companies of the network economy such as Google, Facebook and Twitter. After some time the innovations of the upturn are adopted by the mainstream of the economy and society. When this has happened, a downturn is likely to appear again, at least according to the deterministic and rather speculative logic of the theory of long waves.

THE PRODUCERS: FROM INFRASTRUCTURE TO SERVICE PROVIDERS

This section discusses how the 'communication branch' of the economy takes advantage of the technological and economic developments discussed earlier. Since activities in this sector are extremely divergent, it is important to make a clear distinction between the five parties engaged in networks. They are: the manufacturers of infrastructure; those who construct and maintain the infrastructure; the carriers and managers of both public and private networks; the service providers; and the consumers of networks. The last of these parties is discussed in the next section.

Kinds and functions of network producers

In order to understand what is going on in the media sector in general and in the production of networks in particular, it is necessary to make a distinction between the vertical columns of the various networks – of telephony, computer or Internet and broadcasting – and the horizontal layers of the functions performed by them. This distinction is made in Figure 4.3.

Services: content (information and communication)		
Applications	Applications	Applications
Browsers (guides, contact lists)	Browsers	Browsers (electronic program guides)
Operating systems	Operating systems	Menus

Services: transport and management		
Telephone operators	Internet service providers	Broadcasting operators

Services: construction and maintenance		
Telephone companies	Telephone and cable companies	Broadcasting companies

Producers of infrastructures		
Telephone equipment central exchanges	Computers, decoders connections, data centers	Transmission and reception equipment

Telephone networks	Internet	Broadcasting networks

FIGURE 4.3 Layers of supply in public networks

Producers of infrastructure

Most users do not realize that the highest turnover of capital still occurs at the level of material infrastructure, though the levels of transport, management and content catch up fast. For telephone networks and the Internet, the largest sums are spent on the ever expanding data centres, nodes, exchanges and terminal equipment. With broadcasting networks, most investments go to recording, transmission and receiving devices. Sales of cables, switches, decoders and transmitters flourish every time a new network is constructed. Afterwards a shift towards terminal equipment occurs – from single devices to complete company and house systems.

For some decades now, a strong *horizontal concentration* – that is, concentration on the same level in the production chain (see the rows in Figure 4.3) – has been apparent in all production of infrastructures for public networks. In the last three decades, the world market for telecommunications and computer network equipment has been largely controlled by ten companies. Important names in this context are Alcatel-Lucent, Siemens Nixdorf, AT&T, Cisco, NEC and Fujitsu. The companies involved have to make extraordinarily capital-intensive investments and they have extremely high research and development costs. Therefore, high turnovers and profits are required. This is a problem because profit margins on hardware are much lower than those on software in the information and network economy. Usually they are less than 2 or 3 per cent of total revenues. In order to survive, a company needs a vast and solid international market. So, capital and control are being concentrated more than in any other field, although there is some outsourcing to national subsidiaries.

Considering the production of terminal equipment (telephones, computers, modems, decoders, radios and televisions) big companies also are on the rise, and for the same reason: low profit margins. The giants of computer manufacturing are Dell, HP, Lenovo, Compaq, Siemens Fujitsu, Toshiba and Samsung. Big network equipment producers are Cisco, Alcatel-Lucent, 3Com and Linksys. Most dominant producers on the computer and network hardware market are American and East Asian. Traditionally, the production of broadband network equipment is closely linked to that of telecommunications. The same companies dominate. This situation has been slightly changed by the appearance of satellite manufacturers emerging from the space and arms industry.

Network operators and carriers

The construction and maintenance of networks are tasks largely performed or contracted out by network operators and carriers. This is the reason why no attention is paid to them here. The role of network operators and carriers is much more important. They serve as gatekeepers for networks. Telephone operators, Internet service providers and broadcasting operators largely decide who and what has access to networks and how expensive particular applications on networks are.

We have seen that a strong tendency to oligopolization is noticeable in infrastructure manufacturing. But in the branches of the most important customers of equipment – network operators and carriers – an opposite tendency can be observed: one of eroding monopolies. Public networks have lost their exclusive rights of transmission to private networks. In the 1980s and 1990s the big national public monopolies in telephony and broadcasting declined. They were privatized and split in parts with a different function (such as being a carrier or a content provider). The decline was caused by technical factors (insufficient capacity) and ideological economic factors (desirability of competition, deregulation and privatization).

The trend in operating and carrying telephony and broadcasting has gone from public monopolies to private oligopolies. Public monopolies acted on a national scale. Contemporary private oligopolies increasingly operate on an international level. In telephony they are companies such as Vodafone, T-Mobile, AT&T, Verizon and British Telecom. In broadcasting, companies such as Time Warner, News Corporation (Murdoch), Bertelsmann, Canal+, UPC and Microsoft NBC dominate the international market. There are no complete monopolies in telephony and broadcasting – basically, there is competition – but companies can split the world market among themselves, fix prices and benefit from international regulations on standardization and interconnectivity. Increasingly, large international telephone and broadcasting companies cooperate and merge. A handful of conglomerates are preparing to divide the world market. The final result will be a replacement of a national government-controlled public monopoly without competition by a small number of international private oligopolies with limited competition and scarcely any public supervision.

Contrary to the older networks of telephony and broadcasting, operators and carriers of the Internet are still relatively small and fragmented on a local scale. There are countless Internet service providers (ISPs) in the world, though many of them are in fact owned by the privatized national telephone carriers and big private carriers. ISPs have to work close to customers to help people connect to the Internet and with all kinds of other technical problems and they should be able to execute local laws and regulations in delivering content.

The margins of profitability for network operators and carriers also are relatively small. The reasons are, first, strong (international) competition after privatization and deregulation, despite concentrations, and second, technological development. In this development, infrastructural competition and the rise of the Internet in the process of convergence (see Chapter 3) are crucial. Infrastructural competition has grown where the updated networks of telephony, cable and atmosphere (satellite and wireless connections) each are able to carry the three basic services of telephony, Internet and broadcasting. The arrival of Internet services on smart phones is a second technological innovation that tends to reduce the profit margins of telephone carriers. People using instant message services or SNS on smart phones are calling less and they reduce text messages (SMS) in this way eroding the revenues of telephone operators. As soon as the capacities of fixed Internet connections and mobile smart phones rise, the same is going to happen to broadcasters because people start to partially watch TV and listen to the radio via the Internet.

Service providers of content

The top layer of all public communication networks is the service provision of content, the purpose of all supply on the levels below. The applications delivered here are the ones users know best. Presently, they also deliver the highest revenues and profits in the public network sector as a whole. Clearly, revenues and profits have shifted to companies such as Microsoft, Google and Apple. To understand current trends in the public network sector as a whole we have to discuss the processes of horizontal and vertical integration or concentration as they are the main instruments for the companies in this sector to gain control of it and increase their gains.

Horizontal and vertical integration or concentration

To explain trends of integration and concentration in the sector of public networks we will start with Figure 4.3 (page 83). First, *horizontal integration and concentration* means the unification or merger of business activities on one of the four layers in Figure 4.3 in one of the three cells or, in the context of convergence, in more than one cell on the same layer. In the past, we have observed many mergers or takeovers in hardware production of telephony, radio and television equipment and their connections. The same has happened on the layer of telephone and broadcasting operators and carriers creating big international telephone and broadcasting companies.

The second and strategically much more significant trend is *vertical integration and concentration*. This means integration across different levels of public network production and service delivery (see Figure 4.3 again). The strategic goal of this process is to gain more control of network supply as a whole and to increase revenues and profits by selling services of transport, operation and content to their own customers or subscribers. In the past, public monopolies of telephony and broadcasting controlled and delivered all services on each horizontal layer. After the privatization and deregulation in the 1980s and 1990s, services were split. However, after a short time, integration and concentration started again, this time enacted by private companies. Operators and carriers tried to become or to remain the most important service provider on their own network. In the 1990s, telephone, broadcasting and other media companies even tried to become general media companies in the context of the process of convergence that was clearly visible for all. For example, the already very broad media company Time Warner merged with the Internet service provider America Online.

In the first decade of the 21st century, these mergers appeared to be a bridge too far. Time Warner and America Online split again and they returned to their core businesses. However, the tendency of vertical integration remained, primarily in the form of network operators and carriers trying to sell their own services of content to their subscribers and other customers.

On the issue of vertical integration a crucial regulatory fight is going on. This fight is about the principle of *net neutrality*. Some telephone operators, cable companies and Internet service providers at the level of services of transport and management (Figure 4.3) are tempted to give priority to particular applications at the top level or to ask higher prices for them. The principle of net neutrality holds that all Internet content is treated equally and moves at the same speed over the network. These carriers and providers worry about the enormous bandwidth that some applications require (online gaming, downloading of movies and other real-time communications). Mobile phone operators regret that they earn less from SMS and calling because users shift to instant messaging and SNS on smart phones. Cable companies know that particular content is more valuable than other content for users. The temptation is to ask for extra fees. However, if this happened the Internet would start to look like cable TV (Lessig and McChesney, 2006). It would be an end to the free, peer-to-peer network as we know it. Instead, it would become a toll-network. It would also lead to so-called 'deep-packet inspection' of Internet content to see what applications are used with evident consequences for the privacy of users. Fortunately, an increasing number of countries have translated the principle of net neutrality into telecommunication regulation and even in laws. These laws and regu-lations do not rule out that prices may increase for more bandwidth or higher speeds, but they rule out priorities of content.

In the last ten years a very important second example of vertical integration or concentration has appeared, this time on the level of service provision of content. On this level a distinction should be made between the sub-levels of operating sys-tems, browsers and applications (see Figure 4.3 at the top). Here a very heavy *plat-form competition* is going on between the companies of Microsoft, Apple, Google and Facebook that are struggling for control of the Internet. Each tries to get a hold on the nature and the usage of the Internet by offering its own operating systems, browsers and applications as a platform for all important uses of the Internet.

Platform competition: the struggle for control of the Internet
Microsoft

One of the oldest companies acting on the Internet is Microsoft, though it was not the first. It was actually late as it had to imitate the first successful Internet browsers Mosaic and Netscape offering the first version of Internet Explorer (IE) in 1995 together with Windows 95. From the start, Microsoft was a software company for (desk-top) computers providing an operating system (Windows) and office applica-tion software (Microsoft Office). This proprietary (own) software has proved to be a real cash-cow for more than 30 years now. With the integration of Internet Explorer, Microsoft was the first company to bundle an operating system, a browser and a large number of software programs for both computers and the Internet. It was received with suspicion by many national regulatory bodies and courts accusing Microsoft of monopolistic practices. Some courts forced Microsoft to unbundle Windows, IE and the application program Windows Media Player.

Microsoft might be a software company for 95 per cent, but to be powerful in the sector of digital media and networks a company also needs to have a relation to hardware production. A vital condition for Microsoft's success is the fact that its main programs are sold with the majority of new computers and other digital media. Additionally, Microsoft also offers its own hardware such as keyboards, mice, game controllers and the Xbox for gaming. In the context of convergence it has also produced media players for broadcasting and started cooperation with telephone manufacturers such as Nokia to let them build Windows 7 into their mobile phones. See Box 4.5 below.

BOX 4.5
Microsoft's advance in platform creation in 2010–12

MICROSOFT	Main business model: Software and hardware selling	Revenue 2010 $62.4 billion	Profit 2010 $18.7 billion
	TELEPHONE	COMPUTER/ INTERNET	BROADCASTING
SOFTWARE - Applications	Skype and Apps.	MS Office, Bing, Media Player, MSN, Live Messenger and many others	MSNBC MSN TV
- Browser	Internet Explorer	Internet Explorer	Internet Explorer
- Operating System	Windows Phone	Windows	Windows
HARDWARE	Cooperation with Nokia	Keyboards, mice, Xbox, game controllers	Zune Media Player

The second conspicuous thing in Box 4.5 is that Microsoft builds its supply of proprietary software on its own operating system and browser, the core of the company's power. The third phenomenon that catches the eye is that hardware and software are not only offered for computer networks but also for telephony and broadcasting networks. This is driven by the process of convergence and the transition of fixed to mobile computing and communications. It has become a vital interest for Microsoft to have a share in the trend toward mobile computing and communications.

Therefore it has started cooperation with mobile telephone producers such as Nokia and Blackberry. It purchased Skype in 2011. To a lesser extent, the same goes for broadcasting as multimedia content and Internet videos will increasingly be watched on TVs.

Microsoft's business model is to sell primarily its own software (operating system, browsers and applications) that is proprietary and not an open source. The revenues of this business are huge: 18.7 billion dollar of profit on a revenue of 62.4 billion in 2010, that is 30 per cent. The company benefits from a feature of the information economy: high development costs, but low (re)production costs. Microsoft's mission is to 'create opportunities in the communities where we do business, and to fulfil our commitment to serving the public good through innovative technologies and partnerships'; further Microsoft wants 'to increase customer satisfaction and improve experiences with our products, programs, and services' (Microsoft website). However, in fact Microsoft primarily benefits from the fact that companies and people want working standard applications according to the law of network externality. At the time of writing it is not surpassed by open source software such as Linux. However, the revenues of its cash-cow software will dwindle in the future. Therefore Microsoft is shifting to cloud computing and mobile or ubiquitous computing.

Apple

Right from the start of PC development at the end of the 1970s, Apple has been a competitor for Microsoft in both hardware and software supply. More than Microsoft, Apple operated from the solid basis of its own hardware. At the start of the 1980s, Apple experienced a breakthrough with the Apple Macintosh PC. The prime characteristic of Apple is that it keeps all supply to itself with both proprietary hardware and software. The company has only been able to do this because it continually offers innovative hardware and software that is very attractive for users and has built a large number of fans of its products around the world. Spectacular innovations have been the Macintosh PC, the PowerBook, the iMac, the iPod with iTunes, the iPhone and the iPad. Unsurprisingly, Apple's company mission is to 'bring the best personal computing experience to students, educators, creative professionals and consumers around the world through its innovative hardware, software and Internet offerings' (Apple website).

However, Apple could not just keep producing terminal equipment or devices. It had to enter the world of networks, specifically telephony, the Internet and broadcasting to hold its position on the market. The company managed to do this by offering its own operating systems (OS) and browsers (Safari) in its popular hardware. In 2011 it introduced its own version of cloud computing: iCloud. It did not only offer these software means for computing and the Internet, but also for telephony and broadcasting (TV and iTunes music). See Box 4.6.

As compared to Microsoft, which mainly depends on the software of Windows, Internet Explorer and office software, the core of Apple's business model are its

BOX 4.6
Apple's advance in platform creation in 2010–12

APPLE	Main business model: Hardware and software selling	Revenue 2010 $65.2 billion	Profit 2010 $14.0 billion
	TELEPHONE	COMPUTER/INTERNET	BROADCASTING
SOFTWARE - Applications	Apple Apps	Many	iTunes
- Browser	Safari	Safari	Safari
- Operating System	iOS	Mac OS X	IPTV
HARDWARE	iPhone	Mac Pro/Book; iPod; iPad	Apple TV

popular devices. While Microsoft primarily remains a computer company, Apple has shifted to mobile electronic devices for communication and entertainment. However, it increasingly earns its money by selling applications (in its own App-store) for these devices. As hardware has a lower margin of profit, the ratio of revenue to profit is lower than with Microsoft, in 2010 it was a share of 'only' 21 per cent of profit from $65.2 billion of revenue.

Google

The old computer companies of Microsoft and Apple experience increasing competition from companies that have appeared as Internet companies right from the start such as Google, Yahoo, MySpace, Facebook and Twitter. By far the most important of these is Google. It has an entirely different business model from Microsoft and Apple as it is based on the selling of personalized advertising. The software it offers is free and open source. It even tends to give away devices such as laptops if only its software with accompanying advertisement is used.

Google primarily is an information and advertising company, not so much a software and hardware company. Google's original mission was 'to organize the world's information and make it universally accessible and useful' (Google website), notably by means of Google Search. However, after some time, Google added two other missions. The first was to add users' own information or content to the Web. This was done by copying or making accessible as many books as possible in Google Books. A second popular series of free programs was Google Maps, Google Earth and Street-view. The second additional mission contains the explicit goal to create a platform on the Internet: the offer to store all users' programs, individual files, communications and collective efforts in cloud computing (see Chapter 3). The services of iGoogle (personal portal), Google Docs, GMail, Gtalk and the social networking facilities of Orkut, Buzz and Google + belong to this part of the mission.

This extremely ambitious mission can best be realized when Google also offers its own operating system (Chrome) and browser (Android). At the time of writing, Chrome is not a big success, but Android is because it is stored into an increasing number of mobile phones and tablet computers supplied by other companies. Realizing the importance of a grip on hardware supply, Google has started to cooperate with companies such as Samsung, Sony and Asus. It also offers its 'own' Google phone. See Box 4.7.

BOX 4.7
Google's advance in platform creation in 2010–12

GOOGLE	Main business model: Personalized advertisement	Revenue 2010 $29.3 billion	Profit 2010 $8.5 billion
	TELEPHONE	COMPUTER/INTERNET	BROADCASTING
SOFTWARE - Applications	Google Apps	Google Search, Maps, Books, Gmail, Gtalk, Buzz, Orkut, Google + and many others	YouTube
- Browser	Chrome OS	Chrome OS	Chrome OS
- Operating System	Android	Android; also using others	Android
HARDWARE	Google Phone	Samsung, Asus and others. Tablets with Android	Google TV and Sony

Ninety-nine per cent of Google's $29.3 billion revenue in 2010 was from advertising. As it also has to invest billions on free software development and on enormous computer data centres spread across the world, it has left a profit of 'only' $8.5 billion or 29 per cent in 2010. It is matter of life and death for Google that users massively keep using their largely free software applications. Otherwise they cannot sell adversiting. In order to achieve this, Google has to create its own platform based on Android, Chrome and cooperation with hardware manufacturers.

Facebook, Twitter and other social media companies

An enormous threat for the platform ambitions of Google (in particular) is the rise of social media companies on the Web. They are the 'new kids on the block' that also are typical Web companies and that also have to earn their money with advertisement. Google's social networking applications are not a success (Buzz, +) or are only dominant in a few countries (Orkut in Brazil and India). Only Google+ is growing faster. In fact, Facebook has the same ambitions as Google, only it frames its information supply in the social context of users. Facebook's core idea is that when people have a question they first turn to the proximate people they know and trust and not to an abstract search engine in the outside world whose findings they cannot always understand and believe.

Facebook also develops an idea of the nature of the Internet that is different from Google's. Just like Twitter and other social media producers, it defines the Internet not primarily as an information medium but as a social medium of contacting and communication. What Internet users want is visible in the choice of the opening page on their computers, tablets and phones. When Facebook becomes the opening page for the majority of users of PCs, tablets and smart phones, it has the best chance of winning platform competition. Integrating Twitter or other micro-blogs and instant-messaging services it could sell a steadily increasing quantity of advertisement that is even more personalized than Google's and it could start selling its own or others' apps for phones, tablets and PCs.

Causes and consequences of platform competition

Why are these companies so eager in their ambitions to offer an exclusive Web platform for all kinds of applications? Why are they so keen on promoting their own hardware, operating systems and browsers? The prime reason is that by means of vertical integration or concentration (see above) they can get a grip on the most profitable part of the public network business sector: selling applications and advertisement. They have to encapsulate as many Internet users as possible and keep them to their own attention and service. This is the reason why Microsoft, Google, Apple and before long Facebook all want to invite users to sit on *their* cloud of cloud computing.

The background lies in three powerful laws of the Web (see Chapter 2). The first is the law of network externality which says that the more people participate in a network, the more others are likely to join. This is the reason why the companies in this sector want as many customers as possible. By cross-selling services to people they can make more money. This law also explains why fast-growing Facebook, for example, becomes ever more attractive to users and tends to drive back other SNS.

The second cause is the law of network extension. The Web has become so big and it offers so many and divergent applications that users need intermediaries they can trust to benefit from its opportunities. If anything, Google, Facebook, Apple and Microsoft want to build trust among their customers. This also explains why Google offers a Google application for just about everything you can imagine on the Web.

The last background is the power law acting in networks. Every use and each user is drawn to the most popular. The biggest players on the Web become ever more popular. This is why companies should belong to the biggest players and drive others out.

The strong and seemingly totalitarian ambitions of the big Web companies to create their own all-embracing platform, has particular consequences. They try to design the nature of the Internet following their own strengths and business opportunities. In this way this most-important public network tends to become designed by commercial private companies. Google wants the Internet to be an information medium. Facebook turns it into a social medium per excellence. Apple makes it into a medium for communication, entertainment and popular apps or gadgets. Finally, Microsoft labels the Internet as a series of everyday, practical, business, office and home applications performed online.

Fortunately, we can observe that ultimately the users and consumers decide what the nature of the Internet will be. The four main companies discussed here have often been surprised by apparent needs of users. Microsoft was late in discovering the importance of web browsers and very late in coming to meet the need for mobile communications. But it has earned so much capacity for investment that it can make up for its mistakes by buying other companies. Google was early in learning the importance of useful instruments of information search, but actually missed the boat in social networking. Apple has made very useful and attractive devices and apps but does not have much to offer for the Internet as a social and information medium. Facebook has a long way to go in offering anything other than social applications inside a social media environment. All players were surprised by latent needs of Internet users that suddenly became manifest, such as the attraction of mobile and ubiquitous computing, social media and online gaming. To explain these blind eyes we now turn to the customers of networks.

CONSUMERS: THE PUSHERS AND THE PULLED
Company and government pushes versus consumer pulls

Initially, in the 1980s and early 1990s, the demand for computer networks, hardware, software and services by small and medium enterprises (SMEs) and households or individual consumers lagged far behind the demand by big (trans)national corporations. In the first two decades of new media development, big companies and governments were the pushers. They invested in computers and networks. At that time, individual consumers could only be pulled. Clearly, this illustrates a general pattern of adoption of the new media: first the large enterprises; then their professional employees and people working in departments of higher education; afterwards the SMEs; and finally, a long way behind, the mass of households and individual consumers. However, the adoption of the new media by the last group is essential to pay for the high investments in large-scale infrastructures. This explains the desperate scramble by the IT industry in the 1980s and 1990s to bring on to the market one new medium after another. As almost all of them failed until the middle of the 1990s, these attempts may be termed a *technology push*.

In the 1980s and the first half of the 1990s, there was an impressive series of (consumer) market failures in the supply of new media devices and services: the videophone, the videodisk, videotex, CD-I, the first generation of personal digital assistants and the systems of (home) video on demand, to mention just the most important.

Only since the middle of the 1990s have we witnessed a partial breakthrough of PCs, digital and mobile telephony and, later on, Internet connections in households. It was partial, because at that time the digital divide of physical access (see Chapter 7) was still a major phenomenon, even in developed societies.

Reasons for the mismatch of design and demand

What are the main reasons for these evident past and present failures of the new media on the consumer market? To answer this question one has to appreciate that the introduction of new technologies is a matter of *design by producers* and *domestication by consumers* (Silverstone and Hadden, 1996). Domestication is the appropriation of new technologies by consumers in households, workplaces and other private places, making them acceptable in their own familiar everyday lives. Domestication is anticipated in design, and design is completed in domestication (ibid.: 46). So, it appears that design and domestication have become separated in the recent drive for adoption of the new media by households and individual consumers. Three interrelated characteristics are responsible for this mismatch.

First, a *supply-side view* dominates design, production and marketing of the new media. They are held to be so superior in features like speed, mobility, comfort and other benefits or communication capacities, like those described in Chapter 1, that their demand is taken for granted when their prices drop to a reasonable level. Therefore, unprejudiced market research before and after introduction is scarce. Rarely user groups are invited to participate in design. Of course, the new media are designed and constructed with users in mind. But putting them on the market remains a matter of trial and error instead of real and valid experiments. When a new medium appears to be reasonably successful, all bets are placed on it; when it does not catch on, it is simply dropped. In both cases there is insufficient learning about the causes of success or failure. So far, the trials of the Apple supply of new devices have been most successful. People were standing in line before the shop opened every time a new iPhone or iPad appeared. Eagerly, these phones and tablets were imitated by Apple's competitors. However, they probably still don't know the reason for the success of these devices.

The second characteristic of the introduction of the new media is the dominance of *technical* design. Technicians develop most hardware and software. They are so devoted to the presumed splendid technical capabilities of their artefacts that they neglect real user perspectives and pay insufficient attention to user-friendliness. They simply cannot imagine that a particular target group will not use their technically superior products. It would not be rational to refuse them. They do not realize that the adoption of new technologies is a social and cultural affair as well. Many consumers will stick to their old habits, daily routines and emotional attachments to old technologies for personal and social reasons, which go much deeper than simple utilitarian, rational objectives.

Here we encounter the third and most basic reason for the mismatch between design and domestication. In the offer of new media products, a *device perspective* (hardware) or *service perspective* (software) is taken instead of a social and contextual perspective. A good example is the technical convergence of the computer and the television. Technically speaking, it has become easy to watch TV on a multimedia computer and to display Internet services on TV screens. However, this does not mean that these are dominant social and personal practices in the real settings and daily routines of households. Computer use is mainly an individual affair, with people working and playing close to small screens with extended keyboards, usually in a study. TV viewing is both an individual and a collective activity, with people entertaining themselves watching large screens using a limited remote control, most often in the living room, kitchen or bedroom. Perhaps the use of tablet computers and smart phones everywhere in the house will make a change, but it will not remove the needs of a home cinema in the living room and a secluded working environment in the study.

The simple technical availability of multi-functional computers and TVs does not mean that they will be accepted in the social settings and relationships of households. This is the heart of domestication. The same goes for information, communication, entertainment and transaction services, which are believed by their designers to be superior in use and enjoyment, but do not manage to become embedded in the daily routines of households and individual consumers. Surprisingly little attention is given to research into the social and contextual environments where the new media are supposed to work. The spatial characteristics and usage patterns in living, working and cultural places are neglected, as are the social relationships of gender, generation, status and power in households (see Morley, 1986; Silverstone and Hadden, 1996).

However, the main reason for the failure of most new media on the consumer market, at least until the middle of the 1990s, is the very rational reason that they have simply offered insufficient *surplus value* as compared with the old media. These days, most observers take it for granted that the new media will not replace the old ones completely, but will be added to them. This is one of the most striking effects of media history in the 20th century. It means that new media should have a particular surplus value of their own.

Lessons of media history

All these rather sceptical perspectives do not imply that present and future new media have continued to fail on the consumer market. Currently, many more of them are successful than in the 1990s. It just means that success has taken considerably longer than the new media industry hoped for. The final adoption of the new media by the mass of consumers is often different from the one expected. This is another striking feature of media history. For example, the telephone was designed to be a medium for business and emergencies, not for social talk between people, especially women (Moyal, 1992). Radio users were expected to become broadcasters at the beginning of the 20th century, but they ended up as listeners. Computers were designed to calculate or process data and certainly not to play games with.

The most important type of application of the new media in households is not yet known either. The continuing dominance of business and professional uses makes one part of industry think that information (services) and transaction (electronic commerce and ordering things) will be the so-called 'trigger applications' of the new media for the mass of households as well. Another part, primarily the vested interests in the media industry and telecommunications, expects that it will be primarily entertainment, social networking and communication, since they correspond to the mass applications of broadcasting, the press and telephony in the 20th century.

More successful introductions of the new media might be driven by the opportunity for differentiation, individualization or personalization of demand they offer. Taking advantage of mobile, wireless and ubiquitous computing, users are much better able to choose the time, place and kind of application according to their own individual needs for information and communication than with the old media. These very specific, local and individualized needs in households, working places, schools and mobile environments make the removal of the mismatch between design and domestication all the more necessary. After all, the contexts of consumption become much more complicated.

CONCLUSIONS

- The second communications revolution (the digital revolution) can be explained by the needs of control in the complex processes of the contemporary economy. The new media are able to support the flexibility, efficiency and productivity of organizations, to improve all kinds of logistic processes, to replace transportation of goods and people by the exchange of information, and to reach a differentiated public of consumers.

- The new media assist in creating a flow economy that links scale extensions and scale reductions in production, circulation and consumption. Production is decentralized, while capital and control are centralized.

Increasingly, economic flows are immaterial processes with exchanges of information and knowledge.

- The global capitalist economy adopts the characteristics of a network and information economy, not a 'new economy'. These characteristics are partly responsible for the recent financial crisis. The only new aspects are a partial reversal of the value chain and a far-reaching dematerialization of the information economy.

- Networks, in all kinds of concrete configurations are shaping a new mode of organization in between hierarchies or bureaucracies and the market. They are a compromise between control (planning) and (market) freedom in an increasingly complex environment. One of these configurations is Enterprise 2.0 that focuses on flexible labour conditions, knowledge management and the use of social media in companies.

- The production of new media and networks can be understood by an arrangement in a layered model of telephone, broadcasting and Internet networks with infrastructure production at the bottom and service provision (operating systems, browsers and applications) at the top. This model shows the consequences of convergence in attempts of horizontal and vertical concentration. The goal is to get a larger part of the most profitable part of production: services of content and advertising.

- To achieve this goal some operators and carriers want to ask higher fees for particular applications, harming the principle of net neutrality. At the level of services, the big producers on the Internet (Microsoft, Apple, Google and Facebook) each offer their own platforms with their own operating systems, browsers and applications.

- Initially, the consumers of communication networks were businesses and governments engaged in process innovation. From the second part of the 1990s onwards, individuals and households have adopted the new media on a massive scale. Many new media failed on the consumer market, while others succeeded. With the popularization of the Internet and other new media, consumer needs increasingly shape success or failure.

5 POLITICS AND POWER

About this chapter

- The core concept in this chapter is power. We may all lose power introducing media networks because they rest on a very vulnerable technology. Accidents such as the breakdown of networks, cyber-wars, cyber-crime and hacking are discussed.

- Network politics appear because the political system obtains a network structure. This may lead to the spread of politics in society and to the opposite: further concentration of politics in an (authoritarian) state.

- A popular view is that the Internet is a tool for democracy. Is the Internet democratic by nature? Which views of democracy related to ICTs exist anyway? Is it justified to talk about Facebook and Twitter revolutions against oppressive regimes?

- One of the tools for democracy on the Internet is e-participation by citizens. What does it mean? What are the most important applications?

- The second part of this chapter turns to the power in organizations. Are networks changing the relationship of power inside organizations? The popular idea is that networks are flattening organizations and that they help to transform bureaucratic, top-down organizations into efficient, horizontal types of organization based on teamwork and cooperation. Does this really happen?

- The last part of the chapter is dedicated to power at the level of the individual. It is about privacy and personal autonomy. Both might be at stake because networks are large-scale structures in which individuals may be just a pawn in the game. Several types of privacy and ways to defend them are discussed. A discussion about personal autonomy and basic freedoms of people in networks closes this chapter.

THE VULNERABILITY OF NETWORKS
Causes of vulnerability and potential solutions

People often tend to forget that we may all lose power when we become dependent on networks. Computer networks, at least, appear to be extremely vulnerable technologies. How should this vulnerability be reduced to make computer networks viable communication structures for everybody?

Everybody knows by now that things can go wrong with computer networks. We are informed again and again of yet another hack, virus, criminal offence, violation of privacy and system breakdown. In the last 25 years, countless congresses and seminars about the security of information systems have been offered. And in spite of, or perhaps as a result of, the problems being reduced to concrete technical, organizational and legal proportions, fully satisfactory solutions remain to be found. Problems only seem to get worse. No daily newspaper appears without any news about them.

It is remarkable how the problem of network vulnerability is reduced to aspects of technical security. In fact, most harm is caused by human mistakes, not by technical errors. Moreover, vulnerability is a problem much broader than technology. It is about *the stability of the entire social system* working with new ICTs. The system is making itself dependent on powers over which it has no (complete) control. When technology fails, the system cannot function anymore – 'the network is down' – or only continues to function with problems, sometimes big ones.

Furthermore, networks can generate internal forces opposing the use of technology, resisting the effects or even destroying them. This can happen when internal opposition rises to the way networks are introduced and governed when they exclude certain people and harm particular interests, norms or freedoms. Spiteful employees who have lost their jobs or positions and hackers that do not agree with particular technical solutions are to be found everywhere.

Finally, the power of the system as a whole can be threatened from outside by forces who are hostile to the system: enemies, extremists, hackers or plain criminals. National sovereignty is at stake because nations are conceding their grip on their own economy, culture and politics to the networks of international broadcasting, the Internet, global industry and, most important of all, international financial markets working with networks of ICT.

Unfortunately networks possess certain characteristics enhancing their vulnerability in daily usage. *Size* is a network's most important characteristic. A network's reach largely determines its power and usability. At the same time, the network becomes harder to control for any network management. The chance of something going wrong increases. More than separate machines and applications, a network depends on the quality of all hardware and software engaged. A chain is as strong as its weakest link.

Integration of central and local sources or carriers of information, and their *multifunctionality* are also strong features of networks. However, precisely these features cause a direct or indirect effect across the entire network if there is a failure in one section. Clear examples are computer viruses and computer hacks – most often they can 'travel' unhindered within and between networks. A network's technical design is able to minimize the failures caused by them, but only at the expense of accessibility, flexibility and efficiency.

Another characteristic is that many networks are *patchworks*. In order to increase interconnectivity, hybrid connections are made between private, advanced and well-protected company or government networks and open, less advanced and protected public networks such as the Internet and public telephony. Here goes again: a network is only as strong as its weakest link.

Accessibility for many interconnected users is one of the strong features of a network, but at the same time it is one of its weaknesses. The chances of ignorant and unauthorized people having access to the network increase proportionally.

Networks enhance the *complexity* of information systems in comparison with separate units. Numerous new communication problems arise. Furthermore, complexity increases as local units (intelligent terminals, PCs, smart phones) become able to do more by themselves. As a network becomes more complex, the chances of failure increase in proportion.

Increasing complexity usually leads to *dependence on a few experts*: technicians and network operators. The potential drop-out or unreliability of these experts – caused by illness, a strike, incompetence or fraud – make networks all the more vulnerable.

Most solutions to these problems in fact limit the positive features of networks. Some strategic options have far-reaching consequences: should networks be reduced in size or made less functional, integrated and interconnected? This can be achieved by installing smaller networks for one purpose which can be interconnected, but do not have to be. This, however, strongly reduces the usage value of a network. Another option is to keep the connection itself as 'basic' as possible. This means 'intelligence' is stored at the centre and in the terminal equipment alone. The latest attempt to achieve this is cloud computing which completely centralizes network operations and sources. However, this makes the centre more vulnerable and attractive for external assaults. And the end-users, both companies and individuals, lose control and start to become negligent in applying safety instructions.

Access for all was the most attractive network feature right from the start. However, it was also the first feature to be restricted. Most existing technical and organizational security is based on restrictions. Besides, any limitation of accessibility conflicts with the distribution of knowledge and power which safeguards against dependence on a few experts.

To summarize: this list shows how most solutions limit or even nullify the usability of networks. Some solutions increase vulnerability in new directions. This means that the result must be some kind of compromise between the security and the freedom or usefulness of networks.

Network-centric warfare and cyber-wars

The vulnerability of networks is both exploited and combated by military and security agencies in the most spectacular ways. They take advantage of the weak links in the networks of other countries engaging in experiments with network warfare or espionage.

Conversely, they try to repair these links in their own country's networks as a matter of defence and counter-intelligence. Society has become so dependent on networks that vital infrastructures can be harmed by cyber-attacks with relatively small means. Electrical power, the water supply, nuclear power stations, communication and transportation infrastructures, the government, stock markets, banking and finance and hospital systems, all may be vulnerable to disruption. Soon, it will be far more effective to destroy the country of an enemy by network warfare than by bombardments.

Three concepts should be carefully distinguished on this issue: network-centric warfare, network- or cyber-war, and cyber-attacks of hackers. *Network-centric warfare* has existed since the 1990s when it was first practiced by the American army. It is contemporary high-tech warfare with conventional means such as fighting jets and rockets. In this type of warfare, satellites, air-force command and equipment (jets, precision rockets and bombs), ground command, troops and intelligence sensors everywhere are linked in a single network system. The intention is to reduce errors ('collateral damage'), enhance precision, increase the speed of command and flatten military hierarchies (Alberts, 2002; Alberts et al., 2000).

A *network- or cyber-war* is only waged on the Internet. Clarke (2010) has defined cyber-war as actions by a nation-state to penetrate another nation's computers or networks for the purposes of causing damage or disruption. Cyber-war is considered to be the fifth domain of the military after land, sea, air and space. Several armies in the world are *preparing* for such a war as a potential part of future warfare. Fortunately, such a war has never taken place. In recent years countries such as Russia, China, the United States, Iran and Israel have often been accused of cyber-attacks. Exaggerating them, they are called wars. Russia may have disrupted a large part of the Internet in Estonia in 2007 after the removal of a Soviet-era war monument and may have done the same in Georgia in parallel to the Russian invasion in this country in 2009. In 2010 China was accused of attacks on American government agencies and companies such as Google. In 2009, during the 'Green revolt' the US may have supported attacks on Iranian government websites. In 2010 Israel was presumed to have attacked Iran's nuclear enrichment facility after already having used cyber-attacks against Hezbollah and Syria in the years before.

However, there is hardly any evidence of such government involvement (Mueller, 2010). It is difficult to prove where a cyber-attack comes from anyway (Morozov, 2011). Afterwards, nationalist or oppositional action groups, perhaps stimulated by security organizations, often appeared to be the perpetrators. In that case these attacks belong to the following category.

Hacker-attacks

At the time of writing, one reads in the newspapers about hacker-attacks on company and government websites nearly every day. Currently, this is by far the most common category of Internet assaults exploiting its vulnerability. Hackers often use so-called *Distributed Denial of Service (DDOS)* attacks on websites of governments and companies: a so-called 'botnet' of thousands of computers that are linked and infected by malicious software, often unnoticed, continually tries to get access to a particular site, in this way bringing it to a standstill. These attacks can have a political motivation. In this case, sometimes the word 'hacktivism' is used. For example, in December 2010 hackers attacked the sites of Mastercard, PayPal and Visa because these companies would have betrayed *WikiLeaks* leader Julian Assange. A second traditional hacker motivation is to warn sites of their bad security, such as the attack on Lockheed Martin in May 2011 preventing the theft of classified information. However, the most frequent and fast growing category of hacker attacks has a pure criminal motivation. They entail blackmail and the theft of valuable information or money resources. These attacks are often kept secret by the victims.

NETWORK POLITICS
The political system obtains a network structure

The relations between all actors involved in political activities in the widest sense can be subsumed in a comprehensive model of the political system (see Figure 5.1). In the previous chapter, the manifestation of the infrastructure of the network society in the economy was described in terms of networks within and between companies. Goldsmith and Eggers (2004) have demonstrated that government is also increasingly shaped through networks. Figure 5.1 shows that even politics in general are organized in a network structure. This is a clear example of the law of network articulation (Chapter 2). All the relations between the different actors of the political system can be interpreted both as political relations (of power) and as relations of information and communication. Media networks and their applications increasingly organize and shape these relations. Figure 5.1 should be seen as a model of the political system, able to show how some relations and actors achieve central importance while others drop out or become peripheral.

In one of the chapters of the book *Digital Democracy*, I reached the conclusion that ICT enables both a spread and a concentration of politics (van Dijk, 2000a). The use of ICT enhances existing centrifugal forces in the political system, because in the heart of the system, institutional political forces have to give up some of their powers in favour of international bodies, (inter)national companies, legal institutions, privatized agencies and individual citizens and corporations sharply calculating according to their own interests. With the aid of a public network, they can start their own relations of information and communication and simply bypass the core of the system in the national government. Thus, they can shape a politics of their own. Unlike a state, a computer network has no frontiers. This spread of politics leads to less power for national states (Mueller, 2010).

On the other hand, networks serve attempts to register and control the citizenry by governments and public administrations. In Figure 5.1 it is easy to see that the core actors are linked to every other unit in the system. In authoritarian states this enables surveillance and censorship. In democratic states these links strengthen the power of civil servants over parliaments as these servants are in control of the information systems of government. Additionally, the ever expanding databases of citizens managed by the government enable citizen control. So, ICT also supports

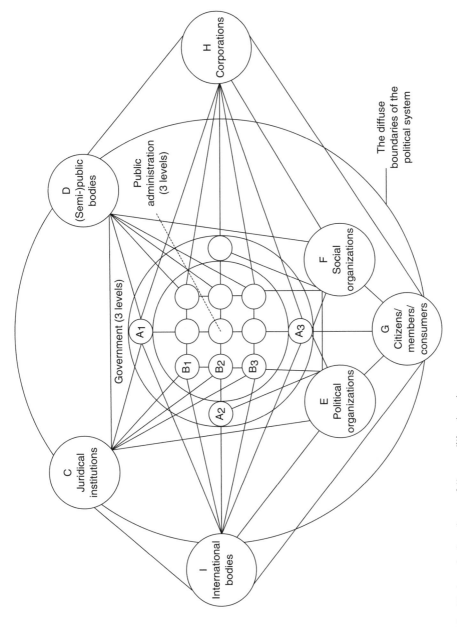

Government (3 levels)

Public administration (3 levels)

A1 A2 A3
B1 B2 B3

C Juridical institutions

D (Semi-)public bodies

E Political organizations

F Social organizations

G Citizens/ members/ consumers

H Corporations

I International bodies

The diffuse boundaries of the political system

FIGURE 5.1 Network structure of the political system

attempts to concentrate politics (van Dijk, 2000a). Departments of the government and the public administration are among the first to introduce ICTs on a large scale. The concentration of politics increases the power of national states. Authoritarian governments amply use this potential (Morozov, 2011). So, the basic idea of those who think that the Internet is decentralizing on a global scale and necessarily undermines the national state is just as one-sided as the opposite idea of the centralization of control by the national state. The state will not wither away or even dissolve into virtual relationships of horizontal types of organization appearing on the Internet.

Both visions are one-sided, since networks consist not only of (horizontal) connections but also of (vertical) centres and nodes. Furthermore, they do not float in the air. They connect actors of flesh and blood (people) and material resources (in households and organizations). In a network society, networks do not replace society, but they increasingly connect and organize its constituents. In any case, the state still belongs to the strongest (assembly of) actors in society. Therefore, politics and democracy, primarily operating at the level of a single society, are not doomed. As Slaughter (2004) has argued, the state is not disappearing, but disaggregating into its component institutions linked by networks.

Network politics consists of attempts to fill the relations in the network political system (Figure 5.1) with various applications of the Internet and ICT in general. The relation between governments (A) on the one side and citizens (G) and their social and political organizations (E, F) at the other is filled by *online democracy* and *web-based election campaigns* (Chadwick, 2006; Chadwick, 2008; Chadwick & Howard 2009; Davis et al. 2009). The relation between departments of the public administration at the national, regional and local levels (B) is supported by shared computer systems in so-called *joint-up government* (van Dijk and Winters-van Beek, 2009). The relation between the government with its public administration (A, B) and (semi-) public bodies (D) or corporations (H) is enhanced by *networked government* in public–private partnerships and by *outsourced government* in privatization using systems of ICT (Goldsmith and Eggers, 2004). Finally, the relations between governments or public administrations and international bodies are intensified by *global networking*, also amply using the Internet and ICTs (Slaughter, 2004, Mueller, 2010).

THE INTERNET: A TOOL FOR DEMOCRACY?

Technology of freedom or control?

Without doubt, the diffusion of communication media and an increasing level of education have been the most important factors in the worldwide revival of the movements for civil rights and democracy during the 1980s and 1990s. The spread of international networks of mass communication and telecommunication had a big impact on the collapse of the communist regimes in Eastern Europe and on the rise of movements fighting for democracy in developing countries. Considering the daily broadcasts of western radio and television programmes and the increase in international telephone calls, it seems like the fall of the Berlin Wall and the collapse of the Soviet Union were inevitable in the long run.

The thesis of information and communication technologies presenting a 'lethal' threat to *traditional* totalitarian political systems, based on the centralization and control of all information and communication in a particular territory, can easily be defended. It is impossible to centrally register and control all individual activities of small-scale production and large-scale distribution across any border using these technologies. No traditional totalitarian regime can remain in power after the massive introduction of PCs, diskettes, faxes and all sorts of new audiovisual equipment. On the other hand, several new types of rule with a totalitarian flavour are conceivable using this new technology, as one of its capacities is to enable central management, surveillance and control (see Beniger, 1996; Burnham, 1983; Gandy, 1994; Lyon, 2003; Morozov, 2011; Mulgan, 1991). Especially after 11 September 2001, the day of the terrorist attack on the World Trade Center and other US targets, many governments have stepped up surveillance for so-called security reasons (see Lyon, 2003; O'Harrow, 2005).

To get a true view of these new types of rule, one should abandon the idea that they need *direct* supervision (in the Orwellian sense) or *total* control of every level of production and distribution of information. Central political and economic power only has to be wielded when citizens, workers or consumers cross one of the carefully chosen lines guarded electronically by large-scale, interconnected systems of registration and surveillance. There are methods of checking on people and their activities that are much more efficient than direct supervision, whether electronic or by eye. They allow plenty of room and freedom, but when a certain line is crossed, a 'red alarm' is triggered at some central control. See the final section of this chapter for further discussion of this dark perspective.

In view of the contrast presented in the previous paragraph, it is no surprise that there are opposing views concerning the effects of ICT and the Internet on freedom, democracy and organization. To some, ICT is a *technology of freedom* since it enhances the freedom of choice for individuals and intensifies horizontal (bottom-up) relations in networks of organizations and individuals (Pool, 1983). Others claim that, since the design and introduction of ICT is determined by leaders in governments, public administrations, businesses and other organizations, it is primarily a *technology of central registration, surveillance and control.* They are accused of using ICT to get a firmer grip on their organizations and subordinates (Burnham, 1983; Gandy, 1994; Garfinkel, 2000; Loudon, 1986; Lyon, 2001; Zuurmond, 1994).

Views of digital democracy

Before going into detail discussing the democratic potential of the Internet and ICT at large, it might be appropriate to answer the question of what democracy actually means. Various implicit and explicit answers have been given to this question (see Abrahamson et al., 1988). In my view, there are at least six views of democracy in this respect. The first five are coined by Held (1987) as *models of democracy.* Their supporters appear to have different preferences for applying ICT in the political system (van Dijk, 1996; 2000a). The basics of these views are that the goal of democracy is either decision-making or opinion-making and that the means of democracy are either representative or direct. See Box 5.1.

BOX 5.1

Six models in two dimensions of political democracy

PRIMARY MEANS	DECISION-MAKING		OPINION FORMATION
REPRESENTATIVE DEMOCRACY	LEGALIST		
	COMPETITIVE		
			PLURALIST PARTICIPTORY
		LIBERTARIAN	
DIRECT DEMOCRACY	PLEBISCITARY		

Source: van Dijk (2000b: 39)

The first two views on democracy lead to the use of ICT for the *reinforcement of institutional politics*, which is the centre of the political system (see Figure 5.1, A and B, the actors of the government and the public administration). With the spread of politics and with the erosion of the national state compared with other (inter)national forces, institutional politics have ended up in a perilous position, which will only be aggravated by ICT. Yet, the most dominant political forces in western democracies are striking back, using ICT to fortify the positions of the state. The so-called '9/11' and other terrorist attacks give them the occasion to prioritize security issues and to organize a strong state. The classical western view on democracy supporting this move is *legalist democracy* – a so-called procedural view of democracy with the aim of decision-making. This view regards the constitution and other laws and rules as the foundations of democracy. The three basic principles are: separation of powers (legislative and executive power, the judiciary); a system of checks and balances between the government, the public administration and the judiciary; and representation. In this view, the lack of information gathered by the state is currently the most important problem to be solved with the aid of ICT. So, ICT has to bring about an effective administration of government, a strong state and more security. Furthermore, it can help to improve public support for the government and the administration by offering more and better information in both directions.

The second conception of democracy is called *competitive democracy*. It is mainly supported in countries with a two-party or a presidential system. According to this view, parties and leaders compete for the support of the electorate. This rather elitist view of democracy emphasizes representation and efficient decision-making by leaders. The Internet and ICT are first and foremost used for information campaigns and election campaigns. In the United States, a lot of experience has been gained with this use of ICT (Bimber, 2003; Davis et al. 2009; Newman, 1994; Rash, 1997; Selnow, 1994; Sunstein, 2001). Party information systems and opinion polls on the Web can help voters in their choice of the best leaders and policies. Social media and email are used to create the suggestion of a personal relationship with voters.

The other four views of democracy have a completely different strategic orientation. Supporters of these views fight for a *socialization of politics* – a further dispersion of politics through the system as a whole (referring to the actors around the outside of the model in Figure 5.1). This implies a more prominent role for social organizations and individual citizens. The assumption is that the Internet will enable them to have a direct influence on politics, and even to bypass institutional politics or replace it with their own political relations. Figure 5.1 clearly shows that relations can be created in this way (bypassing the centre). While views intending to strengthen institutional politics are mainly supported by politicians and administrators, these alternative views are defended by many social organizations and intellectuals.

The most radical view concerning existing political practice is *plebiscitary democracy*. According to this view, political decisions have to be made through referenda or plebiscites. This implies a preference for direct democracy instead of representative democracy. The opportunities offered by the Internet to hold telepolls or telereferenda and to have electronic discussions have had an immediate appeal to the supporters of this view. They are said to revive direct democracy as practiced in the Athenian agora. The term 'teledemocracy' has been introduced (Arterton, 1987; Barber, 1984; Becker, 1981), which means that citizens and social organizations are able to directly determine at a distance, using ICT, what goes on at the political heart of the political system. See also Becker and Slaton (2000) and van Dijk (2000a), on the possibilities and limitations.

Another alternative view is *pluralist democracy*, sometimes also called *deliberative democracy*. In this view, opinion formation within and between social organizations is emphasized. Democracy is not the will of the majority but that of a constantly changing coalition of minorities. Its most important value is pluralism in social and political discussion and in the media. It is a combination of direct and representative democracy, since representation is exercised not only by politicians but also by the organizations of civil society. ICT offers numerous opportunities for pluralism in public debates, among them Internet debates, and for discussions within social organizations, for example, by using an intranet.

The fifth view discussed here is *participatory democracy*. Its supporters promote a socialization of politics, encouraging active citizenship. The emphasis lies on the broadest possible opinion formation about political affairs and on a particular combination of direct and representative democracy. Its most important instruments are public debates, public education and citizen participation in general. If the new media are to play a positive role in enabling these instruments, access for all is vital.

The last view on democracy has appeared as a dominant model among the pioneers of the Internet community. This does not mean that the political views behind it are entirely new. Many observers have noticed the affinity of the Internet pioneers to the radical social movements of the 1960s and 1970s in most western countries. These views range from classical anarchism and left-wing socialism to all kinds of libertarianism. The last are most important in the past two decades. The *libertarian view* is close to the pluralist and plebiscitarian views in several respects, as the opportunities for (virtual) community, telepolling and teleconversation are proclaimed. Specific to libertarianism is the emphasis on autonomous politics by citizens in their own associations using the horizontal communication capabilities of the Internet. In its most extreme form, institutional politics and the national state are held to be obsolete and to be superseded by a new political reality collectively created in networks. The basic problem to be solved, according to this view, is that the centralism, bureaucracy and backwardness of institutional politics are such that it fails to live up to expectations (the primacy of politics) and is unable to solve the most important problems of modern society. A combination of Internet democracy and a free-market economy will serve as a replacement (see Jon Katz, 1997, and for a critique of this view labelled as 'the Californian ideology', see Barbrook and Cameron, 1995).

The preference for Internet applications such as electronic debate, social media and telepolling implies that the libertarian model is both a substantial and a procedural conception of democracy and that it is much closer to direct than to representative democracy.

The Internet: democratic by nature?

The rise of the Internet in the 1980s and 1990s coincided with the fall of the Berlin wall, communism and other undemocratic systems in the Third World. At that time, the democratic opposition benefitted from old media such as international satellite television and telephony and new media such as VCRs, faxes and PCs. It was no surprise that the newborn Internet with so much potential for free expression was seen as the very climax of democratic aids. Particularly after the start of Web 2.0, following the year 2004, the Internet came to be seen by many as a medium that is democratic by nature. Box 5.2 contains a number of Internet characteristics inspired by the Web 2.0 perspective that all seem to favour democracy, particularly according to the four views at the bottom of Box 5.1. Benefitting from these characteristics, the use of the Internet would, in a manner of speaking, overturn undemocratic states of affairs by itself (Leadbeater, 2008; Shapiro, 2000; Shirky, 2009; Surowiecky, 2004).

It is not the first time in modern history that such a view comes forward when a new medium appears. Dispersed electrical power, the telegraph, the telephone, radio, television, the VCR and cable (TV); all of them were once seen as media with a democratic potential that would end wars and dictatorships and usher in an era of freedom (Morozov, 2011; Winston, 1998).

BOX 5.2
Characteristics of the Internet viewed as a democratic tool

- An *interactive* medium that departs from the one-sided communication of existing mass media.
- An *active and creative* medium enabling users to transform from viewers, listeners and readers to participants.
- A *direct* medium in which individual users are able to determine, at a distance, what happens in the centre of politics and the mass media, among others.
- A *platform* on which everybody is equal in principle as assumed expertise has to prove itself before being accepted.
- A *network* medium enabling the collective creation of products online, not primarily by individual authors or businesses.

However, the advocates of the Internet as a tool for democracy are so much focussed on the presumed splendid features of the tool that they forget the users, the actual usage and the social and political context of use. They have an instrumentalist view on technology and fall victim to Internet-centrism (Morozov, 2011). Against this view it has to be argued that it is always the social and political context of use that decides whether the Internet will have a democratic impact. The second basic mistake they make is to ignore the negative characteristics of the Internet concerning democracy such as unequal access and skills for Internet use or privacy intrusion. They also disregard the downside of the positive characteristics. 'Failing to anticipate how authoritarian governments would respond to the Internet, cyber-utopians did not predict how useful it would prove for propaganda purposes, how masterfully dictators would learn to use it for surveillance, and how sophisticated modern systems of Internet censorship would become' (Morozov, 2011: xiv).

Even the characteristics in Box 5.2 have their downside. Interactivity does not mean that there is no supply-side anymore: the interactive interface designed can prove to be very manipulative. The fact that the Internet is an active and creative medium does not guarantee that users actually will be active and creative. Most use is still relatively passive and already politically-motivated elites may be the active users (see Chapter 7). That the Internet is a direct medium does not mean that a system of direct democracy can easily be built on it. Contemporary society is far too complex for that (McLean, 1989). Moreover, most experiments with direct democracy in history have led to totalitarian systems. That the Internet is a platform for Web 2.0 user-generated content does not mean that everybody's voice on this medium is equal. In Chapter 9 we will observe that group dynamics appear in the 'wisdom of crowds' on the Internet. 'Big mouths' may prevail in discussions while sensible people with well-considered opinions keep silent. Finally, the opportunity of collective creation in networks might equally benefit extremist groups creating hate speech or bombs and groups of citizens creating new policies or public opinions.

The claim that the Internet can be used by both sides, by democratic and authoritarian forces, does not mean that it is a neutral tool. Networks have properties that both support and undermine democracy (van Dijk, 2011). First of all, current political trends are amplified whether they go in the direction of more democracy or not (the law of trend amplification; see Chapter 2). The laws of network externality and small worlds support democracy because they entail a drive to connect for growing numbers of people more or less freely exchanging information. Opposed to that, the power law and the law of network extension may lead to concentrations of power and attention in the hands of those already powerful (Hindman, 2008). Promoting democracy in political and regulatory action requires a detailed assessment of the democratic and undemocratic characteristics of a medium in a particular social and political context. Only this can lead to sensible policy proposals supporting democracy according to a particular view.

Facebook and Twitter revolutions?

Clear cases of an instrumentalist view of the Internet as a democratic tool appeared in the mass media during the revolts in the Middle East between in 2009 and 2011. There was much talk about so-called Twitter revolutions in Iran and Tunisia, and Facebook revolutions in Egypt and other Arabic states in revolt. Commentaries were so much focused on the presumed liberating potential of these Internet applications that they ignored the social, economic and backgrounds of the upheavals and the question whether they could be called revolutions at all. They overlooked the fact that in Iran, for example, during the 2009 'Green revolt' there were only 19,235 Twitter accounts registered or 0,027 per cent of the population (Morozov, 2011) and that in Egypt only about 5 per cent of its population had access to the Internet at all in 2010. Twitter, Facebook and other social media are powerful instruments of mobilization for the, mainly young, vanguard of the revolts using them and they are important publication and information media in countries without press freedom, showing the brutalities of armies and security organizations. In China, the micro-blogging system of Weibo supports a more or less free public sphere. However, to organize a revolution much more is needed than mobilization with social media or mobile phones.

In his book *The Net Delusion*, Morozov (2011) completely demolishes these popular ideas. However, even a serious social scientist such as Manuel Castells (e.g. 2009) only describes the liberating potential of the Internet and mobile phones, scarcely paying attention to its downsides (van Dijk, 2010b). His analysis shows that with social media and mobile telephony, a new type of communication appears between interpersonal and mass communication: *mass self-communication* (see Chapter 7). This type of communication is supposed to be liberating for users while it undermines all existing institutions, among them political institutions. In Chapter 7 we will see that this is partly true, but that one should not forget the downsides. The following increasingly forceful counter-moves are made by authoritarian regimes.

First, they themselves are using the social media and mobile telephony for a complete *surveillance* of oppositional forces, often arresting the people concerned shortly afterwards. Unwillingly, Facebook and Twitter are helping them because all communication in their media is open and because they give no priority to privacy protection at all. The same goes for mobile telephony that can be tracked everywhere. There are no better tools to make a complete chart of the opposition than social media and mobile telephony.

The second counter-move is increasingly sophisticated *censorship* of dangerous oppositional voices on the Web. The blunt first-generation types of censorship, simply cutting web addresses and forbidden words overall, have been replaced by much smarter strategies. The so-called second and third generation censorship techniques are much more focused (Deibert et al., 2008). Particular IP addresses, keywords and domains are programmed in routers and software packages at key Internet choke points such as major ISPs and international gateways, for instance, they enable 'just-in-time blocking' when a demonstration is announced. Increasingly, ISPs and Internet companies are stimulated to assist with self-censorship. In countries such as China, self-censorship has become common practice.

The third counter-strategy is to launch *counter-information campaigns* that discredit and demoralize opponents. Authoritarian regimes themselves use social media to distribute their own propaganda. Any false step that is made in a Twitter or Facebook message by the opposition is used to discredit them. Nationalist and religious messages are distributed to gain support for a regime or to create confusion among the population.

E-PARTICIPATION

What is e-participation?

Now I want to turn away from this rather sceptical analysis of the prospects of digital democracy that had to be made to confront unrealistic beliefs in the new media as automatic tools of democracy to strike a more positive tone. I will discuss a series of real possibilities of using the new media to improve the participation of citizens in democratic government. They are called e-participation and they are a part of e-government.

In my (broad) definition, *e-government* comprises all processes of information processing, communication and transaction that pertain to the tasks of the government (the political and public administration) and that are realized by a particular application of ICT. E-government has an internal and an external dimension. The internal dimension concerns the internal government and its administration increasingly using networks and databases to rule the country and to administer the affairs of citizens, corporations and the public administration itself. However, this chapter focuses on the external dimension, the relation between governments or public administrations and citizens. After all, this chapter is about politics and power.

E-participation can be defined as taking part in public affairs by governments and citizens by means of ICTs to shape these affairs in a particular phase of the institutional policy process, from agenda-setting through policy evaluation (van Dijk, 2010c). This definition implies that e-participation can be the initiative of both governments and citizens. Governments invite citizens to participate offering particular Internet applications and citizens use these applications or their own ones to participate. Box 5.3 contains the most important contemporary applications of e-participation listed in the order of the policy process. Concepts will be explained below.

Agenda-setting

Governments sometimes not only inform citizens about their policies on government websites, but also invite citizens to reply or to have an input with their own ideas, suggestions or complaints. Information provision is the most frequently used application in e-participation. However, information provision is not sufficient to talk about participation. At least an invitation to react to the information supplied should be added.

In many countries, citizens initiate or use *e-petitions* to put single issues, complaints, or requests on the political or government agenda. In Scotland this has become an official initiative of parliament. Here citizens are invited to fill petition lists on a website. E-petitions are likely to become very important tools in countries with a legal right to put issues on the parliamentary agenda, after having collected a particularly large number of signatures. The Internet is a much more powerful tool to reach this goal than traditional means of signature collection. A couple of years ago, such a petition had an impact on decision-making in the UK. The Brown government withdrew a plan for road pricing after a first petition against it reached mass support.

Policy preparation

During the years of the Internet hype, many western governments launched *official online consultations* of citizens to discuss government plans that were already prepared. The intention was to engage more citizens in the process of making plans than only those citizens that were known as more or less professional lobbyists gathering on official meetings. In general the results were disappointing as the same kind of lobbyists showed up as before and because governments did not accept results as they were deemed to be not representative.

However, in the meantime, the opportunities for online plan consultations have increased because more citizens are able to participate and because a number of popular innovations in plan consultations are introduced, such as the visualization and simulation of plans (Botterman et al., 2009).

BOX 5.3

Main applications of e-participation in the policy process (initiative of governments or citizens)

Phase in the policy process	Application of e-participation
Agenda-setting	• Open online consultations (governments and public administrations) • E-petitions and e-activism (citizens)
Policy preparation	• Online plan consultations (governments) • Online forums for policy-making (citizens) • Online knowledge communities and social media serving policy-making (citizens)
Decision-making	• E-voting (governments; election committees) and e-voting guides (citizens) • E-campaigns (citizens and politicians)
Policy execution	• E-maintenance of the law (by citizens invited by governments) • E-complaints (initiated by citizens)
Policy evaluation	• Quality panels and individual evaluations of online public services (government initiative) • Citizen control sites and information services for public or government policy (citizen initiative)

Since the advent of Usenet groups more than 30 years ago, Internet users have discussed all kinds of societal issues in *online forums*. They offer the opportunity of contributing to discussions 24 hours a day and from every location without the necessity to meet. Evidence shows that online forums do not draw more people into these discussions than in traditional meetings, with the important exception of a part of the young generation (Brundidge and Rice, 2009; Katz and Rice, 2002). Rarely, they are representative for particular populations as they are dominated by well-educated middle-aged men (ter Hedde and Svensson, 2009). Therefore, governors complain about the lack of representativeness. However, as these forums are so popular with many thousands of participants in every country, they must have some effect on the consciousness and knowledge of policy issues among citizens (van Dijk, 2000a).

In e-participation applications using discussions such as online forums and social media, civil servants of public administrations are invited to discuss government affairs directly with citizens. In this way they tend to lose their role as executives and, perhaps unwillingly, adopt the role of political representatives. This is a basic and often neglected problem of e-participation and e-government in general.

Increasingly, *social media* (both social networking sites (SNS) and knowledge communities), video exchange sites and weblogs have policy discussions as a main or side effect. This can happen on the initiative of citizens or of governments who have discovered the popularity of SNS. Of course, their prime focus is social networking, the exchange of knowledge, and entertainment. Exceptions are political weblogs who are primarily political. Other exceptions are citizens' watchdog communities such as *WikiLeaks* that publish and comment on leaked documents. In Box 5.3 the latter are subsumed under citizen control sites.

Decision-making

Potentially, computer networks offer new channels for *e-voting* in elections and in referenda or official opinion polls. A distinction should be made between electronic machine voting and electronic distance voting. It is the latter kind of e-voting that we will discuss here. It offers new opportunities for people who live far from a polling station, have a lack of time or have a disability. However, most evidence, in the few instances where online e-voting is already practiced – mainly among expats and in Estonia and Switzerland – shows that these opportunities do not, or only scarcely result in a higher voter turnout.

The Barack Obama campaign has shown how important *e-campaigning* can be for elections. With his Internet applications he gathered more than 500 million dollars of funds and organized an army of campaign volunteers as participants in his campaign. Email, YouTube, social networking sites and his own extended website were very frequently used.

Citizens themselves can also use e-campaigns to put pressure on governments. This also happens outside election times. On the Internet we have thousands of pressure groups trying to influence government decision-making. However, currently the most important applications of e-campaigning for citizens are *e-voting guides* that are very popular in several European countries. They are decision-support systems offered by more or less independent public policy and research institutes helping voters to choose the best party, candidate or referendum option on the basis of a number of positions and statements.

Policy execution

Of course, governments use the digital media extensively to control for criminal acts and the offence of rules and regulations. However, the government can use additional eyes to survey what happens in society. This certainly is a kind of participation in policy execution. We are talking about municipal and police sites on which citizens are able to report all kinds of offences, from child pornography to having seen someone driving a car using a mobile phone that is not hands-free. These types of *e-maintenance of the law*, also called 'snitching sites' in popular language, are ever more popular among the population. Increasingly, citizens also launch such sites themselves, as in the case of hunting down paedophiles. This present-day version of the pillory used in the Middle Ages shows that these applications have some worrying aspects. Finally, it has to be observed that e-maintenance of the law can also turn against governments as it can be used to report offences by civil servants and to launch complaints against government acts.

Citizens themselves are also able to launch sites for *e-complaints* against wrong or badly executed government policy. This happens, for instance, in environmental, juridical, mobility and minority or immigration issues and even cases of corruption. Here it appears that these opportunities of e-participation can be a two-edged sword as the same technology can be used to undermine government policies and regulations. For example, sites are available that warn drivers of the exact places where speed cameras are installed along the road.

Policy evaluation

Some governments, mainly on the local level, have installed *online quality panels* or individual feedback systems in their online public service supply. This enables citizens to rate the level of service provision and provide feedback. For governments, this gives them the opportunity to continually improve services.

However, the fastest growing applications of e-participation are all kinds of *control sites* and information services for citizens that enable them to evaluate official policy results on a daily basis and to use them for their own decisions in daily life, such as the choice of a place to live. The issues concerned are not as political as the familiar policy debates on the Internet and other mass media; however, they prove to be very attractive to average citizens, including those with no political motivation. Examples of these control sites are sites where local residents are able to report the level of noise around airports and the pollution of particular regions or waters. Extremely popular are social-geographical cards of quarters and neighbourhoods reporting their statistics of criminality, housing prices and living quality.

General conclusion

E-participation is most frequently used in the first phases of the policy process: agenda-setting and policy preparation. Policy evaluation is a second area, mostly used on the initiative of citizens and their organizations. Governments and public administrations rarely allow entries to the core decision-making and policy-executing phases. They claim that this does not correspond to our representative political system and the responsibilities of the public administration. So, the background for acceptance of e-participation initiatives by governments certainly is a particular view of democracy (see above). The legalist view of democracy is not likely to accept them.

Evaluations of e-participation applications raise the suggestion that applications of e-participation on the initiative of citizens or civilian organizations and new media developers are more successful than those initiated by governments (van Dijk, 2010c). At the end of the 1990s many governments were experimenting with online plan consultations that were disappointing in terms of the extension of participation. Now e-petitions, e-voting guides (made by independent organizations of politically-motivated citizens and software developers), e-complaints and citizen control sites are far more popular than the online open and plan consultations and official online discussions of those days.

These applications of e-participation might be more popular than the traditional ones, but this does not mean that everybody is able to use them. One of the main problems is that they require a number of digital skills added to the traditional skills of citizenship (social skills and knowledge of how the government and decision-making work and what rules and regulations hold). These skills will be discussed in Chapter 7. When this does not change by means of better accessible and usable e-participation tools and by means of more training of digital skills, e-participation will not empower citizens more than old modes of participation (Wilhelm, 2003). Instead, it might raise an additional barrier.

However, the decisive touchstone of e-participation in terms of democracy is the influence on political decisions. On this score, we have to conclude that scarcely any influence of e-participation on institutional policy and politics can be observed yet (van Dijk, 2010c). Few decisions of government, political representatives and civil servants have changed on account of the input of citizens in e-participation, one of the few exceptions being the drop of road-pricing in the UK. The electronic channels of participation used are simply added to the traditional channels. Decision-makers doubt the representativeness, surplus value and quality of the input of the new channels. Few decision-makers are prepared to accept the direct inroads of e-participation on their decisions.

Therefore, it is no surprise that governments and public administrations have problems with the incorporation of the initiatives and results of e-participation in their regular operations and modes of governance. So, in terms of democracy, the sober conclusion is that 'most administrations do not (yet) have mechanisms and capacities in place to cope with a significant increase in participation' (Millard et al., 2008: 76).

POWER IN THE ORGANIZATION
From bureaucracy to infocracy

The previous chapter explained how networks can be used to change the *superstructure* of a (large) business organization. They turned out to support a combination of concentrating power, finance and control and decentralizing production and execution. The *structure within* organizations is also fundamentally changed by the introduction of networks. Here I am talking about changes in management. In the previous chapter, I described how bureaucracy turned out to be an obstacle instead of an innovation for organizations. By modernizing bureaucracy, ICT can help to get rid of this obstacle. According to Max Weber (1922) bureaucracy has five features listed on the left-hand side of Box 5.4.

BOX 5.4
Bureaucracy versus infocracy

Bureaucracy (Weber, 1922)	Infocracy (Zuurmond, 1994)
• Hierarchy of authority	• Business-like central control despite flattening of organizations
• Centralization of desicion-making	• Centralization within a decentralizing framework
• Formalization of rules	• Built into the software
• Specialization of tasks	• Built into the software
• Standardization of actions	• Built into the software

The use of ICT does not make these features disappear. On the contrary, they are integrated in this technology. Frissen (1989) has demonstrated the close relationship between bureaucracy and ICT. This is obvious for three of the features just mentioned. ICT offers much better opportunities for formalizing rules, specializing tasks and standardizing actions than did the old techniques. In using computers and networks, traditional procedures are formalized by programming them in software or even in hardware. Informal solutions have to be rejected as much as possible. People are restricted to their specific tasks more strictly than before, because they know everything they do is registered. Finally, the use of computers and networks leads to an extensive standardization of actions. After all, their use supposes fixed and detailed procedures and strict fine-tuning before one is able to start cooperation through networks.

The relationship between bureaucracy and ICT is less obvious for the first two features mentioned. Many think ICT 'flattens' organizations, as the distribution of network operations requires less hierarchy and centralization of decision-making. So, these features need more detailed explanation.

After having conducted an investigation in a number of Dutch social service departments that used ICTs, Zuurmond (1994) reached the conclusion that hierarchy, centralization, formalization and specialization in these services were decreasing. In some respects, these organizations had become 'flatter'. More teamwork took place at several levels. Civil servants less frequently recorded every step by writing it down. They acquired broader job responsibilities. Even the fifth feature of bureaucracy – standardization – was adapted. Within certain boundaries, civil servants were allowed to produce 'made-to-measure' work in the service. However, the extent of freedom for this work was strictly limited by computerization. Staff were given fewer opportunities than before to take important decisions themselves. Zuurmond has claimed with great emphasis that, in spite of requiring fewer traditional bureaucratic procedures, ICT causes an increase in (central) control over organization.

Thus, an organization can create more horizontal structures, take out hierarchical levels, cancel checks and eliminate paper-devouring file guiding systems
because information architecture can take care of these things. In particular,
(routine) coordination and (routine) communication are being taken over by
information systems. Management no longer has to control this coordination
and communication: very strict procedures, designed to guide these actions,
are allowed to 'disappear'. Now they are inside the system (Zuurmond, 1994:
300–1, my translation from the Dutch).

So, the main part of traditional management's tasks is integrated in information
systems. Modern management *selects* and *steers* these systems. Zuurmond calls his
type of management *infocracy*, the successor of bureaucracy (see Zuurmond, 1998
for an elaboration of this concept in English). The characteristics of infocracy
are summarized in the right-hand side of Box 5.4 and are compared to those of
bureaucracy.

Claiming that (central) control over organizations is increasing, while traditional
hierarchical and bureaucratic procedures are declining, seems contradictory. What
does it really mean? In the previous chapter, I argued that networks combine
horizontal and vertical types of control and coordination. As further explanation,
I want to make a clear distinction between the following aspects of the *infrastructure
of organizations*:

- a structure of *control*, regulation and information coordinating decision-making
  within and between organizational layers; this requires a structure of *authority* in a
  number of organizational layers;

- a *division of labour* distributing functions and tasks within the organization that
  necessitate *coordination*.

Control and authority

The *control of decisions* in networks has to meet high demands. One can meet these
demands by both centralization and decentralization. Mintzberg (1979) makes a distinction between a horizontal dimension (within one organizational level) and a vertical dimension (between organizational levels). Applying these concepts here, the
following possibilities arise:

- *Horizontal centralization*: the highest level of management takes complete control
  (see above); the most important decisions are taken away from staff members,
  whose only job now is to shape the information network to enable the development of manageable options.

- *Horizontal decentralization*: increasingly complex information processes give staff
  functionaries more authority in the organization's management: the so-called 'line
  structure' (management) loses some of its influence to the 'technostructure'.

- *Vertical centralization*: the top layers in management take decisions away from the lower levels and even from employees at the base by means of standardization, formalization and increasing routine; inevitably, lines are shorter and parts of middle management become redundant.

- *Vertical decentralization*: standardization, formalization and increasing routine allow a transfer of decision-making power to the operational levels. They also allow a swift and flexible reaction to changes in the company's environment, an important benefit in the market and in direct relations between personnel and customers or clients.

It is important to note that all four tendencies are technically enabled by the introduction of networks. Which tendency will predominate depends not only on the balance of power within the organization, but also on the type and size of the organization, its diversity and the extent of its computerization. An increase in centralization is to be expected in offices which have had a low level of automation until recently. But most organizations will have to deal with a combination of the four tendencies described. Horizontal and vertical decentralization within a centralizing framework will be the most likely combination, as it is clearly enabled by networks of ICT.

Developments in the structure of *organizational authority* can be shown more clearly. It is common knowledge that the introduction of networks causes a decrease in the number of hierarchical levels. The network 'itself' takes over some of the supervising personnel's coordination tasks. Coordination and supervision are partly replaced by network operations. The work left for supervisors is to watch over and maintain the network instead of supervising and coordinating personnel. Lower and middle management have to give up some of their authority to higher management and staff functionaries on the one hand, and to operatives working independently with the aid of computer programs on the other. From these trends, many people have drawn the conclusion that organizations are getting flatter. But this does not have to be the case at all. It would be more realistic to say that the line between the top and the base is being 'thinned out'. The distance that communications have to bridge is decreasing; the difference in control and authority is not.

Division of labour and coordination

The division of labour within organizations that are supported by computer networks may lead to the integration of tasks (task broadening and even task enrichment) as much as to further specialization (task division and even task erosion). As claimed before, integration of tasks is most likely using ICT. Opening a multitude of programs at one terminal is made easier. Furthermore, task exchanges are supported: it is easier for a person to substitute for someone or to take over for a while. Technology will help to increase the organization's internal flexibility. The strategies of Enterprise 2.0 discussed in the former chapter add to this flexibility. Looking at things from this angle, we will see tasks *broaden*. Whether this will lead to task *enrichment* for the employee involved depends on the extent of power, education and freedom of action within the programs available. With unchanged policies of task divisions within organizations, the standardization and computer programming of traditional craft or expert knowledge often leads to task *erosion*. Task broadening could serve as compensation.

The same network technology, however, may lead to unprecedented task *division* in administrative and industrial organizations: tasks are standardized in programs that assign them to specific functions much more strictly than before. The computer system's access registration controls whether this really happens. Subsequently, the system 'itself' determines the observance of the procedures prescribed.

All this shows that network techniques are not power neutral. They are a clear matter of design, for instance in network architecture. Therefore, let us take a closer look at the *technical options* available in network design. The most important questions in this respect are:

- Will the main processing capacity be placed in a central or a local position?

- Will a workstation have its own connection to a central computer or a shared one?

- Is cloud computing adopted?

- Who is able/allowed to communicate with whom over the network?

- Which programs and files can be used by the various categories of personnel?

The answer to most of these questions is largely determined by the network's technical typology and topology, programmed in the construction and the organization of the standard network layers (see Chapter 3).

PRIVACY AND PERSONAL AUTONOMY
What is privacy?

Now we reach the level of the individual. The use of networks can have major consequences for the power of individuals. Their privacy and their personal autonomy can be violated, but they can use the same techniques to protect themselves and to increase their freedom of choice. The prominence of the issue of privacy and autonomy in networks is a direct consequence of the first law of the web: in the network society the social *relations* are gaining influence as compared to the social *units* they are linking. One of the potential units is the individual that becomes tied up with other units and always loses some of its freedom and autonomy in the structured relationships of social and media networks.

We have to make a distinction between privacy and personal autonomy. Privacy is a freedom. It is a freedom of *individuals*, not of groups or organizations. Personal autonomy is a characteristic of an individual's *relations to others*. It determines the individual's opportunities to gain and protect freedom. Personal autonomy is a synonym for the power of the individual. Here, freedom becomes freedom of choice and control – in this case in the use of ICT. Privacy is a precondition of personal autonomy. Without an individual's freedom in general, any freedom of choice is restricted. Therefore this section begins with a discussion of privacy. First, the meaning of privacy is explained. Subsequently, the threats to privacy caused by the use of ICT are discussed. Finally, there is a treatise on existing possibilities to protect a person's privacy.

Privacy is an abstract concept bearing many meanings. It is so intangible that many people do not realize its importance. Popular descriptions are expressions such as 'privacy is the individual's right to determine whether and to what extent one is willing to expose oneself to others' and 'privacy is the right to be left alone'. A scientifically justifiable definition, however, has to be based on concepts and notions accepted in legal theory, in history or in social science.

Historical and anthropological research have shown that the value attached to privacy varies significantly in social and cultural terms, but that some aspects of privacy may be universal (Roberts and Gregor, 1971). At the end of extensive comparative historical research of ancient cultures, Barrington Moore (1984) reached the conclusion that the *need* for privacy, defined as the need to seclude one's intimate behaviour, to be alone occasionally and not to (have to) show certain views and behaviour to a group or community, is universal. However, *in historical practice* this need is often subordinated to a primitive social organization and technology, according to Moore. In this book, I want to add that, at the beginning of the 21st century, the individual is subordinated rather to *advanced* social organization and technology.

In legal theory, privacy is a particular right of freedom. It is a right of no interference, in this case of private life. Nabben and van de Luytgaarden (1996) even went so far as to call this right the *ultimate freedom*, not to be transferred on to a community and to be weighed against other interests.

In my view, the social philosopher Robert Holmes produced one of the best definitions: 'Freedom from intrusion into areas of one's own life that one has not explicitly or implicitly opened to others' (1995: 18). In this definition of privacy, and in many others, spatial and informational dimensions are evident. Privacy is about the *spatial seclusion* of certain areas, starting with the body and its direct surroundings (private life) which are not to be interfered with. Added to this, *phases of information processing* often recur in definitions: the perception, registration and disclosure of the characteristics and behaviour of individuals.

Following Westin (1987), a distinction is often made between relational and informational privacy. Even though I argue that these two types of privacy often mingle, particularly in the context of networks, I maintain this division and even add a third type: physical privacy. In fact, the body and its immediate physical surroundings are the ultimate private area. This is the main reason why the act of rape is among the greatest possible violations of one's privacy.

Physical, relational and informational privacy

Physical privacy is the *right to selective intimacy*. This applies to the inviolability of the body and the fulfilment of intimate human needs, allowing the presence of only a very small selection of other persons or no other people at all. This may not seem to have relevance to ICT, but, in fact, biotechnology and information technology are increasingly intertwined. The most important link between them is the information code of life: DNA. Charting all genes of the human species and holding DNA tests have everything to do with a registration of personal data. In the future, DNA will probably produce the most important personal data. They will be recorded with the aid of ICT, which will also be used to link DNA data with other kinds of personal data.

Another potential threat to physical privacy is so-called biometrics. These are, first of all, identity checks (such as eye, face, finger and voice recognition) and entrance checks (screening sensors placed on the body). In addition, analogue and digital video cameras intrude into more or less intimate physical spheres of personal life.

Most of the time, checks will primarily affect relational privacy: the *right to select contacts without observation and intrusion*. This is about relationships and behaviour in one's (semi-)private life at home, at work, in forms of transportation (including one's own car) and other less reserved spaces. Being able to determine one's own personal relationships and conduct without other people observing and interfering with them is a fundamental right of freedom. Imagine: few people would dispose the contact list in their phones to everybody. This right might be threatened by all tracking technologies that are used nowadays by authorities and Internet or telephone companies to register people's contacts and messages in mobile telephony, email, instant messaging and social networking sites. 'You are who you know' is a familiar saying about the importance of networks. Tracking our mediated relationships touches a type of privacy that becomes ever more important. This is especially the case because users of SNS, email and instant messaging themselves add to the existing data – freely providing and exchanging all kinds of personal information, contact lists and contact information.

The last type of privacy is informational privacy: *the right to selective disclosure*. In a primitive sense, this type of privacy is as old as mankind (gossip) or writing (the first registers), but the introduction of ICT has made it much more relevant. Information privacy is about the grip the individual has and keeps over his or her personal data and over the information or decisions based on these data. Unfortunately, the concept of personal data has narrowed the common notions of privacy. The protection of privacy has been replaced by the protection of personal *data*, and it is sometimes even reduced to the *security* of these data.

In this book I emphasize the integration of these three types of privacy which have become equally important. Increasingly, they are linked. For instance, databases of personal data of consumers (informational) are linked to their surfing behaviour inside and between sites (relational tracking). In passports, biometric data (physical) of fingerprints, face and iris scans are linked to the personal data also stored on the passport.

Threats to privacy: data-mining and social sorting

More than all previous phases in the development of ICT, the introduction of networks is a threat to all types of privacy. The threats to informational privacy are most obvious, but relational and physical privacy are endangered as well when the spatial and physical spheres of personal life are opened up. I will discuss the most obvious contemporary threats of privacy in the order of technological development. The most traditional type of privacy intrusion comes from using databases and data-mining. This type is more than a century old (Garfinkel, 2000). There are many ways for information technology to help establish relations between personal data within and between files. First, relations within files are discussed. Next, relations between files, also known as links or couplings, are described.

Most database files are created to establish relations between individual records and fields (characteristics) in a matrix. This produces information about individuals. As a next step, databases are created to establish overviews of all records and fields or a selection of them. Thus, strategic information is obtained about groups of people – for instance the purchasing behaviour of various groups of people at various times of the day. In most cases, the information can be traced back to an individual. Enabling a company to use all these possibilities, data from several sources are brought together in one database and checked for correctness (a clearing operation). These data collections are called *data warehouses*. Filling these warehouses with large amounts of data to be used in various contexts has become an industry in its own right. Accompanying search techniques are called *knowledge discovery in databases* (KDD).

The next step is *data-mining*: the extraction of implicitly present, formerly unknown, but potentially usable information from data. All kinds of new search techniques are developed for this purpose, based on a combination of statistics and artificial intelligence.

Data warehouses and data-mining help to produce strategically significant information on persons. The people involved are usually not aware of this. They leave their tracks everywhere, for instance in using customer cards, savings cards and chip cards, or by filling out reply forms, thinking this will not be of any consequence to their privacy. Then, suddenly, the data deposited everywhere return to the person concerned like a boomerang. Many institutions turn out to have a surprisingly wide knowledge of an individual and appear to be able to take decisions, and not always the right ones, for the customer, employee or citizen. This knowledge can result in very interesting product offers, but can also result in being turned down for a job interview, in not being granted a loan, or in having an income tax return refused.

More possibilities appear in the production of links between data in several different files – a process known as *file coupling*. This process can vary from simple comparisons to the actual coupling of files, enabling the use of KDD's advanced search techniques.

Combining two or more files may lead to a complete integration of these files in one file. This integration can help to make *profiles* of a person (and a group or organization). These profiles are created using behavioural psychology and statistics to estimate the chance that someone with specific characteristics will do certain things (Rothfelder, 1992).

These profiles become more and more influential in management and marketing information systems, in personnel information systems of labour organizations and in the suspects lists of police and security organizations. According to Lyon (2007) they lead to a widespread practice of *social sorting and categorization of people*. Contemporary surveillance classifies people in terms of risk management. This practice is already very old in the commercial sector where lists of reliable and unreliable (in terms of payment), regular, occasional and one-time customers are maintained.

Governments have trailed behind the business sector considering profiling. Tax offices may have had black lists of tax payers that have committed fraud, and social benefit organizations may have had lists of potential fraudulent clients, however, a systematic categorization of particular suspected groups of citizens and migrants appeared after the 9/11 terrorist attacks on the US. Suddenly people were suspects because they were Arab, Muslim, migrant or just because they have no flight return ticket. The problem with social sorting and categorization is that they easily lead to discrimination and to the exclusion of social categories from particular services. The people concerned are mostly unaware of this categorization and they are unable to act against it. They cannot correct mistakes made.

In all data-mining, file-coupling and risk categorization the distance between the data combined and the source is great. In these combinations, new data are created that often have a different purpose than the original data. Nevertheless, these data are interpreted as valid and reliable information by these systems. The person involved is hardly ever informed of these adaptations and new purposes. It is strategic information, yet, mistakes and inaccurate presuppositions are easily made.

The elusiveness of file combination and adaptation in networks means that the distance between the reality of individuals, the data on these individuals and the decisions based on them is increasing, while the influence of individuals on the total process is decreasing accordingly.

Threats to privacy: tracking technologies

An average citizen or consumer is not only registered in hundreds or even thousands of databases with more or less permanent data, (s)he also is continually trailed by all kinds of tracking technologies recording temporary traces of behaviour. Let's describe a regular day of an average person that has a job, acts as a consumer and surfs on the Internet.

Mr. Jones is awakened by an alarm on a mobile phone. He gets up and carries his switched-on phone all day. In this way, not only his time of awakening but all his steps, whereabouts, messages and talks during the day are recorded via the antennas in the fields he is passing and stored in gigantic log files of his telephone operator. At breakfast he is looking at a number of TV channels that are automatically recorded by his digital TV service provider. He checks for new messages on his Facebook page, adds a number of new contacts and updates his profile ignoring the fact that all of these acts are stored by Facebook and forwarded to his 'friends' and advertising agencies. Mr. Jones also is a Twitter fanatic who sends around about 20 tweets a day telling of all his adventures.

On his way to work he wants to use public transport as he has a relatively cheap electronic train subscription card in his name. By using this card, all entrance and exit stations he is passing and his precise travel times are registered. Unfortunately, the public transport union is on strike and he has to use his car. On the motorway the registration number of his car is flashed a couple of times and he has to stick a card twice in a toll booth.

Arriving at his work he turns on his network terminal, inserts his user name and password and from that time onwards every move on the keyboard and every program chosen is log-filed and liable to inspection by the local area network operator when this is deemed appropriate.

During lunchtime he is able to go shopping in the local mall. His mobile phone is very advanced and can be recognized by some shops he is passing that know him from their customer database and that inform him of the offers of the day. He is one of the first consumers in his town that uses his mobile as a wallet; in this way he does not need a bank card anymore. Instead all his purchases are listed and he can check them every night to see whether everything is okay. His mobile also has an app installed that lets all his acquaintances know where he is, in case a good friend that happens to be nearby is close and wants to meet him to have a cup of coffee. Unfortunately, the local street burglar was one of these 'acquaintances' and he managed to break into his house in broad daylight! Jones had forgotten to switch on his electronic house protection system, which tracks every move around the house, when he left for work this morning.

Returning from work he logs on to the site of his insurance company. He does not need to fill in his user name and password because a 'cookie' is installed on his computer that is used every time he visits the insurance site. It appears that he gets no refund of the property stolen and the damage done to his house because the company found in the log-files of the protection system linked to their system that it was not switched on. The company took this hard attitude because other, so-called 'third-party cookies' (other websites are engaged) had registered that he recently visited the sites of competitor insurance companies and looked for interesting offers.

This, admittedly not quite normal, day in a life shows a number of things:

1   Tracking technologies are everywhere and in all parts of life; it is impossible to escape them completely. Many people are not even aware of their workings.

2   Originally, tracking technologies were installed by institutions and companies applying them in their own interest; currently, users themselves are adding

personal information to them, using social media such as SNS and Twitter and new apps for mobile telephony.

3   Though users benefit from some handy applications, interest and power shifts to the institutions and companies installing them.

4   The popular phrase that someone who has nothing to hide does not have to be afraid of these technologies is extremely short-sighted. This does not only go for passwords and credit card details enabling identity fraud but also for the everyday things Mr. Jones has to hide: his whereabouts for burglars and his forgetful and surfing behaviour for the insurance company.

5   Tracking technologies are linked to personal information databases of service providers and other institutions (in this case the mobile phone and broadcasting operators, Facebook, the public transport company, the registry of car numbers, the employer, a number of shops and the insurance company).

So, tracking technologies are related to both relational and informational privacy. They also help to intensify existing pressures in contemporary communications technology to *be within reach at any time and place*. All kinds of new facilities in mobile telephony and the social media achieve this. The explosive demand for these kinds of facilities proves how much people have adjusted to continuous communication. However, simultaneously they cause the individual to be traceable to the deepest crevices of the social fabric and in all environments. Almost every place becomes a social space. It is becoming hard to avoid being accessible at any time and place. And even if one tries and succeeds in switching off devices and using blocking options, the chances of having to *justify* oneself are increasing. This is a threat to personal autonomy (discussed below). Our natural space to withdraw and to be left alone is shrinking – though this space is not divided equally in social terms – yet, this space has always been useful to the efficiency of communication. Being accessible at any time and place will lead to a sharp increase in the quantity of communication appearing to be (almost) irrelevant afterwards. This phenomenon of *communication overload* is discussed in Chapter 8.

Threats to privacy: biometrics and physical tracing

In the use of biometrics and physical tracing (for example, with video cameras in public places) our physical privacy is at stake. As biometric attributes of people are increasingly stored in databases and used in transit (security controls on airports and the like), they integrate database and tracking technologies. Our face and iris scans and fingerprints are not only stored in passports but increasingly also in government databases. The DNA of a growing number of criminals and minor offenders is gathered in police files. Police and customs officers have mobile devices to locally check for biometrics.

Tracking is considerably reinforced by technologies for material goods and products such as inbuilt RFID (Radio Frequency IDentity) chips. People wearing and bearing these goods and products might be double traced.

The technology of CCTV (Closed Circuit TV or video cameras in private, semi-public and private places) is progressing rapidly. Until recently, the pictures and videos concerned could not be automatically related to particular personal identities, and therefore they were not considered to be a database containing personal information that was touched by privacy law (see Chapter 6). However, automatic facial recognition is processing so fast that the stored facial biometrics of particular people, not only criminals but also persons that are allowed to have entry to a particular location, can be linked to the faces instantly recorded by sophisticated cameras. When this type of physical tracking is combined with the information and communication tracking technologies discussed in the last paragraphs, we are reaching a situation of *total surveillance*.

Defences of privacy

Of course, these technologies can be legitimately used as privacy always has to be weighed against other vital interests such as safety, the fight against crime and the freedom of expression of people that have a legitimate right to reveal something personal about someone, particularly when this is a political or government representative. This consideration will be amply discussed in the next chapter. Nevertheless, the picture described above is very distressing and worrying for people who consider privacy to be an important right of freedom. In the last decade, a large number of books have appeared with main or subtitles such as 'the end of privacy'. CEOs and CIOs of well-known Internet companies producing software and social media have claimed that we are entering a totally transparent society and that people, especially young people, do not value privacy anymore. I do not agree with them, as will become evident in the remainder of this book. To start with, I will now turn to a more optimist picture of the potential defences of privacy. It will become evident that both privacy intrusion and defence are a deliberate choice of people with a particular interest and that they are not a matter of necessity.

Box 5.5 contains the five most important categories of the defence of privacy. I will describe them in the following paragraphs.

BOX 5.5
Categories of privacy defence

1 Privacy design
2 Usage protection: measures by users and providers
3 Legal protection
4 Technical alternatives

Privacy design

The defence of privacy is most effective when preventive measures are taken. The technology concerned can be designed in such a way that it becomes more difficult to harm the privacy of users. The choices made in design clearly show that privacy intrusion and defence are matters of interest and power and that they are often a deliberate choice. I will explain the following five principles of privacy-friendly design.

1　The first principle is to *separate goals* of new applications and registrations. Many have several goals combined. For example, most smart energy meters in the home are designed in such a way that both consumers and electricity companies are able to continually register the use of energy. The goal of the consumer might be to save on energy and the goal of the company might be so-called grid control (managing peaks of usage). This combination of goals leads to unnecessary privacy risks. First, the amount of data registered is maximized, while for privacy a minimum of data is always better. Second, the combination of goals often leads to so-called 'function creep': for example, the police might also be interested to have an energy meter tap when a person is a suspect. An alternative design would allow the installation of a local registration that could be used daily by consumers while the company is only able to tap into it once a year to prepare the bill. The company has other ways to realize grid control.

2　The second principle is to *store locally*. Central storage is always most risky for privacy. Moreover, central databases are very vulnerable because hackers usually have more interest in them than in local storage (however badly protected this may be). For example, the biometrics stored in the chips of modern passports (fingerprints, face and iris scans) is simultaneously stored in large national or regional databases in a number of countries. This is not necessary because the identity of the passport holder can be checked locally, comparing the biometrics in the passport with the ones measured on the spot. Meanwhile, the large central databases also lead to function creep: police and security organizations are eager to use them for other purposes, for example, to search for criminals.

3　One of the most important principles of data protection is to *keep data as anonymous as possible*. Not all information has to be registered under a name. Identification is not required with a large number of applications. Often authentication and authorization are sufficient (e.g. the person holding this card is entitled to use this service). For example, in privacy terms, an anonymous public transport card without a number or with a number that cannot be linked to a particular person, and only containing a credit of travel distances loaded on it, is always better than a card with a number and a name linked to a particular database. Another opportunity is to distribute attribute cards that not even contain a number, but a balance or a permit for a particular service, for example, a free bus riding card for seniors with a picture on it. Using the principle of maximum anonymity, the EU Prime Program has developed an application to be loaded on computers and mobile phones that on every occasion only reveals those parts of the identity of the person using this application that the service provider really needs. A web-shop in fact only needs a valid postal address and a bank account name and number. A young person trying to buy alcohol in a shop only has to reveal his/her age.

4   The next principle is that people should *own their data* as much as possible. People should always have access to their own data stored in a particular place, to be able to correct mistakes and to see whether they are exchanged with other databases. Many web-shops only partly allow for doing this. Fortunately, recently many applications have been developed that enable users to have more control on supplying data and keep an eye on their destination. Examples are the just-called Prime program and online pay systems that reveal less personal data and that are safer than credit cards.

5   The final privacy design principle to be mentioned here is to *install the goals of registration in the hardware and not in the software*. A device that simply is not able to register particular personal information is always the best option for privacy protection. Hardware and software design simply are technical choices. For example, these days many camera systems along the road registering car registration numbers simply store all numbers, while afterwards the software excludes the 'no-hits' of cars that make no offence or mistake or are not searched for. This also leads to function creep (see above) because all these data are kept much too long. An alternative in this case is to install hardware using smart sensors, registering only those numbers that commit traffic offences or that are on a stolen car search list.

Self-regulation: protection by users and providers

Users, providers and the organizations representing them such as consumer and business organizations can protect privacy in self-regulation by taking particular actions and measures. First we have *individual* self-regulation that consists of the attempts of users to safeguard privacy by their own expertise, actions and technical means. They can choose particular privacy settings in the Internet options of their browsers, they can exclude cookies, spam and spyware and erase search histories. They can take a further step by adopting available search engines that do not store IP numbers, SNS that do not use private profiles for marketing purposes and email that is encrypted (e.g. by Pretty Good Privacy). They can even hire professional privacy services and software helping them to filter and negotiate their personal data with online service providers. Examples are the Platform for Privacy Preferences (P3) and TRUSTe.

Unfortunately, most Internet users are very careless and apparently disinterested in using these means. The first reason is that, to them, privacy threats are abstract and cannot harm them; the second is that they always have to take the initiative themselves. It would be better if potential privacy problems were automatically solved by the hardware and software used (see privacy design above) or if options could be presented to users in a pop-up screen when risks run high. Moreover, some of the privacy software options are time-consuming and require a fairly high level of digital skills.

Some privacy-minded users with less technical expertise simply refuse to fill out names and credit card numbers on the Internet or leave false information instead. A lack of trust leading to simple refusals is more effective than one might expect. It is one of the reasons for the disappointing start of electronic commerce in the 1990s and the early years of the 21st century. So, offering privacy guarantees will become one of the most important quality standards of services in networks. For this reason many producers and service providers offer privacy statements or codes of conduct and good privacy practice on their own initiative, in an attempt to convince consumers. Unfortunately, these statements and codes are only read by a small minority of users (Beldad, 2011).

Because individual privacy protection demands so much from users, *collective* self-regulation has come forwards to support them. Increasingly, official privacy commissioners, consumer organizations, user groups, trade unions and civil organizations negotiate with producers, employers and public administrations about the privacy conditions of using personal data in computer files and on the Internet. They might be able to prevent misuse, instead of trying to cure things afterwards.

When privacy commissioners and consumer organizations are allowed to participate in privacy design and have a say in the conditions of personal data processing this could prevent much unnecessary privacy harm. It could be better than legislation and technical or organizational measures of protection afterwards. For instance, personnel assessment and personnel information systems in companies, which often needlessly threaten privacy, currently can only be stopped or changed by collective agreements between employers and trade unions or works councils.

Legal protection

In the following chapter we will conclude that legal protection remains necessary because self-regulation needs a framework to be effective. Otherwise the rule of the most powerful prevails: the rule of governments that give priority to security and the fight of crime, the rule of the most popular software providers such as Google and Facebook that simply need detailed personal information for effective advertisement and the rule of employers that simply enforce personnel information systems on their employees, to mention just three examples.

Unfortunately, legal protection is still very inadequate. Almost all of the countries in the world have either a constitutional or a legal right to privacy. A country can have legal privacy protection at three levels: the constitution, specific privacy law, and common law (this is law based upon decisions of judges and customs instead of written law). The legal protection of privacy is inadequate, in particular with regard to networks, for several reasons.

First, privacy regulation and legislation are at a low level of development and effectiveness. Constitutions are very broad. They have no immediate and indisputable practical implications. On the other hand, privacy laws are often very specific. For instance, the United States has adopted an impressive series of privacy acts at the federal and state levels. This has produced a complete fragmentation of privacy legislation, making it weak and capable of being mastered by juridical experts only (Perritt, 1996).

By contrast, the EU has developed very comprehensive and ambitious privacy legislation, based upon the long-standing principles and guidelines of the OECD and the Council of Europe. However, the execution of the comprehensive European privacy laws takes so much effort and social support that they are difficult to put into practice. Moreover, the effectiveness of all privacy legislation is uncertain as personal data in networks are transferred across borders with different jurisdictions and because the legislation has a rather low status: it is most often civil law and common law rather than criminal law. So, prosecution and punishment for privacy offences are rare.

This brings us to a second reason: privacy is not viewed as an absolute right of individuals. It is always weighed against other rights and interests, primarily the information and communication freedom of others and the security rights of the government. More and more, privacy regulation is overruled by other laws and by national security or emergency regulation.

The third weakness of legal privacy protection is that it traditionally deals almost exclusively with informational privacy. It is a matter of *data* protection. However, in the former paragraphs we have seen that relational and physical privacy become more and more important. As a result, applications such as email, video surveillance, all kinds of monitoring of Internet use and certainly the currently popular social media and mobile phone applications where users themselves freely submit personal data, are poorly protected (see Chapter 6). The same goes for physical privacy.

Finally, the most important weakness of legal privacy protection is that it always lags behind the development of technology, as do so many laws. In the 1980s, laws were made in which computer registration was assumed to be a static affair of producing and consulting fixed files managed by controllers who could be identified and alerted to their legal obligations. In the 1990s, it was discovered that registration in computer networks is a dynamic affair of continually collecting, processing, editing, changing, consulting, using and transferring data. The *European Directive of 1995* took this dynamic process as its main point of departure in the adaptation of privacy law (European Commission, 1995). However, in 2002 it was already forced to update legislation in the *Directive on privacy and electronic communications* (European Commission, 2002; also see Korff, 2002). In 2010 it was observed that current directives run the risk of becoming outdated again by the rise of ubiquitous and ever more intrusive computing, advanced profiling, globalization of data processing and user-generated web content (European Commission, 2010a and 2010b).

Technical alternatives

Developing technical alternatives might be the best structural solution to the problems concerning privacy. A small number of scientists and technicians have been working hard on such alternatives from the 1990s onwards. They build their work on four alternative network characteristics: local control; concentration of intelligence in terminals; more offline equipment; and privacy-enhancing technologies. *Local control* means that smaller networks are constructed, one each for every organization or department, which are able to protect their own files containing personal data. *Concentration of intelligence in network terminals* or stand-alone machines enables more unregistered use of computers. Using *more offline equipment* for personal registration, such as chip cards or smart cards instead of large online databases, also offers more privacy protection. However, user control of these remains necessary because most often smart or chip cards are simply plugged into computer networks and their central registrations. It goes without saying that cloud computing (see Chapter 3), which goes in the opposite direction, is viewed with great suspicion by these technicians of privacy.

The fourth alternative, *privacy-enhancing technologies*, seems to be the most promising concerning privacy protection. This is the reason why I will now go deeper into these technologies. The same techniques that cause risks to privacy can also be used to protect it. In the 1990s, we saw the breakthrough of all sorts of techniques to encrypt information and communication in networks. Defenders of the right to privacy increasingly consider these *privacy-enhancing technologies* to be their most important weapons. But that is only after it has been determined that the registration of personal data is necessary anyway.

The observation that the identity of the individual is of no importance to the greater part of the process of registration is the basic principle of these techniques. Individuals can be given a pseudo-identity that replaces their real identity in the process of registration. In registration by ICT systems, the following phases usually follow each other:

1 authorization (permission to 'enter' the system);

2 identification and authentication;

3 access control (in particular applications);

4 auditing (check and justification of the use of the system);

5 accounting.

According to a report by the Dutch and the Canadian official data registrars (van Rossum et al., 1995a and 1995b), the user's true identity is needed only in particular cases at the beginning (authorization) and at the end (payment). However, in all cases (when desired) and in all intermediate phases, both of them can be replaced by a *pseudo-identity* protecting the true identity. The following privacy techniques are used for this purpose.

The *digital signature* is the digital alternative to the written signature. A digital signature cannot be copied, since it consists of the unique combination of a private key, known only to the owner, and a public key, known to the other party involved, for instance a service provider. The private key is not some sort of personal identification number (PIN) code, since this code is known by other parties – at least by the distributor, for example, a bank. The private key is compiled by the user from a unique series of randomly chosen numbers. The private key and the public key are combined when a certain process requires identification of the individual by an institution. This combination is another key. When the combination is decoded by the institution concerned using the public key, the authenticity of the signature is confirmed. At that point in the process, it is not necessary to know to whom the signature actually belongs.

The second technique is the digital pseudonym. By using the same combination as used for digital signatures, users can take a pseudonym authorizing them to receive a certain amount of services from service providers. The providers are paid for the amount as a whole. A different pseudonym can be used for every service and service provider.

The techniques mentioned above do not have to be used until some sort of identification or authorization is needed, for example in a transaction or in an electronic payment system (Chaum, 1992, 1994). They can be used to protect both transfers and the contents of messages and transactions. In the latter case, they block access to a message for everyone but the addressee. These codes or encryptions have been designed for email, for instance. Until well into the 1990s, messages by email could be opened by others fairly easily. Pretty Good Privacy (PGP) was among the first techniques for encrypting email.

The latest techniques for encryption are extremely hard to track and decode. They can also be used for privacy protection. Some of them are based on *steganography*. This technique enables the user to make a message invisible by hiding it in another message. Seemingly harmless texts, videos and audio sources may contain criminal messages written 'between the lines'. In this case, the police and security organizations do not even know where to look for them. It will be harder and harder to intercept illegal communication in transit. Gradually, the solution will be to search at the source and at the destination – the sender and the receiver of messages – where the encrypted or hidden messages are bound to disappear from, and reappear in, the analogue world. Photographs of child pornography have to be taken somewhere. Criminal deals and the theft of digital money will leave traces or lead to actions in non-virtual reality.

Integrated protection

The most important conclusion concerning the four means used in the protection of privacy is that none of them can be omitted. They presuppose each other. Legislation will not be effective without the practice of self-regulation and the security of data. Conversely, self-regulation will be unrestrained without a legal framework of enforceable rights: they will promote the power of the strongest, usually big business and government interests. Finally, the conclusion has to be drawn that technical solutions will not cure all evils either. They have to be embedded in legislation, self-regulation (such as participation of consumers and employees) and managerial practices. Most solutions are two-edged swords. They can just as easily endanger as protect privacy. Encryption can be used equally by the Ministry of Justice, by criminals and by respectable citizens. The association between the means to defend privacy shows once more that networks are not neutral technical tools. In all kinds of ways, they are related to power in society, in organizations and between individuals.

The next chapter will continue the discussion about privacy protection.

Personal autonomy

The conclusion just reached will be even more evident when we take the step from privacy to the personal autonomy of individuals in the choices they have to make when dealing with media networks. To estimate the chances of autonomy that people have in networks, we have to realize that media networks have the character of a system. They connect several end points or terminals. At these points, human individuals are working, studying and living. These simple remarks evoke the most fundamental questions concerning power in networks. To what extent do individuals, as members of an organization, as citizens, employees, clients or consumers, have a say in whether or not they are *connected* to the network, and how much influence do they have on the *use* of the network once they have been connected?

The questions above concern the control human beings have over their technical means. However, a network cannot be compared with a machine that one decides to purchase. A network is *not a stand-alone instrument* just replacing or simplifying human communication and activity. A network is a *medium with a system character*. It links separate machines and their human operators and it streamlines their communications and activities. Already in the 1980s, Kubicek and Rolf (1985) claimed the necessity for an entirely different approach to get a grip on network technology. The traditional approach stems from a *machine* model: hardware and software are considered to be detached and locally or functionally confined instruments. Their effects can be calculated and changed directly. This model no longer works in network technology. It has to be replaced by a system model. This model not only assesses all nodes, connections, protocols, terminals and programs separately, but also their *combinations in a system* and especially their *implementation in existing organizational and social processes*. These are aspects of the law of network articulation emphasizing system relations and of the law of network externality signalling the effects of networks on their environment (see Chapter 2).

Introducing networks as organizational and technological means the whole organization or other social unit changes in both its internal and external relations. Many corporations and administrations have discovered that the network phase of automation causes more radical changes than the preceding phases when only separate machines are installed. The consequences are harder to foresee and control. For individuals, the distance to places where decisions are made becomes even greater. For them, this technology usually appears to be extremely large scale, opaque and intangible. For example, few people understand how the Internet works – they simply use it and are surprised when particular things happen or appear to be out of control.

From the following list of examples it appears that networks have both positive and negative consequences for personal autonomy.

As *citizens*, individuals have become completely dependent upon their political representatives and governors concerning decisions on whether and how the government will record data in online services. At best, they will get rights of access to, and correction of, their data. Police and intelligence agents are able to ignore privacy legislation on many issues and to shut off their own networks from political control. On the other hand, citizens are able to use networks such as the Internet to learn about their government, public administration and political representatives and put them under pressure. Among other ways, they can express their own opinions in online forums and social media.

As *employees*, individuals have to accept that their workplaces are integrated in a company network, perhaps abolishing any autonomy they previously possessed. Trade unions and other organizations of employees are not able to stop these fundamental changes, even if they want to. Usually, they lack the power and knowledge. Management and personnel information systems increase the power of executives. On the other hand, employees are able to use organizational networks for task extension and enrichment through vertical decentralization (see above) or for better and more empowering communication with their colleagues in Enterprise 2.0.

As *clients* of a company or government institution, individuals simply have to accept that services move online. The only hope of those who have no access to the Internet or have few Internet skills is that companies and governments will maintain a *multi-channel approach* for a long time to come: keeping service desks, call centres and printed forms as service channels (Pieterson, 2009). On the other hand, clients are also able to benefit from one-stop services and portals of the government and commercial providers where all information and services are gathered. On the Internet, the position of clients and consumers is strengthened by software enabling them to compare the price and quality of products and services.

Finally, as *consumers*, individuals face the constant pressure of a 'technology push' to go online. As long as the majority has not yet done this, the customer seems to be king and offline facilities keep being offered. But from the time concerts, theatre performances and flights are rapidly and fully booked electronically, the potential online customer will no longer feel free to say no to them. And this freedom to say no will probably disappear completely when the vast majority has been connected. This is a consequence of the law of network externality. Then the crucial question will arise as to whether old technologies and personal face-to-face services will be kept in supply.

CONCLUSIONS

- When media networks such as the Internet are used to support or change social relationships, some people gain power while others lose it. They are not neutral technological tools.

- Media networks are a vulnerable technology on which we increasingly depend. Network breakdowns, cyber-attacks and even preparations for network wars are difficult to prevent. Trying to do this will inevitably reduce network freedom.

- Politics will increasingly be networked. Gradually, Internet politics will replace television and press politics. Internet politics will not necessarily be more democratic. The Internet is not democratic by nature. Both democratic and authoritarian governments try to control the Internet. Social media in themselves will not cause democratic revolutions.

- The Internet offers many instruments for e-participation of citizens in government. Presently e-participation on the initiative of citizens is more successful than e-participation on the initiative of governments. Most governments do not accept inroads on their decision power.

- Power in the organization shifts from bureaucracy to infocracy. Both horizontal and vertical types of control and coordination are installed in organizational information systems. In this way, organizations are not necessarily getting flatter: the distance of communication between all members of the organization is reduced, not the distance of control and authority.

- Without protective measures, computer networks will lead to a serious threat to privacy. The vast registration capacity, traceability, permanent reachability and visibility of people and their behaviour, together with the integration of biometrics, deeply touch our informational, relational and physical privacy.

- However, privacy can be defended by a combination of privacy design, self-regulation of users and producers, privacy law and technical alternatives.

- The personal autonomy of network users is also at stake because computer networks are not devices under direct individual control, but systems. Personal autonomy is decided in the daily struggle for power over networks.

 **LAW**

About this chapter

- In Chapter 5 it appeared that networks change the distribution of power at every social level and that they can make us all less powerful because they are so vulnerable. This could lead to less freedom and equality and to unacceptable risks of the network technology for society. We would expect the law to offer some protection, but what happens to the law itself? At first sight, it appears that the law also is undermined by network technology.

- Making a claim on the law is one of the ways to control networks, specifically the Internet. But who actually controls the Internet? In the 1980s, governments (primarily the US government) and the early user communities were the most powerful on this network. However, with the diffusion of the Internet via the Worldwide Web from the 1990s onwards, commercial interests and technology companies became ever more powerful. What technical and business instruments do these companies use to control the Internet?

- The second part of this chapter discusses three of the most important rights and legislations on the Internet. These should be known by social and communication scientists because the issues concerned actually fill the newspapers every day: information and communication freedom; intellectual property rights; and privacy rights. Of course, Internet law touches many more parts of the law, but I have to make a choice.

- For each of these three rights we will examine what the legal, self-regulatory and technical solutions are to uphold them.

THE LAW UNDERMINED BY NETWORKS
Challenges of network technology

The law and justice have lagged behind new technology in almost every period in history. This is understandable, as new technology must become established in society before legislation can be applied to it. Furthermore, the consequences of new technology are not always clear right away. That is why the legal answer usually has the character of a reaction or an adjustment of existing principles. In civil society, this character is enhanced by the principle of civil law, in which individuals initially act freely and the law subsequently makes corrections. Legislation in advance, for instance to stimulate or halt the development of a particular new technology, would be state planning. This idea does not fit well with the principle of free initiative in technological development in capitalist societies.

Justice in general, and legislation in particular, increasingly lag behind information and communication technology development. Incredible to believe, but in 2011 even the most basic terms such as 'information', 'data', 'program' and 'communication' had not yet been defined unambiguously and fixed in legislation. Jurisprudence is the most important weapon against misuse of these new technologies. It is created by judges who often tend to make things easy for themselves – perhaps because they have little knowledge about ICTs – by simply declaring existing legal terminology applicable to new technical realities. Before legislation has dealt with any phase in computerization, the next phase is already happening. More than any preceding technology, networks test existing legislation. This happens for at least seven fundamental reasons.

The first challenge, as preceding chapters have stressed, is the intangible, geographically free and continuously changing character of information and communication in networks. By contrast, existing legislation depends on *clearly demonstrable, localizable and liable legal persons and ownership titles*. Information and evidence have to be, or must be able to be, set down on a data carrier that preferably still has to be comparable to printed paper.

Second, when legislators have managed to develop and lay down new legislation for the utilization of networks, the problem of *implementing these laws* arises. Networks are connected to other networks and they are not terminated by frontiers. This causes three essential problems:

- *perception* of the violation of the law, an offence or a crime: activities in networks are non-transparent and hard to trace;

- *evidence* of such activities: evidence can easily be destroyed, changed or hidden in digital networks;

- *prosecution*: jurisprudence differs across countries and the accuser and the accused may come from different jurisdictions, especially when international crime is involved.

Third, network technology has become international very quickly. Laws, on the other hand, are mainly national, particularly with regard to the actual prosecution and punishment of crime. International regulation usually stops at general declarations and basic principles agreed upon by international institutions. No matter how important these declarations and principles are as an impetus to international legislation, they do not themselves have decisive effects. Moreover, they are usually pretexts for international political action and economic protectionism, rather than genuine protection against the unacceptable consequences of a new technology.

Fourth, existing legislation is still bound to the material reality of the industrial revolution and the first communications revolution, or even pre-industrial trade and craft. This explains why some juridical discussions still deliberate whether information is a commodity and whether communication by computers can be treated as equivalent to a 'conversation'. Without a thorough (re)definition of basic terms such as 'information', 'data', 'program', 'electronic communications', 'information service', 'file', 'owner', 'editor', 'controller' or 'processor' of (personal) data, and so forth, any legal grip on the consequences of network technology is bound to fail. This is a basic requirement following the law of network articulation (Chapter 2) highlighting relations instead of separate units.

Fifth, existing legislation is still tied to preceding phases in economic development. However, the international concentration of capital and power, combined with decentralization of production, the creation of a global 'flow economy' and the enormous growth of an elusive financial sphere, together cause a new economic reality to arise. It can hardly be controlled with existing means, and certainly not with existing legislation.

Sixth, around the turn of the millennium, existing legislation was still based on rapidly obsolete technological boundaries. Network technology ends the old divisions between tele-, data and mass communications and between the various media within these types of communications. Separate legislation is no longer adequate for integrated networks. Obviously, a *general framework of communication and information legislation* is needed. This will have to be based no longer on concrete material technical differences, but on much more abstract distinctions of information and communication, such as the information traffic patterns discussed in Chapter 1 and the network layers dealt with in Chapters 2, 3 and 4. The information traffic patterns, based on relationships of (rightful) power can provide a useful beginning. The network layers also provide useful distinctions for the general framework required. They put together related activities that should be regulated in a similar way.

Seventh, most new legislation is characterized by fragmentary adjustments and by (often) contradictory jurisprudence. There is no integral readjustment. Instead, detailed alterations are made to existing legislation including technical definitions that will soon be outdated. For the larger part, they are economic emergency regulation in copyright, contract law, certification or authentication law (concerning orders and payments), legal responsibility and the like. The only non-economic legislation of any importance consists of freedom of information or communication and privacy acts in some countries. Fragmentary adjustments to legislation are not suitable for the regulation of large-scale networks and their far-reaching consequences to individuals and society at large. Overall adaptations are required in preparing framework legislation, to be worked out subsequently in more specific legislation and self-regulation.

General solutions

The main principle for governments and other authorities in adapting current legislation is that rules that go offline should also be(come) valid online. This seems to be a sensible and wise principle in the first development stages of a new technology. Indeed, it has served as a way to fill the main lacunae of existing legislation concerning ICT. However, I do not think it will work in the long term. This conservative principle does not take into account the fundamental differences between offline and online environments such as those discussed in this book. And it does not take sufficiently seriously the special problems and characteristics of a network such as the Internet. Fundamental differences are derived from the fact that one environment is virtual and the other physical or material and that the distinction between public and private is blurred in online environments. A further basic problem is that the accountability of things that happen in these environments cannot clearly be ascribed to the technology or to human effort. Moreover, the division between collective and individual property rights in networks is not easily made (see one of the following sections). Other difficult-to-solve problems are derived from the peculiar hardware and software architecture of the Internet with its network layers and codes, which are discussed in the next section.

To solve the legal problems of the online environment in a really fundamental way, new legislation has to be designed that does not depend on particular technologies and their characteristics but on basic principles of law in contemporary constitutional states. To combine these principles, legislators could prepare framework legislation that covers a broad range of laws. The main point of departure should be the constitution of a country, which contains the basic rights of information and communication freedom, rights of protection (among others, privacy rights) and property rights that all have to be balanced. Framework legislation does not consist of concrete pieces or articles of law but of political-legal documents proposed by governments and parliaments. Once a country agrees on the framework, concrete laws can be made or changed.

WHO RULES THE INTERNET?

What model of media regulation can be applied to the Internet?

As has been stated, legislation cannot keep pace with technological and economic development, just at a time when we are confronted with new risks. The same can be said about 'politics'. Nationally and internationally, states are losing their grip on information policy owing to three tendencies which took place at the end of the 20th century:

- media networks increasingly crossing borders;

- the growing world market of transnational corporations, operating freely and communicating through their own networks, and the rise of global financial markets largely out of control of global and national regulation as demonstrated by the current credit crisis;

- the policies of privatization and deregulation of public goods and services dominating the last three to four decades.

This state of affairs reveals that individual governments have only weak control over the Internet. However, this does not mean that this network of networks is not ruled by other actors or instruments. This section shows that a fierce struggle is going on between government, corporate, technological and self-regulatory control of the Internet.

First, I want to compare the regulation of the Internet to the regulation of older media such as broadcasting, the press and telecommunications. McQuail and Windahl (1993: 211) have compared the broadcasting model, the press model and the telecommunications model of regulation of public media, among others, with the help of the information traffic patterns discussed in Chapter 1. I want to start the discussion in this section by adding the Internet model of regulation (see Figure 6.1). It appears from this figure that the regulation of the Internet has more similarities with the press model and the telecommunications model than with the broadcasting model. As the Internet combines public and private communication, it looks like the press model when considering public communication (websites) and like the telecommunications model regarding private communication (such as email and SNS). Traditionally, broadcasting meets strong regulation. Both infrastructure and content have high levels of regulation. The access of senders (channels) has always been controlled by governments and regulatory committees. In the past, the reasons for control were the powerful role of the centre (the channels and their programmes), the scarcity of frequencies and the pressures of particular cultural policies. For example, TV is considered to be a penetrating visual medium with potential negative effects such as those caused by violence in programmes. In undemocratic societies, the reason for regulating broadcasting was political censorship.

The Internet looks like a relatively free press model because publication of Internet content is just as open as that of press media and because this content is scarcely controlled by media law. Later in this chapter, I will discuss why governments and media law have no effective grip on Internet content. However, contrary to the press, the Internet meets with high infrastructure regulation and access limitations for receivers. The Internet rides on the heavily regulated infrastructure of telecommunication and cable networks. As it is also used for private communication, it would have to offer the same level of protection as telephony. In fact Internet regulation is weak. Neither strong regulation nor personal protection has

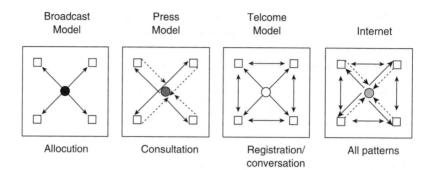

FIGURE 6.1 Four contemporary models of media regulation in democratic societies

	Broadcast Model	Press Model	Telcome Model	Internet
Infrastructure Regulation	High	None	High	High
Content Regulation	High	Low	None	Low
Central Regulation	High ●	Low ●	None ○	Low ●
Sender access	Closed	Open	Open	Open
Receiver access	Open	Open	Closed	Limited

currently been realized on the Internet. Email is far less protected than telephone calls. Regarding regulation there is much discussion about net neutrality – the principle that all Internet content should be treated equally (see Chapter 4). Those in favour of net neutrality want an Internet with a low measure of regulation regarding transportation (only equal transportation of content on a first-come-first-served basis is asked for); those against this principle long for a higher extent of regulation similar to the one we know from the cable and telephony sector to realize a particular tariff structure. However, those in favour of net neutrality can also be advocates of more regulation to protect Internet privacy.

Four competitors for Internet governance

The limitations discussed above will grow. When broadcasting and telephony are integrated in the Internet and powerful software companies are competing for platform control of the Internet (see Chapter 4), there is a risk that the largely public Internet will lose public and legislative control. To understand this risk, it is important to list all actors and forces that are able to control the Internet. This activity is usually called Internet governance. According to a document of the World Summit on the Information Society (2005) 'Internet governance is the development and application by governments, the private sector and civil society in their respective roles, of shared principles, norms, rules, decision-making procedures and programmes that shape the evolution and use of the Internet' (WGIG, 2005). In this definition three actors and competitors for governance of the Internet are mentioned: governments; businesses or market actors; and civil society. This list is not quite complete. Solum (2009) distinguishes five Models of Internet Governance: 1. self-regulation by the Internet community; 2. software code and Internet architecture; 3. transnational institutions; 4. traditional legislation (by governments); and 5. market regulation. In his book *Code, and other Laws of Cyberspace*, Lessig has listed similar constraints of all Internet activities: the law; the norms of the Internet organizing committees and user communities; the market; and the whole technological architecture of the Internet summarized under the name 'code' (Lessig, 1999: 87–90). Following Lessig and Solum, I will list and discuss four competitors for Internet governance and their types of operation (see Box 6.1). The goal of this discussion is to answer the question: who actually rules the Internet? I will argue that in the first decade of the 21st century, control has shifted from governments and Internet communities to the market and the technical standards that are all but neutral technologies, both of them backed by new legislation.

BOX 6.1
Competitors and types of Internet governance

Competitor	Type of governance
Governments	Legal control
Internet communities	Self-regulation
Corporations	Market control
Designers of software, architecture and security	Technological control

---

Governments and legal control

For reasons discussed above, legislation has only weak direct control on Internet activities. The following sections give numerous examples illustrating computer abuse, international property rights, privacy laws and juridical aspects of information and communication freedom. Generally, control is confined to national jurisdictions. To rule the Internet flows of information and communication across borders, governments have to forge international agreements. These appear to be difficult to create, maintain and enact (discussion follows). Increasingly, governments try to exert indirect control calling in the help of market actors, such as ISPs, hardware producers and software agencies. The major part of new legislation addresses these actors. For example, ISPs are asked or forced to act as surveyors on behalf of governments. New legislation may also back the technological protection standards and security instruments proposed by others, such as software, architecture and security designers acting on behalf of business interests.

Finally, there are many examples of how, despite all limitations, governments can be effective in imposing their will outside their jurisdiction (Goldsmith and Wu, 2006). For example, the US gives fair credit to foreign judgments and decrees unless they are contrary to US policy. However, the most important cause is the globalization of production and trade. Governments who host transnational companies simply have to accept particular laws and regulations of other countries where their companies want to run a business.

Within their borders, less democratic governments try to exert control on free Internet exchange. They can do this themselves surveying and filtering suspected oppositional sources by their security agencies. For example, in the Peoples Republic of China, about 40,000 government officials are daily screening and filtering available websites (Mueller, 2010). They can also order or request ISPs and web-organizations, continually screening the Internet for particular contents, to filter and block oppositional sites, blogs, social media and email messages. These attempts used to be far from effective, but present-day surveillance has become much more sophisticated and manages to find and filter large parts of the oppositional voices considered to be dangerous (Morozov, 2011; Mueller 2010). In supposedly democratic countries, the same methods are used to screen, filter and block all kinds of illegal content. This goes far beyond the most wanted type of content: child pornography.

Internet communities and self-regulation

It is a widespread mistake that the Internet has no central organization and that it has to be controlled from outside. The Internet started as a decentralized network for academics and for the American Departments of Defense and Commerce who initiated its design, operation and organization. Internet design (architecture), organization and technical standards have been enforced through self-regulation by the pioneers – mainly technicians and academics – of the Internet community under the supervision of these American departments.

The most important organization is the Internet Engineering Task Force (IETF). This committee of more than 100 working groups takes care of the Internet protocols such as TCP/IP and other standards. Membership is open to all Internet users in principle. However, members of its leading body, the Internet Architecture Board (IAB) are nominated and appointed according to the expertise they have demonstrated. The second most important organization is called the Internet Corporation for Assigned Names and Numbers (ICANN) that decides which domain names and IP addresses can be used and registers these names worldwide. The third organization is the Internet Society (ISOC), founded in 1992, which is intended to be the future 'government' or 'United Nations' of the global Internet community. Most countries in the world currently have such an Internet Society. They are NGOs with both individual and organizational membership. The ISOC deals with all policy aspects of the Internet concerning technical, juridical, economic and tax issues and it advises national governments on these issues.

The mission of these self-regulatory bodies is to work only in the interest of the Internet and its users. They mainly take technical decisions to manage the exploding growth of this medium, to keep it working and to defend security. Since the end of the 1990s, they have gradually been pulled away from the umbrella of the American departments. They have been privatized to be hired and followed by most governments in the world.

However, the Internet community does not only consist of these self-regulatory or semi-private and public bodies. Millions of newsgroups, online forums, virtual communities, peer-to-peer networks and regular organizational websites rule their own matters of content with comparatively great freedom. In the 1990s, many participants of these online groups or their spokespersons and Internet ideologues held the view that the Internet was creating a new democracy in the media and society at large. The arrival of governmental controls on the Internet was considered to be a threat, more than that of business interests, because this can also be the interest of small Internet companies and cooperatives. The libertarian view of democracy and the self-regulation model of Internet governance support this type of Internet control. They have been very popular in the Internet community of the 1980s and 1990s. Benkler (2006) and Mueller (2010) belong to the contemporary advocates of this model.

Corporations and market control

In the 1990s, powerful business interests and controls arrived and extended their influence on most Internet activities. The rise of e-commerce requires secure payments and conditional access. The increasing criminal abuses of the Internet make governments want to cut back on freedom of information, communication, privacy and personal autonomy, both in the general and the business interest. Free downloads and copies of source material with copyright urge both businesses and governments to protect intellectual property rights with all the technical means and legislation at their disposal.

Yet it is not these evident attempts of corporate control, backed by legislation that should have the main focus of attention in describing the growing market control of the Internet. It is no surprise that they try to defend their intellectual copyright, their patents, their online earnings and secure payments at all cost. I would like to once again call attention to the all-pervasive platform competition between the big players on the Internet (Microsoft, Google, Apple and Facebook) as I did in Chapter 4. Without any doubt these players try to control what happens on the Internet to support their business strategies in the long term. They want to sell their own type of software, social media, mobile phone apps and devices, tablets, television and video services and in this way they also have a strong influence on the type of activities of Internet users. In Chapter 4 we saw that each of these four players has a vision of how the Internet could best be used and in fact they try to impose this vision on Internet users. The most important instruments to achieve this are their own operating systems, browsers and applications for most kinds of Internet activities.

The model of Internet governance by the market is not only in the interest of the big players. One of the wonderful things about the Internet is that it offers very cheap, sometimes even free means of production for everyone who has the skills, a computer and an Internet connection to start one's own business. Even Google was started in a small garage. Peer-to-peer networking also offers opportunities to start all kinds of collectives and cooperations. In his book *The Wealth of Networks*, Yohai Benkler (2006) strongly defends these opportunities. So, the self-regulation model of Internet governance in peer-to-peer networking can be combined with the market model.

Software designers and technological control

The architecture of the Internet is not a neutral communication infrastructure. It is the central nervous system of this network defining its character (see Chapter 3). The core of the Internet is the TCP/IP protocol that enables its decentralized structure of end-to-end exchange and peer-to-peer networking. This architecture becomes increasingly important and it is contested by all parties that are trying to achieve a bigger control of the Internet. According to Lawrence Lessig, a shift of regulatory power over the Internet is occurring that goes 'from law to code, from sovereigns to software' (Lessig, 1999: 206). With 'code' he means all apparently neutral technical standards and protocols that are ruling Internet activity. In fact, these technical means are manipulated by all parties to get a bigger grip on the Internet. However, these means comprise more than code; they also contain particular hardware options at the bottom and application software control at the top. The model of network layers described in Chapter 3 is able to serve as an analytic tool to list them all (see Table 6.1). I will describe the most important Internet control instruments following this model from the bottom to the top.

At the *physical* layer of networks, all kinds of options to connect PCs, tablets, smart phones and other digital media and to get access to them and the network are built into the devices, for example, installed blocking chips for particular content, routers, switchers and central exchanges. The big computer and Internet hardware companies are all tempted to enforce their own standards here. Additionally, there are proprietary access devices such as different smart cards for different devices. This will be extended by devices using biometrics for access (electronic fingerprints, iris scans or face and voice recognition). Implementing these technical means on a massive scale will have an enormous effect on potential competition, privacy and personal autonomy on the Internet.

At the *data link* layer, enabling computers to 'talk' with each other as they use the same so-called 'frames', we find protocols that are built into the hardware such as Asynchronous Transfer Mode. This is a favourite tool of the telecom companies and local area network (LAN) operators as it enables much more central control than the present decentralized and hardware independent TCP/IP protocol that is installed on the two layers above the physical and data link layers. Unfortunately for them, and fortunate for Internet and mobile phone users, they are losing this struggle, as for the

TABLE 6.1   Network layers and control instruments

Nature	Network Layer	Control Instruments
Content	Application	Software control: proprietary sources (e.g. Microsoft, Apple) versus open sources and open sources that actually are under business control (e.g. Google, Facebook)
	Presentation	All translations: encryption, conversion, compression
Code	Session	ID: username + password; digital signatures and certificates; Public Key Infrastructure; codes needed for cloud computing, electronic payment systems, digital rights management systems; 'cookies' and log files.
	Transport	Transmission Control Protocol: decentralized package routing
	Network	Internet Protocol: end-to-end principle
Basis	Data link	Among others: Asynchronous Transfer Mode
	Physical	Hardware features (e.g. installed blocking chips, biometric access devices)

time being the TCP/IP protocol has won: observe the transition to this protocol in most digital media connected to the Internet.

The TCP/IP protocol at the *network and transport* layers *is* the Internet as we know it. Without this protocol the relatively free and potentially anonymous decentralized exchange of information and messages on the Internet would be impossible. See Chapter 3.

Most likely this situation will change. The architecture of the Internet is incorporating traits of the traditional telecom networks with central traffic control (Hain, 2000). The IP protocol Version 4 is in the process of being replaced by Version 6, which not only offers much more address space but also contains much more intelligence and options for central control. For example, it contains *IP Sec(urity)*, which enables better encryption of the packages of Internet data streams and also labels them with numbers that allow operators and security agencies to identify the packages, to steer them and to tap their senders and receivers. Since 2000, ardent discussions have been going on in the working groups of the IETF about ways to reconcile this version with the end-to-end principle of the Internet (see www.ietf.org/html. charters/wg-dir.html). The result will be decisive for the character of the Internet as we know it.

Presently, government, corporate and other private interests that try to control Internet traffic have to rely on the codes of the *session* layer. These codes enable user identification and message authentication. Every Internet user knows the screens that request user name and password for identification. To secure the message authenticity, a codification system of digital signatures and certifications with an optional use of a Public Key Infrastructure has been created (see 'Intellectual Property Rights' below for an explanation). Subsequently, electronic payment systems and digital rights management systems have been installed that debit the personal accounts of users and consumers. All these codes at the session layer are visible for users. This does not go for the hidden session codes contained in log files and cookies. They allow businesses, governments, service providers and network operators to trace all Internet use. However, at the presentation layer the user is able to hide internet messages using encryption.

At the session layer a new type of control instrument appears: cloud computing. This means that every session is moved, organized and stored on central computers of software companies. As we have seen in Chapter 3, the big question considering cloud computing is to what extent the users will keep in control of their software and its products. Potentially, there is a shift of power to the software companies.

On the *application* layer, numerous other instances of software control of Internet use could be discussed. I have already amply considered the control the big Internet companies try to reach in their platform competition. The move from proprietary software (Microsoft, Apple) to open software (Google, Facebook) does not necessarily mean that less control is realized in practice.

Summarizing the argument, it has to be concluded that technological control of the Internet offers powerful tools. They might change the character of the Internet from a relatively free, public and user-controlled medium into an instrument of corporate, government and private control. All in all, there is a shift from government control, be it mainly by the US government and Internet community rule in the 1980s and 1990s, to market and technological control in the 21st century. This shift is backed by new legislation and self-regulation after the advent of the Worldwide Web as we will observe in the next sections. We will also see that this support can be given for good and bad purposes.

The political spectrum of Internet governance

How do these four types of Internet governance relate to political perspectives on the contemporary and future rule of the Internet? Clearly, Internet activities escape the control of individual nation states more and more. However, all contemporary politics is still based on the sovereignty and rule of nation states, either democratic or authoritarian. What are currently viable political perspectives of solving this problem? Milton Mueller (2010) has constructed a useful typology of the political spectrum of Internet governance in two dimensions: national versus transnational and based on networking (decentralized control) versus hierarchy (centralized control). I have slightly extended and adapted his typology (Figure 6.2).

Let me explain this spectrum design by taking the axis of networking versus hierarchy first. As we have seen, the rule of the Internet can be realized by the producers and users themselves in market control or self-regulation by individual users and user groups. This is the decentralized dimension of networking. However, we have also seen that networks have centres too; they are embodied by government, big business and technological (standards) control. This is the hierarchical dimension of Internet rule.

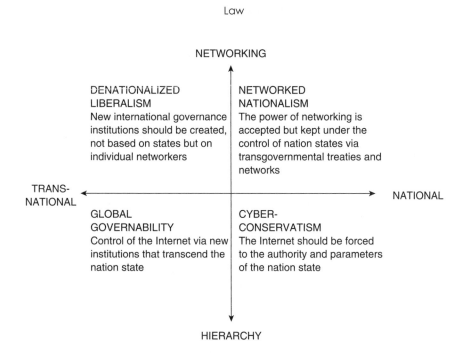

NETWORKING

DENATIONALIZED
LIBERALISM
New international governance
institutions should be created,
not based on states but on
individual networkers

NETWORKED
NATIONALISM
The power of networking is
accepted but kept under the
control of nation states via
transgovernmental treaties and
networks

TRANS-
NATIONAL

NATIONAL

GLOBAL
GOVERNABILITY
Control of the Internet via new
institutions that transcend the
nation state

CYBER-
CONSERVATISM
The Internet should be forced
to the authority and parameters
of the nation state

HIERARCHY

FIGURE 6.2   The political spectrum of internet governance

Source: Mueller (2010: 256)

The axis of national versus transnational governance addresses the question of to what extent the globalizing Internet should be kept under the control of nation states. The processes of globalization and international communication make nation state control increasingly difficult. Some political views accept these processes and try to adapt to them by internationalizing political rule of the Internet through new transnational institutions. Other views do not accept this and want to keep the Internet under the control of the nation state to defend the nation, either in its authoritarian or democratic form (as national parliaments currently are the only truly elected bodies).

Following this two-dimensional spectrum, Mueller has formulated four political positions on Internet rule – see Figure 6.2 again. In the upper-left quadrant is *denationalized liberalism*. This is the favourite position of Mueller himself, being a defender of libertarian democracy (see Chapter 5). 'It recognizes the individual network participant, not states or corporations as the fundamental source of legitimate global internet governance and proposes to create new governance institutions around them' (Mueller, 2010: 259). It favours Internet self-regulation by producers and users and peer production processes.

The second position in the lower-left quadrant, *global governability*, wants control of the Internet via new institutions that transcend the nation state and also enact some central rule. 'These new institutions are most likely to be private sector based and created to advance business interests though they could be multi-stakeholder and public–private partnerships' (Mueller, 2010: 258). I think Mueller is primarily referring to extensions of contemporary Internet bodies such as ICANN and the Internet Societies discussed before.

In the upper-right quadrant is *networked nationalism* which accepts the power of networking but wants to keep it under the control of nation states via trans-governmental treaties and networks. This position 'wants to cope with transnational problems through a mix of trans-governmental networks, delegation to private actors, or formal intergovernmental treaties, but all international institutions would be rooted in states' (Mueller, 2010: 258). This could be seen as the United Nations of the Internet.

The last position in the lower-right quadrant is labelled *cyber-conservatism;* Mueller even calls its supporters 'cyber-reactionaries'. This position wants to force the Internet to conform to the authority of the nation state at all cost. As if globalization and the coming of the Internet and other communication networks have not changed the world. This position is taken by authoritarian states such as China and by American conservatives who think the Internet can be kept under the control of the United States or otherwise be ignored as much as possible.

What would be the position of the author of this book? As a true internationalist who is in favour of networking he would belong in the upper-left quadrant. However, in the way this is defined by Mueller, he thinks this would currently be an unrealistic and even dangerous position. It is unrealistic because unfortunately self-regulation is weak and nation states cannot be missed currently. Organizations of users and consumers on the Internet have no power. Bodies like the Internet Societies are completely unknown by 80 per cent or more of Internet users. The position of denationalized liberalism is even more dangerous because it would in practice support the already strong power of big business interests on the Internet. Currently, only states have a countervailing power. They are the only ones who are able to confine giants such as Microsoft and Google. Government intervention is needed 'when network externalities convey too much power to a private group, or when bottlenecks form around essential facilities' (Mueller, 2010: 257). This is exactly what is happening now. The power of the Internet giants has to be confined and one of the biggest problems facing the Internet is the lack of facilities for people with no access or digital skills. National governments are needed to solve these problems.

The second reason why this position is dangerous is that in practice it means a loss of democracy. The strongest bases of democracy still are the generally elected parliaments of nations, both local and national. No elections, for whatever bodies, are in sight for the Internet.

Whether he likes it or not, the author of this book has to rely on the position of networked nationalism. He hopes that international organized power will grow on the Internet in parallel to a growing power of international bodies for other goals, such as the United Nations. The basic lesson is that online power cannot go ahead of power in the offline world – they can only run in parallel. The Internet forces the offline world to react to its ignoring of borders. However, the Internet is far removed from some kind of global ruling position in the world. And it cannot be independent either.

INFORMATION AND COMMUNICATION FREEDOM

The scope of information and communication freedom rights

Citizens' right to information and communication freedom have been established in the constitutions of democratic states and in general international declarations such as the Declaration of Human Rights. In most constitutions, this freedom is confined to a freedom of *expression* by means of a ban on government censorship. For instance, the famous First Amendment of the American constitution ('Congress shall make no law … abridging the freedom of speech or the press') only protects against interference of the government or a public institution performing state action, not against private interference (Perritt, 1996: 263ff.). A logical corollary would be that the freedom to *receive* expressions should be protected as well. Constitutions and declarations are less clear about this legal principle. In practice, there is no guarantee, as sometimes regulatory bodies, cable operators and other service providers still decide what programmes, channels and services can be received.

So, it is important to observe that current legal rights of information and communication freedom offer a passive protection (against interference) and not an active protection (supply of conditions). Further, they mainly protect against government interference, not against intrusions by private conduct. This means that the infringement of this freedom in new media practice, for example, by increasing information inequalities or gate-keeping media monopolies, is not covered by them. These problems have to be confronted by other laws (of privacy and free competition, for instance) and by public information services.

A second point is that information and communication freedom is not an absolute right. The right to information and communication freedom is not absolute where individual and state autonomy are concerned. At the individual level, one person's freedom of speech and right to reception ends where another person's right to privacy, security, identity, dignity ('reputation') and personal material interest begins. At the state level, the right to entirely free (inter)national information traffic conflicts with a state's right to sovereignty, national security, public order, cultural identity and economic interests.

Problems implementing information and communication freedom rights

These conflicts are inevitable and can never be resolved completely. This is even expressed in the essence of the descriptions of information and communication freedom, all of which reveal at least some internal tension. Thus in the discussion on international traffic of data, jurists use expressions like a 'free *and balanced* flow of information' (Freese, 1979) and 'everyone is free to … as long as this does not …'. This means values have to be weighed against each other in legislation. Such considerations can be made in national legislation. Internationally, legislation can have little effect, while international declarations of human rights are too general and their sanctions are too weak to provide a solution. The biggest problem is that the right to state autonomy is being undermined by the free flow of information in cross-border networks. In addition to the legal aspects, this right also has economic, political, military and cultural aspects, as described below.

First, in the *legal* sphere, international networks can be instruments to evade national legislation. They enable not only extremely fast file transfers from one country to another, but also a division of the parts of information processing between the most advantageous countries – which means the cheapest and least regulated countries. Data are gathered in one country, edited and stored in another, and distributed and used as information in yet another country, thus avoiding taxes, rights of ownership and privacy legislation. Some countries are already known as *data paradises* or *data-free havens*. One just picks a country where there is little or no sanction against a particular wrongful act, or even a crime, and makes sure one has access to an international network.

Second, in the *economic* sphere, states increasingly miss out on income because taxes are imposed only on data carriers and not on the content and the production of these data, which are usually worth a lot more than the carriers. It is impossible to install 'gateways' to serve as a kind of customs in every network at the point where it crosses a border. In the past, Brazil tried to do this, but very soon had to give up its attempts.

Third, in the *political* sphere, the (exclusive) use of information can be of great interest to a country. Most countries want to have crucial information stored on their own territory to make sure they are not completely dependent on others in cases of emergency. Many countries in debt discover the importance of the exclusive use a country has over its own data at the moment when the IMF or the World Bank presents an austerity plan based on far more advanced processing of a country's own data than it is capable of doing itself.

Fourth, the *military* importance of a country's information sovereignty closely relates to the political. Passing on confidential data can cause a threat to national safety. What is more, international information networks are gaining importance as military instruments. At this point, the United States has taken the lead. Until recently, the networks controlled by the Pentagon, the Central Intelligence Agency (CIA) and the National Security Agency (NSA) were vastly superior to anything else in this field. Currently, countries such as China and Russia are catching-up fast.

Fifth, the *cultural* identity of poor or less developed countries and of closed communities is overruled by broadcasting satellites, the Internet, and the powerful databanks of the rich western countries (see Hamelink, 1994).

A country's autonomy should not be absolute either. This would oppose the information freedom and material interests of other countries and, in particular, the country's own inhabitants. In order to disguise this opposition, countries often use false arguments. For instance, countries regularly use arguments about the protection of national sovereignty and culture as a reason to restrict the information and communication freedom of their own citizens. Pure economic protectionism often hides behind claims of legal, political or technological sovereignty.

The rash and uncontrolled development of the new media, the Internet in particular, appears to offer a refuge for anyone who wants to escape prosecution for offences against information and communication law. That is why it is viewed suspiciously by governments, security organizations, regulatory bodies and all kinds of interest groups. The conduct of criminals, terrorists, slanderers, racists and (child) pornographers is more or less controlled in the old media. How should one try to regulate the same conduct in the new media? The groups mentioned are among the heavy users of the Internet. Evidently, they threaten the freedom and safety of others and of society at large. There is a growing consensus that the law should apply to both old and new media, including the Internet as a public mass medium. What are the problems, then, with this application? Some of them are fundamental – the three most important follow.

First, what is the character of the new media? They are in a process of convergence, blurring many of the distinctions between the old media. Should the new media be modelled on the press model, the common carrier (telephone) model or the broadcasting model (see the previous section)? At the start of the 21st century, most of the more or less democratic countries tend to follow the press model regarding the Internet. However, for authoritarian states, the broadcasting model (ability to block channels) and the common carrier model (capacity for surveillance or monitoring) are far more attractive. They want to benefit from the economic necessity or opportunities of the Internet, simultaneously controlling the communicative and expressive capacities of this medium. This is not an easy thing to do, but for the time being a country such as China fairly successfully 'rides the back of this tiger' (the Internet) using sophisticated monitoring, manipulation and censorship (see Chapter 5). Simultaneously, this country develops an advanced knowledge economy with the aid of the same medium, the Internet.

The second basic problem is that the new media also blur other traditional distinctions such as those between social spheres of living and the public and private sphere. This will be emphasized in Chapters 7 and 8. It has immediate consequences for new media legislation. The Internet is both a mass medium and an interpersonal medium. This clearly is the case for the social media. They combine mass media applications, such as blogs, Twitter or YouTube, and interpersonal applications like SNS and peer-to-peer networks. SNS themselves contain both private and public profiles and they enable both interpersonal communication and marketing. What type of legislation and regulation should be applied for this? Traditional media law made clear distinctions between mass media law and private communication law (e.g. for telephony and letters). Traditionally, the regulation of information and communication freedom in mass and interpersonal communication has been rather different. What is left free in private and personal communication, for instance obscenity, may not be allowed in mass communication. So, the question is how all the new applications of the Internet should be rated.

The last problem to be mentioned here is that of the extremely volatile, dynamic and perhaps encrypted nature of network communication crossing many borders and jurisdictions. This makes criminal behaviour of all kinds – obscene, indecent and defamatory expressions, violations of human rights like privacy and other offences – extremely difficult to trace, investigate, prosecute and prove. These activities are very time-consuming for the police and security agencies, so even when an offence is detected, the chances are small that someone will be charged and convicted.

Legal solutions

There are three kinds of solutions to these problems, which have already been mentioned in Chapter 5 and reappear several times in the next sections: legal solutions; self-regulation; and technological protection. It is one of the most important claims of this chapter that they are only effective when used in combination. Box 6.2 shows both the most important problems and solutions in handling information and communication freedom. Here it is evident that most solutions are created to handle the elusive character of global networking.

BOX 6.2
Problems and solutions in handling information and communication freedom on the Internet

Problems	Solutions
Convergence:	Legal solutions:
model of broadcasting, common carriers or the press?	- adaptation of legislation and regulation - international agreements
Crossing jurisdictions	Self-regulation solutions:
Blurring interpersonal and mass communication	- public and private definitions by producers and users
Elusive character of global network communication	- delegation of monitoring to private actors - blacklisting and blocking (monitoring service) - codes of conduct; self-censorship - hot lines (reporting offences) - rating and filtering systems (self-service)
	Technological solutions:
	- protection codes and encryption - scrambling and blocking (software) - rating and filtering systems (software)

The adaptation of legislation and other regulations in the field of ICT remains necessary, however great the difficulties mentioned. One of the main difficulties is the crossing of jurisdictions by the Internet, of course. This is a problem that can only be solved by international agreements and cooperation such as currently being practiced in the struggle against child pornography. An adequate legal framework will offer protection for all the more or less voluntary solutions to be described below. This will take considerable time, as the technology in question and its uses in daily practice are still maturing. However, some governments have been seized by panic, observing the apparently anarchic nature of Internet use. They have hastily adopted emergency legislation. A clear case was the *Communications Decency Act* signed by President Clinton in 1996. The aim of adopting this act was to limit access to, and prosecute offences in, expressions of violence and obscenity on cable broadcasting, the Internet and online computer services. It subjected these media to more severe prohibitions than those existing in traditional media like free-to-air broadcasting and the press. Only one year later the act was overruled as being unconstitutional by a judgment of the US Supreme Court. Afterwards this has happened more often, for example, with the more limited *Child Online Protection Act* in 2008 (Rustad, 2009). It is interesting to observe that the court stressed the right of freedom of interpersonal communication on the Internet as protected by the First Amendment, while the Decency Act primarily classified the Internet as a medium of mass communication.

Restrictions on the freedom of communication on the Internet have been made by East Asian governments as well (Rustad, 2009, Morozov, 2011). The EU has adopted a *Directive on the Protection of Minors* and a *Resolution on Illegal and Harmful Content of the Internet,* that have forced the member states to adapt their laws for Internet regulation accordingly.

The emergency legislation adopted in the last 15 years has often led to more restrictions on information and communication freedom in the new online world than in the old offline world. Generally, this legislation backed the technological modes of protection and the market- or self-regulation of businesses and service providers on the Internet (Lessig, 1999, 2001). In this way, ISPs were forced to store and open the traffic data of their clients or to filter websites and their contents with rating systems. See the following paragraphs for these solutions.

Self-regulation solutions

In view of the fundamental problems with the adaptation of legislation mentioned above, it is no surprise that soon two other classes of solutions have come forwards: self-regulation and technological alternatives. When interpersonal and mass communication are blurred, analytic law experts could try to distinguish them to adapt legislation, but it would be better when the producers and users concerned would act by themselves. For instance, users of SNS could make a clear distinction between their private and public profiles and suppliers of SNS services could facilitate this in the rules they keep to, such as limits to the publication of content in public profiles and solid privacy protection of private profiles.

The most important current self-regulatory solution in these matters is delegation by legislators of maintenance of the law to private actors. Intermediaries such as ISPs and organizations of web-screening with a particular goal, such as the Internet Watch Foundation (UK) and PervertedJustice.org (US) continually hunting for child pornography on the Web, are charged with the responsibility for monitoring and enforcement of the law (Mueller, 2010). Only some ISPs object, arguing that they are not the police. Most access providers assert that they have no control over the messages they carry, just as the telephone companies do not. They claim not to be editors or suppliers of websites and programs. However, for the service providers that offer content, the claims must be different: consensus is growing that they are liable for the content of their services. To help them, two solutions have become extremely popular: *blacklisting* and *blocking*. Web-screeners with a particular expertise compile and distribute lists of banned sites to ISPs similar to spam block-lists, with the call to remove them. This method is the favourite way for governments to block unwanted content from countries outside its jurisdiction. See Mueller (2010) who discusses the problems with this rude method: – often perfectly legal content is also blocked.

The access and service providers themselves propose a basically different type of self-regulation than this web-surveillance from above: *codes of conduct and self-censorship* in refusing subscribers, sites, programs and files which might get them into trouble. Moreover, they introduce special addresses serving as *hot lines* for their own clients to report child pornography, racism and other potential violations of the law. By the end of the 1990s, so-called *rating and filtering systems* had emerged as prime protectors against illegal and harmful content on computer networks under the control of the users and service providers themselves. In fact, these systems are a combination of self-regulation and technology. The quantity and quality of items such as sex or violence are rated on a scale that is attached to a service or site to be rated and is presented in browsers. Then the software of the filtering systems installed by the users themselves is able to offer whatever nature and level of protection are required by parents, educators and in fact any other kind of authority. Users are also able to include them in their own personal information selections.

Technical solutions

For this reason, and others, more effective solutions are being looked for in technology. Some observers are very optimistic about this. For example, the American law professor Reidenberg has proposed a *Lex Informatica* that would be able to solve most problems discussed in this chapter by technological means such as encryptions and other codes of protection (Reidenberg, 1998). As a matter of fact, rating and filtering systems are included in operating systems, search engines and other software and they might even be programmed in hardware. The introduction in the 1990s of the so-called 'violence chip' in TV sets was a precursor to this option. Scrambling messages in programs or blocking them by some kind of code are increasingly 'popular' techniques. However, just like self-regulation these technological solutions are a two-edged sword: They both protect and threaten information and communication freedom as encryption is also used by people harming freedom. They are indispensable as solutions, but to strike a balance in using them in a right, justified and equal way, the adaptation of legislation and self-regulation remains vital.

INTELLECTUAL PROPERTY RIGHTS
The problem of knowledge as a product

Information and communication freedom does not only clash with rightful personal and societal interests (e.g. harm done to them), but also with rights of ownership, first of all intellectual property rights. The latter conflict is even harder to resolve than the former. On the one hand, many people consider information to be a social product that should not be exclusively appropriated by private interests. On the other hand, information has become one of the most important economic products in the modern economy and it should therefore be submitted to the principles of the market economy like any other good. This contrast can be derived from four special characteristics of a more or less fixed kind of information: *knowledge as a product*. (See Chapter 8 for the difference between knowledge and information.)

- The production of knowledge demands far greater investment than its distribution and use. Knowledge is produced once, but it can be used endlessly. The use of networks reinforces this characteristic.

- Every time knowledge is produced or used, risks are taken: one can never be 100 per cent certain in advance about producing useful results. This is why scientific research is subsidized by the government and why the reliability of a knowledge supplier is crucial to the consumer.

- Knowledge is an intangible product. Unlike a material good, it cannot be transferred from one owner to another, giving the new owner the exclusive permission to use it. On the contrary, knowledge is shared. After transfer, knowledge is owned by both senders and receivers. A person is able to 'acquire knowledge' without the producer losing any of his own. This characteristic is also reinforced by networks.

- Knowledge is a result of both individual and social labour. It is hard to place a dividing line between them. For this reason, the protection of individual achievements is a problem and solutions are always temporary. Because networks link individuals and their contribution in a social exchange, they highlight this characteristic too.

These four characteristics offer arguments for both the production of knowledge as a property (the first two) and the free disposal of knowledge (the second two). The existence of networks weakens the arguments of the first two and strengthens those of the second two. Networks simplify and expand the possibilities for exchanging and duplicating knowledge. Knowledge in networks (data, programs, information) is at the disposal of numerous users without losing any quality or intellectual value. Increasingly, it is passed on to multiple users in licence agreements (passing on the right to use the information), and decreasingly it is transferred in strict sale agreements or hire agreements (passing on ownership). *Without doubt, networks add to the socialization of knowledge.* This makes it even harder to protect the ownership of knowledge passed on in networks. Most legal instruments to do so are faulty and outdated (see below).

The socialization of knowledge, and the problem of its private appropriation in digital environments in general and networks in particular, explain the enormous efforts made by governments to protect the billion-dollar interests of the copyright industry and to adapt the legislation of intellectual property rights accordingly. They tend to make it even more rigid than it used to be in the analogue environment.

Intellectual property right in a digital environment

Intellectual property rights consist of three basic parts: the right of *publication* of a work of unique creative effort (authors' right), the right of *reproduction* (copyright) and the right of *distribution* (for instance in broadcasting and on stage). We must recognize that continental European legislation is more concerned to protect (cultural) authors' rights, while American and English legislation tends to put (economic) copyright first. That is why the American law is called the Copyright Act, while the Dutch law is called the Auteurswet (Authors' Law).

The most important fact concerning new media intellectual property rights is that communication in computer networks links the acts of publication, reproduction and distribution. It is the process that becomes central. For example, making a website with hyperlinks and files to be copied blurs their distinction. Therefore, the question arises, which of the three rights mentioned will be emphasized in new legislation? For fundamental reasons concerning the development of authors' rights in a digital environment (see above and below) and for historical reasons (that is, the rise of corporate power and privatization), it is very likely that reproduction and distribution rights will be defended most. The rights of authors as the protectors of creative effort will be threatened (Lessig, 2001). However, there are fundamental difficulties in protecting *all of these rights* in the digital network environment.

First, authors' right and copyright only protect the *form* of an idea, concept, procedure, method of operation or discovery, not the *content*, that is, the facts and ideas embodied (see Perritt, 1996: 421ff.). In content, one encounters the cultural heritage of society: one never knows exactly where this heritage ends and the original expression of creators begins. This was already a basic problem for works created in analogue media. Using digital media, the problem appears to be insoluble for the following two reasons. First, in digital environments the content changes continuously and it soon acquires a general public character. The recognizable artistic content of the age of simple commodity production, clearly visible in paintings, sculptures and books, is lost in digital signs which are very easy to manipulate, reproduce and exchange. Moreover, the form can be changed just as easily. Computer programs are adapted continuously, both by producers and by users. Databanks contain more or less automatic summaries and abstracts of forms and pieces of information. For these reasons, infringements of authors' right and copyright are extremely difficult to prove.

Second, all existing laws of intellectual property right only protect works that are *fixed*, enabling their originals to be copied and multiplied. In the dynamic digital environment of computer networks, this point of departure is untenable. As has been argued above, the process of creation, re-creation and reproduction will replace fixed forms.

Legal solutions

These fundamental problems lead to the conclusion that any authors' rights solely based on the protection of the unique creativity of products of the mind will become untenable in digital environments. A clear case is the problem of computers creating computer programs themselves. The rights to these programs are granted to the owners of the technologies concerned. Other cases are judicial decisions mentioning the added or surplus value of new computer programs, the new composition or reworking of data in databanks or the production of new information out of existing data. More and more, judges and lawyers speak about the protection of *labour* effort instead of creative effort. In this way, authors' rights move from a cultural into an economic sphere. This is an essential change, unnoticed by many people.

In the practice of using software and information services, this evolution of intellectual property towards economic property goes yet further. Here one can observe the shift from property right to *usage right*. All kinds of licences and contracts between producers and business or household consumers become ever more important. In these cases, one buys not a copy of the original but a licence to use it.

In the American and European intellectual property rights legislation of the late 1990s, the fundamental shifts mentioned above were reflected. European proposals moved in the direction of the basic American assumptions of an economic conception of intellectual property rights. Both American and European proposals tried to meet the terms of digital technology. However, I will argue that they did this so zealously and so much influenced by economic interests that essential freedoms of information and communication have been at risk.

In 1998, the Digital Millennium Copyright Act (DMCA) was adopted in the United States (US Copyright Office, 1998). This Act extended the existing Copyright Act to the digital media and gave copyright owners control over every publication, reproduction and distribution of works in a digital form. For example, service providers on the Internet are expected to remove material from users' websites that appears to constitute copyright infringement. Fair use rights traditionally attached to intellectual property rights, such as personal use and use by libraries and schools, are strictly curbed to allow licensed use only. Everyday personal uses, such as making copies of software to use on a second household computer and copying tracks from purchased CDs to make a personal compilation, are not allowed in principle either. Another traditional right of the user, the so-called first-sale right of a book, for instance, meaning the right to use and forward the copy purchased as long as this does not harm the commercial interests of the producer, is also cancelled. So, many technically protected CDs and DVDs do not allow a single copy.

To prevent digital copying and to track every use of protected works, so-called *digital rights management systems* and protections by means of encryption are backed by this Act. With a few exceptions, attempts to circumvent these technological solutions have become illegal. Online service providers are held to be responsible for the report of these offences and for the protection of pay-per-use rules.

Simultaneously, the European Commission adopted the *Directive On the Harmonization of Certain Aspects of Copyright and Related Rights in the Information Society* (European Commission, 2001) – an obligation to adapt copyrights and authors' rights by the member states that is fairly similar to the DMCA. The Directive was extended in 2004 and 2006. It was a bit less severe in fair use rights to be allowed and it still mentioned 'related rights' – referring to authors' rights that were in fact swallowed by copyright in this Directive – but its basic assumptions were the same.

There has been considerable opposition to this legislation in the US Congress, in the European Parliament and by civil liberties groups, free-speech advocates and digital equipment manufacturers. Critics have called attention to the fundamental shift they introduce into intellectual property rights (Catinat, 1997; Electronic Frontier Foundation, 2008; Lessig, 1999, 2001; Miller, 1996; Samuelson, 1996). The balance in existing legislation between creators' and copyright owners' interests on the one side, and the public interest in the diffusion of ideas in fair use and limited copying on the other, has clearly shifted to the benefit of the former, the copyright owners, in the first place. Perritt argues that 'the justification for copyright is to reward new contributions, not merely to increase the revenue for old contributions' (1996: 423). The latter will happen when (fair) individual users, libraries, schools and research institutions will have to pay for uses that so far are free on a non-commercial basis.

With this legislation, the groundwork is laid for extensive and unprecedented tolling on the Internet. This is especially so because the technological solutions to unlimited copying of digital works – all kinds of encryption and rights management software – are strongly backed by this legislation. However, at the time of writing, all countries, both American, European and others with similar new copyright legislation, exhibit several juridical proposals to revise the laws and numerous court cases that deal with inconsistencies and omissions in the new laws.

Self-regulatory solutions

The law revision proposals are also made because legislation (alone) is far from effective. Many Internet users think the Internet is one giant free copying machine and they are only willing to pay for content when they cannot get it otherwise. In the meantime, businesses with intellectual property have explored their own solutions, developing *new business models* to earn on content.

In the last two decades, four new business models have evolved on the Internet as partial self-regulatory solutions for the intellectual property right problem.

1   The *advertisement model* is by far the most important solution. Google, Facebook, and millions of other service providers on the Internet, offer content that apparently does not have to be paid for. In fact users pay in two ways: 1. they have to 'sell' parts of their privacy because the providers want personalized advertisement; and 2. they have to digest a lot of advertising. This is a very successful business model because the market of online advertisement now runs into the hundreds of billions of dollars/euros.

2   The *partly free and partly pay model* gives users many things for free, for example, first tastes of content. Subsequently, they have to pay for really valuable extra content or service.

3   In particular business sectors the *'online is free, but offline and physical products have to be paid for' model* might succeed. For instance, these days the pop-music business earns less from record selling (online and offline) than from concerts, T-shirts and other kinds of merchandizing.

4   *The pay-for-value model* is the ideal model for the copyright industry. Only recently it has started to work in particular sectors. For the first time, quality newspapers and other valuable intellectual content have started to ask subscription and single issue payment. Most likely, this model will grow in the future as more and more really valuable content moves online. However, it might be that only people with high income and education or businesses and educational departments simply needing the services are willing to pay for it.

These models can be combined in business practice. They are not the only business models working in the contemporary, extremely complicated online contents environment. It is also possible to earn from software that is freely available. All kinds of public domain software, freeware and shareware are appearing. Public domain software is free for distribution and for change. It is also called *open code* under a so-called General Public License. The operating system Linux is the most familiar current example. Freeware is called free, but in fact exploitation and change are not allowed. Freeware means that the source code of the software must be made available to other users, not necessarily free of charge. A synonym of freeware is *open source*. Finally, shareware is software that is free until it is actually used; then a licence must be obtained. Generally, licences have become the prime type of transaction in the new media market of intellectual value.

Other self-regulatory means to protect intellectual property rights are not smart ways to earn, but ways to watch who abuses copyright protected sources. These means are the same as the ones we have seen with information and communication freedom. The *monitoring of illegal copying* is left to specialized information agents, sometimes called 'the copyright police'. They are able to make *blacklists* of Internet users that can be reported to ISPs and content providers to *block their IP numbers* from visiting these sites. They can also report them to the real police for persecution under the copyright laws discussed above. In particular countries they can even have their Internet use cut off completely. Recently, the French and Australian governments proposed the 'three strikes and you're out rule': when illegal copying is monitored three times, access to the Internet would have to be blocked. This blunt measure created outrage among the Internet community.

A more respectable self-regulatory solution is the free adoption of *codes of conduct* or *codes of good practice* by organizational users of copyright-protected material (businesses and public organizations). They promise to refrain from illegal use of this material to defend their image and their good relations with content providers.

Technical solutions

In the future, probably the most effective solutions to the problem of illegal appropriation of digital works will be technological ones. The copyright industry and the producers of encryption software are working hard to develop and introduce all kinds of technical means to control any access and usage of these works. To begin with, they can be encrypted like any electronic message. In this case, one only gets a key after payment. A special kind of encryption is a *digital watermark*: a product is equipped with invisible codes which scramble the image in the event of unauthorized use. Again, hardware players (multimedia computers, CD players) have been developed that can no longer make illegal copies: they automatically register what rights a particular user has to use a certain product, and allow access only by payment. For instance, listening to a music number on the Internet might cost the user 5 cents, whereas to buy a copy would cost 1 dollar. This solution comes pretty close to so-called *data-metering*: a built-in chip or a small device connected to a television or a computer registers the use of a certain product in the same way as an electricity meter. Chip cards are a means of payment. However, data-metering might become another great threat to privacy, since all use can (also) be registered in central processors and files.

Of course all these technical protections can be cracked by experts, but the industry will not care much about that when 98 per cent of users pay because for them cracking is too risky, difficult or laborious. When these technological solutions are backed up by legal enforcement, such as that envisaged in the American and European proposals for legislation, the present situation on the Internet and in other new media of uncontrolled illegal copying on a massive scale will be completely reversed (Catinat, 1997; Lessig, 2001; Miller, 1996). No longer will the rights of copyright owners be in danger, but instead the rights of (fair) users, authors (except for the financial protection by their publishers) and the public at large will be at risk. The balance between owners' rights and legitimate public usage will be lost and the scale will tip towards the former. So, while in principle computer networks support an unprecedented distribution and socialization of information, and although technological means are able to protect both owners and users, the practice of our free-market economy will lead information into an (attempted) level of private appropriation as never before.

A list of problems and potential solutions discussed in this section is portrayed in Box 6.3.

BOX 6.3
Problems and solutions in handling intellectual property rights on the Internet

Problems

Current rights only protect forms, not content

Current rights only protect works that are fixed, not digital processes of creation, re-creation and reproduction

Digital contents can be stolen while the owner keeps the property

Solutions

Legal solutions:
- adaptation of legislation and regulation, e.g. DMCA (US) and Copy Right Directive (EU)

Self-regulation solutions:
- new business models for earning on Internet content
- monitoring of illegal copying
- blacklisting and blocking (monitoring service)
- codes of conduct and good practice

Technical solutions:
- protection codes and encryption
- digital watermarks; data-metering

THE RIGHT TO PRIVACY
Legal framework for privacy protection

On a national level, the right to privacy is covered in most constitutions. On an international level it is described in the Treaties of Rome and Strasbourg (European Council) and the Treaty on Civil Rights and Political Rights (UN). To them we can add more general declarations such as the Universal Declaration of Human Rights, and more specific and locally valid ones such as OECD and European Commission guidelines.

Additionally, most countries have some kind of national privacy law. This legislation is often guided by the eight principles formulated by the OECD and the European Council as early as 1980. The following four are the most important of these:

- The *use limitation principle*: the smallest possible amount of personal data should be gathered and used for the purpose given.

- The *principle of purpose specification*: only personal data for strictly specified purposes should be collected and processed.

- *Quality*: the personal data must be correct, complete and up to date. Furthermore, they have to be well protected by means of security.

- The *principle of transparency or openness*: the people involved have the right to know what personal data are collected, to what purpose, who has access to these data, what will happen to these data when they are passed on to others, and to whom they are passed on.

American legislation

The United States has no general and comprehensive privacy (federal or state) law and no other legislation following these principles. However, this country has an impressive number of privacy-related acts dealing with specific issues (see Perritt, 1996: Chapter 3). The Electronic Communications Privacy Act (ECPA) is the broadest of the federal statutes that focuses on communication. Then there are Computer Fraud and Abuse Acts, dealing only with intrusions that cause certain harm after they have happened. These forbid certain actions of intruders and eavesdroppers in computers and their networks, but impose no duties on controllers and processors of personal data (Perritt, 1996: 88). The federal and state privacy acts impose these duties only on government agencies.

The fragmented nature of American privacy legislation leads to a number of weaknesses and loopholes (see Rustad, 2009), for example: medical records are not protected; most often one has to appeal to the constitution in general or to common law; and the results in court are unpredictable.

According to Michel Catinat:

> most of the attempts to improve the legal environment fall short because of the lobbying of businesses including the marketing industry, federal intelligence and law enforcement agencies, and others. All these actors have diverse interests in maintaining easy access to individual data. (1997: 53)

The EU finds American privacy legislation so defective that, according to the directive mentioned above, no export of personal data to that country is allowed. This has forced the US to behave according to particular aspects of EU privacy legislation when its companies want to do business in the EU. However, for the same reasons, the EU accepted the urgent calls of the US to deliver personal data of airline passengers to America and bank account details of European citizens in the fight against terrorism after the '9/11' attacks of 2001, ignoring its own directive. These compromises show that legislation can be globally effective despite its national scope.

European legislation

The EU Directive called *The Protection of Individuals with Regard to the Processing of Personal Data and the Free Movement of Such Data* (European Commission, 1995) is based on the OECD and Council of Europe principles listed before. At the turn of the century, all EU member states adopted privacy laws founded on this directive.

For a long time, the EU directive on personal data protection (European Commission, 1995) has been the most stringent in the world. It has served as an example for many countries in the world. This does not mean that it is an unconditional defence of the civil and human rights concerned. Not for nothing does its long name carry the expression 'and the free movement of such data'. The directive tries to balance the economic interests of global, primarily European, commerce and human or civil rights. According to some critics, it even legitimizes current economic practices of handling personal data with a large potential for privacy intrusion. The economic interest of free movement of data, including personal data, is suspected to be the prime motivation. The directive only afterwards offers some safeguards.

Three essential characteristics of this piece of EU legislation are worth mentioning here. First, it has been technologically appropriate for many years, as it takes the processing of data in networks as the main point of departure. The directive covers the 'collection, recording, organization, storage, adaptation or alteration, retrieval, consultation, use, disclosure by transmission, dissemination or otherwise making available, alignment or combination, blocking, erasure or destruction of all personal data' (European Commission, 1995: Article 2). Personal data 'mean any information relating to an identified or identifiable natural person … directly or indirectly' (ibid.: Article 2). This dynamic approach is considerably better for computer networks than the static approach of taking the existence of single computer files and their exchange as the main assumption for early data protection legislation. This static approach marked the first generation of European privacy laws. Moreover, the broad definition of personal data just mentioned makes the new legislation valid for all multimedia registration as video (camera) and audio recording are protected as well. The same goes for biometrics.

A second advantage of the European directive is the full application of the OECD principles of use limitation, purpose specification, openness and quality of personal data referred to earlier. These data may only be 'collected for specified, explicit and legitimate purposes and not further processed in a way incompatible with these purposes'. The data should be 'adequate, relevant and not excessive in relation to the purposes' and they should be kept up to date (ibid.: Article 6). A controller is held to be responsible – a controller is any agency or body determining the purposes and means of processing personal data. Controllers have to take care of all the actions of processors processing data by technical means on their behalf.

The openness of personal data registration is supported by the demand for prior consent by the so-called 'data subjects' concerned. They have to be informed about the purpose of, and all events subsequent to, the registration, such as passing the data on to third parties. Prior consent is not required when there is a legal obligation or when the registration is part of a contract to which the 'data subject' is a party. However, in any case there is the right of access to one's own data (ibid.: Article 12).

A third advantage of the directive is that the strong obligations it imposes on controllers and processors are enforced not by governments but by independent supervisory authorities such as national data protection registrars (ibid.: Article 28). Controllers have to notify these authorities about the purpose and other features of their processing activities. They are bodies of consultation, investigation and legal intervention or redress. Although the directive is supposed to be a sound legal solution by itself, it strongly encourages self-regulation by codes of conduct and good practice and by the appointment of independent protection officers inside organizations.

However, there are a number of shortcomings to this directive and the national laws based on it. The greatest disadvantage of the EU directive is that it is very difficult and expensive to put into practice and easily leads to bureaucracy. There is much complaint about this among European controllers and processors. This piece of legislation will therefore only work with the help of organizations supplementing it with self-regulation and 'data subjects' being conscious about their assets and defending their own personal data. So, here again, self-regulation is a necessary counterpart of the legal framework. It is no surprise that the EU member states have implemented the directive rather differently and that the national data protection registrars are not able to strongly enforce this law (European Commission, 2010).

The most important shortcoming of the directive and virtually all privacy legislation in the world is that they are not up-to-date regarding technological and Internet use development (European Commission, 2010). The following trends make privacy protection more and more difficult by all means:

- Privacy threats have become *ubiquitous and more intrusive* because our whole electronic environment is packed with technologies touching informational, relational and physical privacy (see Chapter 5).

- The growth of the Internet and mobile telephony *globalize* the transfer of personal data across jurisdictions. The internationalization of data processing, for example, in cloud computing reinforces this trend.

- The technological advance of data-mining has led to a level of *profiling and social sorting* (see Chapter 5) that turns 'data subjects' into mere numbers unable to defend themselves.

- The *rise of social media and user-generated content* has multiplied the amount of personal data created and exchanged by Internet users themselves.

According to a research team charged by the European Commission to screen the directive, these trends do not urge a fundamental change of the broad categories and principles of the directive. However, they should be clarified and specified to take account of them (European Commission, 2010).

Self-regulation solutions

Waiting for an update of clearly inadequate privacy legislation, individuals and organizations simply have to reach for support in self-regulatory solutions. They can be individual or collective. Individual self-regulation consists of measures taken by privacy-conscious Internet users to protect themselves. For example, in the Internet options of their browsers, users are able to define strong *privacy settings*, apply InPrivate navigation, remove browser histories and they can use all kinds of protection against spyware and the like. They can even move to search engines and SNS that don't store IP-addresses.

In the former chapter we observed that the average Internet user is very careless in applying these tools. The most important reasons are ignorance, a lack of urgency (as privacy threats mostly are abstract for users), a lack of digital skills (not knowing how to apply more advanced tools) and the wish to reveal personal data to be effective in applications such as social-networking and online dating. *Privacy rating systems* such as P3 and TRUSTe are rather peculiar, unknown and sometimes rather difficult to apply, indeed. The same goes for special *filtering systems*, blocking sites with bad privacy practices and methods of *anonymous surfing* that are ever more difficult to realize on the contemporary Internet.

Collective means of self-regulation to protect privacy are more or less voluntary offers by organizational websites. Best-known are *privacy statements* drafted on the initiative of these websites. Second are *privacy codes of conduct* that are the result of negotiations with organizations of consumers, employees and privacy commissioners. In the business sectors of electronic commerce, electronic banking, direct marketing, and relation management (job-counselling, online dating and even SNS) these codes of conduct are very important to maintain the trust of users. Finally, we have *professional codes* drafted by medical staff, social workers, researchers, consultants and information service providers.

These instruments can be quite effective, but to support their effectiveness they should be backed, and sometimes enforced by legislation. And the 'data subjects' have to take them seriously, for example, website visitors actually reading privacy statements and codes of conduct. Because this rarely happens, the suppliers have to improve the accessibility and usability of these means, and realize them despite manifest disinterest by many users. After all, their reputation remains at stake when evident privacy intrusions reach publicity.

Technical solutions

Finally, we have the technical solutions for privacy protection described in the previous chapter. They have already been listed and discussed in Chapter 5. Much attention was paid to privacy design principles and privacy-enhancing technologies. In the future they might become the most effective solution as they are able to prevent unnecessary privacy threats. These solutions primarily focus on the principle of *anonymity*. This has been an issue of fundamental discussions in the last 15 years. Clearly, potential anonymity is (ab)used by all kinds of criminals and wrong-doers, including people with improper behaviour in online group communication and social media. However, privacy advocates underline two basic rights people have in this regard. First, the right to anonymity should preserve the same level of protection in online as in offline environments. Currently, this clearly is not the case. For instance it is possible to anonymously glance through books in a bookshop and a library, while online readership at least entails the storage of an IP address. This right says that anonymously sending messages, browsing websites, looking and paying for goods or services and calling with telephones should be equally possible on the Internet and the offline world of sending letters, looking in shop windows, buying with cash and calling anonymously.

The second basic right is that in the online environment one should adopt the same careful balance between the fundamental rights of privacy and freedom on the one hand, and combating crime on the other as we aspire to in offline environments. Currently, this also does not happen. Particularly after 11 September 2001, we observe all kinds of over-reactions of governments who clearly give priority to the struggle against terrorism and crime as compared to rights of anonymity and freedom. In doing this, they amply use the registration capacities of digital media.

Box 6.4 contains a summary of the discussion about privacy rights in Chapter 5 and this section of Chapter 6.

BOX 6.4
Problems and solutions in handling privacy rights

Problems	Solutions
Privacy is not an absolute right	Legal solutions:
Privacy law is either too general or too specific	- adaptation of legislation and regulation, e.g. the ECPA (US) and the Directive on Personal Data Protection (EU)
Privacy law is not international	
Privacy law focuses on informational instead of relational and physical privacy	Self-regulation solutions: - individual privacy settings - anonymous surfing - privacy rating and filtering systems - privacy statements and codes of conduct
Privacy law lags behind technology	Technical solutions: - privacy design principles - privacy-enhancing technologies

CONCLUSIONS

- The law that should protect against abuses of network technology is itself undermined by this technology. It is largely out of government control, respects no borders, and is continually changing and overly complex. To get a better grip on network technology, general framework legislation has to be conceived that is based on legitimate principles of power in networking and that takes account of the individual characteristics of networks. Until the time when appropriate legislation is adopted, the safest principle is to accept that what goes offline should also go online. This should be backed by international agreements.

- The first network to be considered is the Internet. Here, regulation has shifted from early attempts to rule the Internet by (mainly American) government departments and Internet communities, to technological control (architecture and codes) and market rule both backed by legislation. This means a shift from public and self-regulatory rule to private and juridical rule.

- The fact that networks such as the Internet cross borders and undermine the sovereignty of national states can be treated with different political approaches of Internet governance. They follow the power of networks or try to control it by institutions. They are national or transnational. The choice of approach largely determines the institutional and juridical solutions of the crossing borders problem.

- Public computer networks such as the Internet offer both an advance and a threat to information and communication freedom. Freedoms cannot only be defended by legislation. Self-regulation and technological protection are necessary to prevent the censorships of governments and others.

- Networks add to the socialization of knowledge. Therefore it is difficult to protect intellectual property rights in networks. In the American Copyright Act and the European Directive on Copyright, digital intellectual property rights are defended so zealously that the balance between the copyright owners' interests on the one side and the public interest of the diffusion of ideas in fair use and limited copying on the other is lost to the benefit of the former. However, intellectual copyrights cannot be defended by legislation only. Self-regulation that is marked by new business models in the market of intellectual value and technological solutions, such as digital encryption of pay-per-view products, should be added to legislation.

(Continued)

(Continued)

- The same combination is required for privacy protection. Privacy legislation of a level of protection that is at least equal to the EU privacy directive should be the framework for self-regulatory solutions and technological protection (encryption and anonymous computer and Internet use). Privacy is perhaps the most threatened value in network communications; it should be considered as a basic freedom underlying many others that should not be opposed to, and sacrificed for security so easily.

7 SOCIAL STRUCTURE

About this chapter

- This chapter is about the infrastructure of society. One of the core arguments of this book is that this infrastructure is changing under the influence of communication networks. However, the opposite also holds: the changing social infrastructure of society shapes communication technology. These mutual shaping processes create the network society.

- The most basic infrastructure of society is made by the dimensions of space and time. A most popular view is that the constraints of space and time are eliminated in the network society. Is this true? In this chapter the opposite is claimed.

- The social (infra)structure of the network society is marked by blurring spheres of living. Private and public life, work and leisure time, interpersonal and mass communication appear to be merging, for example, in tele-work and distance education. What is to be expected from these tele-activities? A popular view is that telecommuting will reduce traffic jams. Here the opposite is claimed: the new media increase mobility.

- In the first decade of this century, social media appeared that resemble the old peer-to-peer networks of the Internet in the 1980s. Why did they appear so late? What are the characteristics of these media and what are their main social and personal effects? Will they create a new communication infrastructure for society?

- It is often claimed that the use of the Internet is fragmenting the public space and turning it into a multitude of private spaces. Is this true, or are the traditional interpretations of what constitutes a public space perhaps obsolete?

(Continued)

(Continued)

- Networks are able to reduce inequality because they spread knowledge and information. However, in practice they seem to bring the opposite. The problem of the digital divide in the fabric of society is not solved. It is going from unequal access to insufficient digital skills and gaps of usage. Why should a network society create more inequality?

- The whole infrastructure or system of the network society makes the impression of being unstable, especially when we look at the volatility and contagion of processes in all spheres of society. Has the network society become too connected?

SPACE AND TIME IN THE NETWORK SOCIETY
Raising importance of space and time

This section shows how the use of media networks changes even the most basic coordinates of the structure of societies. What can be more basic than the dimensions of space and time? These dimensions are linked to social structures dominated by individual or social, private or public relationships. For example, the globalization of space entails a move from small individual to extended social relationships. The differentiation of time schedules for individuals in the modern world reinforces the social trend of individualization. These examples indicate that, unfortunately, the account that follows has to be fairly abstract. One of the most abstract and general historical processes is *time–space distantiation*. Anthony Giddens (1984, 1991a, 1991b) uses this term to show that human and social time and space horizons tend to widen in the course of history. Traditional society is based on direct interaction between people living close to each other. Modern societies stretch further and further across time and space. Barriers of time are broken by the spread of customs or traditions. Information is stored to be used later or to be passed on to future generations. Barriers of space are broken by the increasing reach of communication and transportation.

With the introduction of global networks reaching into every home and personal space, the process of time–space distantiation seems to be approaching its limit, at least in developed societies. Many take it for granted that we have a 'global village'. Distance and time seem to lose any relevance. Some have spoken about the 'death of distance' (Cairncross, 2001), others about 'timeless time' (Castells, 1996). These popular ideas are partly wrong, however. I want to claim the opposite: that these dimensions are getting more important in the network society! This is the most general instance of the laws of network extension and trend amplification (see Chapter 2). After all, the process of time–space distantiation is marked not only by the extension of space and time, but also by the contraction of space and the compression of time. As a result, time and space in some respects gain importance, instead of losing relevance. Their meaning has radicalized. The explanation is that technological capabilities of bridging space and time enable people to be more *selective* in choosing coordinates of space and time than ever before.

Many examples can be given to support this statement (see also Ferguson, 1990). Nobody will deny the extreme relevance of (clock) time in the most advanced nerve centres of ICT – the stock markets. Hesitating for a second or failing to make a fast connection to another financial market can mean the difference between profit and loss. Millions of dollars are traded on the international online currency markets every second. In companies, the coordination of labour by means of ICT leads to an increase of the relevance of logistics and time registration. In mass communication, the importance of time schedules for broadcasters of programmes and commercials is still increasing, for they want to reach very specific target audiences. The dimension of time is becoming more important for viewers as well, as new concepts of global time (produced by satellite TV and Internet communication) overlie the old ones (marked by local, daily rhythms and routines) (Ferguson, 1990: 155).

In the dimension of space, the same applies to all the fields we have just mentioned. In Chapter 4, it was stressed how selective transnational corporations have become. They are extremely careful in strategically choosing the right places for their departments and computer network nodes in the world, assigning them particular functions. Increasing control over space enables them to choose between the quality of particular places (Graham and Marvin, 1996; Harvey, 1989: 294ff.). They pay five to ten times more for a square meter of office floor in the city centres of New York and Tokyo as compared to floors in their suburbs.

Expansion and compression of space and time

So, the expansion and compression of space and time are two sides of the same coin. They represent the most general expression of the idea of the unity of scale extension and reduction, one of the key threads running through this book. This unity is an expression of the law of network extension (see Chapter 2). Networks connect large scales and small scales, and in between intermediaries serve to realize this connection. The unity also means that control over space and time in a local context by a small social unit can only happen because a larger social unit has control of space and time over a long distance. All our opportunities and facilities in personal space depend upon connections with systems online such as those organizing and delivering water, electricity, gas, information or message supply. In Chapter 1, I pointed out that the modern privatization of local units of living (households) to become smaller units would not have been possible without these large-scale service infrastructures and intermediaries.

In companies, the combination of decentralizing production and centralizing control described in Chapter 4 causes an increase in the need for all kinds of communication channels. Both at home and in companies, the expansion of communication and of information processing over long distances goes hand in hand with an increasing intensity of information activities in the local contexts of the 'intelligent home', the 'intelligent' workstation or mobile space.

In the spatial dimension, global media networks spatially enlarge society – mainly western society in the past centuries – and simultaneously they reduce the size of the world (compression). The spatial expansion of modern society was aptly described by Burgers (1988) as 'the detachment of society from geography'. The natural environment as a relevant context is replaced by, or interwoven with, social environments constructed by people. Simultaneously, natural time is outstripped by the increasing importance of clock time constructed by society (Bolter, 1984; Rifkin, 1987). Communication and information networks more or less complete these processes (Meyrowitz, 1985).

In the temporal dimension, global media networks add different levels of fragmented temporality on top of the continuous local level (expansion). We were already familiar with the fragments of 24 time zones across the globe. In 1998, the first attempt was made to replace clock time by a unitary computer and network time. The Swiss watchmaker Swatch (from Biel) proposed Biel Mean Time (BMT) as a global Internet time consisting of 1000 beats of 1 minute and 26.4 seconds a day. Of course, the British did not want to lag behind; in 2002 they tried to rescue GMT with the proposal of Greenwich Electronic Time (GeT) (www.get-time.org). Both Internet time systems allow only one time to be used in a global web exchange; the computer system then translates this time to the requested local times. According to the Thai philosopher Hongladarom (2002), they enable both the coexistence of different conceptions of time across cultures in the world (expansion) and a return to a 'medieval' conception of unitary time, currently appearing as 'glocal' (global and local) time (compression). However, the artificial time constructs of BMT and GeT are adopted by virtually no one and this is a very telling fact. Local time rhythms and cycles remain dominant.

In computer networks, transmission takes place in 'real time' and messages can be sent and received at any moment. With the shifting limits of natural time, the meaning of socially constructed time becomes increasingly important. The Internet times described above are just the latest example. Even the socialization of time seems to have become complete, as people think time is no longer relevant in the new media environment. So it seems – but in reality the natural (for instance, biological) substratum will continue to exist, of course. For human beings the daily rhythms of the body overrule any other time in the end (an instance of compression as all experience of space and time comes together in our bodies). The consequences and tensions produced by the combination of all these temporal regimes (natural, social and media time) have a big social, cultural and mental impact (Green, 2002; Hongladarom, 2002; Lee and Liebenau, 2000; Lee and Whitley, 2002). This will be demonstrated in the chapters that follow.

Socialization and individualization of space and time

The structural combinations of scale extension and scale reduction and of time and space dimensions described in the former paragraphs run side by side with the combined processes of the socialization and individualization of space and time. I start with the process of socialization: the rising importance of the social and society. A first observation about space is that an *upgrading* of the social environment is going on. Although individual environments remain decisive for individuals, of course, people acknowledge the shrinking relevance of their own environment in the world. *Life is Elsewhere*, as the title of a Milan Kundera (1986) novel says. Burgers has expressed it this way:

> The moment the world is brought into the home via the mass media, the relevance of individual experiences seems to shrink to insignificant proportions. Viewed from the perspective of modern society, the ups and downs of individual life are less and less important and the individual is well aware of this. In relation to the physical environment this means that really important events seem to be taking place elsewhere. (1988: 17, my translation from Dutch)

Second, the social environment is made more *objective*. The social environments made by humans increasingly adopt the character of a natural environment. Individuals therefore feel that they face an anonymous, opaque, inaccessible and uncontrollable reality. Symptoms of alienation and uprooting are widespread. Social and economic crises begin to resemble natural disasters. Who expected the recent credit crisis and who knew its causes? Media networks, which enable more direct communications between the micro-level and the institutions of the macro-level, do not reduce these experiences. On the contrary, I have argued that computer networks both subjectively and objectively tend to enhance opaque and uncontrollable processes. For example, very few people know how the Internet works. And a network breakdown feels like a natural disaster.

In the third place, a *fragmentation* of social environments can be observed. They comprise fewer concrete, continuous and collectively used areas, and more abstract, dispersed areas used for special purposes. For example, squares in cities and villages used to be fully public spaces; today, several parts of them are marked out for special private use such as terraces, billboards, neon lights, kiosks, phone booths and wireless hotspots. And what is more, homogeneous neighborhoods are being gradually divided by all kinds of diffuse, private social networks.

Finally, we perceive a *generalization and a standardization* of social environments. 'Human activities seem to become more uniform after the scale extension of social communications; the same activities are happening in ever more places' (Burgers, 1988: 21). The exchange of experiences through networks on a global level has led to a general diffusion of western urban culture. It is made dominant by western economic and technological strength and it has produced a loss of the particularity and identity of other, less materially strong cultures (Barber, 1996; Castells, 1997). Even the decline of western economic strength and the rise of eastern Asia and other rapidly developing non-western countries, does not make a difference. For example, at first sight, the urban centres in China look like western cities. Almost every airport in the world looks the same.

Again we have to raise attention to the other side of the coin: the individualization of space and time. All trends just described have a countertrend. Both sides are supported by the new media according to the law of network extension (Chapter 2). In modern society the importance of the social environment is not only upgraded but also downgraded. *Individualization* is the most important trend in modern society, at least in western society. According to this trend, the world of the individual reaches the focus of attention. It is the prism from which the individual is looking to the outside world, a prism replacing the traditional prism of the family, neighborhood and village. This is perfectly demonstrated by the opening page of a social networking site: The Facebook opening page has become the window to the social world outside for many contemporary individuals. It has, in fact, become their world.

Second, the social environment is not only made more objective, but also more *(inter)subjective*. Partly as a reaction to the opaque and uncontrollable outside world and the apparent shrinking relevance of their own world, many people are withdrawing into their own understandable lives and environments. The interpretation of the outside world also becomes increasingly (inter)subjective. It is becoming more subjective with the aid of contemporary mass media that pay more and more attention to opinions than to facts according to many media critics. (Inter)subjectivity is growing in the social media (e.g. Twitter and Facebook), exchanging commentary and opinions among people who more or less know each other.

The fragmentation of social environments is compensated by the *unification* of the particular world of an individual, for example, in a social network brought into the scheme of SNS pages and profiles. This makes the fragmented individual world into a particular whole: the Facebook page is a demarcation of some kind of personal garden, a coherent picture of 'my world'.

Finally, generalization and standardization of the social environment meet the opposing trends of particularity and cultural *differentiation*. Beneath the surface of that globalized airport and those Chinese cities one can find the particulars of a local culture. Any modern marketeer knows that every customer is different in particular respects and that marketing should be personalized.

THE BLURRING SPHERES OF LIVING
Multi-functional or connected spheres of living?

As already has become evident in the previous section, one of the network society's most important characteristics is the dissolving of boundaries between the macro-, meso- and micro-levels of social life, between the public and the private spaces and between the spheres of living, working, studying, recreation and travelling. Therefore, tele-work and tele-study are among the most discussed applications of the new media. So far, these tele-activities have not yet proved themselves. The overestimation of their adoption is caused not so much by a lower than expected introduction of the infrastructure required, but by an inaccurate view of existing relations between the personal spaces people are living in and by a strong under-estimation of the social and organizational difficulties involved in tele-activity. Most people assume that our personal spaces, the domestic sphere in particular, will become *multi-functional*. At the same time, it is assumed that people want to perform their activities *in a single place* (except for travelling, of course), preferably at home. Both assumptions are only partly correct. The dissolving of boundaries between the personal spaces of the home, the work and study place and the car or public transport seat is caused not so much by the multi-functional use of these spaces enabled by communication technology, but by the *linking of spaces that remain and are used primarily for special purposes*. Therefore we are witnessing more increases of tele-activity in mobile environments than in homes and other private places. A network's most fundamental technical characteristic is the connections it makes. That enables the combination of multi-functionality and specialization *everywhere*; but this opportunity will only be taken when it is desired.

The opportunity for an increasing multi-functional use of *spaces* in spheres of living cannot be denied. The same applies to the multi-functional use of *time* for that matter (multi-tasking). The new media enable working, studying and entertaining oneself at home, at every hour of the day. In the meantime, workplaces are also provided with opportunities for study, entertainment and mediated conversation with friends, acquaintances and relatives at a distance. Direct links to companies will enable students to gain work experience while sitting at a school desk. And people will be able to work and have conversations while travelling and being entertained by way of mobile and smart phones, laptops, tablets and audio players. Finally, the workaholics among us will be able to work while having a holiday, for instance by taking a tablet to the beach.

Tele-commuting: advantages and disadvantages

However, there are several limitations to a predominantly multi-functional use of space and time. But before these limitations are discussed, we will briefly survey the first experiences with tele-work and tele-study, which already show these limitations. At the start of the 21st century, the number of real tele-workers must be rather disappointing to the advocates of this type of work. In most developed countries, it is less than ten per cent and the majority of this proportion only tele-commutes one day in a week. In a representative survey among Dutch Internet users in 2010 it appeared that 11 per cent of the population tele-commuted every day or week and that seniors above 55 with higher education were the most frequent users (van Deursen and van Dijk, 2010). What is a tele-commuter or tele-worker? According to IDC (1996), they are employees having a formal agreement with their employers that allows them to spend some part of the working week at some location other than the bureau/office using ICT. So, tele-workers are not simply people who have always worked at home, who were mobile workers before, or who have a business of their own. On the one hand, tele-workers are professionals usually working independently (such as programmers, consultants and system designers); and on the other hand,

dissolving of Boundaries

Multi-functional use of spaces in spheres & use of time (multi tasking) they are functional workers undertaking activities such as data entry, data processing and selling goods and services. Finally, there is a group of professionals often working at home, and most often working overtime.

What explains the disappointing frequency of tele-work? Aren't the advantages obvious? Employees need to travel less, they save on energy and help to reduce traffic jams. They are able to plan their own days. Moreover, tele-work can be combined with other activities such as household work and/looking after children. The main explanation is that the disadvantages of a substantial number of hours tele-working each week are currently stronger. They can be summarized as follows:

[handwritten: Advantages to tele-work (same for tele-study)]

[handwritten heading: Disadvantages of telework]

- The *conditions of labour* for tele-workers having functional tasks are poor. Like all people working at home in flexible labour relationships, they have little protection. They have almost no chance of making a career within the organization. Trained professionals often work overtime without receiving any extra payment.

- *Impoverished communication* with management and co-workers affects the quality of the tasks to be performed. The work is routine and it lacks informality and crucial non-verbal aspects. In Chapter 9, I argue that online communication can be richer and more social than people expect. However, tele-work and tele-study in advanced jobs and training require very complex types of exchange, often not available in online communication.

- A consequence, disadvantageous to both management and functional personnel, is that *little support can be given* by management. Not only is supervision unsatisfactory, but there is little opportunity for suggestions (for improvements) and coordination between colleagues. This seems to be the main reason why tele-work in organizations is growing so slowly.

- *Social isolation* of employees working at home is considered to be the most important problem. It can reduce productivity to such an extent that it is noticed by management as well. This is why, in some cases, companies decide to start local tele-work centres.

- Doing tele-work at home makes it *hard to separate work* from other domestic activities. A tele-worker is required to have strong self-discipline. When several members of one household spend more time at home than before, tensions may arise.

Distance education: advantages and disadvantages

The advantages of *tele-study* can be compared with those of tele-work: less time spent travelling, being able to plan one's own day, and the possibility of combining activities. Furthermore, teachers can correct and grade assignments sooner and sometimes even faster. However, the practice of distance education has not experienced a breakthrough either. Only six per cent of the Dutch Internet population daily or weekly followed online courses in the year 2010 (van Deursen and van Dijk, 2010). The disadvantages of tele-study resemble those of tele-work: *Disadvantages to tele-study:*

- Distance education *completely depends* upon two-way communication with the educational department offering this facility. Students among themselves have much more difficulty in consulting other students when they have study problems requiring collective action. Tele-students work more individually than traditional students, though they may send each other messages by email and social media.

- In fact, *interaction* between teachers and students reaches such a *low level* that the quality of education completely depends on the programme, which has to be repeatedly tested and improved.

- Many students cannot handle the *independence* and *self-discipline* required. Direct supervision and help, beyond instruction at a distance, are sorely missed. Dropout rates in distance education are high.

- Distance education is a *socially isolated activity* as well. Students can only lean on their fellow students with online communication. A traditional educational institution serves as a meeting place, a place of socialization and a means of creating a daily study routine. It is therefore highly unlikely that distance education will become the predominant way to educate children and adolescents.

- As is the case with tele-work, separating study from *other domestic activities* is extremely difficult. This division has to be enforced by, for instance, putting the PC in the attic, which can have negative effects on living together. Both too many and too few contacts may lead to tensions in a modern household.

Structural limitations of tele-activity

These disadvantages of tele-commuting and distance education point to a number of structural limitations of this type of online activity and the multi-functional use of spaces listed in Box 7.1. The common denominator in this list is that people usually have had good reasons to perform a particular activity in one place and other activities in another. This conforms to the human needs of orientation, daily routines and change. The opportunity of a multi-functional use of spaces is real but limited. This opportunity has led superficial new media forecasters and strategists to the conclusion that in the future networks would reduce mobility and that people could stay in their preferred places. The future vision of the *electronic cottage* of Alvin Toffler (1980) has proved to be completely wrong. In fact the opposite has happened. The new media increase our mobility, and lead to more traffic on the roads, instead of less. The simple reason is that they give us the choice to perform activities everywhere because they have become increasingly small, portable and wireless. In this way we are able to combine the best of both worlds: our favourite places to domesticate, work, study or to be in transit, and our online places everywhere.

BOX 7.1
Structural limitations of tele-commuting and distance education

1 Original places remain most appropriate
2 Dependence on a centre far away
3 Inadequate communication with managers and teachers
4 Social isolation
5 Difficulty of separation from other activities

THE RISE OF THE SOCIAL MEDIA
Definition and kinds of social media

Another kind of new media environment in which our spheres of living are blurring is constituted by the social media. They link the worlds of the individual and the social and they are a combination of interpersonal and mass communication. The sudden and spectacular rise of the social media will be explained below. First I will have to define who they are and what kinds of social media can be observed. In my view, social media are *Internet applications that enable the sharing of things*. These things can be text messages, photos, videos, music, graphics, pieces of knowledge or information (knowledge networks) and even game acts (online gaming). This large variety of things/messages can be divided according to their media richness. Evidently, the media richness of text is low, while game acts exchanging avatars and 3-D graphics have high media richness. The richer the medium used, the more mental and social effects it produces (see Chapter 8).

A second distinction is the focus of exchange in the social media: this can be the individual sending of messages to others without necessarily receiving feedback or this can be a collective of two or more people exchanging messages in order to get things in return. This two-fold distinction produces a table that lists and categorizes all current social media (Kaplan and Heanlein, 2010) (see Table 7.1). Blogs and microblogs (e.g. Twitter) clearly are individual calls for attention that may not be noticed by anyone. SNS are calls for interpersonal communication that are expected to have feedback but don't have to. In virtual worlds such as Second Life, ones avatar can wander alone or engage into contact. However, a large number of collective social media simply do not work when there is no feedback. Chatting would stop immediately. Knowledge networks cannot have only people who benefit and do

MEDIA RICHNESS

		LOW (text)	MEDIUM (text, audio, video)	HIGH (multimedia; 3D worlds)
FOCUS	INDIVIDUAL	BLOGS AND MICROBLOGS *(Twitter)*	SOCIAL NETWORKING SITES *(Facebook, LinkedIn)*	VIRTUAL SOCIAL WORLDS *(Second Life)*
	COLLECTIVE	CHAT BOXES *(MSN)* COLLABORATIVE PROJECTS *(Wikis and knowledge exchange networks)*	COMMUNITIES OF INTEREST CONTENT and EXCHANGE SITES *(YouTube)*	VIRTUAL GAME WORLDS *(e.g. World of Warcraft)*

FIGURE 7.1 Kinds of social media by focus and media richness (inspired by Kaplan and Heanlein, 2010)

not contribute. The same goes for video and music exchange sites. Not to mention online gaming, which is fully interactive.

Social media as an expression of network individualization

Whether they get feedback or not, the intention of all users of social media is to be social. These media are a perfect illustration of the network society. In themselves they fully combine social and media networks. The social drive behind using them is an important trend of the network society that I have not yet fully covered. I call this trend *network individualization*. Previously Wellman (2000) developed the concept of 'network individualism' that was copied by Castells (2001). However, I think this wording is wrong because of the connotation of egocentrism. The social media in particular have a clear social orientation and sometimes entail altruism in sharing things.

Network individualization means that the individual is becoming the most important node in the network society and not a particular place, group or organization. The social and cultural process of individualization, which appeared long before the Internet, particularly in western societies, is strongly supported by the rise of social and media networks. Networks are the social counterpart of individualization. Using them, the individual creates a very mobile lifestyle and a criss-cross of geographically dispersed relations. Inevitably, it means that individuals will spend more time alone accompanied by technology (transport and communication means) and that they will spend more time being online. However, being online may be fully social, as is expressed in the use of the social media. One only has to look at the opening page of an SNS: this is both the home of the individual as the core of society and the window to his/her social environment.

Social media in between interpersonal and mass communication

One of the most striking characteristics of the social media is that they blur the distinction between interpersonal and mass communication. The intention of writing a blog or a series of Twitter messages can be to create a personal diary or a publication. An SNS contains both private and public profiles that often are not kept apart. The same SNS can be a medium for interpersonal networking and for marketeers to reach an audience with personalized messages.

This blurring of interpersonal and mass communication has been a characteristic of the Internet right from the beginning. After the thousands of newsgroups with special interests created in the 1980s, the 1990s witnessed an explosion of Internet applications in between public and private communication. This means that the sender can be public and the receiver private, or the other way round. It also means that public senders are sending ever more personalized messages for receivers (e.g. target group of marketing) and private senders are framing public messages from a private perspective (e.g. personal websites and weblogs). See Figure 7.2. In the 1990s the number of personal websites, communities of interest (virtual communities), online forums, online support groups and online service subscriber groups multiplied. After the turn of the millennium, social media expanded this trend with a large number of new applications between interpersonal and mass communication. See the boldfaced applications in Figure 7.2. In the two upper cells, social media are listed who come close to mass communication. In the two lower cells, social media are akin to interpersonal communication.

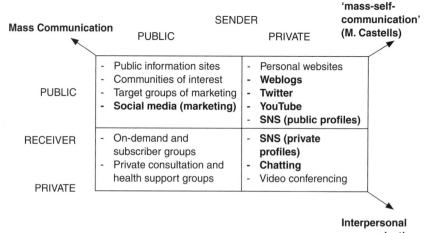

FIGURE 7.2 Social media (boldfaced) between interpersonal and mass communication

The table split between public and private profiles of SNS and between marketing and personal profiles marks the double nature of this medium in a nutshell. On the same issue, Manuel Castells (2009) has developed an interesting concept called *mass self-communication*. It corresponds to the applications in the private–public cell of Figure 7.2 (upper-right) combining mass (public) and self (private) communication. We will see that this combination has important consequences, both for social media use and for society.

The delayed arrival of social media

The rise of the social media on the Internet is no surprise. The only amazing thing is that it took so long. In the first Dutch edition of this book, written at the end of the 1980s, I expected a society based on peer-to-peer networking and exchange at a distance. This was one of the reasons to call the book 'The Network Society'. In the 1980s, the social applications of the Internet were the dominant ones. This was the decade of (academic) peer-to-peer networking and Usenet groups. In the early 1990s, all kinds of virtual communities were created (Rheingold, 1993). However, with the arrival of the Worldwide Web, the Internet took another turn. It became a popular channel for electronic publications, corporate communication, e-commerce and entertainment. With the rise of Internet companies such as Google it evolved into a channel of information retrieval.

The arrival of the social media signifies that the Internet has returned to its origins: a network of exchange and cooperation, not only a source of consumption and information retrieval. How could this happen so suddenly? When the former edition of this book was written in the years 2004–05, the social networking site Facebook had just been born. Blogs were widely available but they served as alternative mass publication media, not as media for a fast exchange of messages to socialize (Twitter). I will list four scientific explanations for the sudden arrival of social media.

First, the use of a new medium has to be learned. This follows, among others, from social-cognitive theory (Bandura, 1986, LaRose and Eastin, 2004). In this theory, social learning and habits of media use are the crucial factors. In the ten to 15 years before the arrival of social media, Internet users learned to use music, picture and video exchange sites and to trade goods on market places such as eBay. They exchanged knowledge to create Wikipedia. Having learned this pattern of using the Internet, the exchange of contacts and messages was a logical next step. The expansion of Facebook started from the exchange of pictures only.

A second obvious explanation departs from human needs. For some time, there must have been a latent need for a social use of the new media, among others to support social contacts. My sociological explanation would propose the trend of network individualization as discussed before. Communication science would suggest uses-and-gratifications theory (Katz, Blumler and Gurevitch, 1974; McQuail, 1987). This theory says that the social media offer a number of extrinsic gratifications (the creation and maintenance of social contacts, ways to organize things and to share them) and intrinsic gratifications (using social media is fun). When conditions are ripe and opportunities become visible, latent needs can suddenly become manifest. The first of these conditions is that a medium has become so popular that more than half of the population achieves access. Regarding the Internet, this happened only after the year 2000 in the developed countries. Here we touch diffusion theory.

explanations cont...

Diffusion of innovations theory (Rogers, 1963) will claim that social media are an innovation that is created by innovators and subsequently spreads into society because it offers a number of advantages as compared to older technologies. Social media have a number of relative advantages: they are faster and more efficient in reaching others or in organizing and exchanging things than, for instance, email, telephony and address books; they can be compared to these older technologies; they are relatively easy to try and to use; and one can observe their use with others which has a contagious effect.

Diffusion and innovations theory also says that innovators prepare the innovation. Indeed, in the 1990s, software developers created new software for exchange sites and knowledge networks. Innovators sometimes have creative insights, such as Mark Zuckerberg, the founder of Facebook, who observed the popularity of the face books of students for dating – he elaborated the basic idea behind this simple instrument into a far more advanced SNS.

The fourth explanation emphasizes diffusion in terms of network effects. This is part of network theory and follows the law of network externality (see Chapter 2). There are two tipping points in the spread of a network medium. The first tipping point occurs when a network reaches critical mass (access rate of about 25 per cent). Than it makes sense to be connected to this medium because sufficient others are available. After this point, diffusion goes faster and faster. Considering SNS, this point has been passed between 2007 and 2009 in most developed countries. The second tipping point arrives when about two-thirds is connected. Then the remaining part feels forced to participate. However, this goes at a smaller rate of increase because here we approach the so-called 'laggards' who actually do not want to participate. At the time of writing, this second point has been reached in the developed countries and it has already been passed some time ago by students, first of which were students of secondary education. They are 'out' when they do not link to Facebook or any other SNS.

Social effects of social media

The former section leads to the conclusion that social media have grown from the deeper personal and social needs of people in contemporary society. If this is true, they must have a similar deep and lasting effect on this society according to the law of trend amplification (see Chapter 2). Discussing these effects actually requires a whole book. Next to frequent references to the social media in other parts of this book I will end this section with a short summary of the effects I think are most important. They are listed in Box 7.2.

BOX 7.2
Social and personal effects of social media

- Blurring traditional dividing lines in life and communication
- The dilemma of privacy and the disclosure of identity
- Higher connectivity and increase of sociability
- Popularization and inequality
- Institutions under pressure
- Information and commmunication overload
- Social pressure and addiction
- Unknown manners

The first societal effect in my view is the blurring of several dividing lines in life and communication, first of all interpersonal and mass communication, as discussed above. This has a number of advantages, otherwise this wouldn't happen. In the context of network individualization, people are able to express themselves in seeking publicity by, for example, Twitter and SNS, sounding out feelings, opinions and identities. In this way you can be someone in anonymous modern society. Social media are used for identity development by teens and adolescents first of all. However, this has a black side. Often people do not know in what kind of environment they are moving in the social media. They think they are engaging in personal conversations but actually they are public. A very large part of SNS users do not make a distinction between their personal and public profiles.

Actually, SNS are (inter)personal media but, on account of their popularity, the whole marketing sector and other types of persuasive communication have jumped on them immediately. In this way they can reach an audience with effective personalized messages. However, these persuaders should be aware of the tactics of their operations; otherwise they will be experienced as spam by many. Some of them will seek real personal SNS and partly leave Facebook and the like. Conversely, users should create new public–private dividing lines in the social media to protect their privacy and liabilities of publicising private information of others (for example, delicate pictures).

To understand the behaviour of social media users it is important to realize that for them risking their privacy is a real dilemma. When people do not reveal personal information in their profiles of SNS and online dating they will not be effective. Teenagers and adolescents just have to do this to sound out their maturing identities. This drive is much bigger than the fear of privacy loss that often is perceived to be abstract. The suppliers of SNS and other social media benefit from this attitude of users because for them the exploitation of personal information is vital for advertising.

Blurring lines: (handwritten margin note)

Disclosing identity: (handwritten margin note)

The rise of the social media has solved at least one fundamental discussion about the Internet. In the last 20 years, a broad debate has been waged considering the question of whether the Internet increases or decreases human sociability. Some observers have claimed that the Internet reduces sociability because it leads to social isolation and even loneliness or depression (Kraut et al., 1998); less real-life involvement producing loners, 'computer nerds' and Internet addicts (Nie and Erbring, 2000); and because it would impoverish social interaction reducing face-to-face interactions (Nie, 2001). Others have claimed that the Internet enhances sociability because Internet use increases so-called 'social capital' in terms of social contact, civic engagement and sense of community (Katz and Rice, 2002; Quan-Haase et al., 2002). 'The Internet complements and even strengthens offline interactions, provides frequent uses for social interaction and extends communication with family and friends' (Katz and Rice, 2002: 326). The first observations of social media use have clearly solved this debate in favour of the last position.

social contact: Social media such as SNS lead to *some* increase of new social contacts for average users, but it is far more important in updating and maintaining existing relationships (Pew Internet and American Life Project, 2009; van Deursen and van Dijk, 2010). There *is* an increase in social contacts, as, for example, 26 per cent of Dutch Internet users in 2010 supported the survey statement 'Via the Internet I have gained more friends that I have really met afterwards' (van Deursen and van Dijk, 2010: 57), but SNS mainly support existing strong ties (Granovetter, 1973). However, they also add a large number of weak ties (Parks, 2010) – this explains the large number of so-called 'Facebook friends' many people are proud of. Though the so-called Dunbar number shows that people are able to really know (cognitively) only 150 others (Dunbar, 1993), many SNS users add more 'friends' to their contact lists. In fact only about ten per cent of Facebook friends are close friends (Parks, 2010). In any case, social media add to the sociability and connectivity of society. They offer all kinds of facilities to maintain and extend relationships. However, one critical position in the Internet sociability debate cannot be ruled out at this moment. The Internet increases social contacts more for some people than for others (Cummings et al., 2002; Robinson et al., 2003; Robinson and Nie, 2002; van Dijk, 2005). Those already having many contacts are adding more. This 'the rich are getting richer effect' is an instance of the power law of the Web that we will come across several times below.

Despite this potential rise of relative inequality it has to be argued that the social media have reached enormous popularity among all sections of the population in a short period of time. These media are just as popular among people with low as compared to high education. They have slightly more interest among females as compared to males. The young generations are the first adopters, but people of medium and higher age are currently catching up fast (Pew Internet and American Life Project, 2009; van Deursen and van Dijk, 2010). The social media have given a great boost to the popularity of the Internet at large among the population (van Deursen and van Dijk, 2010, forthcoming). However, this does not mean that everybody is able to use them equally. The threshold of starting to use them is low (even eight-year-olds seem to be able to open a Facebook page), but in fact communication skills are needed to design a really effective SNS or online dating profile (van Dijk and van Deursen, forthcoming).

The following societal effect of the social media is that they put vested institutions under pressure. Sharing all kinds of things among peers is a horizontal process that collides with vertical, top-down directions of communication in traditional institutions trying to control communication flows (Benkler, 2005). With the rise of the social media, all kinds of traditional advertisement, marketing and government information run into difficulties because people start to inform themselves using their own social contacts instead of the official sources of information from outside. In Chapter 4 we have seen that this might give Facebook the opportunity to beat Google.

In politics this is also happening. Authoritarian governments are under pressure from oppositional forces with parts of them amply using social media. However, in Chapter 5 we have seen that so-called Facebook and Twitter revolutions are an overstatement. Institutions are able to strike back, when they want to. Still, forward looking corporations and government departments in democratic societies will not do this. They might be so wise as to benefit from the information and marketing potential of the social media.

Potential social media effects:

At the end of the list of potential social media effects I want to call attention to some effects on the level of the individual using social media. The first is the information and communication overload the social media happen to produce. *communication overload*

These concepts are discussed in the next chapter. The number of messages and other things to share in the social media is increasing rapidly, sometimes even at an exponential rate. However, who is able to consume all these messages and pieces of information about others? According to Hindman (2008) it is easy to speak on the Internet but difficult to be heard. Most Tweets and blogs are read by nobody. Most new personal information on SNS is certainly not noticed by all 'friends'. Large parts of social media messages are trivial and annoying. But perhaps it is not fair to look at this user-generated content from a rational and economic point of view of receivers. It might be better to see social media contents as *expressions* of people having a particular value for the sender first. From a rational point of view, most everyday communication of human beings is communication overload. However, this view tends to forget that this serves an informal, personal and relational need.

Internet addiction is an accepted disorder in the meantime. This is not yet the case for social media addiction; empirical research is lacking (Rutledge, 2010). It is important to depart from a good definition of addiction here. Very frequent social media use does not have to be addictive. Addiction means the observation of compulsory behaviour, withdrawal symptoms and harm to other vital activities of human beings such as sleeping, eating, physical exercise, going outdoors and having sex. All these phenomena happen to occur with a small minority of social media users; in their mildest forms they are much more common (Porterfield, 2010). Many people check their Facebook and Twitter pages all too often in a compulsory way, *internet addiction* sometimes at night and before breakfast. After all, the social pressure to keep up with social media activities is enormous.

The last (inter)personal effect to be discussed is the unknown manners that belong to this new type of social networking and other social media use (e.g. Twitter). As social networking entails personal relationships, many sensitive issues are likely to appear. A first issue is annoyance number one in SNS: unsolicited invitations of people one scarcely knows and impersonal calls. A second source of disagreement is bringing personal news about others before the people concerned can do this or even before they know it. The main topic of this news is broken relationships. A final source of argument is the publication of personal or even intimate pictures, videos and confidential information of others without asking permission. The publisher is responsible, of course, but who knows this? Evidently, this type of 'netiquette' – see following chapters – has yet to grow.

issues of social media

UNITY AND FRAGMENTATION: A NEW SOCIAL COHESION

The duality of social and media structures

In the previous sections and chapters I stressed the combination of scale extensions and scale reductions, socialization and individualization, and the like repeatedly. I also emphasized merging or blurring types of social relations and communication several times. Readers might be annoyed by this and think that this author is not able to make a stand and always seeks compromises. Therefore I have to clarify the background of this type of reasoning. The most general one is the law of network extension: extension of the network leads to adaptations of scale and shifts in the combination of scale extension and reduction. This is about structures and relates to a second background: the so-called *duality of social structure*. This duality has been noted by many theorists of high modernity or postmodernity, notably Barber (1996); Castells (1996; 1997); Featherstone et al. (1995); Giddens (1991a); Lash and Urry (1994); and van Dijk (1993a). These theorists argue that society simultaneously reveals aspects of growing homogeneity and heterogeneity, integration and differentiation, unity and fragmentation. Usually they have to argue against simplistic notions of a fragmenting society and in favour of the existence of homogeneity, integration and unity. With every modern and technological development it seems as if the sociologist's classic nightmare of a society falling apart returns. The arrival of the new media is no exception.

Against people expecting a break-up of American society into subcultural clusters of race, religion, ethnicity and gender – a process supposedly reinforced by a fragmented media system of countless cable channels and Internet sites – Meyrowitz and Maguire have contended that 'the current trend is towards integration of all groups into a relatively common experiential sphere – with a new recognition of the special needs and idiosyncrasies of individuals' (1993: 43). According to them, television and other electronic media have made the divisions between social groups

188

more visible and permeable. 'Current media, then, continue a trend towards greater homogenization in one way and greater fragmentation in another. Traditional groups are bypassed in both directions: individuals experience more diversity and choice, but traditional group cultures are overlapping, losing identity and blurring into each other' (p. 45). This goes for broadcasting as well as for (new media) narrowcasting. Television has bridged the lives of people living in different physical and informational spheres. The Internet goes even further in offering the opportunity to connect by direct interaction with both people of the same origin and different people or environments.

So, we also may observe a *duality of media structure* closely corresponding to the duality of social structure in society. According to 'medium theory' (Meyrowitz, 1985, 1997), media have their own characteristics, producing social contexts that foster certain forms of interaction and social identity.

They are both defining and enabling, just like the communication capacities described in Chapter 1. Meyrowitz claims that oral media in traditional societies fostered a homogenization of relatively small communities ('us against them'). Opposed to this, the diversity of print media in early modern societies produced a compartmentalization and specialization of social groups and simultaneously supported the unification of nations by a single official language. This duality returns in the history of broadcasting. At first, radio and TV unified national and local societies with a single or a few network(s). After the multiplication of channels and the advent of pay TV, audiences became fragmented again, while keeping many similarities and overlaps. For example, audiences actually choose a handful of broadcasting channels among a much larger number, and broadcasters or advertisers still prefer the mass market (the common denominator).

In the new media, the duality of media structure increases once again. They are both mass and interpersonal media and they offer new types of media in between, for example, the social media discussed in the previous section. The new media are individualizing media, mainly because they are based upon individual human–computer interaction, and they are media to be used collectively as these computers are connected in networks. The huge plurality of potential applications enables both divisions and commonalities among users and audiences. So, the actual result of the duality of media structure is defined by the unifying and fragmenting trends in society, in other words the duality of social structure.

The reconstruction of public space

These dualities can also be used in a response to an urgent question: will the new media primarily bring us together, or will they tear us further apart? This is a question about the future of the public sphere, that we will call public *space* here – an abstract concept to be distinguished from concrete public *places*. The most popular answer to this question emphasizes fragmentation as well. The reasons are evident. At first sight, three conditions of modern public space, as we came to know it in the 20th century, disappear in the new media environment:

Conditions of modern public Sphere } that disappear in the New Media environ.

1 the alliance of public space with a particular place or territory;

2 the presumed unitary character of public space;

3 a relatively sharp public–private distinction.

A short explanation will be sufficient here. As to the first condition, members of a particular community or nation are no longer tied to a given territory to meet each other and build collectivities. Public spaces are no longer confined to the street, the market, the coffee house or pub; there are innumerable public spaces now, both offline and online. People might use old media such as the press, the telephone or satellite broadcasting, and new media such as the Internet to (re)construct their own public space and form imagined communities (Anderson, 1983) or virtual communities.

Second, what binds people in contemporary public space is not a fixed number of common situations, views, habits and other social, cultural and political characteristics. It is an extremely diversified and shifting complex of overlapping similarities and differences, particularly in the growing number of multicultural societies. The 'common ground' of the unitary nation or mass society is an idea from the age of national broadcasting through a few channels. It is still rooted in the minds of the intellectual political and media elite of the nations concerned, though it was never firmly based in reality (Keane, 1995; Meyrowitz and Maguire, 1993).

Finally, the imagined borders of every public space in modern society become blurred, as has been demonstrated in many earlier sections. Public affairs become private in home television viewing, radio listening and surfing the Internet. The private becomes public in the pouring out of intimate affairs in talk shows and reality TV, in the personalization of politics on TV and on Facebook or Twitter. The new media, the Internet in particular, add a new dimension to the blurring public–private distinction as new kinds of association and communication appear between inter-personal and mass communication as we have seen in the section on social media.

Does this mean that the three conditions of modern public space will disappear completely and that all common ground for societies at large will dissolve? No, it just means that the conventional idea of a single, unified public space, and the accompanying ideas of a distinctive public opinion, a common public good and a particular public–private distinction, are obsolete (see Keane, 1995). Instead we get a 'complex mosaic of differently sized overlapping and interconnected public spheres' (1995: 8). The Internet itself, with its hyperlink structure of connections and its numerous overlapping discussion forums and Twitter exchanges, is a perfect model of this mosaic. The rise of the social media has added many other venues to this differentiated public space. Presently, on Twitter, Facebook, YouTube and in blogs, social, political and cultural discussions are going on that overlap and are linked to both older mass media and the street. These days, public spaces appear on radio, TV and the press, on blogs, in Twitter exchanges or moderated online forums and on street markets, terraces and pop festivals. And all of them are linked, both online and offline. In the mass media an increasing number of cross-references and cross-fertilizations appear between new and old media, such as newspapers and television programmes referring to websites and vice versa. I would like to conclude that public space has flourished as never before.

However, contemporary public spaces are far more privatized than they used to be (Papacharissi, 2010). This happens more on account of the development of (at least) western society that is individualizing than by means of the Internet. Types of societal participation have been changing: they went from institutional to personal participation and from physical to mediated participation. This trend precedes the Internet; it is only reinforced by the arrival of this medium (van Dijk, 2010c). Institutional participation entails membership of political parties, trade unions, churches or other large-scale societal organizations, voting or working for these organizations and attending their meetings. This kind of participation has steadily been replaced by a more personal kind that is no more or less than an epiphenomenon of individualization. Personal characteristics, interests or concerns are deciding, not group identities given by birth and kept all life. Conversely, these persons approach societal organizations in a functional way from a personal view and interest. They do not become members, but they draw their cheque-books. Nevertheless, the Internet does enable individualized citizens to keep in touch with these organizations and society at large, much better than before. They are able to be kept informed, to exchange knowledge and to discuss views with other individuals more than ever before.

So, the three conditions mentioned will reappear in different forms. We will get a new type of social cohesion and a far more complicated public space with contours we cannot exactly anticipate yet. The public–private distinction may blur, but it will not vanish. New distinctions will be negotiated in struggles for privacy and personal autonomy. Internet users will create new dividing lines between public and private life or between working and leisure time. Among others they will make new distinctions between private and public parts of SNS. Finally, public communication will be less tied to the parameters of time, place and territory than ever before. But this does not mean that place, propinquity and face-to-face communication are no longer relevant (see following chapters).

The argument in this section is summarized in Box 7.3.

old v. new public space

BOX 7.3
Old and new public space

Old public space	New public space
Alliance of public space with a particular public place or territory	Public space as a multitude of online and offline spaces
Supposedly unitary character of public space	A mosaic of different, but overlapping public spaces
Relatively sharp public–private distinction	Public–private distinction blurred by individualization in public space

NETWORKS AND SOCIAL (IN)EQUALITY
Uneven and combined global development

Contemporary globalization of production, distribution and consumption is a process of uneven and combined development. From the command centres of transnational corporations and developed states, the division of labour (a number of relations) is becoming more selective and more encompassing than ever before (see Barnett et al., 1998). Media networks are the most important infrastructure for this process (see Chapters 2 and 4). Nowadays, information processing is spread globally. Philippine programmers produce online software ordered by American companies: they may be paid only a third of what programmers in the United States demand as a salary. Indian call-centre operators serve the whole English speaking world because they are relatively cheap. Considering the role of ICTs, uneven and combined development is a direct consequence of the first law of the Web – the law of network articulation: relations gain importance as compared to the units they are linking (see Chapter 2). The process is also related to the law of network extension as it reveals a particular combination of scale extension and scale reduction.

At first sight, the examples given appear to add to the diffusion of employment and therefore to social equality worldwide. In fact, the positive effects of this transfer of employment to less developed countries are disappointing, since this kind of employment is highly selective and limited. The tasks are designed from the perspective of the needs and interests of the centre and not from the perspective of a better organic development of the region concerned. Therefore, we might observe increasing differences in the number of telephone and Internet connections between rich and poor countries, while at the same time the latter are being connected to ultramodern international networks.

The negative effects of this transfer of employment for the developed countries, on the other hand, may be greater than expected because simple industrial and administrative work is disappearing rapidly. Moreover, it could add to a further segmentation of the labour market in western countries. This process is sometimes referred to as the First World countries partly resembling the Third World (Castells, 1998): in developed countries, there are enclaves of economic activity with conditions close to those of the Third World. The employment structure created is characterized by high-quality jobs at the centre, usually in a western or east Asian capital, carefully selected according to criteria of logistics and management. Simultaneously, it is marked by relatively low-skilled jobs at the periphery of the system, selected just as carefully and located all over the world.

This network economy stands alone as a system within traditional economic environments: global relations are lifted from the organic environments of the units they are linking. Streams of products, goods, services and information initially flow *inside* (inter)national networks. This observation is crucial for any regional or national economic policy and for every local geographic plan (see Harrison, 1994). The importance of spatial frontiers and proximate areas decreases in a global network economy, though the selectivity of space increases for the structure as a whole. This structure does not seem to 'care' that millions of unemployed Indians live around Bangalore, as long as this region provides sufficient cheap software programmers and call-centre operators with direct connections to the global communication networks. Actually, it would 'prefer' such unemployment because it keeps the wages of programmers and operators low.

The result of this global network structure is diffusion and division of jobs all over the world (combined development). These days there are computer programmers almost everywhere, and even the poorest country is connected to the Internet. At the same time, the quantity and quality of jobs in the global economy across countries and regions is becoming more unequal (unequal development). Without measures that help to increase the spill-over of wealth created in the enclaves of the global economy into their local environment, these inequalities will increase. Moreover, the spatial distance between the poor and rich parts of the global networked economy is decreasing. For example, top executives, high-tech specialists and financial experts, when coming home from work, run into beggars on the street and people working in sweatshops. This might have great consequences for social cohesion in a particular area. Think about the London riots in 2011: in this city the enormous wealth and over-abundance of consumer society are less than a mile removed from the extreme poverty of people who see this wealth all day but have no access to it.

type of employment > extent

The class structure of the network society

Regarding the subject of social inequality, the *type* of employment being created or disappearing is even more important than the extent. In the broadest sense, we will have to deal with the question of the influence of networks on *class structure*. This question first appeared in this book in Chapter 5, when the future of middle management in organizations was discussed. Following Erik Olin Wright (1985), I want to define social classes with the dimensions of (a) ownership of means of production; (b) control of organization; and (c) ownership of skills and qualifications.

social classes defined by:

As we have seen before, the Internet offers relatively cheap means of production. On this network it has become easier to start one's own business. Freelance work also offers more jobs. Obviously, the decentralization of production leads to an increase in the number of formally independent companies, agencies and workers. In the ICT sector, they relatively often consist of one or a few persons. Many independent companies are created in service provision, consultancy, research, software programming and creative design. Richard Florida (2003) has called them the *creative class*. There is no great barrier that prevents people from entering the market: only a single network connection and a small amount of starting capital are needed. The most important asset required is a number of skills (see below). However, only a fairly small minority is really successful in exploiting

independent companies creative class

inequalities
b/c of technology

these accessible means of production. Those are the ones with a fast growing business or a business that is taken over by larger companies after a short period of time. Concentration in the media sector continues to grow (see Chapters 4 and 8). Inequality is huge among independent companies and workers. Many small companies and freelancers earn less than people with a steady job, particularly in times of economic recession.

In Chapter 5, we saw how the use of networks is able to change the ways organizations are controlled. Traditional middle management and supervision are replaced by top executives and technical staff controlling the organization with information systems on the one hand, and executive personnel working with the same systems on the other hand. A polarization between top management and technical staff with increased power to control, and executive staff working with a selective, electronically controlled set of tasks and under flexible conditions, is the most likely development. Other possibilities were described in the same chapter, but this one is the most likely. However, in all cases, supervisors and middle managers are replaced by technicians and information staff managing and maintaining networks. If this observation is correct, the use of networks will increase the almost unbridgeable gap between groups of employees with different skills and qualifications that is starting to appear in larger organizations. Promotion within the organization, from the bottom of the shop floor to top management via supervisory work and middle management, will become nearly impossible.

So, acquiring skills and qualifications will be even more important than it used to be. In any case, having many digital skills offers a skill premium in the level of wages (Goldin and Katz, 2008; Nahuis and de Groot, 2003). Differences of digital skills possessed will create more inequality on the labour market – see the next section. At first sight, ICTs seem to create a lot of high-skilled jobs and make low-skilled ones redundant, particularly in transportation and administration. Generally speaking, the complexity and autonomy of labour in the information and network society are increasing with the rising use of ICTs, according to empirical research in the Netherlands (Steijn, 2001). The more one uses ICT on the job, the higher the complexity and autonomy of the job with the exception of data entry and the like (2001: 105).

However, the last observation points at something particularly important: polarization. When considering individual positions, one also is able to observe a polarization of the consequences of ICT for the different types of labour.

> With regard to autonomy on the job, it is primarily managers and professionals who produce a high score; service personnel and semi-professionals show relatively low scores. Concerning complexity, the scores of (chiefly) managers, professionals, and semi-professionals are high, and the scores of commercial and service personnel and manual labourers are low (Steijn, 2001: 108, my translation).

We can draw two conclusions from these findings. The first conclusion is that not having access to ICTs on the job, or using them less, provides fewer opportunities for increasing the quality of labour (complexity, autonomy, acquisition of skills) for the employees concerned. The second conclusion is that having access to ICTs on the job and using them more extensively can have very divergent consequences for a user's labour position and content, depending on the type of labour organization and labour function. Entering data all day and working with spreadsheets and databases is a type of ICT labour that is completely different from working with advanced search systems and decision support systems, designing programs, or programming software.

It is well known that the number of women is lower in the first segment (i.e. the high quality jobs at the centre) than in the second. An important part of 'female' employment, in administrative and partly in low-skilled commercial work, may even disappear from the second segment. But apart from this, female employment is not particularly threatened by the introduction of networks. Other sectors employing mainly women, such as care and education, cannot easily be fully automated and transferred to self-service. We can expect an increase in employment for women in these sectors. Much more important for the future of 'female' employment, and from an emancipatory point of view, is the estimation that network society will increasingly require a lot of communicative, didactic and commercial skills. In the next section we will see that females have equal digital skills as compared to males. However, in communicative, didactic and commercial skills they might be better according to current divisions of labour, gender roles and gender identities. Precisely these skills are gaining importance in all segments of the job market in the network society. So, the position of women on the labour market of the future might be better than it was in the 20th century.

The future is considerably less bright for migrants and ethnic minorities with low education in a network society dominated by natives and ethnic majorities. Computer networks offer strong assets for migrants and ethnic minorities because they support communication and organization at a distance. However, many lack digital skills and, what is worse, they do not speak or command the native or dominant language sufficiently. So, they run the risk of missing out on the technical and communicative skills required in a network society. The major handicap is having insufficient command of the majority language. The only exception is to be able to speak and write in English. Without the command of either the majority language or the English language in a particular country, one is not even able to do simple terminal work at the level of data entry.

THE DIGITAL DIVIDE

Causes and consequences of the digital divide

This section summarizes the main themes of a book I previously published (*The Deepening Divide, Inequality in the Information Society*, van Dijk, 2005) and of a book I will publish shortly: *Digital Skills: The Key to the Information Society*, van Dijk and van Deursen (forthcoming). At the end of the 1990s, a new term appeared in the discussion about the consequences of the new media for society: the digital divide. Commonly, the digital divide is defined as the gap between those who do and do not have access to computers and the Internet. While the focus in the previous section was on social classes and groups, here the attention shifts to individuals, including their relationships with other individuals.

My research and analysis of the digital divide has the following characteristics. First, a distinction is made between four successive kinds of access to the new media or ICTs. These are: motivation; material or physical access; skills and usage, a distinction to be explained below. Second, the causes and consequences of inequalities to be observed with these kinds of access are made explicit in a theory of inequality in the information and network society. I start with the second characteristic, with a theory I call *resources and appropriation theory* (van Dijk, 2005).

The direct cause of unequal access to digital technology in society is the distribution of a large number of resources. These are not only material resources, such as income and the possession of equipment, but also temporal resources (having the time to use the new media), mental resources (sufficient technical knowledge), social resources (networks and ties that help to attain access) and cultural resources (the status and other cultural rewards that motivate people to get access). The way these resources are distributed among people can be explained by a large number of personal and positional inequalities in society. Personal inequalities are age, sex, ethnicity, intelligence, personality and health or disability. Positional inequalities are defined by a particular job or occupation, a specific level of education and a life in a poor or affluent country and in a particular household role (parent or child, husband or wife). All these inequalities appear to be related to the amount of access different people have to the new media (van Dijk, 2005).

The potential of access to a particular medium is also shaped by the technological characteristics of the medium concerned. Access to TV sets and telephones is not the same as access to computers and networks. All media have characteristics supporting and impeding access. Computers and their networks support access because they are multi-purpose or multi-functional technologies enabling all kinds of information, communication, transaction, work, education and entertainment. So, there are useful applications for everybody. Moreover, the extension of networks produces network effects: the more people gain access, the more valuable a connection becomes. However, multi-functionality also results in extremely different applications, both advanced, with many opportunities to learn and build a career, and simple, mainly focused on entertainment. Other characteristics decreasing equality of access are the complexity, expensiveness and lack of user-friendliness of many contemporary new media.

The consequences of unequal access to ICTs can be conceived as more or less participation in the most important fields of society (van Dijk, 2005). It can be shown that new media access is necessary for an increasing number of jobs, for making progress in almost every career on the labour market and to start one's own business. In social networking, access is required to create new ties and to maintain old ties, as explained earlier in this chapter. Those without access will be isolated in future society. In spatial terms, these people will stick to local opportunities for jobs and social and sexual relationships. They will have to leave the most promising opportunities to mobile people conversant with digital media. In the cultural field, those without access will not be able to benefit from the many splendid applications and types of expression offered by digital culture (see Chapter 8). In politics, citizens who have access are participating relatively more in government, political organizations and all other bodies of public decision-making in society. Finally, even the institutional participation of citizens (equal access to social benefits, scarce public resources and future electronic polls) may be affected.

Unequal participation in all these fields of society reinforces the existing personal and positional inequalities and unequal distribution of resources. Here both a power law and the law of trend amplification are at work, as I will explain below. After all, the new media are important new tools (resources) that help people to obtain better positions in society and to improve their personal characteristics in relation to others, particularly in relationships of power.

Four successive types of access

In the early years of the discussion and investigation of the digital divide, the concept of access was confined to physical access to computers, the Internet and other digital media. Most people thought that the digital divide would be closed as soon as everyone had a computer and Internet connection at home, or was able to use them at a public place. After a while, a number of critics appealed for going beyond access and emphasizing the use and the skills needed to apply digital media. This has been called *the second level divide* (Hargittai, 2002, 2004). In fact, the digital divide and the question of differential media access are even more complicated than these critics have suggested. In a series of publications (van Dijk, 1997b, 2000b, 2004; van Dijk and Hacker, 2003) I have distinguished four successive kinds of new media access as portrayed in Figure 7.3, which is explained in the following paragraphs.

second level divide = divide based on used skills of digital media

Motivation for access ①

The process of appropriating the new technology starts with the motivation to achieve access. Motivation influences the decision to purchase a computer and network connection, to learn the requisite skills, and to use the interesting applications. Some people are not sufficiently motivated. They may be people who do not want to use computers because they do not like them or even fear them (suffering so-called computer anxiety or perhaps even 'technophobia'). Others have used computers and the Internet in the past, but have stopped using them, or they have only temporarily used them. Finally, there are people who have no real choice or opportunity to obtain access to computers and the Internet because they lack the material means or the mental and educational capacities. They are the truly

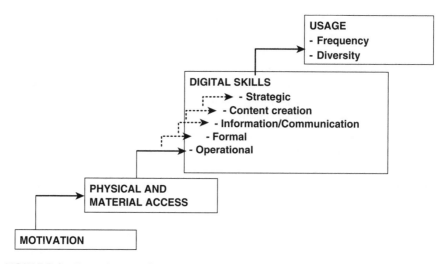

FIGURE 7.3 Four stages of access to digital technology

unconnected. The dividing line between the 'want-nots' and the 'have-nots' is not sharp and it is ever shifting.

The direct causes of this lack of motivation may be insufficient temporal, mental, material, social and cultural resources. They are a lack of time, of technical knowledge and affinity, of money, of social relations that inspire and help people to appropriate new technologies and of cultural lifestyles and identities that fit to computer and Internet use. In their turn, the lack or the availability of these resources are explained by personal inequalities first of all. It is well known that, on average, young people and males are more motivated to adopt and use computers and the Internet than elderly people and (older) females. Intelligence and personality also count (Finn and Korukonda, 2004; Hudiburg et al., 1999). Positional inequalities are less important for motivation. Nevertheless, having or wanting a particular job or education urges people to obtain access. The same goes for inhabitants of high-tech countries where it is becoming obligatory to have a computer and Internet connection.

Physical and material access ②

After acquiring the motivation to get access, the challenge for new users is to act on it. They may purchase a computer and Internet connection themselves, or they may use those of others. This may be done privately at work or at school, or with family and friends, or in public places at a particular access point. Public opinion, public policy, and all kinds of research are strongly preoccupied with this second kind of access that I call physical or material access. Many people think the digital divide will be closed as soon as everyone has a computer and a connection to the Internet. This is completely wrong because inequalities in other types of access will come to the fore. However, physical or material access remains a necessary condition for the other types of access: the requisite skills and the actual use of the technology. Material access is broader than physical access: it not only refers to the opportunity to use computers and the Internet at a particular place, but also to access particular channels, programs or sources of information. Increasingly, this is limited by conditional access when subscriptions have to be paid for always-on facilities and when the familiar screens of user name and password appear.

It can be shown that in the period between 1985 and 2000, all divides of physical access to computers and the Internet increased in both the developed and developing countries (van Dijk, 2005), except for the gender gap and the gap between people with and without disability. However, after the turn of the century, in most developed countries, the categories with relatively high physical access entered a phase of saturation, while the categories with low physical access, which had started later, have been catching up fast. This means that the physical access divide concerning basic computer and Internet technology is closing in the developed countries. Conversely, this divide keeps widening in the developing countries as long as the high access categories grow faster than the low access categories (ibid.).

The most important resources enabling material or physical access are material resources (household income), temporal resources (sufficient time to work with computers) and social resources (a social network that inspires and helps people to obtain access). Decisive positional categories appear to be the labour market and educational positions (having a particular job or schooling), followed by the contextual positions of being part of a particular type of household (for example, with school-going children) and a developed country or region. The most significant personal category appears to be age, followed by gender and disability (all data published in van Dijk, 2005).

Digital skills

After having acquired the motivation to use computers and some kind of physical access to them, one has to learn to manage the hardware and software. For this purpose, at least two types of technical digital skills are needed: operational skills and formal skills. They are called medium-related skills here because every medium requires different skills to use it: reading a book is different from browsing the Internet. However, to benefit from medium use every medium also asks for more substantial content-related skills: information and communication skills, strategic skills and content creation skills. My definition of *digital skills* is the collection of skills needed to operate computers and the Internet, to search and select information in them, to communicate with them, and to use them for one's own purposes, for example, by the creation of new web content. Box 7.4 lists the definitions of these six types of skills (van Dijk and van Deursen, forthcoming).

> ## BOX 7.4
> ## Media-related and content-related digital skills
>
> **Media related**
> - *Operational skills*: successfully operating digital media ('button knowledge')
> - *Formal skills*: mastering formal structures – file and menu structures, web-browsing and navigating
>
> **Content related**
> - *Information skills*: valid search, selection and evaluation of digital media content
> - *Communication skills*: being effective in the exchange of meaning via digital media, e.g. email, chat, designing profiles in SNS
> - *Content-creation skills*: being able to contribute acceptable software, websites, blogs, Tweets, postings, profiles, etc.
> - *Strategic skills*: being able to use digital media as a means for a particular personal or professional goal

In a series of performance tests in a media lab at the University of Twente, a cross-section of the Dutch population – more than 300 subjects – were given 90 minutes to undertake nine big Internet tasks supposed to reveal different kinds of digital skills. It was found that, overall, the operational and formal skills tasks in using the Internet were performed better than the content-related skills (van Deursen, 2010; van Deursen and van Dijk, 2009, 2011, van Deursen, van Dijk and Peters, 2011). All types of skill tasks were performed significantly better by people with higher education. In content-related skills, the gap was bigger than in medium-related skills. Males and females scored approximately the same in all skills. Considering age, a spectacular observation was made. Young people scored much better on operational and formal Internet skills than people with medium age and seniors. However, the older generations were better in information and strategic skills – other content-related skills were not measured in these experiments – provided that they possessed an adequate level of operational and formal skills. This observation puts popular talk about the so-called 'digital generation' in quite another perspective – see the following chapter.

The series of performance tests, that continues at the time of writing, repeatedly shows that the six types of digital skills applied to Internet skills expose a rising level of inequality (from top to bottom in Box 7.4). Most inequality is in the content-related information and communication skills, the content-creation skills (in the context of Web 2.0) and the strategic skills. Those having a high level of traditional

[handwritten margin note: skill tasks performance]

[handwritten note at bottom: where you see most inequality↑]

literacy also possess a high level of these content-related digital skills. Obviously, this type of inequality rests more on the distribution of mental than of material resources. However, the second most important type of resource for digital skills is social and cultural resources. The social context of computer and Internet users is a decisive factor in the opportunities people have for learning digital skills. They learn more from practice and their everyday social environment than from formal computer education and guidance.

Both positional and personal categorical inequalities are responsible for the unequal distribution of these resources. The positional categories of having a particular education and employment define the social contexts that enable computer and Internet users to learn digital skills in practice. The personal categories of age and level of education appear to be the strongest individual determinants of digital skills (van Deursen, 2010).

Usage

The fourth kind of access may be called usage access. This is the ultimate aim of the appropriation of any new technology. The kinds of access described above are necessary, but not sufficient conditions of usage. A user may be motivated to use computers and the Internet, have access to them physically, and command the digital skills necessary to use them, but nevertheless have no need, occasion, obligation, or time, or make no effort to actually use them. Usage data indicate that many skilful users only use their computers and Internet connections once or twice a week. Usage access has its own grounds, although the resources and positional or personal categories concerned overlap with those determining the other kinds of access. Candidates for explanation might be a particular job or school training, a certain level of education and age.

Usage access can be measured in a number of ways. First, actual use can be observed, because having a computer and an Internet connection does not have to mean that they are used. Second, usage time and frequency can be observed in time-diary studies or surveys. Third, the diversity or the type of applications used on computers and the Internet can be listed. The final ways to investigate usage are to look for more advanced types of computer and Internet use by means of content creation.

Digital divide research after the year 2000 has shown that the divides of motivation and physical access have narrowed in the developed countries (van Dijk, 2006). Currently, the big majority in these countries has a very high motivation to have access to computers and the Internet. Some countries already have physical access rates far above 90 per cent. However, the situation in terms of digital skills and the amount and variety of usage is completely different. Here gaps persist and some of them even widen. The situation is very complicated. The level of operational and formal digital skills is rising while the level of content-related skills, such as information and strategic skills, is not, or it is distributed extremely unevenly between people with high and low education. As we have seen, young people may be good in operational and formal skills but not in information and strategic skills.

In terms of usage, the situation is even more diversified. Clearly, the Internet is getting ever more popular among the population as a whole in the developed countries. In the year 2010, some kind of 'social revolution' of Internet use was observed in the Netherlands (home Internet access rate of 94 per cent in 2011). For the first time in history, people with low education used the Internet more hours a day than people with high education, the precise opposite from the 20–30 years before (van Deursen and van Dijk, 2010, forthcoming) However, the differences in types of Internet application remained pronounced. People with low education significantly used more chatting, gaming, SNS and online market places – applications requiring more time – while people with high education preferably used more news, government or travel services and tele-working (ibid.). The differences of using particular Internet applications between the younger and the older generations, and between males and females, were even bigger (see below). My expectation is that with increasing Internet popularity, all existing socio-cultural differentiations in society will be reflected in Internet use and, by means of this use they will be reinforced, instead of reduced (according to the law of trend amplification).

The material and mental resources that are decisive for physical access and digital skills are less important for usage. Here, temporal, social and cultural resources, lifestyles included, come to the fore. The personal categories of age, sex, race, intelligence, personality, and health or ability primarily account for the differences observed.

The appearance of usage gaps

One of the most revealing facts about inequalities of usage is the diversity of computer and Internet use by all positional and personal categories of people. Here, all inequalities in the other kinds of access discussed above come together. Subsequently, they are mixed with all existing economic, social, cultural and political inequalities in society. In the first 1999 English edition of this book, I proposed the thesis of a *usage gap* of people with different educational backgrounds using different types of Internet applications that looks like the *knowledge gap* thesis considering mass media use of the 1970s (Tichenor et al., 1970). Similar observations supported by survey data have also been made by others (Bonfadelli, 2002; Bunz, 2009; Howard et al. 2001; Madden, 2003; van Dijk and Hacker, 2003; Zillien and Hargittai 2009). The common denominator in all these studies is that people with better social positions and higher education use significantly more so-called information and career-related Internet applications that help them forwards in their work, careers, business and studies while people with the lesser positions and lower education use more entertainment applications. In a 2011 study, van Deursen and van Dijk made a distinction between information and news, education and career, social communication and entertainment and shopping and commerce Internet applications being four clusters of 15 applications of a total of 31 observed (van Deursen and van Dijk, forthcoming) – see Box 7.5.

BOX 7.5
Clusters of Internet applications with a particular usage purpose

Information and News

- using search engines
- using news services
- reading online newspapers or magazines

Education and Careers

- following online courses
- independent learning
- finding online courses and training
- searching for job vacancies

Social Communication and Entertainment

- chatting
- using social networking sites
- online gaming
- downloading music or video
- uploading music or video

Shopping and Commerce

- online shopping
- searching products and comparing prices
- using eBay (and other auctions)

In this Dutch study an education, age, gender and Internet experience usage gap was observed. Contrary to the expectations of the investigators the usage gaps of age and gender were bigger than the education gap. The education gap was largely supported because people with higher education used significantly more information, news, education and career applications while people with lower education used the social communication and entertainment applications more, which are listed in Box 7.5. However, the gap was bigger among people from different age groups. Young people use all the applications listed more than seniors. The gender gap was pronounced too: (Dutch) females were more likely to use the Internet for social communication and entertainment functions with the exception of up- and downloading music and video files that is done much more by (young) males. (van Deursen and van Dijk, forthcoming). At first sight the usage gap looks similar to the classic *knowledge gap:* 'As the diffusion of mass media information into a social system increases, segments of the population with a higher socio-economic status tend to acquire this information at a faster rate than the lower status segments' (Tichenor et al., 1970: 159). However, the knowledge gap is only about the differential diffusion and development of *knowledge or information.* While traditional media enable active mental processing, the Internet requires users to interact with interfaces. A minimum level of active engagement with the medium is required, and the possibility of interactions, transactions, and interpersonal communication is offered. Using the Internet constitutes *action, interaction and transaction.* So, the usage gap has a much broader scope than the knowledge gap.

The appearance of a usage gap, particularly an education gap and an Internet experience gap supports the assumption that those who already have a large amount of resources at their disposal benefit first and most from the capacities and opportunities of the new media. This phenomenon has been called the 'Matthew effect' by the sociologist Robert Merton (1968), because according to the Gospel of Matthew: 'For to everyone who has, more shall be given' (Matt. 25:29, New American). A popular version of this might be: 'The rich get richer.' This phenomenon is an instance of the power law of the Web that was explained in Chapter 2.

The tripartite network society

The important point is that usage gaps are likely to grow, instead of decline, with the larger distribution of computers and networks among the population. Concurrent with the popularization of Internet use that makes usage times of the Internet more equally distributed, the type of usage is diversified. Existing social and cultural diversities and inequalities are intensified (as an instance of the law of trend amplification). If this turns out to be true, the difference between advanced or serious types of use contributing to careers and social advance on the one side and relatively simple and entertainment uses for daily consumption will increase. The consequences of this systematic pattern of unequal use will be more or less participation in all relevant fields of contemporary and future society, first of all the job market (see van Dijk, 2005 for more arguments and data). Increasingly, the old media and face-to-face communications will become inadequate means of full participation in society. Progressively, more people will be completely excluded from particular fields of society when they do not have Internet access or have a low level of digital skills using only the simplest of applications. The result will be first, second, and third-class citizens, consumers, workers, students, and community members.

This division would mean structural inequality. What exactly is *structural*? Absolute exclusion from the network society and new media use is a clear case of structural inequality that can be demonstrated empirically. It can be shown that people who have no access to computers and the Internet whatsoever have less chance on the labour market and less educational opportunities (van Dijk, 2005). It can also be demonstrated that a complete lack of Internet access will lead to shrinking social networks and cultural resources. This lack will also give them less chances of participation in politics and citizenship entitlements such as public benefits and healthcare (van Dijk, 2005).

The effects of relative exclusion, which means having less motivation, physical or material access, digital skills and usage than other parts of the population, are more difficult to demonstrate, as they require detailed investigations into the amount of participation in particular fields of society and its consequences for specific positions of affluence and influence. However, in the long run, relative exclusion can also lead to clearly perceptible structural inequalities.

Structural inequality appears when, on the one hand, an 'information elite' strengthens its position, while, on the other hand, those groups already living on the margins of society become excluded from communications in society because these are practiced in media they do not possess or control. The differences become structural when the positions people occupy in networks and other media determine whether they have any influence on decisions made in several fields of society. Here we can refer to Chapter 5, which explains the importance of positions in networks for the exercise of power.

So, the picture is not the usual simple one of a two-tiered society, or of a gap between information 'haves' and 'have-nots' as two clearly separate groups of the population. On the contrary, the pattern described is increasingly complex social, economic and cultural differentiation. A better representation would be a continuum or spectrum of differentiated positions across the population, with the 'information elite' at the top, a more or less participating majority of the population in the middle, and a group of 'excluded people' at the bottom.

The digital divide amplifies such a situation of structural inequality that was already growing before (van Dijk, 2005). It can be portrayed in a simplified picture of a tripartite, instead of a two-tiered, network society (see Figure 7.4). This diagram sketches a (developed) society with an information elite of about 15 per cent of the population; a majority of a variable size that participates to a certain extent in all relevant fields of society, with both social and media networks; and a class of outsiders that is excluded from the new media networks and has a relatively small social network. The information elite, in the first ring, consists of people with high levels of education and income, the best jobs and societal positions, and a nearly 100 per cent access to ICTs. This elite in fact makes all important decisions in society. It lives in dense social networks extending to a large number of strategically important long-distance ties. Most people belonging to this elite are heavy users of computers and the Internet. Some of them form a 'broadband elite' that continually works with these media and perhaps uses more than ten different types of applications each day.

In a second ring we find the majority of the population, which participates significantly less. It contains a large part of the middle class and the working class. This majority *does* have access to computers and the Internet, but possesses fewer digital skills than the elite – information, communication and strategic skills in particular. Moreover, it uses fewer and less diverse applications. These applications are less focused on a career, a job, study, or other ambition and more on recreational and entertainment uses. The majority has a smaller social network and fewer weak ties spanning large distances.

Largely excluded from participation in several fields of society and having no access to computers and the Internet, voluntarily or not, we find the unconnected and excluded outside the rings of the drawing. They comprise 20 to 30 per cent of the populations of (even) the most advanced high-tech societies. Increasingly, they consist of the lowest social classes, particular ethnic minorities, and a majority of (new) immigrants. At this stage of new media diffusion, the unconnected still contain a large proportion of elderly people, some of higher social class, but isolated socially and without access to computers and the Internet.

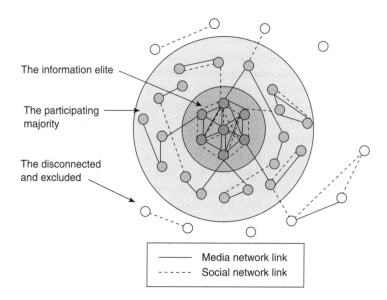

The information elite

The participating majority

The disconnected and excluded

Media network link
Social network link

FIGURE 7.4 Tripartite participation in the network society

THE INSTABILITY OF THE NETWORK SOCIETY

A network society under tension

Reading the previous sections, it becomes obvious that the structure of the network society is full of opposing tendencies. Space and time become both less and more important. Moreover, global and local spaces and times are both merging and clashing. The traditional distinction between public and private spaces is both dissolving and reconstructed in new ways. Social media blur interpersonal and mass communication. In general, networks are both spreading resources and dividing them more unequally than before.

As a general tendency, the laws of the Web, as discussed in this book, articulate social structures and intensify or even polarize them. This puts unknown pressures on the social system as a whole. By nature, the network society is an unstable social system. The reason for this instability is not only the speed of technological development and the vulnerability of media networks as explained in Chapter 6, it is also caused by the nature of networks as an infrastructure that increasingly organizes society. Before this is explained in a more abstract way, I want to list a number of apparent instabilities of contemporary societies that are reinforced by networks.

Contagion and volatility

In the economy, we cannot ignore the increasing volatility of the stock and currency markets, with sharply rising and falling prices, which puts a continuous pressure on the economy. The exchange of monetary values has surpassed the exchange of goods many times. Electronic networks run this exchange and they reinforce the speeds of prices going upwards and downwards. They have inspired numerous speculative bubbles in stocks and currencies. Crashes in stock markets, currencies and stakes of individual companies are always imminent and they happen increasingly often. They aggravate the periodic recessions and upturns of the capitalist economy and they multiply financial crises. The recent credit crisis was only the last occasion of many. It is most striking that this volatility seems to be more driven by contagion and crowd behaviour than by rational decision-making in buying and selling.

In politics, we can observe the drifting of voters that are less faithful than ever to their favourite parties and political leaders. With the help of the media system, TV in particular, voters jump from one candidate with a strong media appeal to another. Populism is on the rise. Voter drift is not only supported by broadcast networks but also by computer networks, such as the Internet, that serve grass-root or central mobilizing agencies and electronic pressure groups. The image of a political leader can be broken in a few hours when accusations, with or without good reason, spread on TV and the Internet.

In social relationships, increasing connectivity and density of social networking, strongly supported by the social media, cause ever faster changes in the composition of contact lists. Old friends and acquaintances are easily rediscovered and added; existing contacts are 'defriended' in a single keystroke. What happens to 'real friendships' lasting a lifetime?

In culture, existing tensions between subcultures and religions can explode in a few hours when a particular accident or violent attack happens and is broadcasted via television, Facebook and Twitter. Such explosions take far less time than the months or years needed for reconciliation.

In the media, all kinds of rumours, fads, fashions, hypes and innovations are spreading faster than ever before. The diffusion power of broadcasting, telephony and computer networks multiplies the speed of the age-old transmission of gossip and local news in social networks. It leads to all kinds of message cascades. The life-cycle of fashions, hypes and innovations is shorter than ever before. Still, their impact on society rises accordingly. The impact can be measured instantly as the topics of search engines and Tweets reveal what's going on in public opinion in minutes.

In eco-systems, various kinds of human and animal diseases are spreading across the world in a few days via air networks. The same happens, with even greater speed, to viruses and worms in computer systems. The instability of both kinds of systems has increased substantially with their internal transportation speeds and their vulnerability to contagion.

Too much connectivity?

These examples of instability and contagion make us think that we have reached a stadium of too much connectivity. Is this true? In Chapter 2, it was argued that networks increase the adaptive capacity of systems, in this way continually restoring broken stabilities. This would mean that rising connectivity increases adaptive capacity and stability. This happens to be in agreement with the contemporary theory of networks and complex adaptive systems. However, Stuart Kauffman (1993) has shown that while too few connections may result in insufficient change and adaptation of systems, *beyond a particular level, too much connectivity decreases adaptability*. Large networks with thousands of members adapt best with less than ten connections per member. Mulgan (1997: 162) explains that with increasing connectivity 'too much time and energy is spent on them. Conformity spreads too fast and dampens innovations. Watts adds that:

> networks that are not connected enough prohibit global cascades because the cascade has no way of jumping from one vulnerable cluster to another. And networks that are too highly connected prohibit cascades also, but for a different reason: they are locked into a kind of stasis, each node constraining the influence of any other and being constrained itself. (2003: 241)

Let me give an example of this very abstract argument. Observers of Twitter, Facebook and online newspaper discussions following a particular news event may have noticed that these discussions are often running around in their own circles and rarely extend to other discussion environments. Moreover, they hardly ever lead to clear-cut conclusions. Within one or two days they dissipate. Because of too much connectivity inside the clusters where they are going on, these discussion circles are constrained in themselves. When they disagree, discussants run separate ways and perhaps immediately jump to other currently fashionable topics in other discussion environments.

The exchange of ideas may spread too fast because the social contagion of ideas spreads even faster than the biological contagion of diseases. This is driven by the three degrees of influence rule rolling on the waves of the six degrees of separation in the law of small worlds (see Chapter 2). Every single disease contagion is independent from the other and has the same chance of occurring, while social contagion is strongly dependent on the number of others infected by the new idea (Watts, 2003: 223). Traditional hypes or fashions already ran harder and harder in the past, but their speed is multiplied many times in contemporary media networks. Gossip on the Internet spreads in a few hours. In the next chapter it will be observed that this extremely rapid message exchange may lead to the phenomena of information overload and over-communication increasing noise and instability in social systems. Fortunately, too much connectivity is refrained by the law of the limits of attention (see Chapters 2 and 8): a rising number of messages simply cannot be digested.

CONCLUSIONS

- Space and time are becoming not less, but more important in the network society. There is no 'death of distance' and no 'timeless time'. Media networks enable more selectivity to choose the right times and places. Space and time are both expanded and compressed.

Networks connect large scales and small scales, and in between intermediaries serve to realize this connection. This is a consequence of the law of network extension.

- Social and media networks cause a blurring of all spheres of living. However, these spheres continue to exist. Networks only link them more directly than before and this enables more activities in particular places and all activities in mobile spaces. Mobility is not reduced by tele-activity but growing.

- The spectacular rise of the social media is part of the popularization of the Internet. It is explained by latent needs of social networking that were ready to be satisfied when a large part of the population reached Internet access and practiced sharing things on the Web. In the social media, interpersonal and mass communication are merging. This brings both opportunities (identity making, personalized marketing) and risks (privacy loss). The social media strongly contribute to the connectivity of society.

- Public space will not become a unity on account of the increasing density of network links; neither will it be fragmented in all kinds of subcultures. Public space will be reconstructed as a complex mosaic of distinct, but overlapping and interconnected public places. Public space and the idea of a society will continue to exist, albeit in much more differentiated shapes.

- Although networks serve to spread knowledge and information more than ever before, they also tend to increase inequality. They have a polarizing effect on class structure. The digital divide is not closing or widening, it is deepening: gradually the digital divide shifts from inequality of physical access to unequal digital skills and usage patterns. Chances are that a tripartite network society appears consisting of an information elite, a participating majority and an excluded minority.

- The network society is an unstable type of society. This is for the paradoxical reason that it is both too much connected and too much divided. Connectivity increases the volatility of processes and the contagion of opinions, feelings, attitudes and behaviour. Growing divisions produce more social tensions.

CULTURE

About this chapter

- This chapter is about the special characteristics and consequences of digital culture. What is digital culture? Is it only the culture as expressed by people using digital media? Or has the use of digital media also special consequences for our culture and media use in general?

- We will start with having a look at a number of conspicuous appearances of digital culture. The ubiquitous use of screens, the multimedia collage of all kinds of cultural forms, the active and creative contributions of users and the speed of change in cultural practices are striking characteristics. Are they substantially changing our culture at large?

- The quantification of expressions in digital media also catches the eye. Are they leading to a daily overload of information and messages? If there is such an overload, how do we deal with it?

- Clearly, digital media are first explored by young people. A special youth culture has appeared among the so-called 'digital generation'. What are the common patterns of this culture? Are they foreshadows of the future of digital culture and media use in the society as a whole?

- The consequences of digital culture are a number of trends in new media use. For example, digital culture is marked by convergence (multimedia), hypermedia and user-generated content. What are the consequences for media use at large? Will the old media be replaced by a single medium (the Internet) that links them all in digital shapes? In case the Internet 'swallows' all other media, will the result be more media concentration or the opposite: an endless number of media or websites to choose from?

WHAT IS DIGITAL CULTURE?

A culture is a set of coherent values, expectations, expressions and artifacts shared by a group of people. A culture is both a creative process, as it is continually in the making, and a result in the shape of products or artifacts. A digital culture is a creative process and set of products that are made by means of digital media. This definition runs the risk of conflating culture with technology (Deuze, 2006). This is not what I intend to do here emphasizing both the social context of digital culture in the network society (the process) and changes in media use enabled by characteristics of digital media (the result). Charlie Gere (2002) thinks digital culture is not as new as it might appear, and that its development ultimately is not determined by technological advances. However, he also thinks that digital culture does refer to ways of thinking and doing that are embodied within technology (2002: 13).

What is embodied in digital technology that potentially helps to create a new or special culture, called digital? To answer this question we first have to look at the *characteristics or shapes* that digital culture possesses and subsequently whether they influence contents or practices of culture at large. After all, the definition of digital in Chapter 1 also emphasizes forms: digitization means that every item can be translated into separate bytes consisting of strings of 1s and 0s. Admittedly, this is a question about the effect of technology but otherwise we cannot analyze the meaning of 'digital' in the term digital culture and we would only be able to describe the practices of people engaged in using computers, mobile phones, the Internet and other digital media. These practices are called *cyber-culture* among others. In the following section we will start the analysis with a number of appearances characterizing digital culture. Box 8.1 lists these characteristics.

BOX 8.1
Characteristics of digital culture

- Pre-programming and creativity
- Fragmentation
- Re-assembly: collage
- User-generation
- Acceleration
- Visualization
- Quantification

CHARACTERISTICS OF DIGITAL CULTURE

Pre-programming and creativity

In popular literature on the new media, the suggestion is made that these media will create unlimited choice from our sizeable cultural heritage and a new creative potential among the population, as people are enabled to create their own works of art and other products with multimedia. However, the chances that we are dealing with a 'new and original type of work', in the terms of Dutch copyright law, are decreasing. More and more often we will be processing, reworking or adapting things other people have created. This is just the next phase in the evolution of art. In the course of (modern) history, the work of art has been taken away from the artist step by step and put into the hands of consumers. After the era of large-scale technical reproducibility of art (Benjamin, 1968), we are now entering an era enabling people to create their 'own' works of art consisting of all the bits and pieces of the cultural heritage. Multimedia encourage users to make all sorts of video collages and images, to sample and compose pieces of music from a CD, to decide the ending of a film by picking one from several scripts, and to create their own abstract Mondrian-style painting from red, yellow and blue squares. Of course, professional and popular art have always been a matter of reworking and adapting the cultural heritage, but now we are taking one essential step further. Qualitatively more means are inserted between source and result. There is more than pencil, pen and ink on paper and paint on canvas. The means of production offered by digital media are (pre-)programmed themselves and they partly work automatically. They only have to be adapted by the user to gain some craft. The material worked upon is not empty, but it is filled with existing cultural content. In this way, creativity is put in an entirely different perspective. The same can be said of the presumed infinite options in digital media. In fact, the whole thing is about options from a menu, in other words, entirely pre-programmed. Usually, the user is able to make general choices only. Allowing users to choose from details would require too much pre-programming work.

Nevertheless, these options do lead to both a differentiation and a standardization of culture. The amount of content from which one can choose is increasing. At the same time, however, the elements of this content increasingly resemble one another. Everything is arranged in similar (menu) structures. Sources of information that used to be separate are combined in multimedia. Under certain circumstances, this may lead to diluting sources of information and eroding contents (see below).

Fragmentation and collage

Digitization causes a technical division of analogue sources into bits and bytes. This enables an unrestricted division of the content of these sources. Digitalization and processing of analogue sources by multimedia equipment have already had a fragmenting effect on our culture. Michael Heim (1987) pointed out this trend many years ago by analyzing changes in text caused by word processing. Text is provided with a pointed structure. The argument is structured in advance and divided into separate subjects, items and paragraphs.

Items can easily be added or deleted later on – which may result in some loss of the course of the argument. Another example is the structure of the Internet. The content of websites is spread over several pages and images which can all be accessed in one click. In this way, the traditional linear processing of content is replaced by the making of links, jumps and associations.

Finally, we come to the content of pieces of music and films processed by using interactive programs. Interactive music CDs are composed of separate, accumulated layers and fragments that may be easily isolated, manipulated, sampled and (re)combined. This *modularization* quickly causes the unity of a creative work to be lost. For the idea is to give listeners the opportunity to create their own collages. Many traditional artists, designers and producers find this anathema. They think the unique construction and coherence they have made is the essence of their creation. They dissociate themselves from the results obtained by the consumer, or accept them only because it pays to do so.

User-generation

Digitization makes it easier for the users of digital technology to contribute themselves to higher forms of culture such as writing publications, making drawings, pictures and videos and even creations considered to be art. The means of production of these higher forms are spread among larger sections of the population. They require fewer skills to master them than the traditional instruments. This is an opportunity of historical proportions. In the first decades of the evolution of the Internet this was not yet visible because the Internet was in fact a publication medium: an electronic version of print and audio-visual media. With the rise of Web 2.0 this has changed, as we have seen many times before in this book.

It is easy to downgrade the result of user-generated content on the Internet as Andrew Keen (2007) has done, calling it *'the cult of the amateur'*. Keen deplores the decline of traditional quality media by the Internet because their economic position is undermined by ubiquitous free copying. What comes instead, in theory, gives amateurs a voice on the Web. In fact quality is low, whether it concerns information or culture produced. User-generated content does not reduce the remaining gap between professionals and amateurs, it only accentuates this gap.

I would certainly agree with this statement, but stress something different. This is that producing user-generated content is not as widespread and popular as it could be. In 2009, 30 per cent of American Internet users above 18 shared content on the Web, 15 per cent remixed cultural items, 19 percent used Twitter and 11 per cent had a blog (Pew Internet and American Life Project, 2009). In 2010, 43 per cent of Dutch Internet users posted some content on the website of others, 25 per cent on one's own website, 11 per cent on Twitter and eight per cent on one's own blog (van Deursen and van Dijk, 2010). The most popular type of user-generated content was creating a personal profile in an SNS (60 per cent). Evidently, the majority of Internet users prefer the consumption of contents on the Web above their own production. Probably, the prime reasons are a lack of motivation and a lack of digital skills to create (see previous chapter).

Acceleration

Digitization allows a considerable increase in the production, dispersion and consumption of information and the signals of communication. In hardware, 'fast' has become the key word: fast computers, fast modems, fast lines, fast programs. The hunger for speed is never appeased. This gives all the more reason to believe that the popular assumption of the irrelevance of time in the new media is wrong. On the contrary, the importance of time is radicalizing (see Chapter 7). Saving time is immediately followed by new needs to be filled and created.

The need for speed is determined by motives in the economy (maximization of profits on the surplus value of working time in capitalism), the organization (efficiency) and consumption (immediate fulfilment of needs). Driven by a swift increase in technical capacities, these motives call into existence a *culture of speed,* (Miller and Schwarz, 1998; Virilio, 1988). This means our culture changes substantially as well. The following examples may be useful. First, expressions of culture date quickly. Trends follow each other at high speed. In the modern world, various trends exist side by side, competing for popularity. Second, information is sent in increasing amounts, ever more frequently and at ever higher speed just to attract attention. This phenomenon is called information and communication overload (see below). The result is shallowness in the perception of cultural expressions. This is a fact producers are anticipating and reinforcing. Furthermore, communication and language have increased to such a speed that we cannot sit down to think about a message, such as writing a letter or starting a conversation. Instead, we immediately pick up the phone and give ad hoc answers by calls, voicemail, SMS or email. Language also changes under the influence of the new media. This will be discussed in the next chapter. It acquires an abrupt style (like staccato) and contains increasing amounts of jargon with innumerable abbreviations. The final example is the rising importance of images in our culture, a type of data that is presented and consumed much more quickly than the others (speech, text and numbers).

Visualization

The fact that screens are increasingly being used for the *presentation* of cultural content has the most visible and direct effect on human perception and understanding. The screen is everywhere in the network society. It is not merely a medium for reproduction but it increasingly dominates all communication. These days people physically co-present have to fight for the attention of others as screens often call attention for remote sources. Smart-phones and tablets have considerably extended this phenomenon as compared to traditional mobile and fixed phones. Screens have become split-screens of several windows and they have become touch-screens for swapping images. Screens have become the window to our world and our second front door. What are the basic consequences of this visualization in digital culture?

The rise of the screen as a means of communication will lead to a partial replacement of text on paper, of separate audio and of direct physical transmission of signs in face-to-face communication. The last replacement is a much more basic development than the other two. The current replacement of reading printed texts by watching images on screens, together with the transformation of listening to the radio and to audio as a main activity into using them as a background, have been judged far too easily by intellectuals and culture pessimists as signs of blunted culture and losses of creativity and imagination.

The Flemish expert in audiovisual semiotics Jean-Marie Peters (1989, 1996), has convincingly challenged these opinions. Peters (1989) has opposed the popular assumption that watching and understanding images takes only a small mental effort, claiming that all sorts of imaginative thinking are required. Even the simplest image is very complex: it contains a large amount of symbols to be perceived and interpreted simultaneously. Peters has also disputed the idea that an image cannot have any depth, given that readers and listeners are themselves urged to employ abstraction and creativity by calling images to mind. He argues that images have not only the capacity of reproduction and representation, but also symbolic and creative values. Viewers are able to discover and shape these symbolic and creative values themselves (Peters, 1989). From this line of argument, he also challenges the assumption that a culture of images is smothering creativity and imagination. Perhaps people who have been raised in a culture of reading have forgotten how to look properly?

Extending Peters' argument, we may say that the most important problem concerning the replacement of text on paper with audiovisual display is complication, not simplification. Screens will contain large amounts of information. They are able to present image, text, numbers, graphics and visual augmentations of sounds, close to each other and in extremely complex shapes. In audiovisual entertainment, we have already become acquainted with the rise of a 'staccato culture' containing a bombardment of stimuli growing stronger and stronger: brief, flashing, swift and full of action.

Intellectuals or culture pessimists should worry less about the decline of reading and listening in itself than about the decay of a particular kind or method of reading and listening that is called 'deep reading' and 'attentive listening' (see the next chapter). Even in a culture of images, reading and listening will quantitatively increase rather than decrease.

The growing presence of screens in all spheres of living leads to an accumulation of similar activities. Currently, people in developed societies spend more than half of their waking hours watching screens. For example, in 2009 an average American spent at least eight and a half hours a day watching a television, computer monitor or mobile phone screen, So, half of Americans used them even longer (Council for Research Excellence, 2009). Often more than one screen was used simultaneously. According to ergonomists the acceptable amount of working time spent in front of a computer screen is five hours a day, but for many workers the actual amount is far more. An excessive use of screens can have negative consequences in terms of the variety of physical exercise people need, the mental pressure they experience and their attention to face-to-face communication.

Mediated communication is always marked by some kind of adaptation to the technical characteristics of the medium concerned. Obviously this has consequences. The power of screens is the attraction of human attention. The biggest contemporary problem in this regard is that attention is slackening fast. The stimuli offered become ever shorter and more powerful in an attempt to prevent the slackening of attention. Short and impressive news-flashes, fast shots full of action in films or video clips and sparkling shows tend to fragment contents. Background information and reflection disappear or are pushed to the sidelines. They are considered to be boring. According to many media critics, this will result in shallower media content produced and consumed, although we have seen that the form of images is becoming more complicated. A recent example is Nicholas Carr's *The Shallows* (2009) that will be discussed below.

However, the most fundamental result of the universal presence of screens is undoubtedly the gradual replacement of a person's direct personal experience and direct interaction by observation through glass and camera lenses, usually someone else's, and by mediated interaction. This is one of the first psychological aspects to be dealt with in Chapter 9. There is a danger that people will start living in an artificial reality offering less room for personal experience and experiences shared directly with others. People become dependent on the nature and quality of images produced by the various media with their more or less limited communication capacities. Debord (1996) speaks about a *society of the spectacle*. However, attending a football match is a completely different experience from watching that same match on television. Going out shopping cannot be compared with tele-shopping. Meeting a friend will always be different from communicating over the best videophone imaginable.

The aspects of the culture of images described will mainly be considered negative. This impression has to be qualified, for several reasons. In the next chapter, we will stress that visual perception and visualization are the most important perceptual and cognitive mental capacities of humans. Perhaps these capacities have been under-used in the history of linguistic media. In that case, a further visualization of culture might mean progress.

The argument has to be refined in two other ways. In the first place, the results discussed only apply to the extent to which screens will *dominate* all media of presentation and the extent to which they will *push aside* other types of mediated communication as the most visible type. In the second place, we have not taken into account the educational and cultural policies trying to confront the negative effects. Their first priority might be an adjustment of teaching courses in language(s), information and computer science, social studies and the humanities. These subjects should be used to teach students an active and conscious engagement with our visual culture and to give them (some) insight into the shape, the content and the selection processes of visual communication. Cultural pessimists might better use their energy in these ways than in futile attempts to restore the reading of printed texts as the presumed most important type of intellectual activity.

THE QUANTITY AND QUALITY OF NEW MEDIA CONTENT

Exploding quantities of data and information

Digital culture is marked by exploding quantities of data and information derived from data. After all, information consists of data that have acquired meaning for human beings. Digital technology has made it far too easy to multiply data that are supposed to contain information. The supply of *data* in our society is increasing rapidly, perhaps even exponentially. In 2007, the data universe consisted of 281 billion gigabytes; the increase expected for 2011 was ten times the size of 2006 (Gantz et al., 2008)! Pool et al. (1984) have assembled a large amount of data and research indicating an increase in *data* supply of some eight to ten per cent each year that already took place between 1960 and 1980. However, demand in the form of *information* lagged behind with an increase of about only three per cent each year. The increase in the amount of *knowledge* our society extracts from this information is even less. Information supply overlaps and repeats itself many times, and in receiving information we have to deal with selective attention, selective perception and a surplus of information. The most astonishing and dramatic conclusion, however, is about the effect of all these data and information. The impact of information in *affecting behaviour* (pragmatics) appears to be marginal: the activities of individuals and organizations are highly insensitive to information once a particular stage has been reached. Compared with 50 years ago, public institutions and companies turn out to be using more information to reach the same kind of decisions (van Cuilenburg and Noomen, 1984: 51). According to these Dutch communication scientists, decision quality has not improved very much. Similarly, Dordick and Wang (1993) have referred to the well-known 'productivity paradox': information technology produces fewer productivity gains than expected, especially in the service sectors.

How should one explain these daring and disturbing conclusions? They certainly do not mean that information technology is not working. On the contrary, they may indicate that the level of complexity of our societies, organizations and personal lives has grown so dramatically that we would no longer be able to handle that complexity without this technology. Imagine a present-day corporation or government department without it. They would get stuck in old types of bureaucracy and paper work. The best explanation might be the conjecture that ICTs are barely able to keep up with the complexity of social, economic and cultural life we have produced.

Information overload

Anyway, the difference between the increase of information and knowledge on the one hand and their application on the other produces too much information or information overload: too much information is produced in relation to its use. Furthermore, it points to a phenomenon Van Cuilenburg and Noomen have called 'information dud' (1984: 52): an increasing amount of information does not offer answers to questions asked, but produces answers to questions that still have to be posed. Indeed, the production of information has partly become an autonomous, self-augmenting process. David Schenk (1997) calls these phenomena simply 'data smog'. He claims our information supply is so contaminated with useless and redundant data that information is no longer valuable or empowering, but is overly abundant and is making us helpless. 'At a certain level of input, the law of diminishing returns takes effect; the glut of information no longer adds to our quality of life, but instead begins to cultivate stress, confusion and even ignorance' (ibid.: 15).

Humans typically have two solutions for information overload. The first is selective perception and cognition: part of the information is simply ignored. For human minds, information overload is not a problem until we are forced by our environment to select too much information and knowledge from an overwhelming amount of data in a short period of time. Examples are the preparation of an exam at school or a project plan for work that have both been started too late. Only in such cases, information overload leads to stress. On other occasions, people simply do not perceive the surplus of signals. Humans have several mental mechanisms to prevent signals coming into their minds, and these mechanisms will work even stronger in times of stress, until they break down and nothing at all is recorded any more (see Milgram, 1970).

The second solution for information overload is scanning. This means to spend less time on each input. Low-priority signals are ignored. This is the most common reaction in using the Internet. Web-pages and links are quickly skimmed in a desperate attempt to scan as many potentially relevant sources as possible. Most web-pages are viewed for ten seconds or less (Weinreich et al., 2008). Adding 100 words to a web-page extends this reading time by only 4.4 seconds, which on average enables 18 words to be read (Nielsen, 2008). So, only 18 per cent of extra words are read. According to Nicholas Carr (2009) scanning might be necessary in the contemporary world of the Internet, but it also leads to a much more fragmentary and superficial kind of reading, sacrificing quality for quantity (see Chapter 9).

Communication overload

Another question is whether we are also dealing with *communication overload* and *communication duds*. After all, the quantity of media and messages is also increasing fast. When the law of the limits to attention – see Chapter 2 – is true, communication overload has to occur too. Every new sender on the Internet will have difficulty in finding an audience. People already had this impression in the old media of broadcasting when they started to offer 500 channels or more. On the Internet, the number of channels/sites is so large that only a tiny percentage can ever be used by an individual. Indeed, some of them are used by (almost) nobody. Portals, search engines and direction services simply have to be used to make selections among the overabundance.

Considering messages of interpersonal communication, the situation might be different in theory. Interpersonal communication is a process requiring two or more sides, otherwise this kind of communication simply is not realized. Even so, communication overload occurs here as well. Digital technology makes it far too easy to produce and send messages. When they cannot be received and replied to immediately, they can always be stored. SMS and instant messages are sent by the dozens or even hundreds a day. Almost every email user complains about the number of messages in their mail-box, even excluding spam. People invite, or do not deny a number of news alerts, RSS and other feeds on the Internet which are impossible to read. When they engage in SNS they get daily updates of members of their social network that at least partly have to be ignored. Most messages of Twitter users and bloggers simply cannot be read by a large part of followers. Many outside listeners to mobile phone calls have the impression that they contain 'nothing' of any value. Isn't calling three times in ten minutes to tell a relative that the airplane or train has almost arrived, an instance of communication overload?

Yet, it is difficult to objectively decide that a particular number or content of messages should be called communication overload. Both sender and receiver would have to subjectively agree. External observers are mainly looking at the assumed burden for receivers, but they tend to forget that messages have an expressive function for senders too – think about the motives to send tweets – and that interpersonal communication also has the informal function of bondage and staying in touch continually.

Anyway, the solutions people are using for communication overload are equal to those for information overload. They are selective reception or reply and the scanning of messages. Regarding interpersonal communication they have the ability to inform communication partners about the desirability of their messages in all kinds of ways.

Information agents as a solution

Technical solutions to both information and communication overload are being developed and introduced rapidly. All kinds of personal or information agents, systems to filter all incoming information and messages, and search engines are offered. These techniques will become essential in the information and network society. A matter of decisive importance, however, will be the extent to which we use these means. We should not rely on them completely, as three great risks with fundamental consequences are associated with them.

The first of these risks is to *rely too much on their intelligence* and to allow one's own ability to judge to remain weak. Systems do get smarter, but their users might become more stupid. In fact, these systems possess all the pros and cons of artificial intelligence (see Chapter 9). Intelligent systems are able to adapt to changing user preferences. However, people's standards, values and emotions are changing much faster. And what is more, they differ depending on innumerable contexts. They cannot be entirely (pre-)programmed.

A second threat is that by continuously using these information agents, people might cut themselves off from new and surprising impressions and contacts.

People may even lock themselves up in a personal 'information prison' (Schenk, 1997: 120). We may settle down in environments that are as safe and controllable as they are limited. We may create a personal subculture locked away from the rest of the world or society, perhaps not in principle but very often in practice. The growing supply of personalized media content on the Web (see below) runs this risk.

The final risk is a threat to the *privacy* of users who increasingly entrust their personal preferences and characteristics to systems of registration. In the 21st century, your information agent will inform your contacts who you are. Authorities and corporations will be very interested, without doubt.

So, it is necessary to use these systems critically and in a selective manner and to retain control over all important steps and decisions made by them.

Quality of content

To a certain extent, the appreciation of information and communication quality is an arbitrary affair. Therefore, we need to develop particular criteria for the quality of information and communication. This last section will consider quality criteria in terms of the substance and pragmatics of new media content.

According to standards concerning the substance of information and communication, the huge quantities supplied in the new media do not necessarily lead to better quality. The so-called pyramid of knowledge is often presented to clarify this statement. A better term would be the *pyramid of information processing*, for knowledge is only one of the results of processing information mentally and technically (see Figure 8.1).

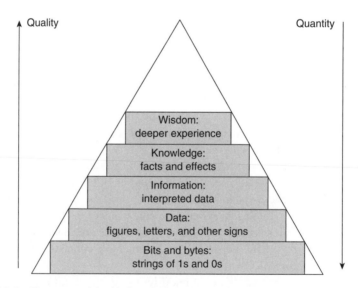

FIGURE 8.1 The pyramid of information processing

In the process of digitization, at the base of the pyramid, endless amounts of *bits and bytes* are produced. Subsequently, every digital 0 and 1 can be translated technically into certain data by means of computer machine language. These data can be letters, images or other tokens. Then humans are able to mentally translate these data into *information*, for information merely consists of data being interpreted: they are tokens bearing a particular meaning. Data are not interpreted when humans do not consider them relevant. In turn, information is often only temporarily important, or is even trivial. A relatively small amount of information has a lasting importance: this is what we call *knowledge*. Knowledge consists of facts (describing reality) and relations of cause and effect that explain how things work and how we can use them. A specific type of knowledge is called scientific knowledge. Finally, the top of the pyramid contains the scarcest result of human information processing: *wisdom*. This rather vague term represents the deeper experience to be gained by associating specific types of knowledge over time, putting them in a context, offering explanations about backgrounds, and connecting them with the values and standards important to humans.

So, information processing using digital media increases the quantity of information as one descends the pyramid toward the base of bits and bytes, while decreasing its quality. In the opposite direction, as one ascends the pyramid towards wisdom, using digital media will improve quality. However, ascending the pyramid gets harder and harder as one approaches the top. More and more 'data smog' or information and communication overload have to be disposed of to reach the next step. So, the use of digital media as such is no guarantee of higher information quality. It does provide us with more opportunities, but we can only use them by making more and better selections simultaneously. To derive quality from the overabundance of digital sources one has to be increasingly selective and critical. These are properties which cannot be programmed in software; people have to develop them on their own account in experience and education.

DIGITAL YOUTH CULTURE: FORESHADOW OF THE FUTURE?

Patterns of digital youth culture

So far, the forerunners in the adoption of new media applications across the world undoubtedly have been young people. They have been called 'the Wired Generation', 'the Facebook Generation', 'the Multi-tasking Generation', and even 'the Einstein Generation'. The most common and meaningless term is 'the Digital Generation'. Another general term, 'the Digital Natives' at least indicates that young people born after 1990 have grown up with digital technology. It has permeated their complete daily life, almost from birth. Picking up digital technology in the most natural way, they have developed a youth culture that reveals a number of common patterns. Some say this is a global culture, first of all in mobile telephony (Castells et al., 2009) while others argue that local digital youth cultures are different (Goggin, 2008; Katz,

2008). Holmes and Russell (1999: 75) claim that the digital lifestyle of young people has created a 'crisis of boundaries' as it moves them away from traditional institutions of socialization (family, school and the mass media) to their own worlds of experience. It would deeply affect their social networks and relationships with parents and teachers.

It would bring our conclusions about this type of digital culture forwards if we were able to identify these common patterns. Some of them are of a more general nature touching all generations deeply engaged with digital technology, while others relate to the special needs of growing up teens and adolescents, as described in the following paragraph. The goal of this analysis could be to identify a number of patterns that will shape the digital culture of the future: what will the current generation of young people take with them when they grow old?

The most superficial patterns to be observed are the collective identity young people develop with digital technology as expressed in a shared language, such as particular SMS codes, and the individual identity as created in personalized messages and mobile phone fashions (Castells et al. 2009: 144–5). These are temporary by nature. Longer lasting might be new patterns of communication and entertainment. When we make an analysis of the Internet applications young people use most, as compared to people of medium and old age, it is striking that they are scarcely related to information retrieval and commerce. Above all, they are applications of communication and entertainment (Oxford Internet Institute, 2009; Pew Internet and American Life Project, 2010a; USC Annenberg, 2011; van Deursen and van Dijk, 2010). Besides the mobile phone applications of texting (SMS and instant messaging), Internet applications most commonly used by young people are SNS, chat-boxes, online forums, uploading and downloading music, photos or videos and online gaming. Older generations use significantly less texting and more talking in mobile phone use. Considering the Internet, they use more online news and broadcasting, product search and online auctions and finally more online shopping and banking.

What are these potential new patterns of communication and entertainment? In communication, the overarching pattern is shaped by new ways to *control contacts and relationships*. Young people use the communication capacities of selectivity (high level), interactivity and stimuli-richness (lower levels) (see Chapter 1). These capacities are enabled by the choice of asynchronicity and anonymity in texting and online messages. In this way they reach more control of contacting and interacting with others. The low costs of this type of communication are an additional motivation. In the following paragraph we will discuss the function this has for teens and adolescents. This control of contacts and relationships might have an empowering effect for young people in their relationships with parents, teachers and peers.

A second new communication pattern is *a complete integration of online and offline types of communication*. At the start of new media development in the 1980s and 1990s, many communication scholars and people of middle and old age were worried about the subordination of the supposedly superior face-to-face communication by much more shallow computer-mediated communication. Young people are the first mobile phone and Internet users who have explored the combination and integration of these types of communication which will merge completely in the future when advanced mobile and wireless communication media will be used in all sections of daily life. The common observation of a small group of young people standing together and simultaneously using their mobile phone or mobile SNS shows the way young people are exploring the integration of communication types and media.

In new media entertainment *practices of sharing* cultural forms and participating in collective media (exchange sites and peer-to-peer networks) have appeared. Young people have been the first to explore these practices of sharing, first in music and video exchange sites and second in the social media, extending exchanges with contacts, knowledge and games. A second new pattern of digital entertainment, obviously related to sharing, is a *participatory culture of new media use*. Young people generally have no hesitations (of losing intellectual property or other assets) in contributing user-generated content to all kinds of collective media such as YouTube and Flickr. This has introduced a new culture of media use enabled by advertisement and other business models (see Chapter 6).

Special needs of teens and adolescents

For teens and adolescents (years 12 through 19) the new media offer a number of special opportunities and risks. Unfortunately, the risks have drawn much more attention than the opportunities, as parents, teachers and other seniors worry about practices of new media use they don't quite understand. Their main concerns are online solicitations by strangers with bad intentions, online bullying and in general the supposed shallowness or triviality of young people's mobile phone and Internet use. Valkenburg and Peter (2009, 2011) have summarized the main results of research in this field. According to them, young people of this age have three tasks in their psychosocial development that can be supported by new media use. First, teens and adolescents have to develop a sense of self or identity. Second, they have to sound out intimacy to learn to form, maintain and terminate close relationships with others. Finally, they have to develop their sexuality by experimentation.

To achieve these tasks, teens and adolescents need to develop two skills: self-presentation and self-disclosure. Online communication offers three features to work on them: anonymity of messages when desired; asynchronicity of messages to prepare and read them at self-chosen times; and extended accessibility of others that are not always easy to meet in offline environments (Valkenburg and Peter, 2011: 1–2). Strikingly, these are features that deliberately reduce the level of interactivity (see Chapter 1). In her book, *Alone Together,* to be discussed in the next chapter, Sherry Turkle (2011) explains this adolescent behaviour as the wish to hide oneself and to escape personal confrontations that are entailed in calling and meeting each other. I would interpret this in a more positive way, as the desire to have more control over communication in order to satisfy the needs just mentioned and to feel more secure.

According to Valkenburg and Peter (2011), it makes adolescents feel free in interpersonal interactions on the Internet as soon as they try to get to know others, reveal things about themselves – even when they are shy or too self-conscious – and sound out identities under construction to peers. They also provide safe ways to experiment with sexual feelings (as long as they are not doing this with adult strangers).

In empirical research of online communication among peers and adolescents in the last ten years, a number of hypotheses have been tested that have a wider relevance. To begin with, the so-called rich-get-richer hypothesis is opposed to the social compensation thesis. The first maintains that all adolescents (aged 12–19) who already have strong social skills will benefit more from the Internet, while the second states that the Internet is particularly beneficial for lonely and socially anxious adolescents as the controllability of online communication stimulating self-disclosure compensates their fears. Valkenburg and Peter (2011: 4) summarize that the rich-get-richer hypothesis has received more empirical support than the social compensation hypothesis. This means social-psychological support of the workings of a power law on the Web.

A second confrontation comes from the displacement hypothesis as opposed to the stimulation hypothesis. The first maintains that online communication impairs adolescents' quality of existing friendships because it displaces the time that could be spend on interactions with offline friends that are more meaningful because they contain more feelings of affection and commitment. Opposed to this, the second hypothesis says that online communication stimulates the maintenance and depth of existing friendships. Valkenburg and Peter (2011: 4) summarize that the stimulation hypothesis has received more support than the displacement hypothesis. This conclusion entails support for the law of small worlds on the Web: the strength of ties is reinforced instead of reduced by online communication.

Patterns extended in the future?

An important question is whether these patterns of digital youth culture foreshadow future new media use when this young generation gets older. In my opinion they do, as I follow social-cognitive theory in this respect: in the course of time, people's media use is learned in social environments (e.g. online communication) and then turns into habits. The following habitual patterns are to be expected. See Box 8.2.

BOX 8.2
Patterns of digital youth culture

- Complete integration into daily life
- Control on forging contacts and relationships
- Priority of self-presentation
- Priority of self-disclosure
- Sharing information and other things
- Creation of user-generated content
- Participatory media culture

First, technology will be even *more integrated into daily life* than today. The 'digital natives' have learned to use and adapt the new media for about every purpose in their young lives. When they grow older, while digital technology is becoming ever more advanced, they will certainly discover more opportunities and adapt them to their adult goals in life.

Second, the need and the experience to have *more control on forging contacts and relationships* will have grown to such an extent that they shall not disappear from their lives anymore. On the contrary, as the spectacular rise of the use of SNS, even among middle-aged people shows, the need to extend and control relationships online only gets stronger. This is a reflection of network individualization in a new media environment.

A third pattern is the *self-presentation* in online environments that young people have learned. This will certainly be extended and taken to a higher, sometimes even professional level in personal profiles of SNS, online dating and the design of Tweets, weblogs and personal websites. This turns into a crucial skill in the struggle for attention on the Web with its information overload and over-communication.

A related pattern to be extended in the future is *self-disclosure*. In our anonymous individualizing world, self-disclosure will be equally vital for adolescents and for adults when people want to develop meaningful and lasting relationships. The pattern developed by teens and adolescents in texting, chatting and SNS will be continued in online dating to find a partner and in SNS use at a higher age. At that age most people with matured identities will feel secure enough to alternate online and offline communication in an effective way.

Growing up with peer-to-peer networking, young people have learned to *share information without hesitation*. Probably, this will be continued as they get older when some young people may engage in the 'new ways of working' and Enterprise 2.0 discussed in Chapter 4. The idea that networking as a practice of giving and taking is more productive than keeping knowledge and information to oneselves as a personal asset will prevail on most occasions with the exception of particular patents, licences and other extremely valuable assets.

A pattern that is less than ten years old is the *creation of user-generated content* on a substantial scale. Young people have taken the lead here, be it mainly for entertainment purposes. Their experience will certainly be extended to other fields, for example, in higher education and in jobs. Perhaps, in creating content for more serious applications they will develop new types of learning and working that are more active and creative (see Chapter 9). Currently, the gap is widening between the world of self-guided learning by teens and adolescents in all kinds of individual and collective Internet applications and the world of school that still is predominantly a world of traditional classroom learning with books and chalkboards. This gap has to close in one way or another to make both the Web and classroom modes of learning more effective.

Creating and sharing user-generated content leads to a *participatory media culture* that has been explored by young people first. This culture does not imply high levels of traditional social and political participation; it is more of a basic kind. According to Jenkins et al. (2009: 3), participatory media culture 'is a culture of relatively low barriers of artistic expression and civic engagement, strong support for creating and sharing creations, and some type of informal mentorship whereby experienced participants pass along knowledge to novices'. Participatory media culture requires the development of a range of new digital skills of a higher, content related type: information, communication and content-creation (see Chapter 7).

This brings me to an important final remark for this section that has to qualify all statements made above. Just like people that are older, young people are very different in the possession of these skills. Most commentary about the so-called 'Digital Generation' is an untenable generalization. Differences among this 'generation' are as big as they are in the general population. Young people of all ages are very much different in all types of access discussed in the last chapter (see, for example, Courtois et al., 2009; Hargittai and Hinnant, 2008; Livingstone and Bober, 2005). Not all of them are equally motivated to use digital media. Many young people in poor countries or in poor households of rich countries have no physical access to computers and the Internet. Most young people have fairly high operational and formal digital skills but they also possess fairly different information and strategic skills, depending on their level of education (van Deursen, 2010). Finally, young people with other demographic backgrounds are different in the new media or Internet applications they prefer (Courtois et al., 2009; Hargittai and Hinnant, 2008).

TRENDS IN NEW MEDIA USE
Convergence

Contemporary new media use is marked by a number of trends that are not self-evident; many actually differ from commonly held views. The first trend is the process of convergence that was a pivotal theme in the early chapters of this book. The integration of the world of the telephone, radio, television and the computer has inspired popular ideas of a complete merge of digital media in a single medium (e.g. a broadband Internet) and of the disappearance of the separate old media. I think both ideas are wrong. They mistakenly assume that technical convergence will automatically lead to convergences in social practices and daily media use and they neglect the trend of media differentiation also present in contemporary society. It is possible to show web-pages and email messages on television screens. One is able to follow a sports game on a smart phone. A confidential business meeting can be held using video-conferencing via the Internet. But have these activities found the most appropriate medium in this way? Probably they have not. Chapter 4 explained that TV use is a matter of (often) collectively viewing large screens in a living room or bedroom, mainly for purposes of entertainment. Until recent times, computer and Internet use was a practice of individuals operating keyboards right in front of a relatively small screen for purposes of information, communication, work or study, taking place in rooms suitable for these activities. The fact that it has become possible to do the same on smart phones and tablet computers everywhere does not mean that favourite places do not matter anymore. People still need private or secluded places where they can concentrate and be left alone. These are all examples of technical convergence not leading to a complete merge of social environments of media use.

The second reason why we are not heading in the direction of a single medium swallowing every other (the Internet) is that contemporary society is in a process of social and cultural differentiation that does not fit with a unitary media environment. A single all-embracing medium that serves all applications and usage contexts is not a realistic prospect. In fact, different social classes, age groups and cultures keep using different media or advanced and simple types of the same medium. Diversity is even increasing, as I argue below.

Multi-functionality instead of replacement

A related popular view is that the new media will replace the old media. This has appeared to be erroneous many times in media history. The most famous example is the TV which was expected to replace the cinema. This time many people think the digital media of computers and the Internet will replace print media, TV and radio.

Longitudinal media research in the last 15 years indicates that the use of the Internet and all kinds of computers in western countries has not, or only partially and very gradually, displaced broadcasting and print media. Television viewing time – excluding viewing television on the Web – is certainly not declining; it even tends to grow (Adoni and Nossek, 2001; Council for Research Excellence, 2009; Ferguson and Perse, 2000; Forrester Research, 2009; Huysmans et al., 2004, Nielsen Company, 2009, SCP, 2010). Only a small part of the young generation increases Internet and cell phone use at the expense of television viewing. This is no surprise, because using the Internet with its relatively active ways of information seeking and message exchange is not functionally equivalent to watching television or listening to the radio as a consumption of information and a relaxing pastime. Neither is it equivalent to reading printed material in a comfortable environment.

At first sight, the decline of the use of print media is dramatic. The readership of printed newspapers and magazines is reduced with percentages every year (see sources above). The same is now happening with books. However, one should realize that, considering reading, these media only change forms. Newspapers, magazines and books are increasingly read on the screens of tablet computers, smart phones and e-readers. The acts of reading themselves are scarcely changing when few interactive and hyperlink features are used. Primarily, the perception of video while reading a newspaper on a tablet computer is changing. So far, even reading online newspapers remains fairly similar to reading a printed newspaper as this is usually also done by a fragmentary scanning of headlines and contents. In the next chapter it will be claimed that the method of reading Internet sources other than the fairly traditional newspaper and magazine versions is fundamentally different, but in these cases the formal structures of the Internet (hyperlinks, hypermedia, interactivity and user-generation) are applied much more.

A second qualification to the evident decline of print media is that this trend precedes the Internet and other digital media. The shift of reading to television viewing already occurred in the 1960s and 1970s. Digital media have only amplified the trend of the rise of audio-visual media in the mass and network society (according to the law of trend amplification; see Chapter 2). We have to conclude that only a gradual and partial replacement of old media by new media occurs. The old media are there to stay. They might change their function (radio has become a background medium) and their form (from printed to screen pages), but their contribution to the media landscape is not disappearing.

One of the reasons for these limited changes is the growing multi-functional use of all media. Until fairly recently, media were used for a particular main purpose: TV for entertainment, papers and magazines for the news, books for education and pleasure, telephony for conversation and computers to process data. The rise of electronic, digital and multimedia technologies enables all these media to become more multi-functional. Television becomes more of an information medium with teletext, continuous news and current affairs programmes with all kinds of banners, boxes and subtitles on the screen. Radio has acquired other functions without losing popularity. Papers, magazines and books have increased their entertainment value with more pictures, short stories, lifestyle information and more fiction in cheap paperbacks. Current telephony offers mobile information, games, pictures and even video or TV. The computer has turned from a number-crunching machine into a multi-purpose information device. The Internet has even become the most multi-functional medium in history.

Increasingly, both old and new media integrate the following functions: information, communication, transaction, entertainment, sociability, education and identity building. To a certain extent, they become functionally equivalent. In the network society, these media are interconnected more and more, and when they cannot be connected they refer to each other inside programs and services.

Contextualization and growing diversity

Again: this multi-functionality does not mean that the differences between media disappear. On the contrary, their special communication capacities (Chapter 1) become even more crucial. People's selectivity in choosing media is increasing. This choice is increasingly context dependent. In the near future, information and a multitude of media will be almost everywhere. Only the most appropriate medium for a particular need in a specific context will draw our attention and invite our use. Here are a few examples. In the living room we want the home cinema, in the bedroom a book, magazine or small TV set. In the kitchen and the car we prefer the less disturbing radio or audio set. While we are on the move, we want to communicate and receive or carry all necessary information on mobile phones and tablet computers. When we are working we need the most advanced information and communication machines: PCs and the Internet. However, rarely are these media exclusively used in these contexts; most often other media and connections are available. Multi-tasking in media use is on the rise, especially among young people.

The diversity of media use also increases when we look at the social inequality of media use. Media diversity is rising much more among people of higher social class than with people of lower social class; among the latter it might even be reduced (Huysmans et al., 2004: 192–4). To use the most familiar stereotype: people of lower social class watch television all day for entertainment, and have done away with the newspaper. The collection of digital media is primarily extended by people with high income and education who have them all: PCs, broadband Internet with additional information services, newspaper subscriptions, smart phones, computer tablets, game consoles, digital HD televisions with large screens and expensive on-demand channels etc. (Pew Internet and American Life Project, 2010b). Compared to this, people with low income and low education have considerably less media, with a concentration on entertainment (big TVs, DVD-players and game devices).

Hypermediation

An instance of changing media forms that is transforming media content is to be found with hypermediation. Hyperlinks and hypermedia in general will cause a revolution in media use. We are just beginning to realize their importance. Until now, media were offered as separate *products*: devices, pieces or bundles of content (books, papers), services and programmes. In hypermedia, they become *processes* of information retrieval, communication and entertainment as people jump from one source to another via the links of media networks. Many visible distinctions between media will disappear. We will go less to a library to borrow a pile of discrete books but we will increasingly consult an electronic library and roam through a large number of sources scarcely noticing that we have moved from one source into another.

Hyperlinks do not interconnect people but content. They will diminish the linear perception and processing of content (reading and watching from the beginning to the end) and turn them into associative modes of perception, processing, memory and learning. In Chapter 9, I argue that this has advantages and disadvantages and contains both opportunities and risks.

The rise of user-generated content

In the Web 2.0 perspective, new media users are using ever more interactive facilities and make their own contributions to the media contents offered to others. This is an extremely important trend that will fundamentally change media use. However, it will not revolutionize it, creating audiences that will be the main editors and editors that will turn into followers. It is by no means certain that a majority of new media users will take advantage of the opportunities of interactivity and user-generation. Many developers of interactive media and programs doubt whether there is sufficient need for interactivity among users. Many media users prefer *relatively* passive viewing, reading and listening, and do not want to make their own contributions. Choosing from (not too) extensive menus serves their needs. Only a minority of Internet users have their own websites, post contributions to discussion lists, regularly exchange music files and videos or produce a personal weblog. Recent survey data from Northern

America and Western Europe show that, as a very rough estimate, about a third of Internet users is engaged in these activities (Oxford Internet Institute, 2009; Pew Internet and American Life Project, 2009; USC Annenberg, 2011; van Deursen and van Dijk, 2010). Perhaps interactivity in media use and active contributions are phenomena that need time to grow among audiences that have been raised in a culture of relatively passive media consumption (Stewart, 1998–9; van Dijk and de Vos, 2001).

Intermediation

A related popular idea is that in the digital media, intermediation of publishers, editors and service providers is no longer needed or needed less. Users are supposed to make their own choices and carry out their own editing. This idea is incorrect as well. In the overly extensive and complicated new media environment, assistance to users is required more than ever before. The rise of portals, information agents, search engines, communication services, auctions, SNS and social media in general confirms this need. It is an inescapable consequence of the law of network extension: the Web has simply become too big (see Chapter 2).

What is actually happening is a transition from broadcasting to narrow-casting and from the mass marketing of homogeneous audiences, via the segmentation and tailoring of parts of audiences, to the customization of media content and the personalization of users or consumers to be reached. This is the following trend to be discussed.

Personalization

After the era of segmentation that has created a multitude of channels and media products for special target groups, we now enter a time of attempts at a one-to-one approach in personalized media forms and content (on demand). However, this is not the end of intermediation, but the start of a host of new services assisting users with making selections – or making selections for them, as personalization may be done by the providers themselves.

Customer-relationship marketing, personalized services and the whole My. X- development belong to the latest strategies in the world of advertising and marketing. Ideologically, they are always presented as being in the interest of consumers as they are supposed to increase choice and service quality. These days, consumers are able to compose their own service packages and adapt the features of shopping, banking and service sites to their needs. Again, the question is whether a majority will use these opportunities, but it has to be stressed that they can be a real benefit for consumers. Unfortunately, there is another side to this trend, when choices of personalization are in fact made by providers. This happens first of all with personalized ads and customized marketing. Consumers are almost never informed about the ratio and the decision formulas behind particular ads and offers to them.

The latest development is that not only ads and commercial offers are personalized but also contents. For example, since December 2009, Google presents a personalized search. This means that search hits are offered in an order that Google 'thinks' will suit your personal preferences. A formula of 57 – in 2009 – characteristics and preferences Google has learned from your previous Internet use is calculated to present the personalized results. Pariser (2011) calls this the creation of *The Filter Bubble* capturing Internet users; previously I have called this the self-selected information prison. The only problem is that these personalized prisons are not self-selected. According to Pariser, these 'bubbles' have three characteristics: 1. You are the only one in a particular bubble; 2. It is invisible to you (you have not selected the criteria); and 3. You have not chosen to enter the bubble. 'For the first time a medium is able to figure out who you are, what you like and what you want' (Pariser, 2011: 217). The problem is that this ability is forced on users and that the criteria behind every personalization are opaque to them.

Pariser stresses the importance of this trend that is not only practiced by Google but also by Facebook, YouTube, Microsoft Live, Yahoo, Amazon.com and many others. First, it could lead to information ghettos in which people only receive information they like and agree with, escaping all other information. Second, it would destroy the main benefit of the Internet: access to a large array of sources, options and opinions. Instead, it would lead to a complete fragmentation of news and information sources. This is an old fear already expressed by Sunstein (2001) who was afraid that the Internet would become a collection of 'echo chambers' for people only seeking and listening to people with the same opinions. Is this fear justified? To answer this question we have to look at another trend first.

Concentration

Another classical fear of media observers is not fragmentation, but the opposite: concentration of media. There are reasons to believe that this is also occurring on the contemporary Internet. Matthew Hindman (2008) has shown that media concentration is currently larger on the Internet than in the traditional mass media of the press and broadcasting. He achieves this surprising result by not looking at the number of senders in the first place – the usual approach – but to the choices of receivers. As a consequence of the law of the limits to attention (see Chapter 2), receivers choose a limited number of very big sites. (The responsible mechanisms such as first page ranks of popular links in search engines only reinforcing their popularity, have been discussed before.) Research of Hindman and others shows that, despite the enormous choice options, the majority of Internet visits in fact goes to Google, Facebook, MySpace, Twitter, YouTube, Microsoft, Yahoo, Apple, eBay and Amazon.com, all of them American companies.

At the other side of the spectrum of Internet sources we have the options that belong to the so-called *long tail* (Anderson, 2006). This concept derives from the figure of a statistical normal distribution that has a bulge in the middle and two tails to the sides. A long tail means that these sides are extremely stretched because there are many options that are chosen by only a few people. Anderson rightfully stresses that about every choice of source or medium, however small or specialized, is made on the Internet. They number in the millions. At first sight, this leads to a fragmentation of Internet supply and demand. However, the total of these little sources is relatively small compared to the total of 'big shots' on the Internet. Moreover, less observed is the striking fact that 'the middle' (medium-sized Internet media) is largely missing (Hindman, 2008). When compared to traditional media of the press and broadcasting, relatively few medium-sized media and other sources present themselves on the Internet. The mechanism explaining this going to the extremes is the power law on the Web ('the rich-are-getting-richer' and 'the poor-relatively-more-poor'), discussed in Chapter 2.

So, the dominant trend appears to be media concentration on the Internet. How can this trend be reconciled with the opposite trend of personalization (fragmentation)? The answer is that they occur simultaneously because they are both driven by user choices in the context of the structures or laws of the Web. Personalization is made according to previous choices made by users and calculated by providers, mostly without asking or informing users. Personalization is one of the potential solutions considering the law of network extension: users need help in making choices on a network that has simply become too big in choice options. It is tempting to take this solution as apparently it is based on one's own characteristics and previous choices.

Simultaneously, these choices result in a concentration of choices on the Internet because 'everyone' goes to the most popular ones. However, this is driven by the law of the limits to attention and by the power law also working on the Internet. The overwhelming majority of small sources and media in Anderson's long tail will only reach the attention of very few people. Opposed to this, a small number of big sources and media draw more and more attention because the already popular are getting even more popular. This does not happen to all big media: they can also lose competition from other big rivals. The winner takes it all according to the power law and the law of network externality. For example, these days 'everybody' is on Facebook and not on MySpace. Facebook defeated and drove back MySpace. MySpace is now turning to the ('missing') middle of Internet media, probably ending up as a niche SNS in the long tail.

CONCLUSIONS

- A digital culture is a creative process and set of products that are made by means of digital media. This culture has a number of characteristics that increasingly shape modern culture as a whole. For example, it produces a culture of speed and of ubiquitous use of screens. It is a combination of pre-programmed and user-generated content, of fragments and collages.

- One of the most striking characteristics is the quantification of sources and messages digital culture produces. This can easily lead to information and communication overload. The solutions chosen for these problems are selective perception and scanning. Scanning entails a very selective and shallow kind of reading Internet sources and messages (Chapter 9). So, more quantity offers no guarantee of higher information and communication quality.

- Digital culture is first explored by young people. They have developed a number of patterns of communication that will, most likely, be extended in the future. They are: more control of contacts and relationships; a complete integration of online and offline types of communication; practices of sharing cultural forms; and a participatory culture of new media use. Other patterns such as the priorities of self-presentation and self-disclosure are first explored by teens and adolescents.

- Digital culture entails a number of trends in new media use. Despite the convergence of media, the new media will not become one – for example, the Internet swallowing all existing media – and they will not replace most old media. Hypermediation and user-generated content will bring basic changes of media use. However, they will not finish all linear processing of media contents and they will not turn the role of editors and users upside-down.

- Internet use is both more fragmented (among others by personalization) and more concentrated than the use of traditional media. Both are driven by user choices in the context of the structures or laws of the Web. Fragmentation occurs by the law of network extension: users make personal choices to reduce the abundance of choices. Concentration occurs by the power law and the law of the limits to attention: in practice users select a small number of big Internet sites.

 **PSYCHOLOGY**

About this chapter

- This chapter is about changes in human perception, cognition, social relationships and personality that occur on account of new media use. Specifically it discusses human-computer interaction (HCI) and computer-mediated communication (CMC). It will try to answer very basic questions such as the differences between human and computer processing. These questions have to be answered to decide whether we want to design computers that equal human beings as much as possible, to gradually *replace* their mental and physical tasks, or computers that are able to *add to* these tasks enabling properly working interfaces between computers and humans.

- The first issues are changes in human perception and modes of communication. What are the consequences of the apparent replacement of direct interaction with physical environments by interfaces with computer operations or contents and by a world of artificial models or simulations?

- The second topic consists of changes in human cognition and emotions. This is the section that will discuss five basic differences between computers and organic human beings and how computer programmers have tried to bridge these differences in HCI.

- The third section will be about the advantages and disadvantages of learning with the aid of the new media. Some have raised high expectations of the educational opportunities of the new media (interactive, associative and multimedia learning) while others fear the distraction and shallowness of hypermedia and Internet use. Who is right?

- The following section discusses computer-mediated communication (CMC). Research in the last 30 to 40 years has started with the basic assumption that face-to-face communication was superior to CMC

> because the latter lacks vital cues such as non-verbal signs. Gradually, one has discovered that the lack of particular cues also has advantages and that after some time CMC equals face-to-face communication. In this way the growing integration of communication kinds is prepared.
>
> - The last section contains much speculation, though empirical observations start to appear. Does all daily work with computers and other digital media change our personalities? We tend to personalize these media and even treat them as human beings. What are the consequences of far-going adaptations to technology for us as human beings?

PERCEPTION AND THE NEW MEDIA

From direct experience to mediated perception

In all mediated communication, some kind of entity is present between human beings and their experience of reality. In allocution we are dealing with a medium–human monologue. In consultation and registration, the patterns shift to a medium–human dialogue. In the pattern of conversation, this is turned into a human–medium–human dialogue or polylogue. In all of these cases, direct *experience* is replaced by mediated and technically supported or affected *perception*. Direct human experience has always been an observation of reality involving all the senses *simultaneously*. This consists not only of knowledge, but also of skills (for instance mental, social and communicative skills), values, feelings and abstractions. Compared with this, mediated communications always involve particular *restrictions.* Here the use of all senses is impossible. Some types of knowledge can be gained, others cannot. Specific skills are used. One medium is suitable for a transfer of feelings, values or abstractions, while another is absolutely incapable of doing this.

In opposition to all the restrictions of the old and new media in relation to direct experience, these media also offer *additions* to experience, of course. Media are the extensions of man, according to a famous expression of McLuhan (1966). To an increasing extent, they help us to overcome the limitations of space, time and lack of information. These forms of help cannot compensate for all limitations, but for many purposes, for instance formal and business communication, this does not have to be a problem. Moreover, the creative human mind is able to fill the gaps, as is argued below.

A second aspect of the transition from direct experience to mediated perception is a partial *pre-programming* of perception and experience in using media. With respect to allocution, this is obvious. It explains the large number of studies about the influence of TV. In consultation and registration, perception is also pre-programmed to some extent by the interface. In mediated conversation, perception is either restricted or enhanced by the communication capacities (for example, stimuli-richness) and the design of the medium concerned. The design of a video-conferencing system requires more pre-programming than a system for simple calls.

Therefore, aspects of comprehensiveness, freedom and the individual's own initiative are at stake in the historical shift to mediated perception. This shift has three characteristics. The first is a historically new type of learning.

From learning by action to learning by symbol systems and visual models

Bruner and Olson (1973: 213ff.) hold that three *modes of experience* fit three *types of learning*:

- the *enactive* mode fits learning by direct action;
- the *iconic* mode fits learning by the observation of visual models;
- the *symbolic* mode fits learning through symbol systems (for instance languages).

With the transition from direct experience to mediated perception, the first of these automatically shifts to the other two types of learning. On the one hand, we could say this does not make any difference. All these types of learning are able to provide the same basic structure of knowledge (Bruner and Olson, 1973: 220). On the other hand, knowledge gained in a particular mode cannot be gained in another mode. Symbol systems (such as languages) merely enable us to process knowledge we have gained in other modes: 'Instruction through language is limited to rearranging, ordering and differentiating knowledge or information that the listener already has available from other sources such as modeling or through his own direct experiences' (Ibid.: 220). A similar point applies to learning through visual models: 'Complex acts cannot be simply imitated unless the performer already knows how to carry out the act' (Ibid.: 218). A person cannot imitate completely unknown behaviour. Imagine that you try to learn salsa dancing by video or DVD instruction only. This will not work. Personal experience in the enactive mode of dancing with a partner is required. Preparing for, or adding to this experience, a video presentation might offer help.

The new media offer new possibilities for all three modes of experience and types of learning, but this applies much more to the iconic and symbolic modes than to the enactive mode. The former modes are aided by all kinds of facilities such as slow motion, rewind, fast forward or searching, and by new ways of presenting information using menus, windows, hyperlinks, graphs, figures and other images. Furthermore, the combination of images, sounds, text and data enables easier usage of several languages/codes at the same time. In this way, new media will only support learning by action in an artificial way, leaning on the other two modes of experience (iconic and symbolic). This is done in simulations or pre-programmed instruction and practice.

On the whole, however, the use of new media will reduce learning by direct action even more than the old media did. As direct action remains the basis of human experience, heavy use of the new media could lead to a decay of this type of learning. Some examples will help to explain this statement. Testing a product in a shop will give you a better impression of the product than reading about its specifications on the Internet. For a long time to come, physical examinations by a doctor will not be replaced in a satisfactory way by medical diagnostic systems. In general, iconic and symbolic modes of experience do not stimulate *active* engagement with the objects and the media concerned. A *comparably* passive mode of perception will prevail: far more is read than written, more is listened to than spoken, more is viewed than depicted, and more use is made of a device/program than of calculation or measurement. The new media will continue this development, which had already been started by the old media. Even though the interactive new media offer more opportunities for active inputs and choices by local units, they start with enlarging the 'weight' and complexity of the medium itself. A lot of viewing, reading, listening and operating has to be done before any active input can be realized. When an overload of information and instructions occurs, this does not stimulate such input either.

Shifts in the modes of symbolic communication

The second characteristic of the shift to mediated perception is a change in the modes of symbolic communication primarily used. Gross (1973) has made a distinction between the *linguistic*, the *social-gestural* (non-verbal), the *iconic*, the *logico-mathematical* and the *musical* modes of symbolic communication. In the course of human history, many alterations have occurred in these general modes of communication and their specifications. The linguistic mode, for instance, has an oral, a written and an audiovisual variant. They were the dominant ones in this sequential order. Several modes of communication, or their variants, have become more important in the first and in the second communications revolutions, and others have become less important. The relative importance of the oral-linguistic and the social-gestural modes of communication, which every human being learns as a child, have decreased in western cultures. The written-linguistic mode and subsequently the audiovisual-linguistic, the logico-mathematical and the iconic modes (photography, film and all sorts of visual signs and designs) have come to the fore.

In the new media, shifts occur once again. Within the linguistic mode, the electronic text and audiovisual variants (texts accompanied by images and sounds) are gaining importance at the expense of the oral and printing text variants. This includes the rise of the iconic mode in the shape of film, photographs, figures, graphs, windows and other pictures and images. This reveals the central position of the screen and the rise of a culture of images. The logico-mathematical mode is also becoming more important. Computer operations dominate not only data processing, but also the interface of human communication with computers. In the new media, the role of the musical mode is not decreasing, but it no longer operates on its own. Increasingly, music is accompanied by images.

The non-verbal (social-gestural) mode is receiving the least attention in the new media. It has disappeared where mediated communication using only speech, text or data has replaced face-to-face communication. Although the non-verbal mode returns in a limited way when video starts to transmit faces and gestures of bodies in multimedia, all expressions and transmissions taken together, this mode has lost space to the verbal or linguistic modes of communication. The intelligentsia's ceaseless mourning of the decline of printed text should not conceal the fact that in the new media one has to read more and more and that the verbal modes continue to gain importance, even where multimedia are concerned. The misunderstanding that reading is getting less important is inspired by the fact that in the new media spoken and printed words have growing audiovisual and iconic support. This enables some people to concentrate on this support and overlook the words (see below).

However, the most basic trend in the modes of communication used in the new media is their advancing *integration*. With the combination of images, sounds, texts and data in a single medium, the modes of communication are also integrating. The resultant multimedia combinations acquire a power of communication unprecedented in human history. They will have a largely unpredictable influence on human perception and cognition. However, a number of assumptions can be derived from known psychological implications of the use of communication modes in older media.

In his classic book *Interaction of Media, Cognition and Learning*, Gavriel Salomon (1979) has explained the psychological differences between 'symbol systems'. This term is comparable to the concept of modes of (symbolic) communication used above. It is taken from the work of Goodman (1968). Salomon distinguishes the following four differences to be related to the mental effects of new media use.

Each symbol system or mode of communication is particularly suitable for the transfer of a specific type of content. For instance, the linguistic mode is used for explanations, the iconic mode for portrayals or expressions and the non-verbal mode for emotions. Abstract notions, arguments and all the things important in a dialogue can be best explained in words. Mediated images are pre-eminently suitable for giving a direct view of reality or for clarifying things usually not visible to the human eye with the aid of a particular visual language.

Symbol systems or modes of communication are either *notational* or non-notational. They contain a set of notations for the clearly identifiable, specific matters they are referring to, or they contain signs not unambiguously referring to a particular thing or matter, for instance all kinds of images with their varied and mostly ambiguous contents (Salomon, 1979: 33). The logico-mathematical mode and the musical mode (represented by stave notation) are notational systems, while the iconic and non-verbal modes are non-notational. The linguistic mode is partly notational, since several interpretations of spoken and written words are possible. In the new media, especially multimedia, the linguistic mode becomes less ambiguous under the influence of strict notational computer language and the advancing integration of texts, images, sounds and data. In multimedia, the iconic mode is joined with the audiovisual-linguistic mode. *All in all, the notational symbol systems or modes appear to be intensified in the new media.* This will have important consequences. Mental processing in notational systems is known to be more complex than in non-notational ones. The appropriate codes have to be learned and subsequently applied over and over again. In non-notational systems, the distance between symbols and representations (for instance images) in a person's mind is shorter (Salomon, 1979: 73–4).

Box 9.1 lists the communication modes integrated and reinforced in the new media.

BOX 9.1
Modes of communication integrated in the new media (boldfaced: modes reinforced)

- Linguistic
  - Oral
  - Text (written/printed)
  - **Text (electronic)**
  - **Audiovisual**
- **Iconic (pure images)**
- **Logico-mathematical (software)**
- Musical
- Non-verbal

Mental skills required for modes of communication

The third characteristic of the shift to mediated perception is that a variety of mental skills for this perception are required. The notational linguistic, logico-mathematical and musical-written modes of communication are primarily processed mentally in the left half of the brain, and the non-notational non-verbal, iconic and musical-auditive modes are primarily, but not exclusively, processed in the right half of the brain (Ivry and Robertson, 1998). So, in general the new media will appeal relatively more to the left half of the brain. However, the expectation of a much stronger simultaneous appeal of integrated new media (multimedia) to both halves of the brain is far more important. An intense dialogue between both halves through their cross-connections is required. This requires all-round mental development. *The ability to benefit fully from all the opportunities of the new media demands a full-grown visual, auditive, verbal, logical and analytical mental development.* Of course, this will increase the complexity of the mental activities required. But the level of this complexity depends on three other crucial factors (Salomon, 1979: 71–2):

New media= left half of the brain

level of complexity depends on:

- the cognitive development of individuals, being related to age, education and experience;

- individual cognitive preferences in perceiving texts, images, sounds or data;

- the tasks to be performed being more or less demanding: study, information retrieval, conversation or amusement.

In conclusion: an *optimum* use of the new media requires full-grown and versatile mental development and a multi-functional use of their capacities.

Various (types of) modes of communication can cause different meanings to be ascribed to one and the same content. Listening to a sound recording of a speech will result in meanings other than those obtained by reading its literal transcription (Salomon, 1979: 78). This is caused not by the contents themselves, for they are (almost) entirely the same, but by the (different) parts of the brain accessed and by the skills and the knowledge of the receiver.

The broader the basic knowledge of the receiver and the better his/her multimedia skills, the less sensitive this person will be to the (type of) mode of communication offered (Ibid.: 79ff.). This means that less educated people depend more on the mode of communication concerned than better educated people do. This must be very relevant to any introduction of the new media because, in theory, the range of options in choosing modes of communication has increased.

In spite of all the myths about the stultifying impact of modern visual culture, almost all psychological research shows that reading in general has a more *compelling* but not necessarily greater appeal to our mental efforts than perceiving audiovisual messages. Conceptual thinking, required by reading, goes beyond perceptual thinking (Peters, 1989). On the basis of these statements we might expect (new) media containing audiovisual presentations to be more easily accessible to less educated people than the (new) media mainly using electronic text and data. At the same time, (new) media would be less instructive for them than for better educated people. The latter are less dependent upon the particular mode of communication offered and they profit more from the increasing elements of text and data.

The (types of) modes of communication not only appeal differently to mental skills, but also help to develop them differently. In order to do so, they have to be demanding and they must force receivers to develop their skills (Salomon, 1979: 82). However, there are several modes of communication, particularly the non-notational types that allow the receiver to choose the line of least resistance. 'The pictorial system of television *allows* (but does not require) shallower processing than a written story or a verbally told one. To generalize, some symbol systems may *allow* shallower mental processing and others may *demand* deeper mental elaboration' (Salomon, 1979: 223, final italic added). 'Notational symbol systems require crystallized ability, based on verbal skills, and non-notational symbol systems require mainly fluid ability, based on spatial and perceptual skills' (Ibid.: 224).

All this has relevance to the new media. In theory, they can help to develop mental skills better than most old media, as they integrate a multitude of modes of communication. In practice they require full-grown mental capacities and a multi-functional usage. The problem is they do not have to be used optimally. The integration of modes of communication in the new media can also be accessed separately and enable a much shallower use. The strength of the audiovisual and the iconic modes offers potential uses that do not stimulate the mental skills required for notational symbol systems. 'The employment of charts, graphs or pictures could save mental effort and make the acquisition of knowledge more effective, but it will impede skill development' (Salomon, 1979: 83). The transition from the (audio) phone to the video phone is a good example. The latter gives more cues and therefore requires less mental skill to understand the conversation (see later in this chapter). People who have to rely on one or two modes of communication must develop the appropriate skills, no matter how one-sided these skills may be. The best case of this until now has been the written linguistic mode.

So, a paradoxical situation arises. On the one hand, the new media (can) make human perception and cognition more complicated and, on the other hand, they (can) facilitate and simplify them. Therefore, the goal and the task of the user determines what happens. Experiments have shown that children learn more from watching television, for instance *Sesame Street* (Salomon, 1979: 225), when they are guided by their parents or by courses for achieving educational goals. Since people with high education in general will be willing to 'do' more with the new media than people with low education, the former will benefit more and will increase their mental advantage. This is the most fundamental psychological cause of the usage gap described in Chapter 7.

[handwritten margin note: Fundamental cause of the usage gap]

COGNITION AND THE NEW MEDIA

The mental combination of different sources and modes of communication

In this section, I am mainly concerned with the fact that the new media require the mental combination of an ever growing quantity and heterogeneity of information and that they call for the mental integration of mediated and face-to-face communications. People are faced with an unprecedented mixture of old and new media. There are no fixed limits to the human capacity to handle information (Neisser, 1976: 97ff.); it is very 'elastic'. For this reason, the effect of phenomena like information and communication overload should not be exaggerated. However, problems arise whenever we begin to combine tasks that have no natural relationship to each other (Ibid.: 101). In the new media, human communication and the handling of data are more and more accompanied by, and increasingly taken over by computers with their own types of data processing and technical communication experienced by using interfaces. The key questions then become whether these forms of process-ing and communication look alike and whether they are able to develop a natural relationship to each other. If the answers to these two questions are primarily posi-tive, there is no reason to worry about any special problems in mentally dealing with the new media. These media will become very useful tools. When, on the other hand, the answer is primarily negative, problems are bound to arise. In the latter case, com-munication between human beings and media/computers will meet limitations and complications.

Similarities and differences of human and computer processing

The *similarities* and possible relationships between processing and communication performed by human beings on the one hand and by media/computers on the other are evident. Computers are used as a metaphor (image) for the description of the human mind, and for good reasons. Terms derived from this source, such as information, processor and memory, play a key role in computer jargon. The same goes for terms derived from communication between human beings, like interaction, interface, dialogue, sign and command. In media technology jargon, terms derived from human perception, symbolization and representation of real-ity, prevail. Media and computers may be considered an extension of or even a substitute for human perception, cognition and communication. They span time and space and they decrease the effects of the limits our body and mind impose upon us.

In answering the two questions posed earlier, a discussion of the *differences* and the possible malfunctions in processing and communication by humans and by media/computers is important. Critics of the new technologies and the accom-panying computer culture and visual culture often phrase these differences in philosophic, humanistic and romantic terms. Human beings, they claim, differ from computers, because they have a broader range of experience, associations, intuition, feelings and emotions at their disposal. Well-known critics in the 1980s and 1990s were J. Weizenbaum, Th. Roszak, J. Searle and H. Dreyfus. Usually, their reactions were much too defensive. This has left them no option other than to stand by and watch how the fifth, sixth and later generations of computers and computer networking seem to be clearing one difference after another. Devoting oneself to modern psychology, and even to so-called cognitive psychology, which actually uses the computer as the most important model of the human mind, would be a wiser thing to do. Additionally, one should take note of empirical studies about the ways humans really use computer hardware and software and one should observe attempts to make designs that take into account the psychol-ogy of the user. After all these efforts, at least five differences will continue to exist (see Box 9.2).

BOX 9.2
Basic differences between human and computer/medium processing

Human processing (cognition)	Computer/medium processing
• Situation-bound	• Context-free
• Total experience	• Separate and successive perception and cognition
• Flexible schemata	• Fixed schemata
• Operant and intelligent learning	• 'Intelligent' learning
• Processing through social communication	• Processing through technical communication

Situation-bound versus context-free processing

The most basic difference can be attributed to the fact that human perception and cognition are *situated physically* in a tangible world. A human being has an active and autonomous relationship to its environment. This is of crucial importance to the versatile perception and cognition in the so-called 'perceptual cycle' (Neisser, 1976). The basic principles of this perceptual cycle are perceptual activities that are controlled by continuously changing mental schemata. This is caused by the *direct intentionality* of the human mind. Intentionality is inspired by the needs and values of human beings as biological and social beings in a particular environment.

This is the basic principle used by neurobiologist Gerald Edelman and his Neurosciences Institute. Edelman's work, summarized and popularized in his books *Bright Air, Brilliant Fire: On the Matter of the Mind* (1991) and *A Universe of Consciousness* (Edelman and Tononi, 2000), firmly supports the five differences dealt with in this section. Edelman rejects the principle of most cognitive psychologists that the human brain can be compared to a computer or to a power plant of neurones. He claims it is more like an organic jungle of continuously changing groups and connections of neurons that are unique for every human being. They are only partly specified by genes. The needs every human being appears to have in their ongoing interaction with the environment cause a continuous *selection* of neurons in the Darwinian sense, changing the human brain ceaselessly. A process of *trial and error* produced by these needs shapes the brain. The workings of the human brain should not be separated into the functioning of hardware (brain) and software (mind), as most cognitive psychologists do. According to Edelman, the complete human brain/mind, but obviously not particular thoughts, can be explained by neurobiology.

Perception and processing in computers or other media, on the other hand, can only start with some kind of *derived intentionality*. Computers are programmed by others and only reproduce or present programs. 'For a computer to have intentional states, it would have to be a robot of some kind', is how one of today's most important cognitive psychologists, Jerry Fodor (1986: 103) phrased the prime difference between man and computer in an interview. The principle of computer processing is programmed *instruction* following algorithms, not neural *selection* as in mental processing (Edelman, 1991).

Computers and media are programmed for various purposes and environments. So to some extent they are *context-free and abstract*. They are intended (instructed by a command) and they follow a rational planning model of the human mind. In her book *Plans and Situated Actions*, Lucy Suchman (1987) has severely criticized this model. In her empirical, anthropological study of the ways people use modern electronic equipment in everyday-life, Suchman came to the conclusion that people do not use this equipment according to a certain plan, the way developers of this equipment expect them to do. Planning models of human action and thinking do not match the reality of 'situated action', which Edelman claims is inspired by neural selection following needs. Large parts of these selections are unconscious, in this way raising doubts about the predominance of conscious will (Wegner, 2002). Suchman feels plans are merely an anticipation and a reconstruction of action. They are a way of thinking, not a real-life representation of action. 'Situated action is an emergent property of moment-by-moment interactions between actors and between actors and the environments of their action' (1987: 179). This interaction has four features that go substantially beyond the three levels of interactivity that computers and media have been capable of supporting so far (two-way communications, synchronicity and, to some extent, control from both sides: see Chapter 1). In fact, these features are an interpretation of the fourth and highest level of interactivity distinguished in Chapter 1 (1987: 180):

- Ordinary interaction between people presupposes *mutual intelligibility* of the parties involved. This understanding is effected during intense cooperation and communication in *fully fledged environments*.

- General communicative practices that people have learned in these environments are designed to *maximize sensitivity to particular partners and occasions of interaction*.

- The use of face-to-face communication includes resources for detecting and remedying difficulties in understanding.

- Human communication is embedded in, and makes use of, *a background of experiences and circumstances*.

Opposed to this, interaction between humans and computers/media is characterized by the following problems. A human being usually understands only partially what the equipment/software 'intends' (its derived intentionality) and why this is the case.

[handwritten: problems between humans & computers]

Equipment and software 'understand' even less of the user's motives (his/her direct intentionality). Equipment/software works according to general schemata that are relatively insensitive to special users and circumstances. Communication malfunctioning will often not be noticed by equipment, let alone solved. Ultimately, the background knowledge programmed in computers/media is not broad and profound enough to fully support the broad range of potential situated (inter)actions.

Of course, developers of software and pioneers in artificial intelligence have been trying to solve these problems for many years now. Some try to make hardware and software more transparent for users (see Norman, 1991, 1993, 1999, 2010; Norman and Draper, 1986). Others want to give users the means to involve their social environment, for instance colleagues, in solving problems of human–computer/medium interaction (see for instance Bannon, 1986: 433ff.). Furthermore, all sorts of 'intelligent' tutor systems and user models are available that are built through 'observation' of the users' successive input. With these systems, the computer should be able to derive the user's knowledge and misconceptions to a certain extent (see Suchman, 1987: 181ff.). In this way virtual learning environments are created that 'learn' from users (Weller, 2007). Finally, computers are increasingly equipped with 'scripts' of concrete situations of a standard appearance that enable them to 'interpret' specific situations. In hardware and software, developers try to offer human cognition more context as well. This happens in virtual reality, in ever more realist games and in artificial environments such as Second Life. The huge problems met by virtual reality and the simulations of artificial environments in achieving their goals reflect the essential differences between human interaction and interaction between humans and computers or other media (Biocca, 1992; Norman, 1991, 2010).

[handwritten: ways to solve problems (try to)]

'Total' experience versus separate perception and cognition

Being physically present in a tangible reality is largely responsible for human experience as well. In a way this can be called 'holistic'. From a varied and active relationship with their environment, from the use of many senses simultaneously and from a whole series of special mental schemata and general conceptual models (among them representations of space and time), people develop a comprehensive view of reality. When we take into account the associations between these schemata or models and the needs, drives and emotions also affecting them, because their neural selection processes all contribute to shaping this comprehensive view, we get the 'total' experience of human beings. Of course this experience is selective, but this is how human beings observe and process objects all at once. Human perception and processing is not a step-by-step process and does not happen linearly.

> Because of their physical condition, human beings first observe the whole with all its internal relations before getting to the specification of aspects. …
> That is how we recognize the face of an acquaintance before noticing certain

details in the person's countenance, such as the eyes. (Coolen, 1986: 144, my translation from the Dutch)

Computers and other digital media operate the other way round, namely according to the principle of instruction. They work with an atomizing perception of one piece of information after another (in the shape of digital bits). Then a piecemeal transmission of these data will lead to step-by-step processing by means of algorithms. So, perception and cognition are separated. It is a sequential and linear process unhindered by indefinite associations, drives and emotions that one cannot program. These fundamental differences in perception and cognition are responsible for the innumerable problems in the interaction between humans and computers or other media and in the attempts to let computers handle human language. For the time being, they will be solved only partially. This even applies to computers working with numerous parallel processors (the so-called fifth generation) and to present neural networks and future neural computers superficially resembling the workings of the human brain.

'Total' experience also means perception, interpretation and interaction in continually changing *contexts* (see above). Most attempts by software developers and artificial intelligence experts to solve the problems just described are aimed at creating some sort of context in the programs and the presentation on a screen. Traditional languages using only commands have been partly replaced by visual overviews – menus from which to choose with the click of a mouse button. The second step was to display several windows on a single screen. Each window is a separate context. It may connect to another window, integrate another window or (partly) overlap. As a result, interaction with computers and other media using screens could be improved (Reichman, 1986). However, it will be far more difficult to create contexts by trying to make devices and software that fit or connect better to natural human language and senses. There has been considerable progress in speech recognition (using the human voice as an input and output medium), in face recognition and in pre-programmed scripts describing contexts for the interpretation of human language.

All these means are useful, but they will not help to overcome the difficulties completely. For example, voice recognition only simplifies human–computer interaction by replacing an oral linguistic communication mode by written linguistic and logico-mathematical and communication modes. A second example are contemporary window systems with independently operating windows that still insufficiently contextualize the perception and cognition of users. Another solution mentioned, programming contexts in scripts, will always prove to be incomplete:

The number of relevant facts needed to completely define a context in theory is unlimited. … On the one hand, you always need a broader context, or you will never be able to distinguish relevant from irrelevant data. On the other hand, you need a final context that needs no further interpretation, otherwise an infinite regression of contexts will occur and you would never be able to start formalizing relevant data. (Coolen, 1986: 137–8, translation from Dutch by the author).

In some fields, computers and other media considerably exceed the performance of human perception and cognition. (For instance, a camera can see/show much more than the human eye is able to do.) But these devices will never be able to fully replace the 'total' experience of humans and their face-to-face communications. The basic reason is that human experience and consciousness are grounded in physical and mental feelings of what happens inside and outside the body according to recent neuropsychological theories (Damasio, 1999, 2003, 2010; Edelman and Tononi, 2000).

Flexible versus fixed schemata

Human cognition is controlled by a series of *continuously* changing schemata referred to as mental maps by Edelman (1991). 'The schema accepts information as it becomes available at sensory surfaces and is changed by that information; it directs movements and exploratory activities that make more information available, by which it is further modified' (Neisser, 1976: 54).

So, schemata are stable to a certain extent without being fixed. This is what makes humans capable of learning and of creative thinking. (See Neisser, 1976 for the schemata and Edelman, 1991 for the concrete neural processes involved.) On the other hand, computer programs, and to some extent other media programs, are relatively fixed. The number of states that the human nervous system is able to adopt is almost infinite, whereas the number in computers is by definition limited (Edelman, 1991). The basis of computer programs is the idea that all human knowledge can be formalized. 'Everything … can be presented in a structure consisting of unambiguous terms linked by formal-logical or mathematical relations' (Coolen, 1986: 134). Fixed forms are the basis. Subsequently they have to be turned into more or less flexible programs. However, formalization, standardization and all sorts of automatization remain present in a prominent way. This is what causes the inevitable communication breakdowns in human–computer/medium interaction. 'The process of achieving mutual intelligibility in face-to-face human communication rests on detection and repair of misunderstandings through the use of a variety of linguistic, contextual and cognitive resources – a capability that current interactive systems crucially lack' (Brown, 1986: 476). This 25-year-old quote can easily be repeated today.

Developers of software and artificial intelligence experts try to compensate for this inflexibility by creating programs able to 'learn' from communication breakdowns and (user) errors (Brown, 1986: 464ff.; Norman, 1991, 1993; Suchman, 1987: 181ff.). These 'intelligent' programs are not designed for a more flexible communication between computer/medium and users or for avoiding errors, but for mutual 'learning' from mistakes and problems deemed to be inevitable.

Another way of compensating for inflexibility is to enlarge the learning capability of the user by increasing the levels of interaction and integration typical of the new media. Extensive psychological research shows how people can learn better and more quickly by using interactive (multi)media and programs. (The next section is dedicated to this issue.) However, these programs will never be as flexible as the schemata of the human mind, for the reasons explained earlier in this section.

Operant and intelligent learning versus 'intelligent' learning

One of the reasons for the difference in flexibility is the structure of the human brain. According to several psychological theorists (for example, see Koestler, 1967; Maclean, 1978; Ornstein, 1986), the 'triune' human brain is a not fully integrated whole of three parts accumulated in a long evolutionary process. These parts are the brainstem with its instincts and reflexes ('the reptile brain'), the limbic system as the source of emotions ('the mammal brain') and the neocortex as the source of intelligence ('the typical human brain'). Computers are designed to come close to the last of these three parts only. In these devices, developers try to simulate intelligent learning. The previous exposition of the differences has shown they have succeeded only partially. All human learning is based on neural processes of *selection* driven by concrete needs and values. Simulation of intelligent learning by computers, however, results from abstract, programmed *instruction*. Furthermore, the human brain is not entirely driven by intelligent learning. Instincts and emotions are essential. Recently, neurobiologists have demonstrated that humans cannot even think without emotions. The classical Cartesian dividing line between reason and emotion is based on a misconception (see Damasio, 1995). Operant learning, a capability of all mammals, in practice often dominates intelligent learning by humans. Operant learning happens when rewarded behaviour is repeated, and punished behaviour is not displayed again. It concerns direct consequences and immediate reactions. It is short-term learning. Intelligent learning, on the other hand, is drawing conclusions from consequences in the long run. This is the basis for planning. Intelligent learning by humans is often influenced by, is competing with, and is often even defeated by much more direct types of operant learning and by the remains of ancient instincts and reflexes. And most of the time this is not a disadvantage. It enables human beings to respond rapidly (to danger for instance) and yet adequately as seen from the person's needs.

Obviously, classical commentary on computer culture (claiming humans are capable of having emotions, contrary to computers and the like) is related to this fourth difference, although it is not based on the psychology concerned. From neuropsychology, neurobiology and the ethnography of human–computer interaction, better explanations can be derived for a large number of phenomena in contacts between humans and computers/media. An instance is Suchman's finding that humans do not use this equipment in a planned way. Furthermore, all kinds of ergonomic observations in psychology become clear: physical signs of stress and even panic if there is a problem, reflexes in the operation of a keyboard, energy-consuming response times, physical aggression towards computer equipment and so forth. In addition, numerous social-psychological phenomena in the contacts of humans with media and networks – see 'The Social Psychology of CMC' later – can be explained by the theories developed by Koestler, Maclean and others: for instance, the uninhibited nature of CMC resulting from the absence of non-verbal cues and immediate sanctions.

Of course, software developers have taken this fourth difference into consideration. Interactive programs are pre-eminently capable of incorporating elements of operant learning. They provide direct output after a particular input, such as error messages. However, this important didactic principle does not help to remove the ergonomic phenomena mentioned above (such as stress in case of malfunctions or error messages). A second pretended solution comes from the world of producing social robots. Here robot pets, babies and robots looking like real adults are constructed with apparent emotions programmed into their behaviour. However, it is easy to recognize that these 'emotions' are unnatural, simplified and inflexible, though this does not have to make much difference for users who project their emotional needs of bondage in these machines and often even treat them like human beings (Turkle, 2011).

Social communication versus technically mediated communication

Human cognition requires communication with other people by using language. Without it, mutual understanding would be hard to accomplish. It makes a great difference, however, whether natural language is used or a (partly) artificial, technically mediated language programmed and transferred by computers and other media. Developers have still not been able to relate artificial languages to natural languages adequately and satisfactorily. The fundamental reasons were explained earlier in this section. In fact, it is wrong to speak of 'communication' and 'dialogue' in human–computer/medium interaction. However, humans have tried to improve the conditions of their natural social communication by using media. In the course of human history, natural types of social communication have been supplemented with, and partially or completely replaced by, technically mediated communication. This means that one or more parts of the communication process are shaped technically. This can be the sender, the message, the medium, the channel or the receiver. This technical *design* can have great influence on the *content* of the communication process and on the mental processing of information produced in it. The number of cues for mental processing can not only increase but also decrease. When using face-to-face communication as a normative reference point, this will be the case almost by definition. However, this may be called the bias of face-to-face communication, as the comparisons made are not fair. In fact, this kind of communication has many disadvantages as well, which may be removed in technically mediated communication. A fair comparison means a study of the decrease *and* increase of cues that the technical parts of a communication process bring about.

Using natural language processing, computers have learned to read and partly 'understand' the languages humans speak (Luger and Stubblefield, 2004). The programs concerned have made considerable progress in the last ten to 15 years enabling more or less acceptable automatic translations of Internet sources and better interfaces between humans and media. However, translations and interfaces are still far from perfect. The main reason is that these programs only partly 'understand' the intentions and meanings behind human language and interaction. ↑ *translators*

LEARNING WITH THE NEW MEDIA
Opportunities of learning with the new media

The new media offer a number of splendid opportunities to improve learning as compared to traditional learning strategies. Unfortunately they also produce a number of risks that may be very harmful for learning. Both opportunities and risks are listed in Box 9.3.

BOX 9.3
Learning with the new media

Opportunities

- Interactive learning
  - Direct manipulation
  - Learn by exploring and experimenting
  - Choice of types of presentation
  - Visualization and simulation
  - Direct dialogue with content

- Integrative learning
  - Addition of new data types
  - Integration of data types and communication modes
  - Associative learning

Risks

- Fragmentation with loss of coherence and argument
- Distraction and loss of focus
- Illusion of multi-tasking
- Illusion of the free availability of knowledge

Let us start with the opportunities. They can be derived from the two structural characteristics of the new media: interactivity and integration.

The *interactivity* of the new media enables a more active and more independent way of learning than we are used to. Interacting with and through these media, the superior type of enactive learning (see the first section in this chapter) is *simulated*, not equalled. In this way, the three modes of learning – enactive, iconic and symbolic – can be combined, as all three of them now use media. With these means, students are enabled to study independently and teachers are gaining another role. Until now, teachers have mainly passed on large amounts of information (allocation). In the future they will mainly be tutors of students studying independently and using a terminal (PC, laptop or tablet) in class or in a special computer classroom, or at home using the means developed for distance education. This will result in a complete, unprecedented transformation of our educational system. This transformation will take at least one and probably two or three generations to complete. The five opportunities of interactive learning can be summarized as follows:

Opportunities of Psychology Interactive learning:

- Students will be able to *manipulate subject matter themselves*. The order, the speed and even the complete contents do not have to be determined in advance. Thus, with enough additional and stimulating guidance from their tutors, they will be able to determine their own course, style and speed of studying.

- Making use of the many choices available in multimedia course material, students are able to *learn by exploring and experimenting* in open environments. Extensive research in education and psychology proves that self-directed and exploratory learning can be highly motivating.

- Students may *choose from several types of presentation*, each with the same content. This content may take the form of text, data (such as figures, graphs and models), (moving) images and sounds. Thus, students with special preferences for reading text or with special capacities for auditive and visual learning may all be served according to their abilities.

- Course material used in multimedia education is extremely suitable for *visualizing, modelling and simulating* information. 'Playing' with this material proves to be a very valuable experience. It helps to clarify and understand abstract matters.

- Finally, interactivity enables the student to start a *direct dialogue* with a program in a device. This combination of hardware and software is called 'intelligent'. Students receive direct feedback and immediately know what they are doing wrong.

The *integration* offered by the new media, particularly multimedia, mainly has consequences for the perception and cognition of students, as discussed in the previous two sections. Three of those consequences can be repeated and renamed in the following way.

Consequences of Interactive learning:

- The *addition of new data types*, such as images and speech, to the traditional ones of text and numbers increases the chances – depending on carefully considered educational designs – of more attention being paid to the subject, more intensive processing and better remembering. The same applies to the addition of audiovisual-linguistic, iconic and logico-mathematical modes of communication.

- These chances can be improved even more when the types and modes mentioned are combined in a didactically appropriate way to allow them to be *integrated cognitively* by students.

- This integration enables perhaps the most basic transformation in education. This is the (partial) transition from *linear learning to learning by association*. Traditional memorizing of a string of words, facts or figures is an expression of linear learning: trying to bang knowledge into the student's head in bits and pieces. This is an extremely poor and ineffective way of learning. It achieves only some result with young people but not much. The larger part of our brain capacity is not used in this process. Associative learning is a quite different mental activity. (Inter)actively dealing with parts of the course material, which can be not only chopped into pieces but also recombined, has much more effect. Neuro-psychological research shows that the right half of the brain is used more and interacts better with the left half in associative learning, among other things with the help of visual cognition.

Learning by association is considerably supported by the rise of hypertext and hypermedia. Learners are no longer confined to the content of a particular book or other source. Provided that they know exactly what they are looking for – a condition unfortunately not often met – the Internet offers an abundance of sources for associative learning.

Risks of learning with the new media

These opportunities were emphasized by innovators in educational science in the 1990s. However, when the Web began to be used on a massive scale by pupils, students and other users, a number of drawbacks also appeared. They have been summarized in the book of Nicholas Carr (2009), *The Shallows, What the Internet Is Doing to Our Brains* that has drawn considerable attention. In this book, Carr claims that the use of the Internet changes our brains, and not for the better. Three risks of learning with the new media are the flipside of the opportunities just discussed.

 The first is *fragmentation* of the contents of learning with a potential loss of coherence and arguments. By combining different kinds of information on the multimedia screen, the Internet can not only integrate but also fragment contents and disrupt concentration and understanding. This occurs when the multimedia learning systems and programs do not combine the different communication modes in an effective way, producing less concentration instead of better understanding. For example, while reading a text one shifts to an accompanying video losing the argument of the text. More in general, hypermedia create a division of knowledge in searchable chunks with increasing chances of a loss of coherence between parts. Take the example of reading this book. It discusses dozens of social aspects of the new media that could be read separately according to choice and preferred sequence. Future electronic versions of this book could hyperlink these fragments internally and externally (to other sources). These advantages would be compensated by the disadvantages of losing the argument of the whole book, for example, about the laws of the Web, and of not understanding the link between several social aspects, for example, the fact that the Internet is both concentrating and fragmenting media use.

By far the most important risk, emphasized by Carr, is *distraction*. When people are using the method of scanning to reduce information and communication overload – see the previous chapter – they are continually distracted by new information stimuli that appear on their screen. This goes at the expense of learning (losing focus) and so-called 'deep reading' of linear texts, such as books. Take the example of this book in an electronic edition again. If its parts were hyperlinked in the way suggested and provided with a lot of illustrations (case studies of new media use) and videos explaining the many abstract arguments in this book, the result of these very attractive improvements would also be continuous distraction. Many readers would lose the argument of the book and not go deep into it. According to Carr, they would learn less of it.

The reason is to be found in cognitive and neuronal psychology: 'The need to evaluate links and make related navigational choices, while also processing a multiplicity of fleeting sensory stimuli, requires constant mental coordination and decision making, distracting the brain from the work of interpreting text or other information' (Carr, 2009: 122). The constant choices that have to be made appeal to the prefrontal cortex, while reading, viewing and understanding text uses other parts of the brain. Together they lead to a cognitive overload and less memory and understanding. Carr refers to experimental research that has proved that reading linear texts showed better results of learning than using hypertext and hypermedia (Carr, 2009: 126–9 and 210–14).

A related risk is created by particular *illusions of multi-tasking*. Of course, multi-tasking is a necessity in the fast and complex world we are living in with its multifarious demands. However, one should not think that it is possible to concentrate on more than one task simultaneously. Virtually all psychological research in this field shows that people can only concentrate on one task while others receive only background attention (for example, Ophir et al., 2009). The art of multi-tasking is to make fast *shifts* between tasks. Some are better in these shifts than others: usually the young and the experienced more than the old and inexperienced. Again, the risk of frequently having to make these shifts is the loss of focus and concentration. Attempts of multi-tasking may lead to the result that no task is performed in a fully satisfactory way.

The final risk to be discussed is the *illusion of the free availability of knowledge* in the new media. A popular view is that with the full and fast availability of knowledge on the Internet, having your own body of knowledge and memory is no longer required. Everything can be found in 'a second' on the Internet. This is a huge mistake. Without basic background knowledge and the understanding of elementary concepts, the knowledge required cannot be found, selected and understood. It would be impossible to distinguish relevant from irrelevant information. Within a few moments, working memory would be flooded by sources of information. A fair amount of linear learning of basic knowledge keeps being necessary. Perhaps this amount is even larger than before the arrival of the new media because the quantity and complexity of sources of information has multiplied.

Nicholas Carr makes a further step claiming that our use of the Internet trying to keep-up with its speed and abundance of stimuli rewires our brains. In our brains:

> the winners are those functions that help us speedily locate, categorize, and assess disparate bits of information in a variety of forms, that let us maintain our mental bearings while being bombarded by stimuli. These functions are, not coincidentally, very similar to the ones performed by computers… (Carr, 2009: 142)

Carr (2009: 120–5) cites a number of neuropsychological studies showing that neuronal connections in the brain change, even after a short time of computer or

Internet use. According to the theory of neuronal Darwinism discussed in a former section, he could be right, considering that every act of learning changes the neurons and their connections in our brains. Then again, the changes can only be temporary. The suggestion of a permanent rewiring of our brains is false. Twenty-five years of computer and Internet use and 15 years of intensive hypermedia use on the Web cannot wipe out millions of years of human brain evolution. Imagine that the heavy users of mobile phones and websites, the so-called 'digital generation' would be deported to an island with no phones and computers. They would feel themselves severely handicapped for a while, but after some time they would become ordinary human beings with the same brains we all have, communicating and informing themselves with all means left.

THE SOCIAL PSYCHOLOGY OF COMPUTER-MEDIATED COMMUNICATION (CMC)

Approaches in CMC research

Next to human–computer interaction, CMC is the most intensively investigated field of new media research in psychology and communication science. This field immediately drew the attention of many researchers, as CMC was accused of being *asocial* (i.e. cold and unfriendly) and even *antisocial* (diminishing face-to-face interaction). Thurlow et al. (2004: 47) summarize that it was held to be 'impoverished, impersonal, ineffectual and emotionally cold'. In the first period of CMC research, in the 1970s and 1980s, the so-called *deficit approaches* to CMC (Ibid.: 48) were the most popular. The accompanying theories have already been introduced in Chapter 1: social presence theory, reduced social context cues theory and information or media richness theory. These theories emphasized the objective defects of CMC as compared to face-to-face communication, which was considered to be the norm and the best quality of communication.

In the 1990s, the deficit approach was severely criticized by the so-called *social information approach*. The theories concerned were also discussed in Chapter 1: the social information processing model, the relational perspective and social identity theory. They stressed that users of CMC compensate for potential technical limitations in actual, information-rich social environments. They accomplish this by great subjective creativity in human communication elaborating all existing CMC cues and adding other cues. According to the social information approach, CMC is all but asocial and antisocial: It might be very personal, even hyper-personal, and it helps to build social relationships online and offline.

Walther (2011) has made the latest overview of theories of CMC concentrating on interpersonal relationships. I want to summarize a broader range of results under the labels of the following five characteristics:

1   technological dependence;

2   assets and deficits of CMC for interpersonal communication;

3   group dynamics;

4   participation and decision-making;

5   standards and netiquette.

Technological dependence

CMC is very much dependent on technology. This applies even more to CMC than to the old media of telecommunication and surface mail. In Chapter 5, I discussed the vulnerability of networks in great detail. Computer meetings, video-conferencing, email and videophony are obviously more vulnerable than traditional surface mail and telephony. The more use is made of computers, complicated switches and video media, the greater the chances of a partial or even complete technical failure of the conversation. It only takes a defective microphone or camera, a wrong communication protocol or a slow switching/processing unit to cause great damage to the entire conversation process. Although such malfunctions do not occur very often, they are always unexpected and hard to repair.

technical pressure:

A second aspect of technical pressure on all mediated conversation is a lower capacity of adaptation to the environment. In traditional meetings, participants are able to repair bad conditions for conversation immediately, for instance by altering the pitch of the conversation and by repositioning furniture, changing seats, closing doors or windows, and so forth. In electronic meetings, most conditions are fixed. Participants are tied to their equipment in all sorts of ways (see Johansen et al., 1979: 24). A third aspect is the pressure of 'having to be available at any given place and time', caused by the new conversation media. This causes an increase not only in *time pressure*, but also in the *pressure to communicate* as a matter of course. Although the new media also offer opportunities to block or to not engage in online conversation and to wait with replies in asynchronous communication, their overall effect is to enlarge the pressure of communication at any place and time. The availability of these media also increases everyone's expectations of each other's communication behaviour. In computer meetings, for instance, quick and well-considered answers are expected (Kiesler et al., 1984: 1125). Most often, the people and devices involved cannot meet these expectations.

Finally, we can point out the *lower sense of responsibility* of groups for a communication process that is so much determined by technology. The burden of taking the initiative of starting and maintaining the communication is left to the technical medium much more than would happen in face-to-face communication (Johansen et al., 1979: 24).

Assets and deficits of CMC for interpersonal communication

Technical mediation of parts of the communication process causes the following *extension* of facilities being perfected in CMC (Weingarten and Fiehler, 1988: 59–60):

extensions of facilities being perfected in CMC:

1 Communication partners do not have to be present in the same location.

2 They do not have to communicate at the same time (synchronously).

3 Computers or media can partially or completely replace humans as conversation partners.

4 The mental processing required for conversation can be replaced (partially) by information processing devices.

The last facility enables users to involve external sources (knowledge, advice) in the conversation process. Users no longer depend on their communication partners' direct knowledge. Online conferences can receive the assistance of databanks and knowledge systems.

Compared with face-to-face communication, each new medium also imposes *limitations* on communication channels. As we have seen, some modes of communication are given room, others are not. The non-verbal mode of communication, body language in particular, is restricted most in CMC. This mode is transferred only in video-conferencing and in videophony, albeit in a limited and altered form. For example, kinetic communication is very limited. It has been known for a long time from experimental research that small images of, for instance, faces in videophony give few more cues than sound telephony; much larger images, on the other hand, will increase cues (Midorikawa et al., 1975). Sign language on a screen comes across differently: it is emphasized and gestures may appear undesirably aggressive (Johansen et al., 1979: 56).

These limitations make it hard to build a good relationship with, and confidence in, conversation partners. Preferably, they already exist when CMC is used. Online conferences and even online dating are not suitable for getting to know people, or for problematic conversations (for instance, in the case of a conflict). *CMC is best used when...* They serve best when the participants already know each other and have a good (business or personal) understanding. Computer meetings (synchronous) and email (asynchronous) are suitable for the exchange of information, opinions and orders, for asking questions, maintaining existing contacts and generating ideas (Vallee, 1978). Apart from face-to-face meetings, video-conferencing is the most suitable medium for complex communication tasks in interpersonal communication. However, high-quality channels for video-conferencing are still very costly and not widely available. Most often only a small number of groups with a limited size can take part, and not all participants can be seen simultaneously. For most business purposes, email, instant messaging and telephone meetings are more efficient and cheaper alternatives.

The consequences of these limitations need to be qualified in three ways. In the *qualifications or consequences* 1.) first place, it is remarkable how well people are capable of compensating for missing cues in images, sounds, text and data by using other cues. In a telephone conversation, most people prove capable of compensating for the lack of visual and non-verbal signs by making subtle adaptations to their conversation style (Fielding and Hartley, 1987). Fielding and Hartley draw the conclusion that ordinary human communication is much more flexible and robust than is expected by most people. It can cope with considerable decline in quality before normal patterns of communication break down (1987: 121). After all, we are dealing with the *totality* of cues people derive from information, even when it is only partial.

Similar effects occur in CMC. Compared to face-to-face communication, it often does not perform worse in formal task performance, quality of decisions and social or group influence and social or personal attraction (Chun and Park, 1990; Dennis and Kinney, 1998; Nowak et al., 2009; Postmes and Spears, 1998; Spears et al., 2001; Walther, 1996, 1997). Performance strongly depends on contextual factors that work in both types of communication: how much the participants know each other and have already used other media reaching each other; the type of group and the task or activity concerned; and the whole social, (inter)cultural and organizational context.

The second qualification is connected to the first. In their comment on the social presence and reduced social context cues approaches, Spears and Lea (1992) and Lee (2004) have claimed that users involve all of their social, cultural and personal group identities when participating in computer-mediated communication. Mantovani has put it this way: 'The social world is not only outside but also inside people, as part of their individuality, and functions even when they sit – physically alone – in front of their computer screens' (1996: 99). Limitations are to be compensated for by the use and amplification of *available* cues. If this is true, the social identity of individuals and groups is more likely to be stressed than reduced in CMC. **2.)**

A third important qualification is the fact that limitations of communication channels are not by definition a disadvantage. On the contrary, they often are a big advantage. They enable the user to gain more control. A cause of the enormous success of the (audio) telephone is the limitation of this medium. It enables users to have a more or less personal conversation without exposing themselves completely to the other person. The opportunity of texting on mobile phones has expanded this ability even more. In the previous Chapter we saw how teens and adolescents take advantage of this ability to control communication and develop identities. Some applications of CMC also enable anonymous communication that is able to encourage self-disclosure in therapeutic and other help sessions. In computer conferences and email, participants can concentrate fully on the text and the data, and they are able to consider these things for longer when communication runs asynchronously. **3.)**

Group dynamics

In CMC, many group dynamics known from face-to-face groups are different. I mention two issues: coordination and discussion. Online groups with simultaneous input of text usually have problems with the coordination of communication. In the first place, participants contribute much more as they can 'talk' simultaneously. A second reason is the lack of non-verbal cues. Coordination problems apply in particular to text-based online conferencing and email, especially when they are used asynchronously. Direct feedback is greatly missed. This is much less the case in audio- or video-conferencing or telephony conferences. Here these deficiencies are partly overcome spontaneously. Ending the contribution and taking turns is accomplished in an organized way.

So, coordination problems are different for each medium of CMC (text, audio, video), but they do have some general consequences. People need more time to build and maintain group organization (Weston et al., 1975). Natural leadership is created far less easily in CMC group sessions (Kiesler et al., 1984). This is one of the reasons why much more time is needed to reach mutual understanding (see below). In CMC, coordination and leadership have to be introduced artificially. The chairmanship and technical organization of online conferences have to meet many more demands than in face-to-face meetings. Moreover, many online conferences are controlled by programs, otherwise all sorts of subjects and lines of discussion get mixed up.

For all these reasons, communication sessions in CMC that are organized for organizational or business purposes are more orderly than face-to-face meetings, as was observed a long time ago by Johansen et al. (1979: 23). Even so, contributions made in electronic groups and forums are less inhibited (Joinson, 1998, 2001; McLaughlin et al., 1995). This might lead to more self-disclosure (Joinson, 2001). However, uncontrolled outbursts also occur regularly. This is called *flaming* (Joinson, 1998; O'Sullivan and Flanagin, 2003; Wallace, 1999). It runs the risk of prematurely ending the conversation by argument or by participant drop-out.

Special group dynamics also appear in online discussions. Deliberating online groups have some important problems that should be solved by moderation, online discussion rules and the filtering of contributions marked by scolding, insults and flaming to make discussion effective. People who believe in the 'wisdom of crowds' exchanging views on the Internet should be aware of these problems. Sunstein (2006: 75–102) lists the following four problems observed in social-psychological research:

1 *Amplifying errors*: existing bias in groups tends to be extended instead of reduced; escalation to a course of action that is failing can often be observed.

2 *Common knowledge effect*: information and views held by a majority of group members have far more influence than minority or individual information/views (that tend to remain silent).

3 *Cascades*: following the lead of others, people go along with the crowd to maintain a good opinion of others though they know better (they also remain silent).

4 *Polarization*: initially different views of individuals turn more extreme instead of coming together.

Participation and decision-making

At the start of the history of CMC, people did not realize these problems. Until the 1990s, most social psychologists were convinced that status, power and prestige had a smaller chance of affecting CMC than traditional communication. The more limited a communication channel, the more the necessary context cues and non-verbal behaviour cues supporting status and power are lost (Edinger and Patterson, 1983).

It is well known that face-to-face meetings with a particular task in organizational contexts are often dominated by one person or a few people. In contrast, it turned out that people who usually keep quiet contributed more to electronic group conversations (see Finholt and Sproull, 1987: 221, for instance), and research also indicated that women were more forthcoming in electronic meetings, particularly in meetings mediated by computers (Turoff, 1989: 115). The result of this removal of traditional barriers in electronic conversation was held to represent an equalization of participation and influence in discussions. The presumed key for it was the *emphasis on content*, as the lack of cues prevents all kinds of (status) distractions.

This common view among psychologists in the 1970s and 1980s was countered by a clearly different situation outside the laboratory in less organized large-scale Internet conversations. In discussion lists or electronic chatting groups on the Internet, everyone could observe a lack of participation and equality among the unlimited number of potential members addressed and a lack of central moderation of discussion, leading to anarchy and the rule of the hard core instead of democracy. The dominant practice is that a relatively small core of people dominate the discussion, while the majority contribute only once in a while or just read the contributions of others (e.g. Rojo and Ragsdale, 1997). The same currently happens in Twitter exchanges and other social media discussions.

The practice of Internet discussions and email conversations in real organizational settings outside the laboratory also has cast doubt on the presumed equalizing effects of electronic conversation. Bikson et al. (1989) tried to show that CMC generally tends to strengthen existing patterns of hierarchy, status and interaction in organizations instead of creating new ones. Rice (1998) even expressed the view that CMC increased rather than decreased status differences in real organizational contexts. Research by Saunders et al. (1994) on the use of online conferences in health care, and research by Scott and Easton (1996) on the equality of participation in group decision support systems, revealed a persistence and even a reinforcement of status barriers. Smith et al. (1988) showed that the vast majority of email messages in the organization they investigated were addressed within the same divisions and hierarchical levels. The same conclusion was reached by Lux Wigand (1998) ten years later when email had become a widespread medium inside organizations.

Mantovani (1996) reaches the conclusion that on most occasions, electronic democracy in organizations is a myth and that the actual use of CMC is determined by decisive social and organizational contexts. He questions the validity of the laboratory experiments, mainly on American students. Spears and Lea (1992) cast doubt on the individualistic assumptions behind these experiments. According to Spears and

Lea, social power not only comes from outside the individual. Individuals will not be released from group and organizational power in electronic environments. Power is a relational affair and it is internalized in the self- and the group-identities of individuals. When status cues are lacking, people will attach more importance to the remaining cues and to the group identities they bring with them in electronic conversations (Postmes and Spears, 1998; Spears and Lea, 1992).

We may conclude that the evidence of more equal participation and influence in electronic conversations is contradictory. Actual social and organizational contexts and the use of particular conversation media (from closed and regulated organizational networks to open and free Internet discussions) or modalities (text, audio, video) appear to be decisive.

Standards and netiquette

Conversation in the new media has not yet developed accepted standards. No socially accepted codes of conduct apply. So, we must be very cautious in generalizing the findings discussed in this section. The limitations of conversation in the new media are not conducive to the creation of group structures with clearly defined standards of behaviour. In computer meetings, email conversations and social media, formal and informal, public and intimate messages run side by side. People do not yet know how to exchange greetings and other courtesies. The right mixture of politeness and efficiency (speed) is not easily achieved.

Groups not having a close mutual understanding prior to the mediated exchange run the risk of adopting an apparently conflictive and aggressive style. So, one should always ask oneself whether an electronic meeting really is the most effective means.

This does not mean that there are no standards in electronic conversations. They are not widely known and accepted, however, and they are always strongly determined by specific contexts (Spears and Lea, 1992). After some time, groups develop their own standards and language systems, such as so-called *netiquette* for behaviour on the net and *smileys* or *emoticons* as a paralanguage – certain key combinations indicating emotions, such as ☺. Group identity and personalities are able to grow in electronic meetings (Walther, 1992, 1996). CMC may even become 'hyperpersonal' (Walther, 1996); it can become more personal, intimate and friendly than face-to-face communication when people feel closer to the people at the other side of the screen than they usually do in meetings. Increasingly, people polish their own identities and perhaps harm those of others in online environments such as those offered by the social media. This is a part of online impression management. As we have seen in Chapter 7, social media have an urgent need to develop a netiquette.

In organizations, new media are also used for less formal communication. They seem to serve as a safety valve for emotions (Finholt and Sproull, 1987). Paradoxically, in these cases it is the presumed 'impersonality' of the medium that enables intimate communication (see Rice and Love, 1987) – a phenomenon with which we are already familiar in sex lines, help lines and the use of personal profiles in social media. In the next section, I try to resolve this apparent contradiction.

Future CMC research

CMC research will have to adapt to changes in technology that might lead to other conclusions (Parks, 2009, Walther, 2011). The vast majority of CMC research in the past 30 years has concentrated on text-based and anonymous communication. The basic research questions were how people would react to the absence of non-verbal cues and the presence of anonymity. The hard core of the research perspective was to find basic differences of computer-mediated and face-to-face communication assuming that the last kind of communication was superior. In the course of time, CMC research has shown that this superiority does not have to exist. After some time, online and offline communication can become similar in many respects. This goes especially when: a) participants know each other offline and regularly interact and b) online and offline communication are alternated and integrated. Box 9.4 lists this and eight other main conclusions of CMC research.

CMC will have to take account of three technological developments. The first is ongoing integration of online and offline communication in daily life, especially where mobile technologies are used. The second is increasing simultaneous use of all kinds of media. This has barely been investigated yet (Parks, 2009). The choice between the increasing number of communication channels is a research topic of growing importance (Pieterson, 2009). The third is the rise of media that use text, images, video and audio and that are no longer anonymous (Walther, 2011). This is typically the case in social media who are certainly not only text-based (such as Twitter) and who are built on personal profiles. However, the most important task for CMC research is to not be led by technology only. We have an urgent need for psychological and sociological theories with a broader scope that explain both CMC and other kinds of communication (Parks, 2009, Walther, 2011).

CMC must take into account:

BOX 9.4
Nine major results of CMC research (1980–2010)

- Dependence on technology makes CMC vulnerable, less adaptive and its conditions less controlled by users.
- CMC is not appropriate for getting to know each other and for difficult communication tasks. It works best when people already know each other.
- The lack of cues in CMC is an advantage for many communication purposes.
- Participation and influence are more equal in free, but not in organizational CMC. However, reaching consensus and conclusions are more difficult.
- Coordination and leadership (moderation) have to be added to CMC to be effective.
- Norms and manners ('netiquette') are not yet established in CMC.
- Individuals in front of computers do not become less but more social.
- After some time, electronic groups equal face-to-face groups.
- In general, face-to-face communication is not superior to CMC.

CHANGES IN HUMAN PERSONALITY?

Anthropomorphization of technology

Several authors expect interaction with computers, the Internet and other digital media to change human personality in the long run. They might be right. Still, their expectations are extremely speculative, though sometimes they are supported by a growing body of empirical research. Sherry Turkle (1984, 2011) has the greatest record of this research with her mainly qualitative studies *The Second Self: Computers and the Human Spirit* (1984), *Life on the Screen: Identity in the Age of the Internet* (1995) and *Together Alone, Why We Expect More from Technology and Less from Each Other* (2011). Other examples can be found in contemporary social-psychological research. Such research shows, for instance, how people with certain personality characteristics are attracted to mediated communication (see below).

The main starting point in this section is the universal approach of ICT in using names derived from the human mind and human communication. This anthropomorphization (humanization) of technology can easily lead to technical influences on humans and their personalities. It is well known that people tend to approach computers as if they are partners instead of devices. Reeves and Nass (1996) have published a large number of experimental cases indicating the *media equation* that media experience equals real life, as people treat media like real people and places. 'When we are confronted with an entity that behaves in humanlike ways, such as using language and responding based on prior inputs, our brain's default response is to unconsciously treat that entity as human' (Nass et al., 1997: 158). People consider contact with a computer to be a dialogue, and technically-mediated interaction with and through other media to be full human communication. This anthropomorphization of computers and media is very understandable. At least three fundamental reasons can be given (Brown, 1986: 459ff.; Suchman, 1987: 10ff.; Turkle, 1984: 281ff.):

- The technologies concerned are *non-transparent*. Computers are like closed black boxes. Large-scale networks are opaque to most people. For example, most people have no idea how the Internet works.

- These technologies appear as *autonomous units responding to questions and commands*. The tendency to talk about devices and even to devices (such as cars and cameras) using terms derived from communication with humans is intensified. Strikingly, the device is always a 'he'.

- These technologies respond as *intelligent equipment/software*. They are *logical* units operating with a *linguistic* mode of communication. They work with languages themselves, and interact with humans. It is no surprise that humans get the impression they are dealing with units similar to the human mind. This impression will be strongly reinforced as soon as speech recognition, spoken output and biometrics (enabling recognition of the user by a computer) enter the world of computer technology on a mass scale.

Humanization of human–computer relations

The result is a humanization of the *relationship* between humans and computers or other new media. Three phenomena are observed over and over again (see Reeves and Nass, 1996; Turkle, 1984):

1 The relationship is *personalized.* People handle computers as if they are other humans. Consulting help utilities or information services gives the impression of a dialogue with a human service provider. During an electronic conversation, people unconsciously compensate for the limitations and impersonality of communication taking place. When computers are built as social robots – serving as toys for children or to take care of the elderly – and can talk and superficially display 'emotions', personalization increases to such an extent that this robot is seen as a good companion and a substitute or even as a better alternative for people (Turkle, 2011).

2 The relation becomes *binding, fascinating or even addictive* to humans, because they have far greater *control* over these relations than over relationships with other humans. A whole series of psychological needs can be fulfilled (to be discussed later). The binding and sometimes even addictive relationships of humans with computers, mobile phones and Internet applications such as SNS are well-known phenomena.

3 A *partnership* develops between humans and computer/media. People consider computers to be partners fulfilling several psychological and social needs. A computer is a powerful projective medium (cf. Turkle, 1984): it is a *second self*, it can be used by humans to project a (desirable) other identity onto it. Subsequently they are able to communicate with this safe environment created by themselves. Twenty-five years later, Turkle found the same projection and relationship development in her studies of user attitudes to social robots, mobile telephony and SNS (Turkle, 2011).

Changes in language and relationships

In humanizing their relationships with ICTs, humans adapt themselves to technology without knowing it. This is most obvious in *language*. I am not only referring to the increasing use of technical jargon and 'techno-babble', but also to changes in 'normal' language. In human–computer interaction, computer conferencing, email, texting in mobile telephony and social media, the number of words used decreases, the sentence structure becomes more rigid, the number of abbreviations, stopgaps and half-finished sentences increases, and the expressions of emotions become less rich and varied (see Wallace, 1999: 9–12 and Turkle, 2011). Other examples have been found in word processing, which appeared to have a fragmenting effect on messages right from the start (Heim, 1987).

The consequences are most evident in *social relationships*. Technology allows strong control in making contacts and turn-taking in ensuing communication.

Aided by our contact lists, these processes can be planned more than ever before. A likely consequence is a reduction in the number of chance meetings we used to have in traditional public places. You are more likely to come across an old friend with the help of your Facebook page than just by chance on the street. Of course, surfing on the Internet and clicking or responding to hyperlinks and addresses also offer opportunities for surprise, chance and adventure, in the same way that people previously ran into unexpected programmes and content in the overwhelming supply of the old media. However, one is not forced to pay attention. The supply is overabundant and there is absolutely no social pressure prompting people to pay attention. In the former chapter we have seen that personalized intelligent agents are offered to select only known or favourite contacts and contents. The most likely result will be that social relations will become more pragmatic, businesslike and rationalized. Another effect might be a decay of traditional social skills, such as responding flexibly to chance meetings in the public sphere, and perhaps even the advanced social skill of flirting!

Indeed, a similar phenomenon is popular *online dating*. This is a good example of the increasing selectivity and control potential of online social contact. Here the fancy romantic ideal of finding 'the only one' by chance is replaced by a more businesslike search for potential partners with particular characteristics. Of course, chance meetings also occur in online dating, as the number of potential contacts is much bigger than in the offline world, but the online dating software immediately reduces this number to manageable proportions. It appears that partners with similar characteristics, attitudes and ideas are (even) more attractive in online than in offline dating (Wallace, 1999: 141–2). Online dating makes things easier for finding someone attractive (Thurlow et al., 2004: 140); it stimulates efforts to be attentive to partners and to disclose oneself. However, it is also easy to drop out of an online relationship and immediately or simultaneously start another. In the long run this may shorten the life span of romantic and sexual relationships. After some time, the traditional skills of courting and flirting may be lost and replaced by skills of online impression management.

John Naisbitt (1982) once stated that human needs and opportunities for social contact will increase as technology develops further. He used the expression 'high tech, high touch'. The problem is, however, that communication technology can serve not only as a mediator, but also as a substitute for social contact. Apparently, this technology relieves loneliness. How can loneliness survive 'in a world where the choice of media contacts with another person is always possible' (Gumpert, 1987: 189)? In order to answer such a big question, one must realize that the initiative in making contacts is placed increasingly on the individual in the process of network individualization. The individual will have to negotiate continuing communication. Some will succeed; others will fail.

Perhaps this (partly) explains the astonishing fact of increasing loneliness in modern western society, following countless social surveys, while the number of contact media at the disposal of this society grows and grows. According to a study of McPherson et al. (2006), the average number of people with whom Americans can discuss matters important to them has dropped from 2.94 in 1985 to 2.08 in 2004 and the percentage of Americans that has no such person at all has nearly doubled in that period reaching 25 per cent. This was before the rise of Facebook. Most likely, this has not reversed the trend. If you have no real friends, Facebook is unlikely to bring them. It will bring only more contacts. Mediated communication with familiar people and with strangers is often no satisfactory substitute, as to some it produces a gnawing feeling of remoteness and asynchronicity of communication – this old statement (Gumpert, 1987: 186) is still relevant today. For others, it may be intimate, personal and even hyper-personal (see previous section). They *feel* connected all of the time (Turkle, 2011), experiencing the connection as a *fear* of losing it, something to be prevented at all cost, and of continuous *hope* for new and more rewarding contacts, checking them all the time. However, in spite of the advantages of online personal relationship building and maintenance at large distances, many modern people continue to long for small-scale interaction in dense social networks and close-knit communities (Gumpert, 1987: 167ff.).

The biggest scarcity in modern relationships is not the number of contacts but the amount of attention. The struggle for attention marks our completely mediated world. This is only reinforced by the law of the limits to attention on the Web (see Chapter 2). This means that this law also, and even especially, goes for those most connected – the young generation. 'Today's young people have a special vulnerability, although always connected, they feel deprived of attention' (Turkle, 2011: 294). In the meantime, the young also have parents that might be more engaged in texting on their mobile phones than, for instance, having an eye from the tribune on the swimming performance of their offspring trying to qualify for a certificate.

Personality changes?

The impact of technology on human language and communication may lead to personality changes in the long term, which means a lifetime. This is the time-frame for personalities. Contemporary psychology is not sure about the possibility of the transfer of personalities to future generations. Influence might be the maximum effect. The speculation discussed here is that, at best, the increase of opportunities for information and communication offered by the new media will contribute to *a universally developed personality*. In the worst case, these changes may lead to the four related personality types described below. Emphasizing worst case scenarios here is not driven by pessimism but by the interesting thought experiments it offers: think under which conditions they would not become true.

The first could be called the *rigid or formalistic personality*. People working frequently with computers or other media and, in doing so, being constantly confronted with the changes in language and (coarsening) manners described above, may start to make the same demands on natural communication with their fellow humans as they do on technically mediated communication. For instance, they might get annoyed with vague, ambiguous and incomplete, in other words normal, human language. They could prefer the use of abrupt language. They could also become irritated by chatter and communication with no clear direction or goal except in places that are explicitly designed for this type of communication such as online chatting, instant messaging, Twitter and other social media. In the end, they might only be satisfied by the quick and clear answers they are used to receiving from their computers or information services.

In interpersonal communications, these people might desire the same extent of control they have gained over their relationship with computers/media. In texting on mobile phones they are able to end the message in a few words: 'Goodbye, I have to go to work'. In voice phone calls ending the conversation might feel to last ages. If the other person does not wish to meet the demands made, the rigid personality will retreat to his/her favourite medium and 'second self'.

> But if the sense of self becomes defined in terms of those things over which one can exert perfect control, the world of safe things becomes severely limited because those things tend to be things, not people. Mastery can cease to be a growing force in individual development and take on another face. It becomes a way of masking fears about the self and the complexities of the world beyond. People can become trapped. (Turkle, 1984: 124)

A second type, often combined with the first, could be called the *computerized personality*. Previously in this chapter we have seen that in our brains those functions that help us speedily locate, categorize, and assess disparate bits of information in a variety of forms have become stronger (Carr, 2009). This is an instance of adapting to computer processing. When the popular comparison between the human brain and the computer is taken too literally, some people may start considering the human brain to be a series of parallel connected processors, and the personality to be programmed and reprogrammable software. In her research among the first generation of computer users, Sherry Turkle already found several indications pointing in this direction. Users defined their personalities in terms of the differences and similarities with computers (and computer programs).

A third type could be called *the second-best social personality*. Computers and other media serve as a safe substitute for direct human company. This applies in particular to all those people who, for some reason or other, are afraid of intimacy, or rather, who want to gain more control over it, such as adolescents.

> Terrified of being alone, yet afraid of intimacy, we experience widespread feelings of emptiness, of disconnection, of the unreality of self. And here the computer, a companion without emotional demands, offers a compromise. You can be a loner, but never alone. You can interact, but never feel vulnerable to another person. (Turkle, 1984: 320)

Turkle (2011) has expanded these observations for the use of social robots, social media and mobile telephony. Social robots, virtual world avatars, Facebook profiles and texting or SNS contact lists serve even more as 'second selves' than desktop computers. All four provide safe substitutes for direct human contact, that is with real humans (instead of robots), in physical games and meetings with friends (instead of online games and meetings) and even in personal voice calls on the mobile phone (instead of mere text calls). They also serve as avatars and 'second selves' substituting the 'first self'. Who are you? Answer: your Facebook profile and your phone contact list. 'You are who you know' was the original popular expression of network theory. Being a 'network guy', I think this is only partially true. Yet, developing second-best social personalities it has become more of a reality than ever before.

An extremely dark potential consequence of the second-best social personality would be the loss of empathy for fellow humans of flesh and blood. Turkle (2011: 292–3) refers to American studies that showed a dramatic decline of this empathy among the young generations in the last 20 to 30 years. She adds:

> an online connection can be deeply felt, but you only need to deal with the part of the person you see in your game world or social network. Young people don't seem to feel that they need more, and over time they lose the inclination. (Turkle, 2011: 293)

My first comment would be that we do not know whether this trend, when it exists at all, is a result of our individualizing society or of the extensive use of media networks. My second comment is that, fortunately, empathy is a basic characteristic of humans that cannot be changed that fast. In my view, any loss of it can only be the result of a total immersion in online life, something rather exceptional at this moment in history. By the way, this is the prime condition of all worst case scenarios described in this section. The current situation is what Turkle herself calls the 'life mix', the start of an integration of online and offline life, not a substitute. The 'life mix' also offers the opportunity of combining the best of two worlds. I will come back to this positive view in the last chapter of this book.

Our final speculative type is the *multiple personality*. The Internet and many computer games enable us to play several roles and to assume several other identities by taking on pseudonyms. A game or simulation, such as a multi-user dungeon or domain (MUD) is based on these opportunities. Seriously playing with identities is a typical activity of modern society. Here, for the first time in history, people are not simply offered a fixed social personality, but have to partly shape their own personalities (Giddens, 1991b). Coolen (1997) claims the use of several identities on the Internet holds a mirror to our eyes. In this mirror, a modern view of people and the world is projected. This reality is not merely counterfeit, for modern identities are not fixed in advance. In (post)modernity, personalities become more multiple as some parts of our identities are revealed in some social contexts and other parts in others.

Sherry Turkle (1995; 1996a; 1996b) used to believe in the positive side of MUDs and all kinds of role-playing on the Internet. They offer the chance to experiment with our identities, as much as we like, and to find an answer to the question: who am I? Adolescents, in particular, could benefit from this. Today she has become much more critical about this (Turkle, 2011). The negative side of this play for the construction of identities is the fact that it does not help us very much in real life. Habitual searching for one's offline multiple identity already causes existential doubt (Giddens, 1991b). Turkle would clearly agree with Coolen (1997) who argued 15 years ago that the problem with Internet creations and games lies in the fact that *this reality does not offer any resistance*. It provides safe environments (see above). Users are not corrected and they can assume another identity when they want to. In this way they try to escape the bothersome and sometimes inharmonious relationships with physically present others. Escapism is the great risk of playing with identities on the Internet.

Becoming cyborgs?

A continuing development of these personality types and the advance of the technical capabilities of ICT and biotechnology may turn humans into some sort of *cyborgs*. This term links *cyber*netics with the human *organism*. This combination results in a system of human and technical components increasingly regulating itself within the environment and constituting a new whole. Little by little this technology is taken out of the sphere of science fiction and films such as *Robocop* and *Blade Runner* and adopted in reality (see Featherstone and Burrows, 1996; Mann, 2001; Thomas, 1996). Cyborgs are humans integrated in technology and technologies integrated in humans. It is a fact that people are more and more often equipped with artificial limbs and other technical devices, carrying them around everywhere and even inside their bodies. On the previous pages, the potential consequences of humanizing technology and of technology taking over more and more functions from humans have been described. The influence of ICT on humans must be greater than that of any other instrument. After all, it is an 'intelligent' technology having a direct impact on the human mind. Thus the means of ICT come closer and closer to the human brain.

In the future, ICT devices will be located not only in front of us, but also on and even inside our heads or bodies. Try to imagine what the mental consequences might be if, in 50 years' time, humans carry around a miniature but extremely powerful multimedia computer in the shape of a head installation for 24 hours a day. A simple oral command processed by voice recognition would suffice to literally see each image or piece of information desired, projected in front of their eyes (through glasses) or perhaps even directly on the retina through an implant chip. This extremely personal computer would serve not only as a second self, but also become a part of our 'first self', increasingly entering our deepest and most intimate personalities. When this time comes, we humans have to know who we are, what makes us different from machines such as computers, and, even more importantly, who we want to be. Otherwise one of our strongest capabilities, the ability to adapt quickly to our environment, will turn into a submission to a technology we would presently call inhuman.

CONCLUSIONS

- In the new media, the historical transition from direct experience to mediated perception is continued. Learning by action is gradually replaced by learning through symbol systems and visual models. This produces shifts in our modes of symbolic communication and the mental skills we need. Within the linguistic mode, the audiovisual variant is gaining importance at the expense of the oral and printed textual variants (not text per se). The growing use of graphics emphasizes the iconic mode and the use of computer language emphasizes the logico-mathematical mode of symbolic communication. The non-verbal mode has become less important, at least in new media without high-quality moving images. However, the most basic trend is the integration of modes in the multimedia.

- The ability to fully benefit from all the opportunities of the new media demands a full-grown visual, auditive, verbal, logical and analytical mental development. The problem is that the new media do not have to be used optimally. The integration of modes of communication also enables a much shallower use.

- The effects of new media use on human cognition depend on the similarities and differences of human and computer processing. The similarities intensify the phenomenon of humanization of our interaction with computers and the differences explain the numerous frictions in human–computer interaction. We have listed five basic differences. Computers realize a context-free and fragmentary perception and cognition that are completely pre-programmed. Computers use fixed schemata and they only achieve artificial 'intelligent' learning, without willpower, drive or emotion. Computers follow instructions, while humans make selections according to their needs. Evidently, computers are not biological and social creatures. Any attempt to fully imitate these human characteristics in computers or robots is bound to fail.

- The new media characteristics of interactivity and integration (multimedia, hyperlinks) enable types of learning far superior to the traditional ones. For instance, linear types of learning things by heart are partly replaced by associative types of learning. However, they can also lead to distraction and losing the argument. The capacity of 'deep reading' can be lost. Illusions of multi-tasking and the redundancy of basic knowledge, because everything can be searched and found, may lead to false learning strategies.

(Continued)

(Continued)

- CMC has proved not to be inferior to face-to-face communication. Users of CMC are able to compensate for technical limitations to produce actual, information-rich social environments. In this way, CMC might become personal, even hyper-personal, and help to build social relationships online and offline. The main problem of CMC is not its supposed replacement of face-to-face communication but its interplay with this type of communication. A satisfactory integration of online and offline communication is needed.

- Whether the new media are able to change our personalities is a speculative issue. It is certain that our relationships with these technologies are humanized. They are personalized, they are binding, fascinating or even addictive and they might even become our 'second self' in identity building. When humans are directly connected to computer media, they come close to being cyborgs. Our interaction with these media might even change our 'first selves'. Less speculative conclusions are that very intensive new media use is able to change our use of language, our social relationships, our view of the world and even our multiple identities in (post)modern society.

10 CONCLUSIONS AND POLICY PERSPECTIVES

About this chapter

- This chapter contains the most important conclusions of the book. First, it comes back to the definition of the network society and to an explanation of the importance of social and media networks for contemporary society. Second, it summarizes the theoretical conclusions on the basis of the seven 'laws of the Web' that have run through the argument of this book.

- Are information and network societies the same everywhere in the world? The answer given in this chapter is that they certainly are not. So far, Northern America, Europe, East Asia and the Third World have created rather different so-called information society development models. Eleven ideal-type models are used to describe the current situation in these parts of the world regarding the promotion of ICTs.

- The last section of this closing chapter proposes a number of general policy perspectives for the network society. Readers might be overwhelmed by the social aspects and effects discussed in this book. Are we able to influence them? Suggestions are made to safeguard access to the network society for all, to make it safe for citizens, consumers and society at large and to design its infrastructures such as the Internet. Should this be left completely to business enterprise or are other options available? The political control and the more or less democratic nature of the network society also require a number of policy suggestions. We have seen that international networks undermine the law. How can this problem be solved? Finally, it is discussed how the network society can bring us more returns, both material and immaterial. All these policy options are given against the background of a number of explicit norms and values such as democracy, equality and freedom.

GENERAL CONCLUSIONS
The scope of the network society

In Chapters 1 and 2, network society was defined as a form of society increasingly organizing its relationships in media networks, which are gradually merging with the social networks of face-to-face communication. This means that social and media networks are shaping the prime *mode of organization* and the most important *structures* of modern society. They are not the whole *substance* of society, as they are in the exaggerations of Manuel Castells (1996, 1997, 1998; see van Dijk, 1999). Society still consists of individuals, pairs, groups and organizations. Of course, they establish external and internal relations, but these relations do not equal society. The organic and material properties of individuals, pairs, groups and organizations with all their rules and resources cannot be cut out of society in order to return it to a set of formal relationships. Even a totally mediated society, where all relations are fully realized by, and substantiated in, media networks, where social and media networks equal each other, would still be based on bodies, minds, rules and resources of all kinds.

The first conclusion of this book is that modern society is *in a process of becoming* a network society, just as it is developing into an information society, a related concept. It is in a transition from mass to network society. Most contemporary societies are not yet full-grown network societies. Virtually all developing countries are still largely mass societies. To take the example of India: large parts of cities such as Bangalore or Hyderabad are strongly connected to the global network infrastructure and they are part of an Indian network society. However, the overwhelming part of the countryside of India still lives in a mass society as it consists of people with a high level of illiteracy and limited old mass media use. Their fast growing adoption of simple mobile phones is only a first step into the network society as described in this book. Developed societies are not 100 per cent network societies either. At least 20 or 25 per cent of the population never uses the Internet and many elderly scarcely use a mobile phone. In these countries, many people also use traditional mass media for information and entertainment, and face-to-face communication for social relationships.

A pervasive infrastructure

The main conclusions of this book will now be summarized in the arrangement of the seven 'laws of the Web' that were first introduced in Chapter 2 and that returned in virtually every chapter that followed. The first of these laws is the *law of network articulation*: a structure of relationships comes forward at the expense of the independence of the units they are linking. In Chapter 4, we have seen that networks are creating a network economy and networked organizations with actors who depend on each other. They serve as a new organizational form in between traditional hierarchies and markets. The new media sector itself is also networked when we take into account how the big new media companies are engaged in platform competition offering their own standards and dependencies. In Chapter 4 and 5 it was shown that the national state is submitted to the yoke of global economic and financial networks. As a reaction, the state itself evolves into some kind of network state. Politics becomes Internet politics. In Chapter 6, we have noticed that our current law system, based on the notion of independent actors, acts and property items is undermined by networks. In Chapter 7 the idea comes forward that the whole social structure of modern society is increasingly built on networks. The structure is marked by network individualization and a polarized class structure of digital divides. Social media and online communities start to dominate social relationships. Chapter 8 has described the rise of a cyber-culture or a digital culture of hyper-linked user-generated content. Finally, In Chapter 9 we have seen that in using networks such as the Internet and mobile telephony we can be 'alone together' (Sherry Turkle), increasingly depending on others we cannot fully reach.

So, a network structure pervades all spheres of society. This makes the metaphor of networks as a nervous system of society an appropriate image. This is also true because the network structure connects all levels of society, usually called the micro-, meso- and macro-level, and merges the private and the public spheres. It was noticed that the dividing lines between these abstractions are blurring. On the Internet, interpersonal, organizational and mass communication come together. Using this medium, we bring the 'whole world' into our homes and workplaces. However, the blurring of traditional dividing lines does not result in their disappearance. It only means that we have to invent new dividing lines. The difference between public and private domains remains important. Interpersonal communication will not become equal to mass communication. It would be very harmful for people to remove every distinction between working time, leisure time and sleeping time because they can check new media connections everywhere and all of the time.

The articulation and pervasion of network structures have many effects that I have described in the previous chapters. However, two qualifications apply. First, this first law of the web is not a matter of natural necessity. In social science, structure, action and consciousness are a dialectic unity, such as that explained in the theory of structuration (Giddens, 1984). Structures appear in communicative action. This leaves room for agency and consciousness. Network structures are not natural necessities, but they are both defining and enabling. They offer choices within particular limits. This is why it is claimed here that the views presented in this book are neither pessimistic nor optimistic. In the first decades of the 21st century, new media such as the Internet are gradually appearing to be 'normal media'. Soon they will not be called 'new' anymore. Because they become normal media they will increasingly reflect all present characteristics and trends of society – both those being viewed as good and bad.

The second qualification is that the effects of network structures on society are not unidirectional. They have a *dual structure*. A combination of scale extension and scale reduction marks all applications of the new media in the economy, politics, culture and personal experience. This combination is the prime advantage and attractiveness of these media. It explains their fast adoption in what was considered to be a communications revolution. A dual structure results in several oppositions explained in the previous chapters: centralization and decentralization, central control and local autonomy, unity and fragmentation, socialization and individualization. To claim that these opposites form a whole and may be observed in both the causes and the effects of new media usage is not the easy assertion of an indecisive author. It is a prime characteristic of network structure itself. Networks both connect and disconnect. They have centres, nodes and relations between them. At these points we find human beings who participate and decide differently and who are central or marginalized, included or excluded.

The pervasiveness of network structures in modern society is enforced by combinations of social and media networks. Media networks are not simply channels or conduits of communication: they are becoming social environments themselves (Meyrowitz, 1985, 1997). They are settings for social interaction, bridging the individual settings or environments of numerous people acting at their nodes and terminals. Media have their own particular characteristics, which are called communication capacities in this book, but we cannot understand how they work out in practice if we do not learn about the social context of their use and their users. This contextual approach explains the attention to the relationship between mediated and face-to-face communication in this book. The central conclusion is that media networks and mediated communication do not replace social networks and face-to-face communication, but are integrated with them. They become interwoven. They create a unified physical and media ecology that hopefully will combine the strong characteristics of meetings and mediation.

Inclusion and equation

The second law of the Web was called the *law of network externality*. Networks have effects on people and things external to the network. First, they contain a drive to connect. When a threshold of about 20 to 25 per cent access is reached, diffusion accelerates. This is what we have seen considering the Internet in the developed countries. Most developing countries are in that stage now. However, when a second tipping point is reached at about 65 to 70 per cent, saturation sets in. The last third of society is far more difficult to include. They contain people who do not want Internet access or have no means (money and skills) to use it. They consist of elderly or poor and low educated people or perhaps they are migrants. These are reasons why the digital divide remains a problem. Even when there is almost universal access, unequal digital skills come forwards.

Another network effect is the drive to standardize and equate. Without this effect, network communication would not be possible. Internet users want standards to be able to communicate with everybody. Standards are not just technical characteristics such as network protocols. They also are economic common forms. In a free market society, this means that a few big network companies are trying to promote their own standards. In Chapter 4 we have seen that Microsoft, Google, Apple and Facebook offer their own standards on their own Internet platform. The winner of this competition, if there is one, will largely control the Internet of the future.

Intermediation

In the early years of the Internet many people thought that this new medium was completely free and under the control of the users. Editors and mass media gatekeepers would no longer be needed. All users could choose, create and exchange contents themselves. This was the idea of disintermediation. It has proved to be completely false. The third law of the Web, the *law of network extension* holds that, in a short period of time, a network becomes so extended that intermediary and mediating nodes simply are required to make things work. This is a matter of scale. We would drown in the vast information ocean of the Internet without search engines. To organize our online social relationships without the intermediary of a SNS would be impossible. Reading an online newspaper or magazine without any conviction that their contents have had a reality check (and even double checked) in an environment of misinformation and rumours, would simply be considered a waste of time. The more information and communication overload a medium contains, the more intermediaries are needed to organize contents and contacts. This means that quality information brokers, contact agents and newspapers have a future.

Intermediaries have become so vital that they tend to gather a lot of power. We have seen that companies such as Microsoft, Google, Apple and Facebook try to control the Internet according to their own design. The design of these American companies is certainly not neutral. We have argued that they have their own idea of the nature of the Internet. They claim to respond to the needs of the average Internet user, but their designs and corporate strategies are not entirely clear to most users. So, users do not know how their Internet behaviour is influenced by these designs. Who is familiar with the formulas behind the search engine Google? Who knows exactly what Facebook is doing with the personal data of its users? What ideas of social networking are behind the typical applications Facebook is offering you to keep in touch with your contacts? What kind of newspaper reading is promoted by Apple's iPad? And, wouldn't it be possible that a culture historian of the late 21st century 'discovers' that Microsoft software of a century ago was a typical product of American office culture?

Connectivity and contagion

According to the law of *network externality*, networks have effects on people and things external to the network. They have the internal drive to grow and to exert all kinds of effects on human behaviour and the organization of things in material production. According to the law of *small worlds*, they increase the connectivity of people, organizations and societies. Presently, connectivity accelerates to proportions never known before. This goes for people that can reach each other in a few seconds or minutes in all parts of the world with an abundant choice of partly overlapping media: telephone calls, voicemail, SMS, Instant Messages, email, fax, SNS messages, Twitter and chat messages. Despite broad and deep digital divides, access rates are growing fast everywhere. On account of this growth, the six degrees of separation, keeping individuals apart, tend to be reduced to five or even four (see Chapter 2).

275

A more recent development is that things are also increasingly connected using inbuilt chip technology. As we have seen, this changes production, distribution and consumption processes.

On the basis of this connectivity, social processes as old as human kind are finding new and ever faster venues. Among others, people imitate each other and their behaviour is clearly contagious. I have discussed the three *degrees of influence* between people (Chapter 2). As this network effect comes on top of an ever smaller number of *degrees of separation*, contagion is accelerating. This is exactly what we can observe: – both good and bad information (rumours, gossip) are spreading faster than ever before. For example, the stock markets have become places of herd behaviour. Here, inaccurate and irrational information processing often overrules accurate and rational processing. Stock prices jump up and down. With the aid of ICT networks, financial trade has become faster and more voluminous than ever before. Networks have become a mode of organization next to markets (Chapter 4). So, in the age of the rule of financial capital, these networks certainly are not innocent to the current credit and debt crises. The laws of contemporary global capitalism are causing this crisis, but evidently networks amplify its workings (Chapter 4).

The most basic consequence of the rise of connectivity and contagion is that the network society is an unstable type of society (Chapter 7). Though networks are able to assist in a better informed and organized society which is more coherent, they also amplify all current tensions in society.

Concentration and fragmentation

According to the law of *network extension*, the scale of a network is likely to extend. However, this can only happen when the internal structure of a network is adapted in such a way that the scale can also be managed via intermediaries and reduced to enable units to connect not only with everyone at random but also, and primarily, with those in a socially close cluster. The combination of scale extension and scale reduction is a structure of networks and the network society that has returned in every chapter. The most important example is a concept under tension: network individualization. Individualization is scale reduction while networking means scale extension.

The opposites of scale extension and scale reduction return in all kinds of opposing tendencies at a lower level of abstraction that have marked the analysis of the network society in this book. An important one is the combination of unity or concentration and fragmentation. Networks help to create a new social cohesion in society but they also serve to increase a social and cultural diversity of countless subcultures. In the media sector, the opposite scales appear as a combination of new media concentration and fragmentation. The Internet is increasingly dominated by a few big companies with the surprising effect that media concentration on the Internet is higher than in the traditional media. At the other end we find the fragmentation of Anderson's long tail: a countless number of small media sources are available on the Internet. Strikingly, the middle that consists of medium-sized Internet media is much smaller. As we have seen, Internet media concentration is reinforced by the *law of the limits to attention* on the Web.

The rich are getting richer, but what will happen to the poor?

The law of the limits to attention on the Web is linked to another law, *the power law*, among others via 'Googlearchy': those sources that are already on top of the list become even more popular because of search engine ranking. This produces concentration and inequality of sources. 'The rich are getting richer' is the most popular expression. In this book it was argued that social and information inequality tends to rise in networks despite the fact that networks are able to connect and to spread knowledge and other resources. Those that already have the most material, social, cultural and personal resources are most likely to acquire the special resource of the Internet and the resourceful opportunities this network brings. They have the best chances to reach physical access and the highest motivations to use it. They develop the best digital skills of all kinds. And they use it to a large degree for serious applications that give them an advance in their studies and careers.

What will happen to the poor? A slinking number is excluded because they have no access at all. A growing number will face *relative* inequality because they benefit systematically less from the new media than those rich in resources. The information elite is likely to grow. Relative inequality is especially important in a network society because in this kind of society, power is built on relationships (van Dijk, 2005). Without defending an instrumentalist view of technology (see van Dijk, 2010a), I have to conclude that the access and use of networks are important tools that work like a lever in the hoarding of opportunities (Tilly, 1998).

Trend amplification

A last conclusion concerns the overall effect of the new media on modern society. Will they have revolutionary implications for society, will they only gradually transform society, or will they have no substantial effect? To put it another way: will the network society be an altogether different type of society? In this book, the answers to these questions are that changes will be evolutionary rather than revolutionary and that the network society will not be an altogether different type of society.

These answers do not oppose the acceptance of the concept of the communications revolution discussed in Chapters 1 and 3. This is a revolution at the level of media development itself. It is not a concept of the revolutionary effects of media on society. On the contrary, the first communications revolution at the turn of the 19th to 20th century, as described by Beniger, was a *consequence* of a revolution – the industrial revolution. In this book, we have frequently observed that the new media intensify trends that have already appeared before and that they reinforce existing social relationships in modern society. According to the seventh law of the Web, the new media are *trend amplifiers*. This comes close to the picture presented by Brian

Winston in his *Media Technology and Society* (1998). In a detailed overview of media history from the telegraph to the Internet, he contends that modern media's most important contribution is the so-called 'law of the suppression of radical potential'. New media technologies, which have a revolutionary promise at first, are later moulded to existing social processes. According to Winston, we should not forget that these processes both promote and hinder the adoption of new technologies. It would be interesting to test this 'law' in the development of the Internet from its revolutionary promise in the 1990s to its 'normalization' in the first part of the 21st century.

However impressive and wide-ranging the potential social consequences of the new media, as described in this book, they will not change the foundation of present developed societies, let alone developing societies. Perhaps ICT has made a contribution to the collapse of the Soviet Union and other communist states, as this technology does not fit traditional bureaucratic authority and planning (see Castells, 1998). However, capitalism is here to stay. It is likely to be reinforced or reinvigorated by the new media in an accelerated, flexible and socially harsher shape. However, instability and crisis potential grow equally fast.

Patriarchy may be in crisis in large parts of the world (Castells, 1997), but it will take a very long time before it withers away, and the new media will have only a small, if any, part in that process. Nor will ecological destruction be halted by the new media. At the most, these media contribute to a dematerialization of the economy and to higher efficiency and effectiveness in helping to save natural resources. The globalization of the economy is not caused by ICT, but is intensified by it. It is to be observed that the national state and sovereignty are undermined by the new media, but they will not disappear. Moreover, a concentration of politics in a surveillance state, party state or infocratic state is a possibility as well (Chapter 5). Rising social and information inequalities are not caused by ICT, but they might be increased by an exclusive appropriation of its opportunities by a relatively minor part of the population. I could carry on in this vein for many more pages, but it seems wiser to continue describing the diverging ways modern societies have tried to fit the advent of this new technology to their existing policies.

THE NETWORK SOCIETY IN NORTH AMERICA, EUROPE, EAST ASIA AND THE THIRD WORLD

The design of the information and network society

Is the information and network society created by policy in a conscious way? This appears to be only partly true. The characteristics of this type of society, as described in this book, are rather abstract. They are not clearly visible and proceed in a creeping way. They change the basic structures (networks) and substances (information) of society. So, it is doubtful whether policy-makers of all kinds (governments, businesses, community organizations and households) are able to develop the visions required to influence the information or network society. Nevertheless, the more or less conscious and autonomous actions of these kinds of policy-makers are really creating the information and network society we are able to observe.

On the other hand, the information and network society lends itself to conscious policy more than previous classifications of society. Information, at least partially, is a conscious activity that leads to other conscious activities such as education policies. Networks are infrastructures that can be built just like roads. So, in theory the information and network society can be designed before it is put into practice. Such designs are actually made in a number of policy perspectives or models for building the information society, the information superhighway, the global information infrastructure or whatever they are called.

In the many designs that have been proposed worldwide in the last 25 years, a number of similarities have appeared. In addition, a number of diverging information society designs have emerged that characterize policies in different parts of the world. I first summarize the similarities and then examine the differences by describing the information and network society policies in North America, Europe, East Asia and the Third World.

Similarities of information society policy perspectives

The most important similarity for its real and lasting impact is the historic decision made in most parts of the world to invite *market forces to take the lead* and construct the nervous system of our future societies. In this age of liberalization and privatization, governments have acquired the role of catalyst and protector of social and legal conditions. Building the (infra)structure and providing the content of the information and network society itself and defining all its opportunities and effects has largely been left to business enterprise. This applies to the policy of every country, from the complete dominance of corporate interests in the United States, through the somewhat stronger public–private partnership in Europe, to the strong stimulus of the developmental states in East Asia (to be explained below).

In this time of cuts in public expenditure, the level of economic investment by governments themselves is low. Most often they do not even have a plan or vision about the shape and nature of a coherent information infrastructure. Therefore business corporations construct this infrastructure according to their own interests and expectations (see Brown, 1997). The governments, perhaps, make corrections afterwards by enforcing competition, interconnection and common standards.

A second similarity is the nature of national policy initiatives and action plans: they are essentially *economic projects*. The predominant intention is to improve nations' positions on the global markets of the future. Clearly, this is a part of the economic race between North America, Europe and East Asia. This means that the economic aspects always come first and the social aspects second or nowhere at all.

A related point of agreement is the *technological determinist nature* of most perspectives and the *supply-side orientation* of the economics concerned. The focus is on infrastructure rather than on the content and the services that the new media are supposed to deliver. The fast diffusion of ICT, and in its wake the information society, are seen as inevitable. The opportunities are simply too attractive to be refused by corporate and household consumers. They just have to adopt the new media. These expectations have been backed by a series of hypes following one after another: first the Internet in general, then e-commerce to be followed by broadband and wireless communications. Finally, the most recent hypes related to the Web 2.0 perspective and the social media.

All policy perspectives adopted by national governments and international bodies and conferences after 1993 clearly are a matter of *promotional action*. The technology concerned was developing for decades and nothing special happened at the beginning of the 1990s. In fact, the Internet and other new media meant nothing to the vast majority of Americans, Europeans and other populations at that time. Launching the so-called information superhighway or national information infrastructure was a matter of raising awareness among corporations and citizens about things to come. Almost every developed country in the world adopted an action plan to support the construction, regulation and promotion of this new infrastructure.

In the 1990s, the things to come were presented in *grand visions* of the immense potential benefits of this technology to the societies and economies concerned. The opportunities were emphasized rather than the risks. The information revolution would produce economic growth, new jobs, better education, a higher quality of life, environmental protection by savings on travelling and energy and a boost to more direct types of democracy. Approaching the risks was a matter of courage and of regulatory protection of universal access, safety, privacy and intellectual property rights.

At the end of the 1990s, propaganda and wild expectations gradually gave way to a more sober view of the information society. In these years, the new media slowly entered social and economic life, producing real problems requiring solutions that were different from the early expectations. After the turn of the century and the collapse of the Internet hype, this trend intensified. Eventually, age-old differences between countries with regard to their economic, social and political systems and cultures drifted to the surface again.

Differences of policies: information society models

To summarize the differences of global information society policies I gratefully adopt the classification of seven information society models that Shalini Venturelli (1998, 2002) has made in a similar international comparison. I have added four models that are especially important to the Third World. See Box 10.1.

BOX 10.1

information society development models (inspired by Venturelli, 2002)

Libertarian model	The information society (IS) should be built by businesses, citizens and consumers. No state intervention.
Liberal market model	The IS should be developed by market forces. States should only regulate when needed.
Public interest model	The business and public interest should be balanced in building the IS. States should regulate and intervene to protect the public interest.
Public service model	The IS should be inclusive as part of a welfare state. Services for every citizen and consumer should have focus of attention.
National cultural model	The IS is not only an economic but also a cultural project. Local cultures should be protected in a globalizing environment.
Development model	State intervention is needed to stimulate the national economic interest in the IS.
Corporate model	States, corporations and their employees should cooperate to build the national IS.
Stage approach	The IS is built in stages, especially in developing countries: first the technical infrastructure, then products and services, and finally education and digital skills of the population.
Leap-frogging strategy	Developing countries are able to jump across stages of development by building cheap wireless infrastructures and enclaves of ICT hardware and software production.
Organic development strategy	Developing countries can only gradually develop. Education, health and basic infrastructures should have priority before ICT.
Combination development strategy	Developing countries should simultaneously invest in technical (ICT), educational and service capabilities.

North America

The United States reveals the similarities described in the clearest way. It is the guiding country in the design of information society plans, products and services. Initially, it looked like the US would be the first full-grown information and network society. However, in the last ten years it has been overtaken by Northern Europe and parts of East Asia that have higher Internet access and usage rates. Yet, the country remains the main centre of ICT development on the world market and it still dominates the Internet because all of the big Internet companies are American (Microsoft, Apple, Google, Yahoo, MySpace, Facebook) and because it has the most influence in Internet bodies such as ICANN. The US leads the market in software and services and, to a lesser extent, (network) hardware.

So, it is no surprise that the centrality of business interest and private initiative with regard to the new media is strongest in the United States. However, according to Venturelli (1998, 2002) this focus manifests itself through three rather different, competing American information society models or 'socio-political frameworks': the libertarian model, the liberal market model and the public interest model.

The libertarian tradition in the US has been dominant among the designers and early adopters of the Internet right from the start (see the discussion of the libertarian view of democracy in Chapter 5). It has been called 'the Californian Ideology' as it is closely linked to the IT industry of Silicon Valley and other Californian regions. Its point of departure is the concept of minimal state influence and a maximum of initiative and regulation by businesses (first of all) to be followed by citizens and consumers as they are the developers and main users of ICT. In this view, 'the information networks of a society should be open and non-proprietary, with strict constraints placed upon state intervention' (Venturelli, 2002: 71). It is averse to control, regulation or monopolization of the information society from above. Conflicts should be resolved by consensus or agreement by the network users themselves in self-regulation. The roots of this tradition can be found in the typical American perspective of the perpetual New Frontier, the continuous conquest of new space, in this instance 'cyberspace'.

Although the early days of the Internet are over, the libertarian model persists in the continuous struggle by many Internet business advocates, academics and electronic pressure groups in the United States for open architectures and open source software, for the preservation of fair use rights for intellectual property and for new business models in the Internet economy.

Far more influential, and in fact dominating the American information and network society policy, is the US liberal market model. This is backed by all large business interests and their representatives in the US government, who also argue for a minimum of state intervention, but they simultaneously ask for a 'powerful legal regime guaranteeing contractual and proprietary rights in the market place' (Venturelli, 2002: 73). In this respect, the liberal market model opposes the libertarian model, which advocates open sources and fair use rights. Another basic difference is an emphasis on legal and market business regulation, while the libertarians propose self-regulation.

So, in the liberal market model, the law should protect contracts and property rights. Anti-trust law is accepted with reluctance, but general laws to protect privacy and consumer interests are rejected. This is the reason why these are so weak in the United States. According to Yao (2003: 433), the prevailing US perspective is to give the market the time to sort out these types of problems themselves and to develop self-corrections. In the long term this would lead to cheaper, better and safer products that would be in the interest of consumers.

The public interest tradition in the United States aims to balance the interests of consumers with those of industry. The markets in the communication sector are not perfect, but they can be improved by regulation covering competition law, fair trade, consumer protection, universal access, educational investment, government investment in innovation, the protection of privacy and of minors, the interconnection of networks and the maintenance of fair use rights, to mention the most important ones (Venturelli, 2002: 72).

The public interest model is supported by a minority that includes consumer organizations, civil rights organizations, trade unions, people working in the public media, many intellectuals and those who are called 'liberals' in the United States. This model has lost ground in the last 25 years. Most attempts at the regulation described above have not been successful. The universal access obligations in telecommunications are almost the only achievement. These have funded many computer access points in schools, libraries, hospitals, community centres and other public buildings.

The result of the competition between these models is a clear victory for the liberal market model. This has made the United States the most competitive economy in the world in the information and communication sector. However, this has happened at the expense of many public interests and the basis of support for future innovation, because many Americans do not have access to the information infrastructure and lack the digital skills required (van Dijk, 2005; Wilhelm, 2004). Private law and contract law are strongly emphasized, but public law has been neglected (Venturelli, 2002: 73).

The low attention to problems of access, skills and innovation, which were thought to be automatically solved by the market, has led to stagnation of the US as compared to Northern Europe and parts of Eastern Asia such as South Korea and Japan. Here broadband access and use have developed much faster (the US was only 15th on the global list of broadband adoption in 2008). This is the reason why, in 2009, a national broadband policy was adopted in the *American Recovery and Reinvestment Act*. This investment plan can be seen as a compromise of the liberal market and public interest models.

In the US market, economic freedom in relation to ICT is not matched by comparable cultural, economic and political freedoms for its users. On the contrary, the US record of restricting this freedom in the name of national security and the fight against crime and terrorism is impressive: the Communications Decency Act, the discouragement or ban of encryption, the proposals of key escrow and all kinds of hardware blocking chips, the infringement of fair use rights as compared to copyright and the Patriot Act are clear examples that were discussed in Chapter 6.

People claiming civil and public rights often lose their case in the courts against business interests and government security (Catinat, 1997; Miller, 1996). This is mainly due to legal shortcomings: one has to make an appeal either to one of the many specific acts or to the very general constitution (see Rustad, 2009 and Chapter 6).

A fragmentary legislation full of holes benefits parties with the best lawyers or well-organized interest and pressure groups.

Compared with the United States, the other North American state, Canada, has produced more safeguards against the effects of corporate dominance, for instance in public information supply and privacy legislation (Magder, 1996). In Canada, the public interest model is much stronger (see Canadian Internet Forum, 2011). In this way, the Canadian information society more closely resembles the models prevailing in Europe.

Europe

In Europe, we have to make a distinction between the EU of 15 member states in the north, west and south of the continent, the 13 (mainly) Eastern European countries that have recently been added to the EU, and the rest of formerly communist Eastern Europe. For the EU, the development of the information society is a matter of the highest priority. The EU risks losing the battle of competition on the global information market with North America and East Asia. It lags behind in hardware production (except for telecommunication equipment), in software and in audio-visual productions. It takes a prime position only in the production of local services and so-called multimedia content because of its allegedly rich cultural heritage.

The biggest difference between the United States and Europe is the European tendency towards government intervention to promote and regulate the information society. This tendency considerably declined in the 1990s. However, according to Venturelli, the EU policy, at least, is still a contest among three principal forms of intervention: the EU liberal market model, the EU public service model and the EU national-cultural model.

Liberalization and privatization substantially changed the European information and communication sector in the 1990s. However, the liberal market model that promoted these changes is rather different from the US liberal market model. European economic neo-liberalism accepts and even expects public intervention in this sector, both by government stimulation and by public law. The European unification project has served as the main legitimation and mandate to accomplish this. In the EU, every policy is subordinate to the task of creating a common market between member states. Information society projects are excellent opportunities for the European Commission, the Council of Ministers and the central directorates to unify Europe with a new mission: to strengthen Europe's position on the world market and to legitimize their own role as coordinating powers of the EU (see Garnham, 1997).

The prime European approach to the information society that opposes the liberal market approach is the public service model (Venturelli, 2002: 76–8). This model derives from the tradition of European countries being welfare states. In this model, the government is needed to guarantee the general welfare of citizens and their access to services that are essential to participate in the information society. This means universal access to telecommunications, high standards of privacy protection, recognition of authors' rights and fair use rights, strong competition rules, standards for the quality of networks and their services and public investment in research and innovation, employment, education and health (Ibid.: 77). The EU public service model should not be confused with the US public interest model. The European model aims to safeguard the constitutional *rights of citizens* in an information society by the distribution of public *services*. In the American model, the only government role is to protect by law the *interests of consumers* and *small producers* against unregulated big corporate power.

European policies are complicated by a third model, the EU national-cultural model. This model of the information society emphasizes the content to be distributed and exchanged in networks; this content should safeguard, support and enrich the different national cultures in the EU. The model stresses that the national communities are expressive (cultural) instead of economic or political unities (Venturelli, 2002: 78). For this reason the national media are protected against the threats of the global, read 'American', market as regards audiovisual policy, content regulation and program production of the new media.

The struggle between the EU liberal market, public service and national-cultural models has led to an indefinite project to build the information society since the 1990s. It is no surprise that EU information society policies oscillate between broader social concerns, such as social inclusion for all, national considerations and a more technology- and market-oriented focus (Henten and Kristensen, 2000: 83).

The provisional result of this competition is that the liberal market model has reached the most dominant position and that for the EU as a whole, the information society has mainly been an economic project. Each year the EU spends several billion euros on information society projects. The legislation of the member states is adapted and harmonized to create a stronger economic position, which is urgently needed from a European perspective. The number of people and enterprises with access to computers and networks in the southern and eastern parts of the EU clearly lags behind the rest of the EU and North America. With regard to innovation, Europe loses the competition with the United States and East Asia (taking hardware into consideration). The so-called 'Lisbon 2000 agenda' – to become the most competitive and innovative economy in the world in ten years – has been a miserable failure.

In 2010, a new attempt was made in the context of the Europe 2020 plan, called the *Digital Agenda* (European Commission, 2010). This Agenda contained, among others: plans to speed up the roll-out of high-speed internet; to create a single market for online content and services; to use EU funds for innovation in the sector of ICT; and to support digital literacy and accessibility. In this way it appears to be a clear compromise between the EU liberal market model and the EU public service model.

An achievement of the European public service model is greater attention to digital access and skills problems than in most other parts of the world. A second accomplishment is a greater civil rights orientation in the information society policy of the EU as compared with the United States and, much more clearly, East Asia. The EU has adopted comprehensive privacy legislation that serves as an example for the rest of the world. It has imposed relatively few restrictions on information and communication freedom; and it is friendly towards encryption and the right to anonymity of communication on the Internet. However, with regard to intellectual property rights, it has adopted roughly the same position as the United States, benefiting the copyright industry and harming the public interests of users, libraries and educational institutions. See Chapter 6 for these differences and similarities.

However, a stronger government role, both European and national, has also enabled the EU to emphasize interconnection and open standards and to confront new monopolistic tendencies on the private market. For example, the EU rather than the United States forced the American company Microsoft to launch a version of Internet Explorer without a media player in 2004.

Eastern Europe lags behind the (rest of the) EU in the diffusion and development of ICT, even compared to southern Europe. The Eastern European countries keep large state bureaucracies. To stimulate new media development, they have welcomed a wild type of capitalism that is no longer present in the EU. As the governments in these countries lack the means for investment in new technologies, transnational media and telephone companies have jumped into the gap and offered commercial broadcasting and mobile telephony. The initial results decreased rather than increased access to information channels for the populations concerned, first of all in Russia (Vartanova, 1998).

However, after the coming to power of president Putin, Russia has fallen back to an authoritarian statist variant of the development model (see Alexander, 2003). See Box 10.1. This means state intervention to control the Internet and to promote, among others, e-government and the connections of schools. The Russian state now controls the majority of ISPs (in order to survey Internet content) while network connections are realized by oligarchic private interests. Internet access approached 40 per cent in 2011. However, it is extremely uneven, divided between city and countryside and between the half of Russian Internet users that has broadband access and the other half that still has to use unattractive and limited dial-up access.

East Asia

East Asia (Japan, China, Taiwan, Hong Kong, South Korea, Malaysia and Singapore) is the second largest actor on the global market of information technology after the United States. It is particularly strong in hardware production. In software and information services it is much weaker. The most conspicuous characteristic of East Asia concerning the information and network society is the large role of the state, which is called a *developmental state* by Castells (1998). In the 1990s, most of the states in this region of the world launched national deployment programmes for an information infrastructure. Examples are the Technopolis and Teletopia programmes in Japan; the Multimedia Super Corridor Project in Malaysia; Singapore One, a nationwide high-speed multimedia network; and the Korea21 Project in South Korea.

The Asian developmental state is not some kind of socialist planning agency (with the partial exception of China). This kind of state accepts the rules of global capitalism and merely aims to transform the economic order in the interest of the nation, neglecting or repressing all other interests like information and communication freedoms in civil society (Castells, 1998: 271). It makes strategic and selective interventions in the economy to promote and sustain development, but it leaves the execution to private enterprise. It guides and coordinates the process of industrialization, sets up the necessary infrastructure, attracts foreign capital and decides on priorities for strategic investment (Ibid.: 256).

This view of stimulating the information society is called the East Asian development model by Venturelli (2002: 80–2). Although hardware production is almost completely privately owned, the telecommunication, broadcasting and other media service sectors have largely remained state-owned public monopolies. However, they have served to support industry and the development of the nation as a whole; but they have not encouraged the civil societies in these countries. These are notoriously weak as compared to the EU and the United States. The public media monopolies have not supported a public sphere with broad participation in debate, there is no large proportion of non-commercial public services in support of the building of communities and associations and no 'educational system that cultivates independent judgment instead of rote learning' (Ibid.: 82). Instead, they have curtailed citizens' information rights with restrictive freedom of information laws and public service obligations for information providers.

This state-led development is combined with a liberalized corporate model that appeared with the global shift toward liberalization and democratization in the 1980s and 1990s. The particular shape this shift adopted in East Asia is a corporatist approach that depends on a close cooperation between the large industrial conglomerates competing on the world market, their workforces and the state.

This role of the state might be very beneficial to the expansion of information technology hardware industries in these countries. In this market, they are extremely successful. However, the logic of the state and of the international market often collide. In the background are East Asian social and cultural values. Family networks and personal relationships organize business enterprise, the state institutions and the links between them. Personal and state protection prevent unfavourable conditions in industry and bad bank loans from resulting in immediate punishment by the market, or independent control and supervision by financial authorities. The problem is not too much protection by the state and financial supervisors, but the wrong protection, biased by proximate private interests.

The second problem is the growing conflict between the developmental state and the information or network society it has brought to life (Castells, 1998: 236). The emphasis on hardware production and diffusion comes at the expense of innovation in software and services, except for the most generally used in e-commerce and Internet service provision (Wong, 2002). The strategy behind this emphasis is a stage approach to development (van Dijk, 2005: 198). The first phase is to boost the industrial production of ICTs that will subsequently lead to a large-scale adoption of ICT by the population at large. The final phase will be the development of digital information skills, information services and advanced innovation. The problem, however, is that the last phase may never arrive, or will arrive much later than in other parts of the world.

The conflict between the developmental state and the information or network society this state has brought to life with hesitation is most clearly visible in The Peoples Republic of China. Here the development model is extremely successful. In a very short time-span, China has become the biggest Internet country in the world. In 2011 it passed the number of 500 million Internet users or 35 per cent of the population. The majority has a broadband connection. For all big American Internet company applications it has developed local alternatives such as the search engine Baidu, the encyclopedia Hudong and the micro-blogging site called Weibo.

Private enterprise and initiatives realize most Chinese Internet hardware, software and applications under the supervision of the state. The problem for the Chinese government is that the Internet helps to create a public sphere that is much freer than it would like to accept. The government tries to control information and communication on the Internet at all costs. In the year 2000 it started with outright censorship of a very blunt type in a project called the *Great Firewall of China*. In the year 2010, 1.3 million websites were shut (41 per cent of the total number of sites) while web-pages kept growing (BBC Asia Pacific, 2011). However, in the meantime much more sophisticated censorship types are being explored, including the use of self-censorship (Morozov, 2011, Castells, 2009).

The conservative and bureaucratic character of the East Asian developmental state does not fit with the continuous innovation, flexibility and openness (debate to improve things) required in a network society. The lack of openness and innovation capacity in developing computer networks is partly caused by restrictions on communication freedom and the outright censorship of the Internet as described.

The Third World

The connection of Third World countries to the global information and communication networks is a clear case of combined and uneven development. It is *combined* because any country in the world has connections to the international telephone system, global broadcasting and data networks such as the Internet. In all countries lives a small elite with advanced new media access and experience. The adjective 'small' is relative, as the elite may consist of millions of people, as is estimated to be the case in India. This elite is working in the cities and nodes that are connected to global networks. Most of the nodes are business and government research centres, financial markets, branches of transnational corporations, software programming departments and defence or security agencies.

However, the development is uneven as well, and increasingly so, because the overwhelming majority of the population does scarcely participate. It is lagging behind compared with the diffusion of new media in the nodes of their own countries, and even more as compared with the developed countries. This majority has little access even to old media such as the telephone, radio, TV and the press and to essential services such as electricity. The only exception is the spread of cheap mobile phones (see below). Some newly industrializing countries such as China, Brazil, Iran and South Africa have experienced a tremendous rise in the use of computers and connections to the Internet. Their rapidly growing middle classes of hundreds of millions of people are already entering the information and network society. However, most fast growing economies of the Third World are typically also dual economies. The majority of their populations lags far behind and remains a poor mass society. Take the example of India. This country, with a lot of software programmers and service providers, only had 8.4 per cent Internet access in 2010, while approximately half of Indian households owned a television.

A consequence of this combined and *uneven* development is a subordination of the organic development required in poor countries to the dynamics of the global economy and its networks (Mansell, in press). The few computers and network connections in developing countries are barely used for applications in agriculture, health, education, public works, water resources, public transportation, public information, population planning, rural and urban land development or public utilities. Instead, they are used by the military, executive branches of government, transnational corporations, banks, major universities and research centres (Sussman, 1997: 248). The populations of these countries mainly use their mobile phones and Internet connections for communication and social networking, far less for work and education.

This last paragraph refers to the potential strategies of models to develop an information society in the Third World. Venturelli has not discussed the models proposed in this part of the world. I will add four strategies or models (see van Dijk, 2005).

The first strategy is to adopt some kind of stage approach, as in East Asia. This means, first, rolling out the technical infrastructure and promoting a local industry of ICT production and software development. The second stage is to invest in operational digital skills, first for those who need them most and then for the whole population. The final stage is to develop usage applications for the masses. A consequence of this strategy might be that government policy focuses on business access at the cost of equitable access (Kenny, 2002). This strategy joins with globalization policies and with the liberal market models discussed above.

A second strategy is an accelerated version of the stage approach. It is considered possible for a Third World country to leap-frog stages of development and go directly to the production of ICT in enclaves of industrial regions linked directly to the world market, as in some East Asian countries and in Costa Rica (chip production) and India, which focuses on software programming (see Press et al., 1999 and Steinmüller, 2001). A technological infrastructure could be built very quickly using wireless technologies and cheap terminal devices (simple computers and mobile phones). The diffusion of mobile phones in the Third World is incredibly fast, indeed. Phones are also used for Internet access. In countries such as India and Indonesia, more than half of Internet access goes via mobile phones. James (2003) suggests this road as one of the solutions for the digital divide in the Third World. However, phones can also widen the digital divide (in the shape of a usage gap) because mobile phones – from the vast majority of simple devices to the small number of very expensive smart phones – are mainly used for communication and simple information retrieval, and barely for advanced information processing that is required in jobs and in education. In a global country comparison, Howard (2007) has found that the leap-frogging strategy barely works in the Third World; it proved to be more valid for advanced economic and technological countries.

The third strategy takes the opposite view of the stage approach. This version contends that Third World countries are able to evolve only gradually from their current stage of development. The massive introduction of ICTs is not a priority at this stage. Instead, all effort should be spent on the improvement of basic material and human resources. This means electricity, transportation, health, traditional education, and old mass media (the press, broadcasting, and the telephone system).

The final strategy is a rejection of all stage approaches by suggesting that investment in technical infrastructure, education and all kinds of usage applications should be made in parallel. Mansell and Wehn have argued that 'the developing societies will need to find ways of combining their existing social and technical capabilities if they are to benefit from the potential advantages of ICTs' (1998: 256). Ideally, they say, investment in both capabilities should be undertaken simultaneously, but when this does not appear to be possible, investment in social capabilities should receive priority.

POLICY PERSPECTIVES FOR THE NETWORK SOCIETY

Strategic characteristics of networks

This book closes with a number of general policy perspectives that can be linked to the conclusions drawn previously. They are general because some kind of action plan is not intended; it would become out of date too quickly. The introduction of networks as the nervous system of our society has seven crucial strategic characteristics: access, security, design, control, legality, returns and content. They will define the framework for every concrete policy that can be proposed. I now describe these characteristics against the background of a number of *explicit social values* that I have determined to be at stake in this book: material and spiritual welfare, social equality, democracy, safety, personal autonomy, information and communication freedom, the quantity and quality of social relationships and the richness of the human mind.

Access

If it is true that networks are becoming the nervous system of our society, access to networks must be the most vital characteristic. No access, or marginal access, simply means social exclusion. In this book, I have argued that people without (sufficient) access will become second-class citizens, consumers, workers, students and community members. However, access is a multi-faceted concept: I have distinguished motivation, physical and material access, digital skills and usage (Chapter 7). How should each of them be accomplished?

The primary kinds of access are motivation and physical access. Influencing the motivation to use computers is a complicated process. It requires the improvement of the accessibility and usability of technology. It also calls for regulation and other measures to remove the repellent practices observed by many people when they start to use computers and the Internet. Physical access is the kind that can be realized by policy most directly. Here we can often meet two policy principles: the realization of universal access and universal service.

Universal access simply means the *availability* of a connection to a computer and a network in equal terms for anyone. Universal service is the availability or supply of *services* everyone needs on this physical infrastructure. Universal access is a condition for universal service. Universal access and universal service taken together may be defined as 'access to a defined minimum service of specified quality to all users independent of their geographical location and, in the light of specific national conditions, at an affordable price' (European Commission, 1996). This telecommunications principle could be extended to the Internet, specifically email, and, within a reasonable term, to broadband connections (Anderson et al., 1995; van Dijk, 1997). In the developed countries the necessity of broadband connections has already arrived. Many governments have realized this and they have adapted their (tele)communications policy accordingly.

Yet, nowhere has the universal access principle been completely realized. When realization seems to be impossible in the short term, most countries step back to achieve principles of public access. In the developed countries, this means access in schools, libraries, and other public buildings. In many developing countries, it comes down to an attempt to connect at least every village or city neighbourhood in tele-centres, kiosks or Internet cafés.

Universal *access* to homes is a realistic prospect in most developed societies; here public access (as the only type of physical access for people) can be considered to be a second-hand option that does not enable full participation in the network society. However, in developing countries only two options form a realistic prospect. The first is the fast development of wireless and mobile connections. This enables at least basic or primitive Internet access for individuals, mainly for communication and consumption. The second option is public access in Internet cafés, community centres, schools, libraries, and other public buildings. These public places enable more advanced community and educational use for collectivities when staff is available.

Universal *service* offers first of all telecommunication services needed to use connections. Others are services of content. Together, these services can be considered the *basic provisions* of information and communication that every inhabitant of a network society needs:

1 Basic connections: extending universal service of telecommunications to Internet connections, email, and (in a reasonable amount of time) broadband in all infra-structures (telephony, cable and satellite).

2 Public information and communication: government information, vital community information services, and public broadcasting.

3 Health information and communication, with basic alarm facilities.

4 Information needed in compulsory education: primary and secondary schools.

The United States is one of the few countries in the world that has a Universal Service Fund that subsidizes from a small part of the telecommunication tariffs (only) public *access* for schools and libraries – that is, only the connections described in item 1 above. The EU concentrates on public *service*, that is, the provisions described in items 2, 3, and 4.

Ultimately, investment in the diffusion of *digital skills* and in the number and variety of network applications used is more important to improve equal access than realizing the necessary conditions of universal access and universal service according to the analysis in this book. This investment requires a transformation of current educational programs at all levels (basic, secondary, higher and adult education). The world of fairly traditional learning with old and new media in schools and the spontaneous types and styles of learning developed by young people themselves using new media have to come together to benefit from each other. Many didactic innovations are required. See Soloman et al. (2002) and van Dijk (2005) for concrete policy instruments in education.

Security

When networks become the nervous system of society, their breakdown will cause the organism, that is society, to come to a halt or at least enter a serious crisis. Perhaps the worst nightmares for sociologists – the breakdown of society – could even become real. However, this is only one side of the story. The other is the opportunity for networks to protect the safety of humans, organizations and society as a whole. Alarm and security systems may prove to be a great improvement for the ill, the handicapped and the elderly. Monitoring and registration systems can help to protect the ecological environment and the security of organizations in general and production processes in particular. Internal and external state security are improved by all sorts of registration systems.

In many respects, we are heading for a society free of risks (Beck, 1992, 2009). Being adaptive structures, networks assist in reducing risks at all levels. States face less surprise (for instance rebellion) because they know more about the mood and the conduct of their subjects. Individual companies are confronted less with overproduction because they have more data about their stock and the daily demand of their customers. Finally, individuals need to communicate less with strangers and unwanted callers or writers because they have greater control over their contacts.

In other respects, the risks for society, organizations and individuals are increased by the use of network technology. This has both a technological and a social dimension. The technological dimension is the ubiquitous threat of a breakdown of critical connections. The social dimension is the potential lack of trust in each other and in the network communication people might have when they use online instead of face-to-face communication.

Networks prove to be a very vulnerable technology. This risk is clearly underestimated by contemporary governments and business leaderships. They do not take full precautions. Few organizations are fully protected against hackers and criminal offences. After the leadership's choice to construct a network or to get access to collective networks, their social unit becomes dependent on a technology full of risks. The pressure of technology on communication processes may increase as well. Sometimes, if there is a malfunction, vital parts of messages are not transmitted and understood anymore.

In Chapter 6, I argued that measures to increase security often have contradictory effects: they might diminish security in other places. Another possibility is that these measures oppose other values. For example, attempts to bring more intelligence in public networks in order to trace the origins, destinations and kinds of messages contained in packets for security reasons (for example, changing TCP/IP to include *IP 6 or Sec*; see Chapter 6) would completely change the character of the Internet as a relatively free and decentralized network. If we want to defend this character, security would actually be best protected by a connection that itself is as 'empty' as possible, and thus less vulnerable to technical failures or attacks, and that has most of its intelligence stored in the terminals. However, with cloud computing, solutions sought are going in the opposite direction. Cloud computing cannot be 100 per cent safe either. Regularly we read in the news that very big companies such as Sony (in 2011) have lost personal information after hacking. Cloud computing also makes the end-user (even more) careless.

Design

Networks are not the inborn nervous system of societies as they are for human beings. They are more or less consciously constructed. Building a social network is at least partly a deliberative activity for humans. Constructing media networks is always a matter of technical and organizational design. However, they are not built like roads, according to a (usually) well-considered local and national government plan. The infrastructure and architecture of media networks are rarely discussed in parliaments and other bodies of representation. Actually, this is a rather strange state of affairs for a technology that is so important for society. The two main reasons have been described above. First, this infrastructure of society was largely privatized and liberalized in the 1980s and 1990s. Second, the people in government and in parliaments usually do not have the expertise and vision needed.

Previously, the telecommunication and mass communication networks were designed by both public and private organizations following the indications of far-reaching government regulation. The Internet was designed by people in the US Departments of Defense, Education and Commerce in cooperation with people from American universities. The military and the academics preferred a decentralized network that would be resistant to attacks. The US Department of Commerce and the Telecommunication and Infrastructure Administration hoped this would boost further privatization and the liberalization of government regulation in the United States and the rest of the world.

With the tremendous growth of the Worldwide Web, the Internet community took its chance to use and strengthen the decentralized and peer-to-peer nature of this network as an outstanding public network. However, since the end of the 1990s, governments, technicians and market interests have tried to regain a central hold on the Internet for reasons of security and commerce (marketing, reliable selling and billing and the protection of copyright). Currently, a fierce struggle for control over the Internet is being waged by businesses, governments, technicians and the Internet user community. This struggle was described in Chapter 6. It appears that the architectural design of the Internet is becoming increasingly important. Apparently technical discussions over 'codes', such as protocols and other standards, are in fact political and economic discussions.

The first thing that should strike us here is that these discussions remain obscure and hidden from the vast majority of Internet users and the population at large. Only experts know about them. Even most political representatives in parliaments and governments do not know the stakes. This means that the design of the infrastructure of our future societies is completely undemocratic. A broad discussion in society, starting with the Internet community itself, is urgently required.

The second observation is that after the privatization and liberalization of communication networks, the construction of this vital infrastructure for society has been completely left to the market. This goes for the technical infrastructure of the networks, their centres, wires and terminals, for the construction, maintenance and operation of these networks and for the vast majority of their content services. In Chapter 4, I showed that, at the level of Internet services, four computer and Internet companies are struggling for hegemony by offering their own platform for all Internet applications: Microsoft, Apple, Google and Facebook. We have seen that this is an instance of vertical concentration on the services level: these companies want us to sell their very profitable services on top of their own operating systems and browsers. Governments and regulatory bodies will not only have to take account of horizontal concentration (mergers which are too big) but also of these attempts of vertical concentration. The prime solution here is *unbundling*. Just like the European Commission once forced Microsoft to unbundle Windows and Internet Explorer and Windows Media Player, the other platforms have to be unbundled. For example, it should become possible to use Apple apps on Android (Google). All apps should be available on all platforms.

The influence of the proprietary software and de facto standards of software companies such as Microsoft, Apple and Computer Associates on the design of the Internet have also become too big. This has provoked an open-source movement developing open source and open code software within the Internet community itself. The result of the fight between proprietary and open software will be crucial for the future of the Internet.

In Chapter 4 I have also stressed that the platform companies of Microsoft, Apple, Google and Facebook have their own ideas for designing the Internet. The users are barely aware of this. Fortunately, they have an influence indicating what kind of applications they like and which kinds they do not. Recently, they indicated that they want social networking and that they want to go mobile. But how much influence did they have on the particular idea of social networking that is behind

Facebook and on the privacy policy of this company? Considering mobile telephony: what other influence do users have on mobile telephony than of choosing a device and particular apps? Telephone companies only respond to market signals. Their users are barely organized.

Governments have plans to construct roads several decades ahead, but they have no idea what the nervous system of the society they are ruling should look like. They are defensive and only react to excesses (security, criminality, child pornography and other harm to children). Again: would it not be a good idea to have more public discussion about the future of the Internet in parliaments, in organizations of users or consumers and among pressure groups for all kinds of issues related to the Internet?

Control

The struggle for the design of the nervous system of the network society is no less than a struggle for its control, which means future freedom and democracy. The result also sets down rules for the privacy and personal autonomy of network users.

Almost every chapter in this book has pointed out that the design of computer networks can result in both centralization and decentralization. This applies to decision-making as well. However, as the initiative for the development and introduction of networks is usually taken entirely by central management, and because network technology is very complex (requiring network management and supervision) and since it is suitable for central registration and control, the centralizing effect of networks at first seems to be stronger than the decentralizing effect. Nevertheless, large organizational units soon meet the limits of central control. Furthermore, it is well known that employee, citizen and consumer motivation is stimulated by local execution with wider margins. This is why all kinds of flexible control and controlled or guided decentralization are gaining popularity in business organizations and political systems.

In terms of *economic* democracy, government and legislation should deal with the rise of large private oligopolies in tele-, data and mass communication (Chapter 4). The technical convergence of these types of communication is a stimulus to corporate concentration within and between the three communication branches concerned. Very soon, fewer than ten companies will dominate the world market in each of them. They will obtain a disproportionate grip on the communication policies of countries, companies and households. From a democratic point of view, this does not mean progress. The public monopolies at least were under some sort of democratic control.

Considering *political democracy*, it has become evident that information and communication networks are a lethal threat to traditional totalitarian rule. However, in Chapter 5 I argued that more ingenious ways to exercise control, to rule and to supervise with these technologies are appearing. They enable states to gain control over their citizens by surveillance and by coupling all kinds of registrations or practising data-mining. On the other hand, the same networks can be used by citizens themselves to ask for better information and to become more involved in political decision-making.

Politicians and civil servants use the new media for different strategic orientations. In Chapter 5, I explained that some are using them for the reinforcement of institutional politics and the state. Their perspective is to create a strong and efficient state that is able to compete with international crime and terrorism, that costs less and that performs better. Others use the new media or networks as means to spread politics and democracy into civil society and to empower individual citizens. Which strategic orientation is the best cannot be determined because it completely depends on the view of democracy one holds.

The *social democracy* of new media use will be decided by the evolution of the digital divide, as portrayed in Chapter 7. Most likely, information inequality will increase in the network society. However, the tripartite network society sketched in this book – a society consisting of a relatively small information elite, a more or less participating majority and a relative large minority of excluded people – must be prevented at all costs from becoming a structural aspect of future society. This would create first-, second- and third-class citizens, workers, students and consumers. See van Dijk (2005) for the concrete policy instruments I would suggest.

Because networks are systems, they automatically take away part of the autonomy of those connected. Citizens, employees, clients and consumers as individuals usually have little choice as to whether they are to be connected to such networks. And once they are connected, they have little control over usage. One way to solve this problem is to increase users' choice opportunities; another is to grant the bodies representing these individuals more control and to extend the area in which they have a say. In particular, this applies to employee organizations. Networks will be a structuring part of any organization, not merely a technical instrument. However, in the few cases where employee organizations have been allowed to interfere in the fields of network technology, they have had little knowledge of issues such as organization structure, management strategy and information control.

The second class of organizations that should organize personal autonomy and choice are consumer and citizen organizations. They should not only comment on final products and prices, but also on the design and regulation of these products, in this case e-commerce and e-government networks, and on the availability of the remaining non-electronic alternatives. The third class, of course, are individual users and user groups themselves. Is it not astonishing that user groups of frequently used and perhaps crucially important websites rarely have any say in their design and services despite all apparent interactivity? When they are not satisfied, the only option they usually have is to click away and go to a competing website. Facebook is likely to react that when users don't like the company's new designs, facilities and privacy settings, they can go to a competitor. But such a reaction would not be fair. Adopting an SNS is not equal to buying a car that can easily change hands. Facebook users cannot be expected to simply transfer their whole social network to another location. This is barely possible according to the law of network externality (see Chapter 2). SNS applications have become important private tools for daily life. They should be under the control of their users.

The introduction of networks implies a greater threat to the informational and relational privacy of individuals than the preceding information and communication techniques. The threat comes from the coupling and the integration of files and the traceability of individuals' daily routines. Privacy harm is no technical inevitability; it is a matter of *deliberate* design by governments and corporations (Chapter 5). Governments simply want our personal data for better surveillance and the struggle against crime and terrorism. Internet companies with a business model of advertising need our personal data to sell more effective advertisement. This means that alternatives of privacy design are possible and most effective. Privacy is not doomed in the network society.

Unfortunately, most countries in the world have no comprehensive privacy law. The EU has one, which in theory is the best (see Chapter 6) and that serves as an example for many other countries, but it does not work properly in practice. Network traffic remains elusive. This applies in particular to the Internet, which crosses every border and is barely regulated. When legal options do not offer adequate solutions, forms of individual and collective self-regulation and technical options of protection will come to the fore. The self-regulation of codes of conduct and (privacy) rating systems should be stimulated, and research programs dealing with new techniques of encryption and digital anonymity should be funded. However, I have argued that a combination of legal, self-regulatory and technical solutions remains the only viable alternative in the long run.

Legality

We expect the law to offer some protection against the wrong use of network technology, but the tragedy is that the law itself, particularly existing legislation, is being undermined by this technology. The first reaction of governments and legislators is to declare that what goes offline should also go online. This might be a safe principle at the start of a new technology, but it does not do justice to the special characteristics of computer networks in the long run. These networks are passing all frontiers and jurisdictions, they show no clear demarcation line between public and private affairs or between collective and individual property rights and they primarily exchange virtual instead of physical goods and services.

For these new online realities, each country will have to develop framework legislation that balances at least three fundamental rights against each other: information and communication freedom, the protection of society and of individuals, and the protection of property rights. This framework should first of all be based on the constitutions of the countries concerned. Subsequently, it should specify the meaning of public and private, collective and individual, virtual and physical, national and international in online environments for all classes of applications: information, consultation, registration, transaction, conversation and entertainment. Within the confines of this framework (a series of political documents) formal laws related to the three rights just mentioned can be drafted or changed.

Repeatedly, I have stressed that governments and legislation cannot solve the problems of legality in networks alone. Legislation has to be supplemented by all kinds of self-regulation created and maintained by businesses, user groups and individual users. Additionally, to make national legislation effective across frontiers, international agreements between governments will have to be made in all kinds of international forums. Networked nationalism with a growing international focus is currently the only viable option of Internet governance (Chapter 6).

The third legal instrument is the backing of technological protection using encryption and other codes installed in the software or operations built in the hardware. As technological protection is a double-edged sword, to be used by the good and the bad, it should always be embedded in self-regulation and legislation.

Returns

What are the returns of the production and use of media networks for society? I first deal with the material returns such as economic welfare and employment. In the next section the immaterial returns are discussed.

As far as economic prosperity is concerned, the new communication technology seems to have a positive effect in both the short and the long term. In this book, I have observed that it helps solve bottlenecks of a general nature in the economy and society: bureaucratic organization; a jamming and polluting infrastructure of transportation and regional planning; and a continuing lack of communication in an increasingly differentiated, fragmented and individualized society. In the short term, the powerful communication capacities of the new media (speed, few restrictions on place and time, large storage and processing potential, accuracy and interactivity) will cause an increase in the effectiveness and efficiency of production and distribution processes and office work.

These capacities are crucial to the process innovations I have summarized in the term 'flow economy'. Apart from improving effectiveness and efficiency, they also help to save on production factors, among them the use of energy and materials. So, they might have a role to play in environmental protection. Furthermore, control of production processes as a whole will increase. Media networks have become indispensable in controlling the widespread chains of companies and other organizations and the increasing division of labour within these organizations.

The main problem of this general rise in economic prosperity is its increasingly unequal division. Network technology is highly selective in its diffusion, application and effects on the social and economic environment. Globally, it supports a tendency for the combined and uneven development of countries (Chapter 7). Locally, it helps to create dual economies of parts directly linked to the global information infrastructure and parts that are not.

This state of affairs touches every regional and national economic policy. Policymakers believe companies can be persuaded by local authorities to set up facilities in their region, and this will have positive effects on activities in the entire region/state. In fact, the international companies determine their own priorities and preferences on a global scale. They are indifferent to the general organic development of a particular region/state and contribute to one specific economic field of activity only. These specific assets of regions and states will be of far greater importance in the future. It will result in uneven development barely controlled by local authorities, except perhaps by stressing the region's strong assets. The problem of uneven development can be solved in the long term only by strengthening international political and economic bodies and regulatory agreements.

On balance, few jobs are created by ICT in the short term. In the network sector itself, the new services, transport, operations and the manufacture of equipment cannot balance the loss of jobs in the old services and the declining labour costs of support and maintenance of new infrastructures and equipment, primarily in telephony and cable networks. On the other hand, the network sector does cause the reduction of a lot of existing activities in production, distribution and administration, mainly through labour-saving data communications. Yet existing authorities do not really have the option to refuse to stimulate this technology. To an increasing extent, network technology is the backbone of any technological innovation considered necessary for lasting economic growth.

All observers and policy-makers agree that the future is innovation in content services and a knowledge economy. This will bring the vast majority of future new employment. The countries discussed in the previous section pursue different policies concerning innovation. Up to now, the United States has been the most successful country, because it has the most competitive market and because it has a very liberal immigration policy inviting ICT specialists and students across the world to work and study in the country. However, the United States risks creating too narrow a base for innovation among its own population, because it is cutting back on public education and because bridging the digital divide is not considered a priority.

The ageing continent of Europe has problems keeping up with the United States and East Asia in the field of innovation. Europe has good assets for innovation because of its rich and varied cultural heritage. However, it has difficulties in organizing these assets because it is stuck in regulation, inadequate national funding of innovation and education, and a fragmentation of activities. East Asia still focuses on hardware innovation. Innovation in software, in content services and in a creative knowledge economy in general appears to be difficult. This might lead to stagnation in the future. The Third World is experiencing a brain drain of young innovative scholars and students to the developed world. Fortunately, many return to their home countries later on. However, there they tend to stay in the enclaves of a dual economy that are directly linked to the global information infrastructure that is primarily serving the developed countries.

Content

Can networks also satisfy social and individual needs: in other words, can they add to our intangible welfare? They seem to intensify the rationalization and commodification of social relations, already characteristic of modern western culture. They do not score too well on communication capacities such as interactivity (relatively low levels), stimuli richness (some sensorial decay compared with face-to-face communication, even in multimedia), complexity (of appropriate communication activities) and privacy. The last of these capacities applies in particular in comparison with face-to-face communication.

A comparison between mediated and face-to-face communication will be made with respect to increasing numbers of activities. In this book, I have argued that it is not right to think that face-to-face communication is superior to mediated communication in all respects. Moreover, ten to 20 years of CMC research have indicated that computer-mediated communication largely equals face-to-face communication after some time. The basic reason is the amazing human creativity and imagination involved in communication. So, the future is all kinds of links and interplay between online and offline communication.

In this book I have emphasized that all kinds of social demarcation lines are blurring on account of the new media. For example, personal and public space, work and leisure time are merging. This trend has a limit. Human beings have not invented these divisions of their daily life for nothing. We will have to discover and explore new dividing lines, setting clear personal limits of new media use if we do not want to be subjected to strong social pressures and a technology that works 24 hours a day.

The new media intensify the historical process of replacing direct experience with mediated perception. The new media may enrich direct experience because they can help overcome barriers of distance, time and lack of information. On the other hand, they may also rob this experience of its 'total' character, its freedom and its ability to take its own initiatives.

Since direct action and experience will remain the basis for human experience in general, excessive and one-sided use of the new media will result in a decay of human experience. This is all the more reason to combine their use with natural experience, learning and action, and communication.

The optimum use of new media capacities requires people to develop themselves visually, verbally, auditively, logically and analytically. For most people, this is too much to ask. So, in fact, the optimum use of the new media requires a many-sided mental development and a multi-functional use of people's capacities. The truth is, the new media do not really have to be used optimally. Simple and superficial uses are also possible. Thus the paradoxical situation may arise of new media making human perception and mental processing more complicated on the one hand, and simpler on the other. People with high education are most likely to use the former, while people with low education will probably choose the latter. In this way, a usage gap will appear that is difficult to resolve (van Dijk, 2005).

Information overload seems to be one of the main substantial problems in the information and network society. I have emphasized that this only becomes a real problem when people are forced to deal with this overload in conditions of work, study and family life. Additionally, being reachable at all times and places and with an increasing number of communication means may create what I have called over-communication. The obvious solutions to information and communication overload are selective perception and a fast and superficial scanning of sources. This may lead to a reduction of 'deep reading and understanding' (Chapter 9). This negative effect is compensated by a large number of positive opportunities of the new media for learning discussed in Chapter 9. Educational innovation is one of the prime tasks for new media development.

If we ignore, or no longer see the fundamental differences between human cognition and computer or medium processing discussed in Chapter 9, the richness of the human mind will be at stake. This could happen if typical human perception and cognition are subjected or adapted to the workings of hardware and software. Perhaps human beings will then even turn into cyborgs – creatures that are half computer and half human. This could happen earlier than we think, namely as soon as information technology and biotechnology are linked via the connection of chips to human cells and the implantation of chips in the human body.

Probably, or perhaps fortunately, these links will not create a balanced unity. The differences between humans and computers or other new media will most likely remain and will cause friction in human–medium/computer interaction. The strong program of Artificial Intelligence, to try to equalize and replace human minds by intelligent agents and software, is a mission impossible. Machines with artificial agents and software will never equal the peculiar biological organism including the minds of human beings developed in evolution. They may become intimately connected by the connection of cells and chips, but it is at that point that it becomes important to know the difference between organisms and machines. The best strategy is a fertile combination of the strong assets of intelligent machines and human beings. Frictions between them should be handled, not denied. We should learn from them. Research, education, including media education, and software or interface development should be directed towards this learning.

People in the network society will also have to learn how to mentally integrate the various impressions and relations offered by mediated and face-to-face communication. Increasingly, they are mixed. When we discover the similarities and differences we can have the best of both worlds. Without a gratifying cooperation and integration we might become tragic personalities torn apart by human and technical characteristics. Socially, we would become alone being together in the network society.

CONCLUSIONS

- Conclusions of conclusions are a bit overdone. It can be emphasized once again that the structures of the network society, in this book largely described in terms of seven so-called laws of the Web, are no natural laws but that they are liable for change. They are made by human beings and given meaning by them. Network structures are strong, but continuous communicative action realizes and changes them.

(Continued)

(Continued)

To mention just two examples: we define what 'friends' are in SNS and we can change the power laws of Googlearchy by using the rankings differently than we tend to do.

- Eleven information society models have been elaborated and applied to the information and network societies currently built in the world. They testify to the conclusion that we can create and design these societies differently.

- The book is closing with a number of policy perspectives for the network society of a very general nature. Evidently, access to this society is crucial, as is the way it is designed. The society should also be safe and under democratic control (in whatever view). Finally, the goal of this society should be more and better material and material returns.

REFERENCES

Abrahamson, J.B., Arterton, F. and Orren, G. (1988) *The Electronic Commonwealth: the Impact of New Technologies upon Democratic Politics*. New York: Basic Books.

Adoni, H. & Nossek, H. (2001) 'The New Media Consumers: Media Convergence and the Displacement Effect'. *European Journal of Communication Research. Vol 26*, No. 1, 59–83.

Aglietta, M. (1979) *A Theory of Capitalist Regulation: The US Experience*. London: Verso.

Albert, Réka, Hawoong, J. and Barabási, A. (1999) 'Diameter of the World-Wide Web', *Nature*, 401: 130–1.

Alberts, D.S., Garstka, J.J. and Stein, F.P. (2000) *Network Centric Warfare: Developing and Leveraging Information Superiority*, 2nd edn (revised). Washington, DC: CCRP Publications.

Alberts, D.S. (2002) *Information Age Transformation: Getting to a 21st Century Military*. Washington, DC: CCRP Publications.

Alexander, Markus (2003) *The Internet in Putin's Russia: Reinventing a Technology of Authoritarianism*. Oxford: University of Oxford, Department of Politics and International Relations.

Anderson, P. (1983) *Imagined Communities*. London: Verso.

Anderson, Chris (2006) *The Long Tail*. New York: Hyperion.

Anderson, R., Bikson, T., Law, S.-A. and Mitchell, B. (eds) (1995) *Universal Access to e-mail: Feasibility and Societal Implications*. Santa Monica, CA: Rand. www.rand.org/publications/MR/MR650.

Applegate, Lynda (1999) 'In Search for a New Organizational Model', in G. DeSanctis and J. Fulk (eds), *Shaping Organizational Form: Communication, Connection and Community*. Thousand Oaks, CA: Sage.

Arterton, Christopher F. (1987) *Teledemocracy: Can Technology Protect Democracy?* Newbury Park, CA: Sage.

Axelrod, Robert and Cohen, Michael D. (1999) *Harnessing Complexity, Organizational Implications of a Scientific Frontier*. New York: The Free Press.

Badaracco, J.L. (1991) *The Knowledge Link: How Firms Compete Through Strategic Alliances*. Boston, MA: Harvard University Press.

Balance, R.H. and Sinclair, S.W. (1983) *Collapse and Survival: Industry Strategies in a Changing World*. London: Allen and Unwin.

Bandura, A. (1986) *Social Foundations of Thought and Action: A Social-Cognitive Theory*. Englewood Cliffs, NJ: Prentice Hall.

Bannon, L.J. (1986) 'Computer-mediated communication', in D.A. Norman and S. Draper (eds), *User Centered System Design: New Perspectives on Human–Computer Interaction*. Hillsdale, NJ: Erlbaum.

Barabási, Albert-László (2002) *Linked, The New Science of Networks*. Cambridge, MA: Perseus.

Barabási, Albert-László and Albert, Réka (1999) 'Emergence of Scaling in Random Networks', *Science*, 286: 509–12.

Barber, B.J. (1984) *Strong Democracy: Participatory Politics for a New Age*. Berkeley, CA: University of California Press.

Barber, Benjamin (1996) *Jihad versus McWorld: How the Planet is Both Falling Apart and Coming Together*. New York: Ballantine.

Barbrook, R. and Cameron, A. (1995) 'The Californian Ideology'. Harrow: University of Westminster, The Hypermedia Research Centre. http://www.hrc.wmin.ac.uk/theory-californianideology-main.html.

Barnett, G.A., Salisbury, J., Kim, C.W. and Langhorne, L. (1998) 'Globalization and International Communication: An Examination of Monetary, Telecommunications and Trade Networks'. Paper presented to International Communication Association, Annual Conference, Jerusalem, 20–24 July.

BBC Asia Pacific (2011) 'China: 1.3 million Websites Shut in 2010', 13 July. http://www.bbc.co.uk/news/world-asia-pacific-14138267.

Beck, Ulrich (1992) *Risk Society: Towards a New Modernity*. London: Sage.

Beck, Ulrich (2009) *World at Risk*. Cambridge, UK & Boston MA: Polity.

Becker, T.L. (1981) 'Teledemocracy: Bringing Power Back to the People', *Futurist*, 15(6): 6–9.

Becker, T.L. and Slaton C. (2000) *The Future of Teledemocracy*. Westport, CT: Praeger.

Beldad, A. (2011) 'Trust and Information Privacy Concerns in Electronic Government'. *Dissertation, Defended March 17, 2011, University of Twente*. Enschede: University of Twente.

Beniger, J.R. (1986) *The Control Revolution: Technological and Economic Origins of the Information Society*. Cambridge, MA: Harvester.

Beniger, J.R. (1996) 'Who shall control cyberspace?', in L. Strate, R. Jacobson and S. Gibson (eds), *Communication and Cyberspace*. Cresskill, NJ: Hampton Press. pp. 49–58.

Benkler, Y. (2006) The Wealth of Networks, How Social Production Transforms Markets and Freedom. New Haven and London: Yale University Press.

Benjamin, Walter (1968) 'The Work of Art in an Age of Mechanical Reproduction', in W. Benjamin (ed.), *Illuminations*. London: Fontana.

Bikson, T.K., Eveland, J. and Gutek, B. (1989) 'Flexible Interactive Technologies for Multi-Person Tasks: Current Problems and Future Prospects', in M.H. Olson (ed.), *Technological Support for Work Group Collaboration*. Hillsdale, NJ: Erlbaum.

Bimber, B. (2003) *Information and American Democracy: Technology in the Evolution of Political Power*. Cambridge: Cambridge University Press.

Biocca, Frank (1992) 'Communication Within Virtual Reality: Creating a Space for Research', *Journal of Communication*, 42(4): 5–22.

Bolter, J.D. (1984) *Turing's Man: Western Culture in the Computer Age*. Chapel Hill, NC: University of North Carolina Press.

Bonfadelli, H. (2002) 'The Internet and knowledge gaps: A theoretical and empirical investigation'. European Journal of Communication, 17(1), 65–84.

Bordewijk, J.L. and Van Kaam, B. (1982) *Allocutie: Enkele gedachten over communicatievrijheid in een bekabeld land*. Baarn: Bosch and Keuning.

Borgatti, S.P. and Foster, P.C. (2003) 'The Network Paradigm in Organizational Research: A Review and Typology'. *Journal of Management 29 (6)* pp. 991–1013.

Botterman, M., Millard, J., et al. (2009) *Value for Citizens, A Vision Of Public Governance in 2020*. Report to the European Commission, Information Society and Media. Luxembourg: European Communities DOI 10.2759.

Brass, D. (1995) 'A Social Network Perspective on Human Resources Management', *Research in Personnel and Human Resources Management, Vol. 13*. Greenwich, CT: JAI Press. pp. 39–79.

Brown, D. (1997) *Cybertrends: Chaos, Power and Accountability in the Information Age*. London: Viking.

Brown, J.S. (1986) 'From Cognitive to Social Ergonomics and Beyond', in D.A. Norman and S. Draper (eds), *User Centered System Design: New Perspectives on Human–Computer Interaction*. Hillsdale, NJ: Erlbaum.

Brown, J.S. and Duguid, P. (2000) *The Social Life of Information*. Boston, MA: Harvard Business School Press.

Brundidge, J. and Rice, R. (2009) 'Political Engagement Online: Do the Information Rich Get Richer and the Like-minded More Similar?', in A. Chadwick and P.H. Howard (eds), *Routledge Handbook of Internet Politics*. London and New York: Routledge, pp. 144–56.

Bruner, J.S. and Olson, D.R. (1973) 'Learning Through Experience and Learning Through Media', in G. Gerbner, L. Gross and W. Melody (eds), *Communications Technology and Social Policy*. New York: Wiley.

Buchanan, Mark (2002) *Nexus, Small Worlds and the Groundbreaking Science of Networks*. New York, London: W.W. Norton.

Bunz, Ulla (2009) 'A Generational Comparison of Gender, Computer Anxiety, and Computer-Email-Web Fluency'. *Studies in Media and Information Literacy Education*, 9(2): 54–69.

Burgers, J. (1988) *De Schaal van Solidariteit: Een Studie Naar de Sociale Constructie van de Omgeving*. Leuven: Acco.

Burnham, D. (1983) *The Rise of the Computer State*. London: Weidenfeld and Nicolson.

Cairncross, Francis (2001) *The Death of Distance, How the Communications Revolution Is Changing our Lives*. Boston, MA: Harvard Business School Press.

Canadian Internet Forum (2011) *The Internet and Canada's Future: Opportunities and Challenges*. Ottawa: Canadian Internet Registration Authority.

Carr, Nicholas (2009) *The Shallows, What the Internet Is Doing to Our Brains*. New York and London: W.W. Norton & Company.

Castells, Manuel (1989) *The Informational City: Information Technology, Economic Restructuring, and the Urban–Regional Process*. Oxford: Blackwell.

Castells, Manuel (1994) 'European Cities, The Informational Society and the Global Economy', *New Left Review*, 204: 18–32.

Castells, Manuel (1996) *The Information Age: Economy, Society and Culture. Vol. I: The Rise of the Network Society*. Oxford: Blackwell.

Castells, Manuel (1997) *The Information Age: Economy, Society and Culture. Vol. II: The Power of Identity*. Oxford: Blackwell.

Castells, Manuel (1998) *The Information Age: Economy, Society and Culture. Vol. III: End of Millennium*. Oxford: Blackwell.

Castells, Manuel (2000) 'Materials for an Exploratory Theory of the Network Society', *British Journal of Sociology*, 51(1): 5–24.

Castells, Manuel (2001) *The Internet Galaxy, Reflections on the Internet, Business and Society*. Oxford, New York: Oxford University Press.

Castells, Manuel (2009) *Communication Power*. Oxford: Oxford University Press

Castells, Manuel, Fernández-Ardèvol, M., Qiu, J.L. and Sey, A. (2009) *Mobile Communication and Society: A Global Perspective*. Boston, MA & London: The MIT Press.

Catinat, Michel (1997) *The 'National Information Infrastructure Initiative' in the US: Policy or Non-Policy?* Cambridge, MA: Harvard University, Center for International Affairs.

Chadwick, Andrew (2006) *Internet Politics: States, Citizens and New Communication Technologies*. Oxford: Oxford University Press.

Chadwick, A. and Howard, P.H. (eds) (2009) *Routledge Handbook of Internet Politics*. London and New York: Routledge.

Chaum, David (1992) 'Achieving Electronic Privacy', *Scientific American*, August: 96–8.

Chaum, David (1994) 'Towards an Open and Secure Payment System'. Speech at the 16th International Conference on Data Protection, 6 September, The Hague.

Cheng, Alex (2010) 'Six Degrees of Separation, Twitter Style'. http://www.sysomos.com/inside-twitter/sixdregrees/.

Christakis, Nicholas and Fowler, James (2009) *Connected, The Surprising Power of Our Social Networks and How They Shape Our Lives*. New York, Boston and London: Little, Brown and Company.

Chun, K. J. and Park, H.K. (1990) 'Examining the conflicting results of GDSS research', *Information management* 33: 313–325.

Clarke, Richard A. (2010) *Cyber War: The Next Threat to National Security and What to Do About It.* Ecco/HarperCollins.

Coolen, Maarten (1986) 'Artificiële Intelligentie als de Metafysica van Onze Tijd', in P. Hagoort and R. Maessen (eds), *Geest, Computer, Kunst.* Amsterdam: Stichting Grafiet. pp. 124–49.

Coolen, Maarten (1997) 'Totaal Verknoopt', in Ymke deBoer and J. Vorstenbosch (eds), *Virtueel Verbonden: Filosoferen Over Cyberspace.* Amsterdam: Parresia. pp. 28–59.

Council for Research Excellence (2009) ´The Video Consuming Mapping Study´. http://www.researchexcellence.com-vcmoverview.pdf.

Courtois, C., Mechant, P., De Marez, L. and Verleye, G. (2009) 'Gratifications and Seeding Behavior of Online Adolescents'. *Journal of Computer-Mediated Communication,* 15: 109–37.

Cummings, J., Butler, B. and Kraut, R. (2002) 'The Quality of Online Social Relationships', *Communications of the ACM,* 45(7): 103–8.

Daft, R.L. and Lengel, R.H. (1984) 'Information Richness: A New Approach to Managerial Behavior and Organization Design', in L. Cummings and B. Staw (eds), *Research in Organizational Behavior. Vol. 6.* Greenwich, CT: JAI Press. pp. 191–233.

Damasio, Antonio (1995) *Descartes' Error: Emotion, Reason and the Human Brain.* New York: Avon.

Damasio, Antonio (1999) *The Feeling of What Happens, Body and Emotion in the Making of Consciousness.* New York: Harcourt Brace.

Damasio, Antonio (2003) *Looking for Spinoza, Joy, Sorrow and the Feeling Brain.* Orlando, FL: Harcourt.

Damasio, Antonio (2010) *Self Comes to Mind, Constructing the Conscious Brain.* New York: Pantheon.

Davenport, Thomas and Prusak, L. (1997) *Working Knowledge: How Organizations Manage What They Know.* Boston, MA: Harvard University Press.

Davis, R., Baumgartner, J., Francia, P.L. and Morris, J.S. (2009) 'The Internet in US Election Campaigns', in A. Chadwick and P.H. Howard (eds). *Routledge Handbook of Internet Politics.* London and New York: Routledge.

Debord, G. (1996) *The Society of the Spectacle.* London: Verso.

Deibert, R., Palfrey, J., Rohozinski, R. And Zittrain, J. (eds) (2008) *Access Denied: The Practice and Policy of Global Internet Filtering.* Cambridge, MA: MIT Press.

de Kerckhove, Derrick (1998) *Connected Intelligence, The Arrival of the Web Society.* London: Kogan Page.

Dennis, A. and Kinney, S. (1998) 'Testing Media-Richness Theory in the New Media: The Effects of Cues, Feedback and Task Equivocality', *Information Systems Research,* 9: 256–74.

De Sitter, L.U. (1994) *Simple Organizations, Complex Tasks: the Dutch Sociotechnical Approach.* Maastricht: MERIT.

Deuze, M. (2006) 'Participation, Remediation, Bricolage: Considering Principal Components of a Digital Culture', *The Information Society,* 22: 63–75,

Dordick, H. and Wang, G. (1993) *The Information Society: A Retrospective View.* Newbury Park, CA, London, and New Delhi: Sage.

Dunbar, R. (1993) 'Coevolution of Neocortex Size, Group Size, and Language in Humans'. *Behavioral and Brain Sciences,* 16: 681–735.

Dutton, W.H. (2008) 'The Wisdom of Collaborative Network Organizations: Capturing the Value of Networked Individuals'. *Prometheus,* 26(3): 211–30.

Dutton, W.H. and Eynon, R. (2009) 'Networked Individuals and Institutions: A Cross-Sector Comparative Perspective on Patterns and Strategies in Government and Research'. *The Information Society,* 25(3): 1–11.

Dutton, W.H., Kahin, B., O'Callaghan, R. and Wyckoff, A.W. (eds) (2005) *Transforming Enterprise: The Economic and Social Implications of Information Technology.* Cambridge, MA: MIT Press.

Edelman, Gerald (1991) *Bright Air, Brilliant Fire: On the Matter of the Mind.* New York: Basic Books.

Edelman, Gerald M. and Tononi, G. (2000) *A Universe of Consciousness: How Matter Becomes Imagination*. New York: Basic Books.

Edinger, J.A. and Patterson, M. (1983) 'Non-Verbal Involvement and Social Control', *Psychological Bulletin*, 93: 30–56.

Electronic Frontier Foundation (2008) 'Unintended Consequences: Twelve Years under the DMCA', http://www.eff.org/wp/unintended-consequences-under-dmca.

European Commission (1995) *The Protection of Individuals with Regard to the Processing of Personal Data and the Free Movement of Such Data*. Official Journal no. L 281, 23/11/1995. Brussels: Office for Official Publications of the European Communities, www.ispo.cec.be.

European Commission (1996) *On Standardisation and the Global Information Society: The European Approach*. COM (96) 359. Brussels: Office for Official Publications of the European Communities, www.ispo.cec.be.

European Commission (2001) *On the Harmonization of Certain Aspects of Copyright and Related Rights in the Information Society*. Directive 2001/29/EC. Brussels: Office for Official Publications of the European Communities, www. ispo.cec.be.

European Commission (2002) *Directive 2002/58/EC of the European Parliament and of the Council of 12 July 2002 concerning the processing of personal data and the protection of privacy in the electronic communications sector*. Retrieved on June 14, 2011 from http://eur-lex.europa.eu/LexUriServ/LexUriServ.do?uri=CELEX:32002L0058:EN:NOT.

European Commission (2010) *Comparative Study on Different Approaches to New Privacy Challenges in Particular in the Light of Technological Developments*. Submitted by LRDP Kantor Ltd. in association with Centre for Public Reform. Brussels: Directorate-General Justice, Freedom and Security.

Featherstone, M. and Burrows, R. (eds) (1996) 'Introduction' to *Cyberspace/Cyberbodies/Cyberpunk: Cultures of Technological Embodiment*. London: Sage.

Featherstone, M., Lash, S. and Robertson, R. (1995) *Global Modernities*. London: Sage.

Ferguson, M. (1990) 'Electronic Media and the Redefining of Time and Space', in M. Ferguson (ed.), *Public Communication: The New Imperatives*. London: Sage.

Ferguson, D.A. & E.M. Perse (2000) The World Wide Web as a Functional Alternative to Television. *Journal of Briadcasting & Electronic Media 44 (2)*:155–174.

Fielding, G. and Hartley, P. (1987) 'The Telephone: A Neglected Medium', in A. Cashdan and M. Jordin (eds), *Studies in Communication*. Oxford: Basil Blackwell.

Finholt, T. and Sproull, L. (1987) 'Electronic Groups at Work'. Research paper, Carnegie Mellon University.

Finn, S. and Korukonda, A. (2004) 'Avoiding Computers: Does Personality Play a Role?', in E. Bucy and J. Newhagen (eds), *Media Access: Social and Psychological Dimensions of New Technology Use*. London: LEA. pp. 73–90.

Florida, Richard (2003) The *Rise of the Creative Class, and How It's Transforming Work, Leisure, Community, and Everyday Life*. New York: Basic Books.

Fodor, J. (1986) 'Minds, Machines and Modules: An Interview of Brown, C., Hagoort, P. and Maessen, R. with J. Fodor', in P. Hagoort and R. Maessen (eds), *Geest, Computer, Kunst*. Amsterdam: Stichting Grafiet. pp. 90–117.

Forrester, J. (1976) 'Business Structure, Economic Cycles and National Policy', *Futures*, 1976: 195–214.

Forrester Research (2009) 'How European Teens Consume Media'. 4 December 2009, www.forrester.com/rb/Research/how_european_teens_consume_media/q/id/53763/t/2.

Fountain, Jane (2001) *Building the Virtual State, Information Technology and Institutional Change*. Washington DC: The Brookings Institution.

Freese, J. (1979) *International Data Flow*. Lund: Studentliteratur (Swedish University of Lund edition).

Frissen, P.H.A. (1989) *Bureaucratische Cultuur en Informatisering: Een Studie naar de Betekenis van Informatisering voor de Cultuur van een Overheidsorganisatie*. Contains a summary in English. The Hague: SDU.

Fulk, J. and DeSanctis, G. (1999) 'Articulation of Communication Technology and Organizational Form', in G. DeSanctis and J. Fulk (eds), *Shaping Organizational Form: Communication, Connection and Community*. Thousand Oaks, CA: Sage. pp. 5–32.

Fulk, J. and Steinfield, C. (1990) *Organizations and Communication Technology*. Newbury Park, CA, London and New Delhi: Sage.

Fulk, J., Steinfield, C., Schmitz, J. and Power, J.G. (1987) 'A Social Information Processing Model of Media Use in Organizations', *Communication Research*, 14(5): 529–52.

Gandy, Oscar (1994) *The Panoptic Society*. Boulder, CO: Westview.

Gantz, J., , Chute C., Manfrediz, A., Minton, S., Reinsel, S., Schlichting, W. and Toncheva, A. (2008) *The Diverse and Exploding Digital Universe*. IDC Working Paper. Framingham MA International Data Corporation.

Garfinkel, Simson (2000) *Database Nation: The Death of Privacy in the 21st Century*. Sebastopol, CA: O'Reilly.

Garnham, N. (1997) 'Europe and the Global Information Society: The History of a Troubled Relationship', *Telematics and Informatics*, 14(4): 323–7.

Gere, Charlie (2002) *Digital Culture*. London: Reaktion Books.

Gershuny, J. and Miles, I. (1983) *The New Service Economy: The Transformation of Employment in Industrial Societies*. London: Pinter.

Giddens, A. (1984) *The Constitution of Society: Outline of the Theory of Structuration*. Cambridge: Polity.

Giddens, A. (1991a) *The Consequences of Modernity*. Stanford, CA: Stanford University Press.

Giddens, A. (1991b) *Modernity and Self-Identity: Self and Society in the Late Modern Age*. Cambridge: Polity.

Gleick, James (2011) *The Information: A History, A Theory, A Flood*. New York: Pantheon Books.

Goggin, Gerard (ed.) (2008) *Mobile Phone Cultures*. London: Routledge.

Goldin, C. and Katz, L. (2008) *The Race between Education and Technology*. Cambridge, MA and London: The Belknap Press.

Goldsmith, J. and Wu, T. (2006) *Who Controls the Internet? Illusions of a Borderless World*. New York: Oxford University Press.

Goldsmith, S. and Eggers, W. (2004) *Governing by Network, The New Shape of the Public Sector*. Washington, DC: Brookings Institution Press.

Goodman, N. (1968) *Languages of Art*. Indianapolis, IN: Hacket.

Graham, S. and Marvin, S. (1996) *Telecommunications and the City: Electronic Spaces, Urban Places*. London/New York: Routledge.

Granovetter, M. (1973) 'The Strength of Weak Ties', *American Journal of Sociology*, 78: 1360–80.

Green, Nicola (2002) 'On the Move: Technology, Mobility and the Mediation of Social Time and Space', *The Information Society*, 18: 281–92.

Greiff, I. (ed.) (1988) *Computer Supported Co-operative Work: A Book of Readings*. Cambridge, MA: Kaufmann.

Grewal, David Singh (2008) *Network Power, The Social Dynamics of Globalization*. New Haven and London: Yale University Press.

Gross, L.P. (1973) 'Modes of Communication and the Acquisition of Symbolic Competence', in G. Gerbner, L.P. Gross and W. Melody (eds), *Communications Technology and Social Policy*. New York: Wiley.

Guéhenno, Jean-Marie (1993) *La Fin de la Démocratie*. Paris: Flammarion. Translation: *The End of the Nation State*. Minneapolis: University of Minnesota Press, 1995.

Gumpert, G. (1987) *Talking Tombstones and Other Tales of the Media Age*. New York: Oxford University Press.

Hain, T. (2000) *Architectural Implications of NAT, RFC2993, 2000*, ftp://ftp.isi.edu/in-notes/rfc2993.txt.

Hakken, David (2003) *The Knowledge Landscapes of Cyberspace*. London & New York: Routledge.

Hamelink, C. (1994) *The Politics of World Communication*. London: Sage.

Hargittai, E. (2002) 'The Second-Level Digital Divide: Differences in People's Online Skills', *First Monday: Peer-Reviewed Journal on the Internet*, 7(4). Retrieved 31 August 2004, http://firstmonday.org/issues/issue7_4/hargittai/

Hargittai, Esther (2004) 'How Wide a Web? Social Inequality in the Digital Age', Ph.D Dissertation, Princeton, NJ: Princeton University, Sociology Department.

Hargittai, Esther and Hinnant, Amanda (2008) 'Digital Inequality: Differences in Young Adults' Use of the Internet'. *Communication Research* 35, 5, October 2008 602–621.

Harrison, Bennett (1994) *Lean and Mean: The Changing Landscape of Corporate Power in the Age of Flexibility*. New York: Guilford.

Harvey, D. (1989) *The Condition of Postmodernity: An Enquiry into the Origins of Cultural Change*. Oxford: Polity.

Hawryskiewicz, I. (1996) *Designing the Networked Enterprise*. Norwood, MA: Artech.

Heim, M. (1987) *Electric Language: A Philosophical Study of Word Processing*. New Haven, CT: Yale University Press.

Held, David (1987) *Models of Democracy*. Cambridge: Polity Press.

Henten, A. and Kristensen, T. (2000) 'Information Society Visions in the Nordic Countries', *Telematics and Informatics*, 17: 77–103.

Hindman, Matthew (2008) *The Myth of Digital Democracy*. Princeton, NJ: Princeton University Press.

Holmes, D. and Russell, G. (1999) 'Adolescent CIT Use: Paradigm Shifts for Educational and Cultural Practices?' *British Journal of Sociology of Education*, 20(1): 69–78.

Holmes, Robert (1995) 'Privacy: Philosophical Foundations and Moral Dilemmas', in P. Ippel, G. de Heij and B. Crouwers (eds), *Privacy Disputed*. The Hague: SDU. pp. 15–30.

Hongladarom, Soraj (2002) 'The Web of Time and the Dilemma of Globalization', *The Information Society*, 18: 241–9.

Horrigan, J. and Rainie, L. (2002) *The Broadband Difference: How Online Behavior Changes with High-speed Internet Connections*. Washington, DC: Pew Internet and American Life Project, www.pewinternet.org.

Howard, Ph., Rainie, L. and Jones, S. (2002) 'Days and Nights on the Internet: The Impact of a Diffusing Technology', in B. Wellman and C. Haythornthwaite (eds), *The Internet in Everyday Life*. Oxford: Blackwell. pp. 45–73.

Howard, Ph. (2007) Testing the Leap-Frog Hypothesis: The Impact of Existing Infrastructure and Telecommunications Policy on the Global Digital Divide', *Information, Communication Society*, Vol. 10, No. 2, April 2007: 133–157.

Huberman, B. (2001) *The Laws of the Web, Patterns in the Ecology of Information*. Cambridge MA, London: The MIT Press.

Hudiburg, R.A. (1999) Preliminary investigation of computer stress and the big five personality factors. *Psychology Reports*, 85: 473–480.

Huysmans, F., de Haan, J. and van de Broek, A. (2004) *Achter de Schermen, Een Kwart Eeuw Lezen, Luisteren, Kijken en Internetten*. Contains a summary in English. The Hague: Sociaal en Cultureel Planbureau.

IDC (1996) *Telework and Mobile Computing 1996–2000*. Amsterdam: IDC-Benelux.

Ivry, R. and Robertson, L. (1998) *The Two Sides of Perception*. Cambridge, MA: MIT Press.

James, J. (2003) *Technology, Globalization and Poverty*. Cheltenham, UK: Edward Elgar.

Jenkins, Henry, with R. Purushotma, M.Weigel, K.Clinton, and A. J. Robison (2009) *Confronting the Challenges of Participatory Media Culture*. McArthur Foundation Report. Cambridge MA, London: The MIT Press.

Jensen, Jens (1999) '"Interactivity" – Tracking a New Concept in Media and Communication Studies', in P.A. Mayer (ed.), *Computer Media and Communication*. Oxford: Oxford University Press.

pp. 160–88. Elaborated as 'The concept of "Interactivity"', in J. Jensen and C. Toscan (eds), (1999) *Interactive Television, TV of the Future or the Future of TV?* Aalborg: Aalborg University Press. pp. 25–66.

Jerome, H. (1934) *Mechanization in Industry.* New York: Publications of the National Bureau of Economic Research.

Johansen, R., Vallee, J. and Spanger, K. (1979) *Electronic Meetings: Technical Alternatives and Social Choices.* Reading, MA: Addison-Wesley.

Joinson, A. (1998) 'Causes and Implications of Disinhibited Behavior on the Internet', in J. Gackenbach (ed.), *Psychology and the Internet: Intrapersonal, Interpersonal and Transpersonal Implications.* San Diego, CA: Academic Press. pp. 43–58.

Joinson, A. (2001) 'Self-Disclosure in Computer-Mediated Communication: The Role of Self-Awareness and Visual Anonymity', *European Journal of Social Psychology,* 31(2): 177–92.

Kaplan A.M. and Heanlein, M. (2010) 'Users of the World, Unite! The Challenges and Opportunities of Social Media', *Business Horizons,* 53: 59–68.

Katz, E., Blumler, J. and Gurevitch, M. (1974) 'Utilization of Mass Communication by the Individual', in J.G. Blumler and E. Katz (eds), *The Uses of Mass Communication.* Beverly Hills: Sage. pp. 19–34.

Katz, J.E. (1997) 'Social and Organizational Consequences of Wireless Communications: A Selective Analysis of Residential and Business Sectors in the US', *Telematics and Informatics,* 14(3): 233–56.

Katz, J.E. (ed.) (2008) *Handbook of Mobile Communication Studies.* Boston, MA and London: The MIT Press.

Katz, J.E. and Rice, R.E. (2002) *Social Consequences of Internet Use, Access, Involvement, and Interaction.* Cambridge, MA and London: The MIT Press.

Katz, Jon (1997) *Media Rants: Postpolitics in a Digital Nation.* San Francisco: Hardwired.

Kauffman, S.A. (1993) *The Origins of Order: Self-organizing and Selection in Evolution.* New York: Oxford University Press.

Keane, J. (1995) 'Structural Transformations of the Public Sphere', *The Communication Review,* 1(1): 1–22.

Keen, Andrew (2007) *The Cult of the Amateur, How today's Internet is killing our culture.* New York, London: Doubleday/Currency.

Kelly, Kevin (1998) *New Rules for the New Economy.* New York: Viking Press.

Kenny, C. (2002) *The Internet and Economic Growth in Least Developed Countries: A Case of Managing Expectations.* World Institute for Development Economics Research Discussion Paper No 2002175, www.wider.unu.edu/ publications/dps/dps2002/dp2002-75.pdf.

Kiesler, S., Siegel, J. and McGuire, T. (1984) 'Social-Psychological Aspects of Computer-Mediated Communication', *The American Psychologist,* 39(10): 1123–43.

Kiesler, S. and Sproull, L. (1992) 'Group Decision Making and Communication Technology', *Organizational Behavior and Human Decision Processes,* 6: 96–123.

Koestler, A. (1967) *The Ghost in the Machine.* London: Hutchinson.

Kondratieff, N.D. (1929) 'Die langen Wellen in der Konjunktur', *Archiv für Sozialwissenschaft und Sozialpolitik,* 56: 573–609.

Kontopoulos, Kyriakos (1993) *The Logics of Social Structure.* Cambridge, NY: Cambridge University Press.

Korff, D. (2002) *Comparative Summary of National Laws, EC Study on Implementation of Data Protection Directive* (Study Contract ETD/2001/B5-3001/A/49). Colchester UK: University of Essex, Human Rights Centre.

Kraut, R., Kiesler, S., Mukhopadhyay, T., Scherlis, W. and Patterson, W. (1998) 'Social Impact of the Internet: What Does it Mean?' *Communications of the ACM,* 41(12): 21–2.

Kubicek, H. (1988) 'Telematische Integration: Zurück in die Sozialstructuren des Früh-Kapitalismus?', in W. Steinmüller (ed.), *Verdatet und Vernetzt Sozialökologische Handlungsspielraüme in der Informationsgesellschaft*. Frankfurt: Fischer. pp. 17–42.

Kubicek, H. and Rolf, A. (1985) *Mikropolis, mit Computernetzen in die 'Informationsgesellschaft'*. Hamburg: VSA.

Kundera, M. (1986) *Life is Elsewhere*. London: Faber and Faber.

LaRose, R. and Eastin, M. (2004) 'A Social Cognitive Theory of Internet Uses and Gratifications: Towards a New Model of Media Attendance', *Journal of Broadcasting and Electronic Media*, 48(3): 358–77.

Lash, S. and Urry, J. (1994) *Economies of Signs and Space*. London: Sage.

Lea, M. (ed.) (1992) *Contexts of Computer-Mediated Communication*. New York: Harvester.

Leadbeater, Charles (2008) We-*think: The Power of Mass Creativity*, http://www.wethinkthebook.net/home.aspx.

Lee, E.-J. (2004) 'Effects of Visual Representation on Social Influence in Computer-Mediated Communication'. *Human Communication Research*, 30: 234–59.

Lee, H. and Liebenau, J. (2000) 'Time and the Internet at the Turn of the Millennium', *Time & Society*, 9(1): 43–56.

Lee, H. and Whitley, E. (2002) 'Time and Information Technology: Temporal Impacts on Individuals, Organizations and Society', *The Information Society*, 18: 235–40.

Lessig, L. (1999) *Code, and Other Laws of Cyberspace*. New York: Basic Books.

Lessig, L. (2001) *The Future of Ideas: The Fate of the Commons in a Connected World*. New York: Vintage Books.

Lessig, Laurence and McChesney, Robert (2006) 'No Tolls on The Internet'. *The Washington Post*, 8 June, http://www.washingtonpost.com/wp-dyn/content/article/2006/06/07/AR2006060702108.html.

Livingstone, S. and Bober, M. (2005). *UK Children Go Online*. London: Economic and Social Research Council.

Loudon, K. (1986) *The Dossier Society: Comments on Democracy in an Information Society*. New York: Columbia University Press.

Luger, George and Stubblefield, William (2004). *Artificial Intelligence: Structures and Strategies for Complex Problem Solving* (5th edn.). The Benjamin/Cummings Publishing Company, Inc.

Lux Wigand, Dianne (1998) 'Information Technology, Organization Structure, People, and Tasks'. Paper presented to International Communication Association, Annual Conference, Jerusalem, 20–24 July.

Lyon, D. (2001) *Surveillance Society: Monitoring Everyday Life*. Buckingham/Philadelphia: Open University Press.

Lyon, David (2003) *Surveillance After September 11*. Cambridge: Polity.

Lyon, D. (2007) *Surveillance Studies, An overview*. Cambridge: Polity Press.

Maclean, P. (1978) 'A Mind of Three Minds: Educating the Triune Brain', in *Education and the Brain*. Chicago: National Society for the Study of Education.

Madden, M. (2003) *America's Online Pursuits*. Washington, DC: Pew Internet and American Life Project.

Magder, T. (1996) 'The Information Superhighway in Canada'. Paper presented at the 9th Colloquium on Communication and Culture of the European Institute for Communication and Culture, 'Virtual Democracy', Piran, 10–14 April.

Mandel, E. (1980) *Long Waves of Capitalist Development*. Cambridge: Cambridge University Press.

Mann, Steve (2001) 'Wearable Computing: Toward Humanistic Intelligence', *Intelligent Systems*, 16(3): 10–15.

Mansell, Robin (in press) 'Power and Interests in Information and Communication Technologies and Development: Exogenous and Endogenous Discourses in Contention'. *Journal of International Development*.

Mansell, R. and Wehn, U. (eds) (1998) *Knowledge Societies: Information Technology for Sustainable Development.* Oxford: Oxford University Press.

Mantovani, Giuseppe (1996) *New Communication Environments: From Everyday to Virtual.* London: Taylor and Francis.

Martin, James (1978) *The Wired Society.* Englewood Cliffs, NJ: Prentice-Hall.

Maturana, H. and Varela, F. (1980) *Autopoiesis and Cognition.* Boston, MA: D. Reidel.

Maturana, H. and Varela, F. (1984) *The Tree of Knowledge: The Biological Roots of Human Understanding.* Boston, MA: Shambala.

McAfee, A. (2009) *Enterprise 2.0: New Collaborative Tools for Your Organization's Toughest Challenges.* Harvard Business School Press.

McLaughlin, M., Osborne, K. and Smith, C. (1995) 'Standards of conduct on Usenet', in S.Jones (Ed.), *Cybersociety: Computer-mediated communication and Community.* Thousand Oaks CA: Sage.

McLean, I. (1989) *Democracy and New Technology.* Cambridge: Polity.

McLuhan, M. (1966) *Understanding Media: The Extensions of Man.* New York: Signet.

McNeill, J.R. and McNeill, W.H. (2003) *The Human Web: A Bird's-eye View of World History.* New York and London: W.W. Norton.

McPherson, M., Smith-Lovin, L. and Brashears, M.E. (2006) 'Social Isolation in America: Changes in Core Discussion Networks over Two Decades'. *American Sociological Review* 71 (June 2006): 353–375.

McQuail, D. (1987). 'The Functions of Communication': a Non-functionalist Overview'. In C.R. Berger & S.H. Chaffee, *Handbook of Communication Science.* Beverly Hills, Londen: Sage Publications.

McQuail, D. and Windahl, S. (1993) *Communication Models for the Study of Mass Communications.* London and New York: Longman.

Merton, R. (1968) 'The Matthew Effect in Science', *Science*, 159: 56–63.

Metcalfe, S. (1986) 'Information and Some Economics of the Information Revolution', in M. Ferguson (ed.), *New Communications Technologies and the Public Interest.* Beverly Hills, CA: Sage.

Meyrowitz, J. (1985) *No Sense of Place: The Impact of Electronic Media on Social Behavior.* New York: Oxford University Press.

Meyrowitz, J. (1997) 'Shifting Worlds of Strangers: Medium Theory and Changes in "Them" versus "Us"', *Sociological Inquiry*, 67(1): 59–71.

Meyrowitz, J. and Maguire, J. (1993) 'Media, Place and Multiculturalism', *Society*, 30(5): 41–8.

Midorikawa, M. et al. (1975) 'TV Conference System', *Review of the Electrical Communication Laboratories*, 23: 5–6.

Milgram, Stanley (1967) 'The Small World Problem', *Psychology Today*, 2: 60–7.

Milgram, Stanley (1970) 'The Experience of Living in the Cities', *Science*, 13 March: 1461–8.

Millard, J., Nielsen, M. M., Smith, S., Macintosh, A., Dalakiouridou, E. and Tambouris, E. (2008) 'eParticipation recommendations – first version, European eParticipation Consortium'. Retrieed January 11, 2010 at: http://www.european-participation.eu/index.php?option=com_docman&task=doc_details&gid=45&&Itemid=82._

Miller, S. (1996) *Civilizing Cyberspace: Policy, Power and the Information Superhighway.* New York: Addison-Wesley.

Miller, J. and Schwarz, M. (eds) (1998) *Speed-Visions of an Accelerated Age.* London: The Photographers Gallery.

Mintzberg, H. (1979) *The Structuring of Organizations: A Synthesis of the Research.* Englewood Cliffs, NJ: Prentice-Hall.

Monge, Peter R. and Contractor, Noshir S. (2003) *Theories of Communication Networks.* New York: Oxford University Press.

Moore, Barrington (1984) *Privacy: Studies in Social and Cultural History.* Armonk, NY: Sharpe.

Morley, D. (1986) *Family Television: Cultural Power and Domestic Leisure*. London: Comedia Publishing Group.

Morozov, Evgeny (2011) *The Net Delusion, The Dark Side of Internet Freedom*. New York: PublicAffairs.

Moyal, A. (1992) 'The Gendered Use of the Telephone: An Australian Case Study', *Media, Culture and Society*, 14: 51–72.

Mueller, Milton L. (2010) *Networks and States: The Global Politics of Internet Governance*. Cambridge, MA and London: The MIT Press.

Mulgan, G.J. (1991) *Communication and Control: Networks and the New Economies of Communication*. Cambridge: Polity.

Mulgan, Geoff (1997) *Connexity, How to Live in a Connected World*. Boston, MA: Harvard Business School Press.

Murray, F. (1983) 'The Decentralization of Production: The Decline of the Mass-Collective Worker?', *Capital and Class*, 19: 74–99.

Nabben, P.F.P. and van de Luytgaarden, H. (1996) *De Ultieme Vrijheid: Een Rechtstheoretische Analyse van het Recht op Privacy*. Deventer: Kluwer.

Nahuis, Richard and de Groot, Henri (2003) *Rising Skill Premia, You ain't seen nothing yet?* CPB Discussion Paper No. 20. The Hague: CPB, Netherlands Bureau for Economic Policy Analysis, www.ideas.repec.org/s/cpb/discus.html.

Naisbitt, J.R. (1982) *Megatrends: Ten New Directions Transforming Our Lives*. New York: Macdonald.

Nass, Clifford, Steuer, J. and Tauber, E. (1997) 'Computers are Social Actors, A Review of Current Research', in B. Friedman (ed.), *Human Values and the Design of Computer Technology*. Stanford, CA: CSLI Productions.

Negroponte, Nicholas (1995) *Being Digital*. New York: Knopf.

Neisser, Ulric (1976) *Cognition and Reality*. New York: Freeman.

Newman, B.I. (1994) *The Marketing of the President: Political Marketing as Campaign Strategy*. Thousand Oaks, CA: Sage.

Nicol, L. (1985) 'Communications Technology: Economic and Spatial Aspects', in M. Castells (ed.), *High Technology, Space and Society*. Beverley Hills, CA: Sage.

Nie, N.H. (2001) 'Sociability, Interpersonal Relations and the Internet: Reconstructing Conflicting Findings', *American Behavioral Scientist*, 45(3): 420–35.

Nie, N.H. and Erbring, L. (2000) *Internet and Society: A Preliminary Report*, www.stanford.edu/group/siqss.

Nielsen, J. (2008) 'How Little do Users Read?' *Alertbox*, May 6, 2008. www.useit.com/alertbox/percent-text-read.html.

Nielsen Company (2009) 'A2/M3 Three Screen Report 1st Quarter 2009'. 20 May, http://blog.nielsen.com/nielsenwire/wp-content/uploads/2009/05/nielsen_threescreenreport_q109.pdf.

Nonaka, I. and Takeuchi, H. (1995) *The Knowledge-Creating Company: How Japanese Companies Create the Dynamics of Innovation*. New York: Oxford University Press.

Norman, D.A. (1991) 'Cognitive Artifacts', in J.M. Carroll (ed.), *Designing Interface: Psychology of the Human–Computer Interface*. Cambridge: Cambridge University Press. pp. 17–39.

Norman, D.A. (1993) *Things that Make Us Smart*. Reading, MA: Addison-Wesley.

Norman, D.A. (1999) *The Invisible Computer*. Cambridge, MA and London: The MIT Press.

Norman, D.A. (2010) *Living with Complexity*. Boston, MA and London: The MIT Press.

Norman, D.A. and Draper, S. (1986) *User-centered System Design: New Perspectives on Human–Computer Interaction*. Hillsdale, NJ: Erlbaum.

Nowak, K., Watt, J. H., & Walther, J. B. (2009) 'Computer mediated teamwork and the efficiency framework: Exploring the influence of synchrony and cues on media satisfaction and outcome success'. *Computers in Human Behavior, 25,* 1108–1119.

O'Harrow, R. (2005) *No Place to Hide*. New York and London: Free Press.

Ophir, Eyal, Nass, C. and Wagner, A. (2009) 'Cognitive Control in Media Multitaskers', *Proceedings of the National Academy of Sciences*, 106: 15583–7.

Ornstein, R.E. (1986) *The Psychology of Consciousness*. Harmondsworth: Penguin.

O'Sullivan, P. and Flanagin, A. (2003) 'Reconceptualizing "Flaming" and Other Problematic Communication', *New Media and Society*, 5(1): 67–93.

Oxford Internet Institute (2009) *The Internet in Britain 2009*. Authors: W.H. Dutton, E. J. Helsper and M. M. Gerber. Oxford UK: Oxford Internet Institute.

Palvia, S., Palvia, P. and Zigli, R. (eds) (1992) *The Global Issues of Information Technology Management*. Harrisburg, PA: Idea Group.

Papacharissi, Zizi (2010) *A Private Sphere: Democracy in a Digital Age (Digital Media and Society)*. London: Pluto Press.

Pariser, Eli (2011) *The Filter Bubble, What the Internet is Hiding from You*. London and New York: Viking/Penguin.

Parks, Malcolm (2009) 'What Will We Study When the Internet Disappears?', *Journal of Computer-mediated Communication*, 14: 724–9.

Parks, Malcolm (2010) 'Who are Facebook Friends? Exploring the Composition of Facebook Friend Networks'. Paper presented at the 60th Annual Conference of the International Communication Association, Singapore, June.

Perritt, Henry (1996, 1998) *Law and the Information Superhighway*. New York: Wiley.

Peters, Jean-Marie (1989) *Het Filmisch Denken*. Amersfoort: Acco.

Peters, Jean-Marie (1996) *Het Beeld: Bouwstenen van een Algemene Iconologie*. Baarn: Hadewijch.

Pew Internet and American Life Project (2009) by Amanda Lenhart, 'Adults and social networking websites'. Project Data Memo, www.pewinternet.org.

Pew Internet and American Life Project (2010a) by Amanda Lenhart, Kristen Purcell, Aaron Smith and Kathryn Zickuhr, 'Social Media & Mobile Internet Use Among Teens and Young Adults', 3 February, http://pewinternet.org/Reports/2010/Social-Media-and-Young-Adults.aspx.

Pew Internet and American Life Project (2010b) by Jim Jansen, 'Use of the Internet in Higher-Income Households', 24 November, http://pewinternet.org/Reports/2010/Better-off-households.aspx.

Pieterson, W. (2009) 'Channel Choice: Citizens' Channel Behavior and Public Service Channel Strategy'. Ph.D Thesis, Enchede: University of Twente.

Piore, M. and Sabel, C. (1984) *The New Industrial Divide*. New York: Basic Books.

Pool, I. de Sola (1983) *Technologies of Freedom*. Harvard, MA: Belknap.

Pool, I. de Sola, Inose, H., Takasaki, N. and Hunwitz, R. (1984) *Communication Flows: A Census in the US and Japan*. Amsterdam: North-Holland.

Porterfield, Amy (2010) 'Study Highlights Growing Social Media Addiction', http://www.social-mediaexaminer.com/study-highlights-growing-social-media-addiction/.

Postmes, T. and Spears, R. (1998) 'Breaching or building social boundaries? Side-Effects of Computer Mediated Communication'. Paper presented to International Communication Association, Annual Conference, Jerusalem, 20–24 July.

Powell, W. (1990) 'Neither Market nor Hierarchy: Network Forms of Organizations', in B. Slaw (ed.), *Research in Organizational Behavior, Vol. 12*. Greenwich, CT: JAI Press. pp. 295–336.

Press, L., Foster, W. and Goodman, S. (1999) 'The Internet in India and China', *First Monday: Peer-Reviewed Journal on the Internet*, 7(10), www.firstmonday.dk/issues/issue7_10/press/.

Prigogine, I. and Stengers, I. (1984) *Order Out of Chaos, Man's New Dialogue with Nature*. Toronto: Bantam Books.

Quan-Haase, A. and Wellman, B. with Witte, J.C. and Hampton, K. (2002) 'Capitalizing on the Net: Social Contact, Civic Engagement, and Sense of Community', in B. Wellman and C. Haythornthwaite (eds), *The Internet in Everyday Life*. Malden, MA and Oxford: Blackwell. pp. 291–324.

Rada, J. (1980) 'Micro-Electronics, Information Technology and its Effects on Developing Countries', in J. Berting, S. Mills and H. Winterberger (eds), *The Socio-Economic Impact of Micro-Electronics*. Oxford: Oxford University Press.

Rash, Wayne (1997) *Politics on the Nets: Wiring the Political Process*. New York: Freeman.

Rayport, Jeffrey and Sviokla, John (1999) 'Exploiting the Virtual Value Chain', in D. Tapscott (ed.), *Creating Value in the Network Economy*. Boston, MA: Harvard Business Review.

Reeves, B. and Nass, C. (1996) *The Media Equation*. Cambridge, MA: Cambridge University Press.

Reichman, R. (1986) 'Communication Paradigms for a Window System', in D.A. Norman and S. Draper (eds), *User-Centered System Design: New Perspectives on Human–Computer Interaction*. Hillsdale, NJ: Erlbaum.

Reidenberg, J.R. (1998) 'Lex Informatica. The Formulation of Information Policy Rules Through Technology', *Texas Law Review*, 3: 553–94.

Rheingold, Howard (1993) *The Virtual Community: Homesteading on the Electronic Frontier*. Reading, MA: Addison-Wesley.

Rice, R.E. (1998) 'Computer-Mediated Communication and Media Preference', *Behavior and Information Technology*, 17(3): 164–74.

Rice, R.E. and Love, G. (1987) 'Electronic Emotion: Socio-Emotional Content in a Computer-Mediated Communication Network', *Communication Research*, 14: 85–108.

Rifkin, J. (1987) *Time Wars*. New York: Holt.

Roberts, J.M. and Gregor, T. (1971) 'Privacy: A Cultural View', in J.R. Pennock and J. Chapman (eds), *Privacy*. New York: Atherton Press.

Robinson, J., DiMaggio, P. and Hargittai, E. (2003) 'New Social Survey Perspectives on the Digital Divide', *IT & Society*, 1(5): 1–22.

Robinson, J. and Nie, N.H. (2002) 'Introduction', *IT & Society*, 1(1): i–xi.

Rogers, E.M. (1963) *The Diffusion of Innovations*. Glencoe, IL: Free Press.

Rojo, A. and Ragsdale, R. (1997) 'Participation in electronic forums', *Telematics and Informatics*, 13(1): 83–96.

Rothfelder, J. (1992) *Privacy for Sale*. New York: Simon and Schuster.

Rustad, Michael L. (2009) *Internet Law in a Nutshell*. St. Paul, MN: West/Thomson Reuters.

Rutledge, Pamela (2010) 'Social Media Addiction: Engage Brain Before Believing', *Psychology Today*, http://www.psychologytoday.com/blog/positively-media/201005/social-media-addiction-engage-brain-believing.

Salomon, G. (1979) *Interaction of Media, Cognition and Learning*. San Francisco, CA: Jossey-Bass.

Samuelson, Pamela (1996) 'Intellectual Property, At Your Expense', *Wired*, January: 135–8, 188–91.

Saunders, C.S., Robey, D. and Vaverek, K. (1994) 'The Persistence of Status Differences in Computer Conferencing', *Human Communication Research*, 20(4): 443–72.

Saunders, R.J. and Warford, G. (1983) *Telecommunications and Economic Development*. Baltimore, MD: World Bank and Johns Hopkins University Press.

Sayer, A. (1986) 'New Developments in Manufacturing: The Just-In-Time System', *Capital and Class*, 30: 43–72.

Schenk, David (1997) *Data Smog: Surviving the Information Glut*. New York: HarperEdge.

Schumpeter, J.A. (1942) *Capitalism, Socialism and Democracy*. New York: Harper & Row.

Scott, C. and Easton, A. (1996) 'Examining Equality of Influence in Group Decision Support System Interaction', *Small Group Research*, 37(3): 360–82.

SCP (Social and Cultural Planning Agency) (2010) *Alle Kanalen Staan Open* (All Channels are Open). Contains a Summary in English. The Hague: SCP, http://www.scp.nl/Publicaties/Alle_publicaties/Publicaties_2010/Alle_kanalen_staan_open.

Selnow, G.W. (1994) *High-Tech Campaigns: Computer Technology in Political Communication*. Westport, CT: Praeger.

Shapiro, Andrew (2000) *The Control Revolution: How the Internet is Putting Individuals in Charge and Changing the World We Know.* New York: PublicAffairs.

Shapiro, Carl and Varian, Hal R. (1999) *Information Rules – A Strategic Guide to the Network Economy.* Boston, MA: Harvard Business School Press.

Shirky, C. (2009) *Here Comes Everybody: The Power of Organizing Without Organizations.* Harmondsworth: Penguin.

Short, J., Williams, E. and Christie, B. (1976) *The Social Psychology of Telecommunications.* New York: Wiley.

Silverstone, R. and Hadden, J. (1996) 'Design and Domestication', in R. Mansell and R. Silverstone (eds), *Communication by Design.* Oxford: Oxford University Press.

Slaughter, A.-M. (2004) *A New World Order.* Princeton, NJ: Princeton University Press.

Smith, N., Bizot, E. and Hill, T. (1988) *Use of Electronic Mail in the Research and Development Organization.* Tulsa, OK: University of Tulsa Press.

Soloman, G., Allen, N. and Resta, P. (2002) *Toward Digital Equity: Bridging the Divide in Education.* Boston, MA: Allen and Bacon.

Solum, L. (2009) 'Models of Internet Governance'. In: L.A.Bygrave and J. Bing, *Models of Internet Governance: Infrastructure and Institutions.* New York: Oxford University Press.

Spears, R. and Lea, M. (1992) 'Social Influence and the Influence of the "Social" in Computer-Mediated Communication', in M. Lea (ed.), *Contexts of Computer-Mediated Communication.* Hemel Hempstead: Harvester Wheatsheaf. pp. 30–65.

Spears, R., Lea, M. and Postmes, T. (2001) 'Social Psychological Theories of Computer-Mediated Communication: Social Pain and Social Gain', in W. Robinson and H. Giles (eds), *The New Handbook of Language and Social Psychology.* Chichester: Wiley.

Sproull, L. and Kiesler, S. (1986) 'Reducing Social Context Cues: Electronic Mail in Organizational Communication', *Management Science,* 32: 1492–512.

Sproull, L. and Kiesler, S. (1991) *Connections: New Ways of Working in the Networked Organization.* Cambridge, MA: MIT Press.

Steijn, Bram (2001) *Werken in de Informatiesamenleving.* Assen: Koninklijke van Gorcum.

Steinmüller, W. (2001) 'ICTs and the Possibilities of Leapfrogging by Developing Countries', *International Labour Review,* 140(2): 193–210.

Stewart, James (1998–99) 'Interactive Television at Home: Television Meets the Internet', www. itvnews.com/. Published later in J. Jensen and C. Toscan (eds), *Interactive Television, TV of the Future or the Future of TV?* Aalborg: Aalborg University Press. pp. 231–60.

Stone, A.R. (1991) 'Will the Real Body Please Stand Up?', in M. Benedict (ed.), *Cyberspace: First Steps.* Cambridge: Cambridge University Press. pp. 81–118.

Suchman, L.A. (1987) *Plans and Situated Actions: the Problem of Human–Machine Communication.* Cambridge, NY: Simon and Schuster.

Sunstein, Cass (2001) *Republic.com.* Princeton NJ: Princeton University Press.

Sunstein, Cass (2006) *Infotopia, How Many Minds Produce Knowledge.* Oxford, New York: Oxford University Press.

Surowiecky, James (2004) *The Wisdom of Crowds.* London: Random House.

Sussman, G. (1997) *Communications Technology and Politics in the Information Age.* Thousand Oaks, CA: Sage.

ter Hedde, M. and Svensson J. (2009) 'Online Discussion on Government Websites: Fact and Failure?', in A. Meijer, K. Boomsma and P. Wagenaar, *ICT, Citizens and Governance: After the Hype!.* Amsterdam, Berlin and Tokyo: IOS Press. pp. 21–37.

Thomas, David (1996) 'Feedback and Cybernetics: Reimaging the Body in the Age of the Cyborg', in M. Featherstone and R. Burrows (eds), *Cyberspace/Cyberbodies/Cyberpunk: Cultures of Technological Embodiment.* London: Sage.

Thompson, G.F. (2003) *Between Hierarchies and Markets – The Logic and Limits of Network Forms of Organization*. Oxford: Oxford University Press.

Thurlow, C., Lengell, L. and Tomic, A. (2004) *Computer Mediated Communication: Social Interaction and the Internet*. London: Sage.

Tichenor, P., Donohue, G. and Olieh, C. (1970) 'Mass Media Flow and the Differential Growth in Knowledge', *Public Opinion Quarterly*, 34: 159–70.

Tilly, Charles (1998) *Durable Inequality*. Berkeley, Los Angeles, London: University of California Press.

Toffler, Alvin (1980) *The Third Wave*. New York: Bantam Books.

Turkle, Sherry (1984) *The Second Self: Computers and the Human Spirit*. London: Granada.

Turkle, Sherry (1995) *Life on the Screen: Identity in the Age of the Internet*. New York: Simon and Schuster.

Turkle, Sherry (1996a) 'Who Am We?', *Wired*, January: 149–52, 194–9.

Turkle, Sherry (1996b) 'Parallel Lives: Working on Identity in Virtual Space', in D. Grodin and T. Lindlof (eds), *Constructing the Self in a Mediated World*. Thousand Oaks, CA: Sage.

Turkle, Sherry (2011) *Alone Together, Why We Expect More from Technology and Less from Each Other*. New York: Basic Books.

Turoff, M. (1989) 'The Anatomy of a Computer Application Innovation: Computer-Mediated Communications', *Technological Forecasting and Social Change*, 36: 107–22.

UCLA, Center for Communication Policy (2003) *The UCLA Internet Report, Surveying the Digital Future, Year Three*. Los Angeles: UCLA, Center for Communication Policy, www.ccp.ucla.edu/pages/internet-report.asp.

US Copyright Office (1998) *Digital Millennium Copyright Act*, www.copyright.gov/.

USC, Annenberg, School of Communications (2011) '2010 Digital Future Report'. Los Angeles: University of Southern California, http://www.digitalcenter.org/pages/current_report.asp?intGlobalId=43.

Urry, John (2003) *Global Complexity*. Cambridge, UK: Polity Press.

Valkenburg, Patti and Peter, Jochen (2009) 'Social Consequences of the Internet for Adolescents: A Decade of Research'. *Current Directions of Psychological Science*, 18(1): 1–5.

Valkenburg, Patti and Peter, Jochen (2011) 'Online Communication Among Adolescents: An Integrated Model of Its Attraction, Opportunities, and Risks'. *Journal of Adolescent Health*, 48: 121–7.

Vallee, J. (1978) *Group Communication through Computers. Vol. IV: Social, Managerial and Economic Issues*. Report R-40. London: Institute for the Future.

van Cuilenburg, J. and Noomen, G. (1984) *Communicatiewetenschap*. Muiderberg: Coutinho.

van Deursen, Alexander (2010) 'Internet Skills, Vital Assets in an Information Society'. Ph.D Thesis, Enschede: University of Twente.

van Deursen, A.J.A.M. and van Dijk, J.A.G.M. (2009) 'Improving Digital Skills for the Use of Online Public Information And Services'. *Government Information Quarterly*, 26(2): 333–40.

van Deursen, A.J.A.M. and van Dijk, J.A.G.M. (2010) 'Trendrapport Computer en Internetgebruik 2010, Een Nederlands en Europees Perspectief'. Enschede: Center for eGovernment Studies, University of Twente, http://www.utwente.nl/ibr/cfes/docs/Rapporten/2010_11_TrendrapportComputersInternet.pdf.

van Deursen, A.J.A.M. and van Dijk, J.A.G.M. (2011) 'Internet Skills Performance Tests: Are People Ready For eHealth?'. *Journal of Medical Internet Research*, 13(2): 1–11.

van Deursen, A.J.A.M. and van Dijk, J.A.G.M. (forthcoming) 'A Social Revolution on the Internet? The Digital Divide Shifts to Gaps of Usage'.

van Deursen, A.J.A.M., van Dijk, J.A.G.M. and Peters, O. (2011) 'Rethinking Internet Skills: The Contribution of Gender, Age, Education, Internet Experience, and Hours Online to Medium- and Content-Related Internet Skills', *Poetics*, 39: 125–44.

van Dijk, Jan A.G.M. (1991, 1994, 1997, 2000) *De Netwerkmaatschappij: Sociale Aspecten van Nieuwe Media*, 1st–4th edns. Houten: Bohn Staflen van Loghum.

van Dijk, Jan A.G.M. (1993a) 'Communication Networks and Modernization', *Communication Research*, 20(3): 384–407.

van Dijk, Jan A.G.M. (1993b) 'The mental challenge of the new media', *Medienpsychologie*, 1: 20–45.

van Dijk, Jan A.G.M. (1996) 'Models of Democracy Behind the Design and Use of New Media in Politics', *The Public/Javnost*, III(1): 43–56.

van Dijk, Jan A.G.M. (1997) *Universal Service from the Perspective of Consumers and Citizens*. Report to the Information Society Forum. Brussels: European Commission/ISPO.

van Dijk, Jan A.G.M. (1999) 'The One-Dimensional Network Society of Manuel Castells', *New Media and Society*, 1(1): 127–38.

van Dijk, Jan A.G.M. (2000a) 'Models of Democracy and Concepts of Communication', in K. Hacker and J. van Dijk (eds), *Digital Democracy: Issues of Theory and Practice*. London, New Delhi and Thousand Oaks, CA: Sage. pp. 30–53.

van Dijk, Jan A.G.M. (2000b) 'Widening Information Gaps and Policies of Prevention', in K. Hacker and J. van Dijk (eds), *Digital Democracy: Issues of Theory and Practice*. London: Sage.

van Dijk, Jan A.G.M. (2001) *Netwerken, het Zenuwstelsel van Onze Maatschappij, Oratie* (Networks, the Nervous System of our Society, Inaugural Lecture). Enschede: University of Twente, Department of Communication.

van Dijk, Jan A.G.M. (2004) 'Divides in Succession: Possession, Skills and Life of New Media for Societal Participation', in E. Bucy and J. Newhagen (eds), *Media Access: Social and Psychological Dimensions of New Technology Use*. London: LEA. pp. 233–58.

van Dijk, Jan A.G.M. (2005) *The Deepening Divide, Inequality in the Information Society*. Thousand Oaks, CA, London and New Delhi: Sage.

van Dijk, Jan A.G.M. (2006) 'Digital Divide Research: Achievements and Shortcomings'. *Poetics* 34: 221–35.

van Dijk, Jan A.G.M. (2010a) 'Conceptual Framework', in *Study on the Social Impact of ICT* (EU-SMART PROJECT: CPP N°55A – SMART N°2007/0068), pp. 1–30, http://ec.europa. eu/information_society/eeurope/i2010/docs/eda/social_impact_of_ict.pdf.

van Dijk, Jan A.G.M. (2010b) 'Review of Manuel Castells, *Communication Power*, 2008'. *Communications*, 2010: 485–90.

van Dijk, Jan A.G.M. (2010c) 'Participation in Policy-Making', in *Study on the Social Impact of ICT* (EU-SMART PROJECT: CPP N°55A – SMART N°2007/0068), pp. 31–79, http://ec.europa. eu/information_society/eeurope/i2010/docs/eda/social_impact_of_ict.pdf.

van Dijk, Jan A.G.M. (2011) 'Network Properties and Democracy', in Jan A.G.M. van Dijk (ed.), *Information Society and Globalisation: Transformation of Politics*, Proceedings of the 10th International Conference of the PSRC Forum, 22 October, Dubrovnik, Croatia. Zagreb: University of Zagreb.

van Dijk, Jan A.G.M. and de Vos, L. (2001) 'Searching for the Holy Grail: Images of Interactive Television'. *New Media and Society*, 3(4): 443–65.

van Dijk, Jan A.G.M. and Hacker, K. (2003) 'The Digital Divide as a Complex and Dynamic Phenomenon', *Information Society*, 19: 315–26.

van Dijk, Jan A.G.M., Heuvelman, A. and Peters, O. (2003) 'Interactive Television or Enhanced Television? The Dutch Users' Interest in ITV Via Set-Top Boxes'. Paper presented at the 53rd Annual Conference of the International Communication Association, 27 May–4 June, San Diego, CA.

Van Dijk, Jan A.G.M. and van Deursen, A. (forthcoming) 'Digital Skills, The Key to the Information Society'.

van Dijk, Jan A.G.M. and Winters-van Beek, Anneleen (2009) 'The Perspective of Network Government', in A. Meijer, K. Boomsma and P. Wagenaar, *ICT, Citizens and Governance: After the Hype!*. Amsterdam, Berlin and Tokyo: IOS Press. pp. 235–55.

van Duijn, J.J. (1979) *De Lange Golf in de Economie*. Assen: Van Gorcum.

van Rossum, H., Gardeniers, H. and Borking, J. (1995a) *Privacy-Enhancing Technologies: The Path to Anonymity*, Vol I. TNO Physics and Electronics Laboratory. Rijswijk: Registratiekamer.

van Rossum, H., Gardeniers, H. and Borking, J. (1995b) *Privacy-Enhancing Technologies: The Path to Anonymity*, Vol II. TNO Physics and Electronics Laboratory. Rijswijk: Registratiekamer.

van Tulder, R. and Junne, R. (1988) *European Multinationals in Core Technologies*. Chichester: Wiley.

Vartanova, P. (1998) 'New Communication Technologies and Information Flows in Russia'. Paper presented at Beyond Convergence: ITS-98 Conference, Stockholm, Sweden, 14–21 June, www.ITS98.org/conference.

Venturelli, Shalini (1998) *Liberalizing the European Media: Politics, Regulation and the Public Sphere*. Oxford: Oxford University Press.

Venturelli, Shalini (2002) 'Inventing e-regulation in the US, EU and East Asia: Conflicting Social Visions of the Information Society', *Telematics and Informatics*, 19: 69–90.

Virilio, P. (1988) *La Machine de Vision*. Paris: Galilée. Translation: *The Vision Machine*. Bloomington, IN: Indiana University Press, 1994.

Wallace, Patricia (1999) *The Psychology of the Internet*. Cambridge: Cambridge University Press.

Walther, J. (1992) 'Interpersonal Effects in Computer-Mediated Communication', *Communication Research*, 1 (1): 52–90.

Walther, J. (1996) 'Computer-Mediated Communication: Impersonal, Interpersonal and Hyperpersonal Interaction', *Communication Research*, 2 (1): 1–43.

Walther, J. (1997) 'Group and Interpersonal Effects in International Computer-Mediated Collaboration', *Human Communication Research*, 23(3): 442–69.

Walther, J. (2011) 'Theories of Computer-Mediated Communication and Interpersonal Relations', in M. Knapp and J. Dale (eds), *The SAGE Handbook of Interpersonal Communication*. Beverley Hills, CA: Sage. pp. 443–78.

Watts, Duncan (2003) *Six Degrees: The Science of a Connected Age*. New York: Norton.

Watts, Duncan J. and Strogatz, Steven (1998) 'Collective Dynamics of "Small World" Networks', *Nature*, 393: 440–2.

Weber, Max (1922) *Gesammelte Politische Schriften*. Tübingen: Mohr.

Webster, Frank (2001) 'The Information Society Revisited', in L. Lievrouw, *Handbook of the New Media*, London, Thousand Oaks, CA and New Delhi: Sage. pp. 22–33.

Wegner, D. (2002) *The Illusion of Conscious Will*. Boston, MA and London: The MIT Press.

Weingarten, R. and Fiehler, R. (eds) (1988) *Technisierte Kommunikation*. Opladen: Westdeutscher Verlag.

Weinreich, H., Obendorf H., Herder, E. and Mayer, M. (2008) 'Not Quite the Average, An Empirical Study of Web Use'. *ACM Transactions on the Web* 2, No. 1: 133-42.

Weller, M. (2007) *Virtual Learning Environments, Using, Choosing and Developing your VLE*. London: Routledge.

Wellman, B. (2000) 'Changing Connectivity: A Future History of Y2.03K', *Sociological Research Online*, 4(4), www.socresonline.org.uk/4/4/wellman.html.

Wellman, Barry (2001) 'Computer Networks As Social Networks', *Science*, 293, 14 September: 2031–4.

Wellman, Barry & Berkowitz, S.D. (eds.). (1988) *Social Structures, A network approach*. Greenwich Conn., London: Jai Press.

Wellman, Barry and Haythornthwaite, Caroline (eds) (2002) *The Internet in Everyday Life*. Malden, MA and Oxford: Blackwell.

Wenneker, Marieke (2009) '*Ze Gebruiken Meer de Mensen om Zich Heen', Een Onderzoek naar de Rol van ICT-Toepassingen bij Kennisdelingsprocessen* ('They Primarily Use the People Around', A Study of the Role of ICT Applications in Knowledge Sharing Processes). Doctoral thesis. Contains a summary in English. Radboud University, Nijmegen, Netherlands.

Westin, A.F. (1987) *Privacy and Freedom*. London: Bodley Head.

Weston, J.R., Kristen, C. and O'Connor, S. (1975) *Teleconferencing*. Ottawa: Social Policy and Programmes Branch, Department of Communications.

WGIG (Working Group on Internet Governance) 2005 'Report of the Working Group on Internet Governance', Château de Bossey June 2005. Retrieved July 12, 2011 from http://www.worldsummit2003.de/en/web/762.htm

Wilhelm, Anthony (2003) 'Civic Participation and Technology Inequality: The "Killer Application" in Education', in D. Anderson and M. Cornfield (eds), *The Civic Web, Online Politics and Democratic Values*. Lanham, MD: Rowman and Littlefield. pp. 113–28.

Wilhelm, Anthony (2004) *Digital Nation, Towards an Inclusive Information Society*. Cambridge, MA and London: The MIT Press.

Williams, F. (1982) *The Communications Revolution*. Beverly Hills, CA: Sage.

Winston, Brian (1998) *Media Technology and Society: A History from the Telegraph to the Internet*. London: Routledge.

Wong, P.-K. (2002) 'The Impact of IT Investment on Income and Wealth Inequality in the Post-War US Economy', *Information Economics and Poverty*, 14: 233–51.

Wright, E.O. (1985) *Classes*. London: Verso.

Yao, Dennis (2003) 'Non-Market Strategies and Regulation in the United States' in B. Kogut (ed.), *The Global Internet Economy*. Cambridge MA, London: The MIT Press. pp. 407–35.

Zillien, N. and Hargittai, E. (2009) 'Digital Distinction: Status-Specific Internet Uses'. *Social Science Quarterly*, 90(2): 274–91.

Zittrain, J. (2008) *The Future of the Internet – And How to Stop It*. New Haven and London: Yale University Press.

Zuurmond, A. (1994) *De Infocratie*. Contains a summary in English. The Hague: Phaedrus.

Zuurmond, A. (1998) 'From Bureaucracy to Infocracy: Are Democratic Institutions Lagging Behind?', in I. Snellen and W. van de Donk (eds), *Public Administration in the Information Age: A Handbook*. Amsterdam: IOS Press. pp. 78–95.

Index